MARKETING STRATEGIES FOR COMPETITIVE ADVANTAGE

Dennis Adcock

COVENTRY UNIVERSITY

JOHN WILEY & SONS, LTD

Chichester • New York • Weinheim • Brisbane • Toronto • Singapore

Other Wiley Editorial Offices
John Wiley & Sons, Inc., 605 Third Avenue,
New York, NY 10158-0012, USA

VCH Verlagsgesellschaft mbH, Pappelallee 3,
D-69469 Weinheim, Germany

Jacaranda Wiley Ltd, 33 Park Road, Milton,
Queensland 4064, Australia

John Wiley & Sons (Canada) Ltd, 22 Worcester Road,
Rexdale, Ontario M9W 1L1, Canada

John Wiley & Sons (Asia) Pte Ltd, 2 Clementi Loop #02-01,
Jin Xing Distripark, Singapore 129809

Library of Congress Cataloging-in-Publication Data

Adcock, Dennis
  Marketing strategies for competitive advantage / Dennis Adcock.
    p. cm.
  Includes bibliographical references and index.
  ISBN 0–471–98169–9
  1. Marketing.   I. Title.

  HF5415.A3234 2000
  658.8--dc21   99-047600

British Library Cataloguing in Publication Data

A catalogue record for this book is available from the British Library

ISBN 0–471–98169–9

Designed and Typeset by Wyvern 21 Ltd, Bristol.
Printed and bound in Great Britain by Bookcraft (Bath) Ltd, Midsomer Norton.
This book is printed on acid-free paper responsibly manufactured from sustainable forestry or which at least two trees are planted for each one used in paper production.

CONTENTS

PREFACE

There are already many books available on marketing strategy and marketing management, so why another one? This question needs to be answered in two specific ways. First, how is this new book different from others, and second, what does it offer to readers that is of particular value to them? These are precisely the questions that every marketer has to ask with regard to the product offerings for which they are responsible, and I would be failing as an author if these aspects were ignored with regard to this book. Of course these questions have to be considered from the perspective of those specific customers (readers) who are the prime target, those for whom this book was written. These are the potential customers and it is their needs that must be considered above all else.

The initial stimulus for this book came from the students studying marketing at Coventry University. Some were mature part-time students with experience in practical marketing operations; others had studied full time the many aspects of marketing, but all required a framework to integrate their knowledge in a way relevant to the various marketing careers they wanted to pursue.

All these students and marketing practitioners already have a good basic understanding of the principles of marketing but now wish to consider the role of marketing in a wider context and with a longer time horizon. They are typically final-year undergraduates studying business and marketing, and hoping for a career start in a marketing-related area, as well as master's level students on an MBA or a more specialist course where the scope of market-based decisions is of more relevance than the operational dimensions of the marketing mix. Both groups understand that market-focused decisions are inseparable from general business decisions in every organization. They also realize the truth in the edict 'No customers – no business!'. However, the issues covered range across all aspects of where and how to compete, therefore the book will be useful to practising marketers who want to explore the various aspects of success in a dynamic, customer-driven market-place in more detail, especially the interrelationship of these.

So, addressing the first question posed above, how does this book differ from others? The first difference is the emphasis on those elements that are vital to compete effectively in today's market-places. This is no longer based on confrontational competition but a more modern approach which embraces the benefits of value added partnerships and the long-term management of customers in order to achieve beneficial relationships wherever possible. This is developed from a study of the key players together with an evaluation of the range of opportunities available that could help to build customer loyalty.

Another difference is that the book does not spend much time on the tools of analysis, which are more than adequately covered in specialist texts. My own experience, 30 years after my MBA studies, is that many of these tools change over time and models in vogue then have long since been replaced. This process will inevitably continue, with new techniques superseding the old, especially as the easy availability of greatly increased levels of marketing data require new ways for marketing managers to extract useful marketing information. The explosion in the availability of data makes it more important than ever that marketers should understand the role of analysis and the risk involved when filtering data to turn it into information. This is a timeless issue and is the emphasis of Chapter 3, which covers analysis, rather than a study of specific, current analysis models.

A final difference concerns the implementation of marketing plans, the crucial stage in achieving success. There is no mention of the traditional (McCarthy) marketing mix; rather the priority is customer care and building relationships in order to meet the tests of *acceptability*, *affordability* and *availability*. If a series of P-words is required then the operational issues can be considered as ways to achieve a competitive *position* through the use of *promises*, *power* and *persuasion*.

As mentioned above, the second question every customer wants to pose is WIIFM (what's in it for me?). In order that an offering can add value it must meet expectations in a satisfactory way, and then go further by delivering real benefits when set against customer needs. The sole judge of this is the customer. However, by concentrating on the key issues of marketing competitiveness, and putting them in a structure relevant to both mature and nascent products, it is to be hoped that the result – this book – will be of real value to all marketing students as well as practitioners.

This book is divided into five parts:

- Part I   The process and players involved
- Part II   Where to compete
- Part II   How to compete

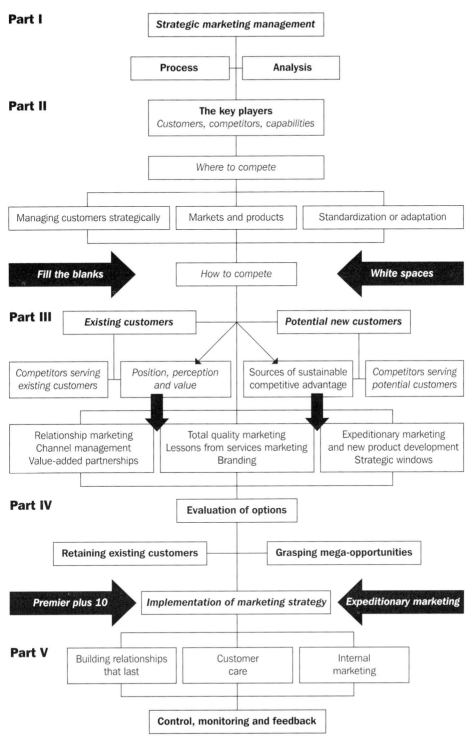

Part I

Strategic marketing management

Process — Analysis

Part II

The key players
Customers, competitors, capabilities

Where to compete

Managing customers strategically | Markets and products | Standardization or adaptation

Fill the blanks | How to compete | **White spaces**

Part III

Existing customers | Potential new customers

Competitors serving existing customers | Position, perception and value | Sources of sustainable competitive advantage | Competitors serving potential customers

Relationship marketing
Channel management
Value-added partnerships | Total quality marketing
Lessons from services marketing
Branding | Expeditionary marketing
and new product development
Strategic windows

Part IV

Evaluation of options

Retaining existing customers — Grasping mega-opportunities

Premier plus 10 | Implementation of marketing strategy | **Expeditionary marketing**

Part V

Building relationships that last | Customer care | Internal marketing

Control, monitoring and feedback

Fig 0.1 Structure of the book

- Part IV   Evaluation and selection of strategy
- Part V   Implementation and control of strategy

Each part is described in a short introductory section, and divided into chapters covering the relevant topics.

The structure for the book is derived from the diagram shown in Figure 0.1, which follows the sequence of issues from *where to compete*, through to decisions regarding existing customers as opposed to potential new customers. While the figure places these groups on separate arms, there are, of course, many overlapping competitive issues which apply to both groups. Therefore the chapters on *how to compete* do include the common aspects of competitive advantage as viewed from a marketing perspective. Nevertheless, there is a distinction that must be made between continued trading with existing customers and, where appropriate, building relationships with this group, and expeditionary marketing, which focuses on new activities. To emphasize this, Chapters 14 and 15 deal specifically with new initiatives. Everything comes back together in considering *implementation* issues such as customer care and internal marketing activities, both issues that are critical to the actual delivery of strategy.

Figure 0.1 has been overlaid with the four categories of the matrix proposed by Gary Hamel and C.K. Prahalad in their book *Competing for the Future*. This 2×2 model has many links with the classic Ansoff matrix, although, as will become apparent, it develops the issue of *product* into a more interesting category of *competence*. Current and future decisions regarding both existing and new customers form the basis of good strategic marketing, therefore this matrix provides a relevant basis for the consideration of the key issues in the text.

The book would not have been possible without the help of my students and the encouraging input from my colleagues at Coventry. To them I offer my sincere thanks. My most sincere dedication must be reserved for my wife Marion, who has encouraged and cajoled me to finish the writing. She has suffered as I spent more time with my computer on too many occasions.

Dennis Adcock
July 1999

ACKNOWLEDGEMENTS

The Publisher wishes to thank the following who have kindly given permission for the use of copyright material.

Academic Press
American Marketing Association
Boston Consulting Group
Butterworth Heinemann
Chartered Institute of Marketing
Elsevier Science
Free Press
Harvard Business School Press
HBS Press
Indiana University
ITPS
John Wiley
MCB Press
McGraw-Hill
Penguin
Prentice Hall
Sloan Management Review
West

Every effort has been made to trace and acknowledge ownership of copyright. The publishers will be glad to hear from any copyright holders whom it has not been possible to contact.

THE PROCESS AND PLAYERS INVOLVED

PART I

This first part encompasses three short chapters that act as a foundation for many of the specific topics in the main body of the book. The first chapter simply discusses the strategic marketing process, and what is strategy. However, it starts with the last element, the implementation of strategy. The ultimate test of all the stages is making things happen for the eventual consumer, so this critical stage is highlighted in order that the requirements are always in the mind of the strategist, and he or she does not become too focused on the beauty of the plans as conceived. The key test of strategy is, of course, that of *suitability*, *feasibility* and *acceptability*. Chapter 1 emphasizes the requirement of achieving a *customer focus*, strong *competitive positioning* and internal *consistency* in order to be successful. It further explores the concept of *positioning* as a key issue in competitive advantage. The crucial decisions on *where* and *how* to compete, which are developed in Parts II and III, are introduced here.

Chapter 2 reviews the key players in competitive marketing strategy. Obviously prime is the *customer*, but all customers must be considered in conjunction with both the *capabilities* of the supply organization and the appropriate *competitors*, forming a triad of key players. Customers are considered as any group with whom the supplier has a relationship. Of course marketing is present wherever such exchanges take place. The discussion of capabilities and competencies is designed to shift the focus away from products and onto the skills and strengths an organization possesses, and, more vital, how these can be utilized to build competitive offerings. Of course customer satisfaction is a comparative measure, hence the need for an organization to identify competitors and predict their future behaviour in a given market-place. This is also discussed in the chapter.

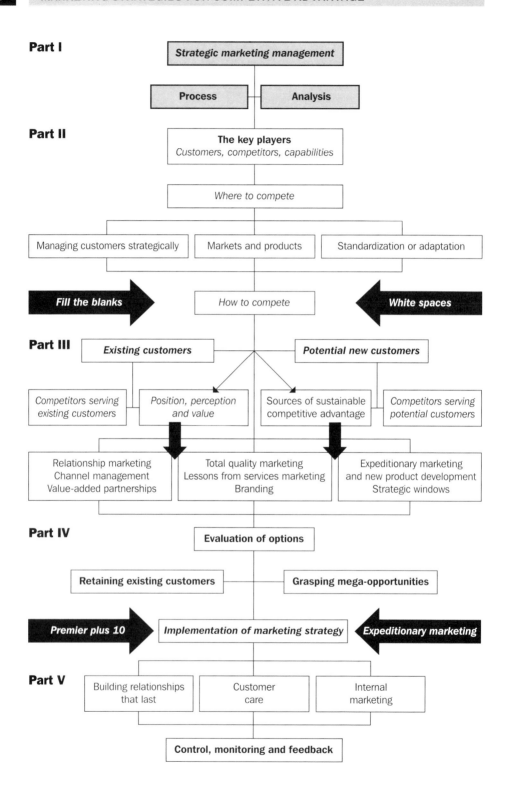

The final chapter in Part I considers the need for good, objective analysis of all the key players. While it is not prescriptive with regards to analytical techniques, it does suggest both a framework of contents and some key issues relevant to the development of good information. That is information which can become a positive input, reducing risks in decision making, and leading towards the development of robust strategies.

The three chapters of Part I are not specifically interconnected; rather, they all discuss issues that affect the context of the following sections on where and how to compete.

Figure 0.1 in the Preface is designed to show the development of the subject as presented in this book. It develops from the general discussion on the background process and the key parties involved through to specific issues regarding the achievement of success in a competitive market-place. Part II covers *where to compete*, then Part III covers many of the issues necessary in order to compete effectively. The final two parts, IV and V, cover the critical evaluation of options and the actual implementation, which was introduced right at the beginning of Chapter 1.

STRATEGIC MARKETING MANAGEMENT

CHAPTER 1

INTRODUCTION: THE MARKETING CONCEPT

Marketing is based on an incredibly simple but powerful idea, that of achieving a profitable exchange between a supplier and a customer.

It is all too easy to lose track of this simple fact when faced with the wide range of decisions that are part of the day-to-day task of marketing management, and when offered the plethora of theories and models all supposed to assist in the making of 'marketing' decisions.

In the practice of marketing, actions speak louder than words. Marketers will not be judged on the logic of their plans, nor on the elegance of the models used to analyse situations and point to the future; they will be judged by the results that follow on from their decisions, both operational and strategic. These have to be proactive; marketers must make things happen. Relationships do not just happen in a world typified by overproduction, where all customers have an abundance of choices. The exchange has to be created by investment and effort.

In a dynamic market with a future that is difficult to predict, the resulting actions stand more chance of success if they are well founded within the basic concept that underpins the exchange process. But it is necessary to blend an appropriate strategy to excellent implementation if real success is to be achieved. Bonoma (1984) summarized this neatly in his classic article '*Making your marketing strategy work*' (Figure 1.1).

The idea of a profitable exchange is encapsulated in the basic marketing concept, and this indicates that the starting point for many marketing actions is a deep

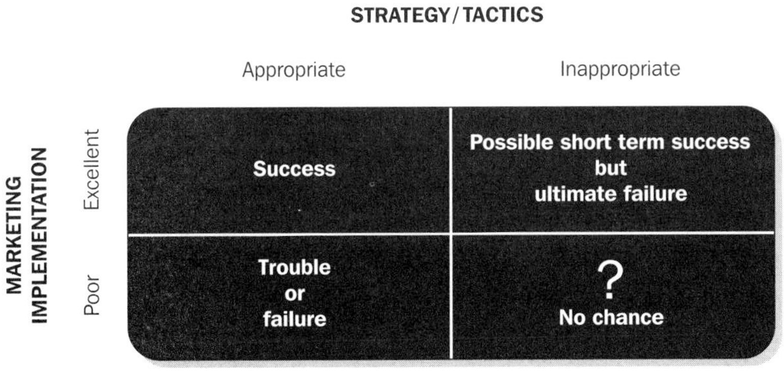

STRATEGY / TACTICS

Appropriate   Inappropriate

	Appropriate	Inappropriate
Excellent	**Success**	**Possible short term success but ultimate failure**
Poor	**Trouble or failure**	**? No chance**

MARKETING IMPLEMENTATION

Fig 1.1 Marketing strategy and implementation diagnosis.
Source: Adapted from Bonoma (1984)

understanding of the appropriate consumer desires. These desires will have been developed from some basic needs, which are then expressed as wants. The wants can then be translated into demands for particular 'products', which can be made available to try to satisfy those demands. The linkage leading from needs to demands can be managed, and I would suggest this is often a *necessary* action if customer satisfaction is to be achieved and a profitable exchange is to take place. In fact, effective marketing involves more than the development of demands; it should include the management of customer expectations, since the way customers evaluate their satisfaction will in some way be based on what they perceive they received when compared to what they expected.

It is important to differentiate between needs, wants and demands when trying to understand a particular customer's motivation. This understanding is vital to good marketing decisions. Kotler (1997) defined these as:

A human need is a state of felt deprivation of some basic satisfaction.
Wants are desires for specific satisfiers of these deeper needs.
Demands are wants for specific product (offerings) backed by an ability and willingness to buy them.

The differences (gaps) that can exist between these factors, as well as between demands and customer expectations, are explored in more detail in Chapter 9.

Marketing is experienced at the point where customers interact with a supply organization. Often a supplier will compromise when developing an offering in order to reflect both the internal capacity of that company and the way it interprets *needs*, *wants*, *demands* and *expectations*. However, this can lead to problems in achieving customer satisfaction, as illustrated in Figure 1.2.

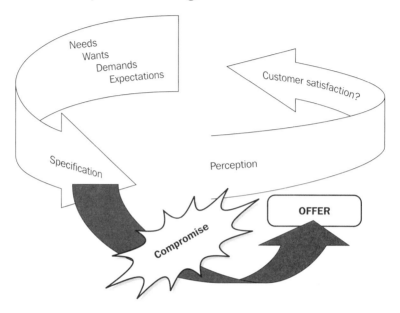

Fig 1.2 Links between customer needs and wants and suppliers' specification and offerings

However, the domain of practical marketing decisions lies within an organization, involving everything that leads to a successful offering to a chosen customer. Of course there is no point in a supplier meeting any demands unless it helps achieve a satisfactory profit. This should, perhaps, be widened to embrace the satisfactory achievement of the supplier's prime objectives, whether financial or non-financial. From a supplier's perspective, it is possible to define a 'perfect product' as:

> A combination of goods and services, unique and impossible for actual or potential competitors to match, which solves a problem for a customer, or meets his or her needs, in a way no other combination of goods and services can do as well, and which can thereby generate a revenue stream, discounted at the company's cost of capital, more than adequate to pay the costs of its development and provision.

There are several types of interaction with customers. The basic exchanges involve the offering (total product) going from supplier to customer with a balancing consideration going the other way; however, there is, in addition, the exchange of information of many sorts from customer to supplier (e.g. marketing research) and vice versa (marketing communications).

Customers receive more than a simple commodity product when they enter into any transaction. Consider any purchase that you have made and this will be obvious. A 'total product' will incorporate both the tangible part of the offering and a number of intangible aspects. In addition, customers will have a view on the value of the offering to themselves (different from the price) as well as the way the product was offered (service issues). Further feelings could well develop after the transaction, either positive or negative. Most basic marketing texts demonstrate that the satisfaction of any want is achieved by the receipt of a 'total' offering rather than a simple physical product or service, and it is through all the factors that make up a 'total product' that any exchange is judged.

All this should be clear from the study of basic marketing principles. These principles must be considered in an environment where there is spreading globalization, or at the very least an ever-expanding radius of competition in many markets. There is an ever-growing number of markets that are reaching maturity, although some others are dramatically new. But the customers in all markets – old and new – are increasing in their sophistication as well as in the critical way they judge offerings.

The underlying principles of the marketing concept are now well understood and accepted in most areas of business. What is more difficult is the actual adherence to the concept inside an organization and, in particular, the implementation of the marketing activities necessary to achieve competitive success.

Implementing marketing

The application of the marketing concept requires a number of specialist functional activities to take place. Usually these will exist in all marketing departments but they can be carried out in an organization that does not have a formal marketing section. Such activities include marketing research, product and service development, advertising promotion and other communication. These activities need to be managed in a coherent way but they are only part of the requirement for success. The most critical areas are all the contacts that take place between suppliers and customers.

Customer contact must be viewed as a continuous activity. There are those activities that take place before any actual trading. Such activities should be aimed at helping to create the right climate for an exchange to take place and could be termed *transaction creating* activities.

Obviously there are the activities surrounding the actual exchange, but following these there is the post-transactional stage when the satisfaction can be increased (or spoilt), and when relationships can be developed. These are the *exchange fulfilment* activities, and all exchanges must be set in the context of a time scale that spans the actual transaction.

These three stages are fully discussed in most standard marketing literature, but as Vandermerwe (1990) suggests, 'this process centres around the buying sequence of a product or service rather than the holistic experience over time'. She argues that it is not enough to understand the benefit a customer receives when a product offering satisfies a particular *want*. Using SKF as an example, she states that 'their customers have one thing in common: they don't want to buy bearings – they want to maximise productivity from their machines'. Goran Malm of SKF has defined his business as 'delivering trouble free operations to customers in the belief that many companies can produce and sell bearings, but few can produce solutions to the problems that bearing users encounter.' Looked at another way, bearings are currently appropriate as the specific demanded product to satisfy a need, but if a new technology offered a new way of doing things then it would not matter how good SKF bearings are when judged against any quality measure (Vandermerwe and Trisholl, 1991).

The author had a similar experience as managing director of a company that supplied pet foods and accessories to Boots retail stores in the UK in the mid-1980s. Boots did not want to sell pet products; rather, they wanted to maximize their financial return from a given retail space. In 1987 they discontinued all pet product ranges although sales levels had always met historical targets.

Organizations really ought to consider the total consumption experiences of their customer and focus their marketing thinking on how to enhance it. Vandermerwe terms the full range of a customer's operations as the Customer Activity Cycle (CAC) and recommends that it should be studied in detail, including the reasons behind some activities. Often suppliers fail to uncover the true *need* because of a focus on achieving a sale. In fact, it could be advantageous to try to predict a customer's lifetime needs (and lifetime value) rather than concentrating on a single purchase transaction.

Both of the above examples show how important it is to understand the customer's activity cycle as a totality. This should lead to a better knowledge of a supplier's real contribution to its customers. It will allow a proper evaluation of the real customer need and will help to fill the 'welfare gap', which has been described by Hooley (1993) as 'the difference between what customers *want* and what they actually *need*'.

Study of the CAC leads onto another basic issue that is important in marketing, that of developing strong relationships with customers. An exchange could be a once-and-for-all single transaction or part of an ongoing series of exchanges where repeat business is the aim. It could be argued that every single customer forms a relationship with the supplier, even in a single transaction. In markets where repeat business is required it is hoped that solid relationships will lead to further exchanges in the future. But in every case, even single transactions, we must never forget the role of existing customers, whether satisfied or not, as influencers of other potential customers.

There will be occasions when the effort involved in developing strong ongoing relationships is not the best strategic choice. A situation could exist when there is always a chance of a share in a particular customer's business but because of the activities of that customer, or other market factors, it would not be cost effective to go beyond each separate transaction. There is, of course, still a need to ensure satisfaction in every transaction that does actually take place but that could be the limit, rejecting further development as inappropriate. What is necessary is to choose carefully those customers where it is worth investing in a deeper relationship, and those where it is not so important. This is more than segmentation, and it is a key strategic issue. Grönroos (1996) has suggested that 'focusing on exchange is too narrow a view. A relationship includes much more than exchanges, and if a trusting relationship between two or several business partners exists, exchanges should inevitably occur from time to time. . . . The relationship is a more fundamental unit of study than the exchanges that from time to time take place in them. Hence the basic concept of marketing is the relationship itself rather than the singular exchanges that occur in the relationship'. While I would agree that relationships can be considered over a longer term than a single exchange, it is the exchange that actually delivers measurable benefits (profit) for both supplier and customer.

It should also be obvious that there are many people inside any organization, not directly part of the marketing area, who are involved in ensuring that a profitable exchange is achieved. Later, there will be a discussion of these 'part-time marketers', as they have been called, which will suggest that good marketing planning and communications are needed for activities inside an organization as well as externally. So the part-time marketers are an important element in successfully applying the marketing concept.

Here we are already making the practice of marketing more difficult because there are so many individuals and issues that impinge on the simple basic marketing exchange.

Achieving success

There is of course another key element in achieving a satisfactory exchange with a chosen customer and that is the competition, both direct and indirect, making offers to that customer. Competitors are probably more unpredictable than customers, but successful marketing in a developed economy is about competitive success, and activities will take place in a fiercely competitive environment – an environment where any new initiative is all too easily copied. A true marketing orientation will combine the three areas of customer focus, competitive positioning and internal consistency. These are reflected in Ohmae's strategic triangle, discussed in Chapter 2.

Ian Wilson, in his book *Marketing Interfaces* (1995), suggests that there are three faces of marketing: *concept, strategies, functions*. He chooses this order deliberately because (fortuitously) the acronym that results, CSF, is also used to refer to critical success factors – the key customer-driven factors that must be present in order to succeed in a given market-place. He shows how both the marketing concept and marketing strategy are firmly rooted in the triad of customer, competitor and our own organization. The concept requires these three to be understood. If a supplier is to continue to develop competitive offerings acceptable to customers then this understanding is another *necessary* condition.

Wilson then suggests that marketing strategy requires that, in the light of this knowledge, the organization follows a coherent and consistent path towards an agreed destination. It is possible to consider the domain of marketing success as the area where:

- customers regard an offer as *acceptable*, in that it meets their needs and wants;
- supply is *feasible* for the producer with regard to the capacity to offer it at a profit; and
- it is *suitable* when compared to other, available, competitive offerings.

This process – known as SFA – has been popularized by Johnson and Scholes (1997). However, it can be adopted for use in many contexts.

These aspects are shown in Figure 1.3 and are discussed further in Chapter 4. One view of marketing strategy could be focused on enlarging the central area where all three circles intersect. Certainly there are opportunities to work on the adjacent areas, where only two components are currently present. This requires improving competitive advantage, acquiring necessary skills/capabilities or increasing demand.

However, strategy is not so simple. By considering the many issues that impinge

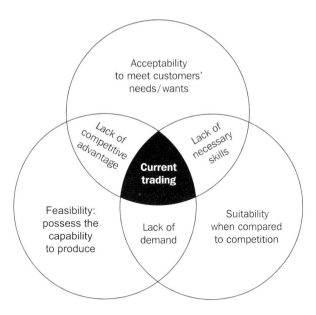

Fig 1.3 The domain of marketing operations

upon an exchange it will be seen that a strategy must embrace a wide range of factors. It is also certain that strategy does not have any prescribed form, nor any limits on the issues that it must consider. Also, as all strategy is focused on the future, there is a poor level of feedback and a high relevance of personal opinion in all strategic decisions.

Marketing strategy

This book is about marketing strategy, and there are several different meanings and uses of the word strategy in business today. It is now a managerial cult word, and a much misused term, so it would be fair to ask *'what is strategy?'*. Originally derived from the ancient Athenian (Greek) word *strategos* (to lead an army), a definition from the first century AD by Frontinus suggested that strategy is 'everything achieved by a commander, be it characterized by foresight, advantage, enterprise, or resolution'. There are some key issues here that translate directly into the modern marketing arena. Foresight involves strategy firmly in actions to be taken that affect future operations; advantage is directly related to winning in a competitive situation; enterprise refers to the capacity to take initiatives; and resolution is the determination to see things through.

So in its original context military strategy should cover that set of policies used for the conduct of a future conflict. If we extend this into business, it should encompass the activity of the organization pertaining to its future operations. In a marketing context this focuses primarily on external dealings and exchanges with customers, but it must include those things necessary inside an organization to support such dealings.

The role of strategy has been discussed by many authors. Mintzberg (1987) suggested a '5P' mnemonic of:

- Strategy as a Plan
- Strategy as a Ploy
- Strategy as a Pattern
- Strategy as a Position
- Strategy as a Perspective

These are all different aspects of strategy, but they can occur at the same time because they are complementary and not exclusive categories. *Plans* are some sort of consciously intended course of action. To fulfil this role the plans must be formed in advance and developed in a purposeful manner. A *ploy* is sometimes part of a general plan, when a particular course of action is undertaken as an attempt to confuse a competitor. Consistent *patterns* of behaviour could be seen as a strategic outcome, although it is not always the case that those patterns are actually intended. The idea of strategy as a *position* to be achieved in a market-place could be seen as a goal or objective, but it is also part of strategy and can be consistent with both predetermined plans and specific patterns of behaviour. A *perspective*, the last category, is more than a pattern of behaviour, a marketing orientation for instance. It is really an ingrained way of seeing the external market and it is very necessary when a company such as Body Shop attempts to take on the major competitors in its market.

Whittington (1993) explores in a structured way 'four very different conceptions of what strategy is and how to do it'. He maps these on a cross matrix, which has the two dimensions of outcomes and processes (Figure 1.4).

The 'classical' rational approach is to be found in most texts on marketing planning. However, practical marketing within most organizations has many of the other dimensions, especially the political issues involving all employees. The idea of a strategy as an emergent pattern of behaviour, or the result of a specific cultural orientation (perspective) is closer to reality in most cases. This text will consider the component parts of strategic marketing decisions rather than a prescriptive procedure to be followed.

Porter (1996) warns about the failure to distinguish between operational effectiveness and strategy. He suggests that in many cases management tools have taken the

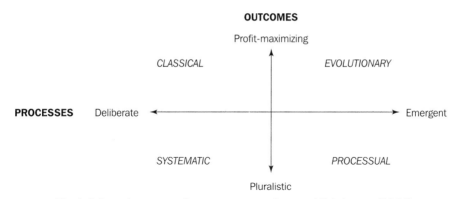

OUTCOMES

Profit-maximizing

CLASSICAL   *EVOLUTIONARY*

PROCESSES   Deliberate ←——————————————→ Emergent

SYSTEMATIC   *PROCESSUAL*

Pluralistic

Fig 1.4 Generic perspectives on strategy. *Source*: Whittington (1993)

place of strategy. In Porter's terms, competitive strategy is about being different, choosing a set of activities to deliver a unique mix of value to customers. Hamel and Prahalad (1996) suggest it is *revolution*, giant leaps as opposed to incremental improvements. But strategy does not always require change; a perfectly acceptable strategy in some circumstances could be no change, but every strategist should guard against complacency as past success can be a real barrier to much-needed future change.

Strategy could be described as the link between objectives and the implementation necessary to achieve those objectives, although the strategy process could include the development of objectives. Strategy can be present at different levels covering an organization as a whole, a part of an organization or even a single transaction such as a salesperson developing a strategy for a sales call on a particular customer. Strategy therefore has many levels.

At the highest level corporate strategy is the equivalent of grand *political* strategy. It will cover decisions on where to get involved and which areas to avoid. In particular, Aaker (1998) suggests 'the scope of a business is defined by the products it offers and chooses not to offer, by the markets it seeks to serve and not serve, by the competitors it chooses to compete with and to avoid'. This is especially important in dynamic and complex markets, and there is therefore a high-level product/market strategy which reflects the question *'what business do we want to be in?'*. This is a fundamental starting point for strategy. It can be answered only by a study of the customers and competitors in the market-place and so is really a key element in high-level marketing strategy.

The term strategic marketing suffers from what Brownlie and Saren (1992) describe as 'strategy general, marketing specific'. There is no reason to create an artificial divide between strategy and marketing. The processes and analytical tools have a commonality; they should exist in harmony, with the marketing emphasis being to integrate the longer term competitive and internal objectives of an organization with those of its selected customers.

Wensley (1996) suggests that *marketing strategy* is an oxymoron. His argument rests on the developments in strategic management, where the study has shifted significantly to consider the processes by which strategies emerge, and the systematic perspective, which is derived from the study of psychology and sociology applied to organizations. This has left the decisions about products and markets and the achievement of competitive advantage where, I suggest, it belongs – with strategic marketers and perhaps industrial economists. I would agree with Wensley that a particular focus for marketing is the behaviour of markets and this is necessary in considering the relationships that are formed around exchanges.

Elements of strategic marketing

The starting point for strategic marketing must be the basic question '*What business do we want to be in?*'

When considering this we could again turn to ancient military strategists. Sun Tzu, the 4th century BC Chinese general and thinker, is reported to suggest that the two factors vital to the choice of battleground are:

- areas that have distinctive advantages
- areas ignored by the enemy.

The choice of product/market reference areas could be categorized in the same way. Peter Drucker (1985) suggested four specific strategies for entrepreneurs, which have a similar foundation.

- being the 'firstest with the mostest'
- 'hitting them where they ain't'
- finding and occupying a specialized ecological niche
- changing the economic characteristics of a product, a market or an industry.

All involve vision as well as good analysis. They accept that in markets where supply exceeds demand, all customers have a choice of what to acquire and who to trade with if such a choice is apparent. Obviously there is much to be gained by avoiding direct competition, but this requires a clear understanding of all those external issues that could affect a competitive situation. To return to Sun Tzu, he goes on to discuss the characteristics of the battleground itself, which should be considered in relation to elements from the wider environment. When translated into the market-place, these require that an organization must know its customers, competitors and itself, as we have stressed already. Such knowledge must be translated into a critical analysis of the issues, and will be part of an analysis that should cover both *industry attractiveness* and *competitive strengths*. These two dimensions are combined in the nine-cell GE matrix, which can be used to develop strategic directions but suffers from difficulties in assessing the key categories in an objective way.

Sun Tzu was a military man and much has been written about the lessons from military strategy that can help business strategy. There are several strong links, especially in the area of beating competition. However, one area where we need to be particularly careful is in our study of the battleground. With military strategy the terrain on which a battle is to be fought could be considered static in many of its characteristics, confined within defined borders. In marketing terms the terrain is the customer, or more precisely the perception as seen by customers, and this is more complex and ever changing. In fact, much marketing effort is aimed at the very difficult task of influencing or perhaps changing customers' perceptions.

I would contend that the choice of product/market, or *where to compete*, is an essential part of high-level strategic marketing but there is an obvious overlap with corporate strategy. While corporate strategists might consider an industry as a complete entity, a marketing strategist would prefer to separate the product from the customer groups (markets). The question can then be split to become *'which customer groups?'* and *'what product areas/customer needs?'*.

Often the product areas are considered to be given by the existing operations of the organization. However, writers in strategic management such as Hamel and Prahalad suggest a new look at such issues which evaluate the competence (or available skills) that an organization possesses. Other writers have developed the theme of capabilities that can be considered as organizational strengths. A good strategic thinker will be able to review what an organization is able to do by taking a dispassionate and objective view of the competencies and capabilities of that organization, and could then define existing operations in a completely new way.

While core competencies and capabilities are internal to an organization, there are, in addition, external 'assets' which are equally important. These will be based on existing trading links and the attitudes customers have regarding the organization. We can consider them as:

• partnership-based assets
• customer-based assets.

The first, partnership assets, are those things derived from the way an offering is made available to the customer. As many items travel along a supply chain before reaching the ultimate consumer, there are issues of the actual network, its convenience and abilities, as well as the various agreements with partners that could affect the ability of competitors to reach customers. These assets can also lead to a level of competitive advantage based on *low delivered costs*, which customers could require.

Customer-based assets cover issues related to the company that are valued by customers or potential customers. They contribute to competitive advantages based on *high perceived value* as evaluated by customers. They are often of an intangible nature such as image, brand names and reputations but they can include more tangible issues such as location, previous performance or known quality levels.

In deciding which product areas to consider a strategist must not confine evaluation to existing products, even though these are an obvious and important starting point. They should include a wide range of product/market areas, but if these are based on existing organizational strengths or 'assets' then there is more likelihood of choosing an area where a competitive advantage could be achieved (Figure 1.5).

However, the fact remains that there are many *high potential old products*, in contrast to the low success rate for new ones. It is said that products are not like people – they do not die of old age. They die of neglect – marketing and management neglect. The history of marketing is littered with success stories of products that would have been written off long ago if the life cycle theory had been the basis of product management.

When an organization is already operating in a defined industry with established customers, then the strength of its position will be a key determinant of how to proceed. If it is possible to defend the position by building ever stronger relationships with existing customers, thus excluding competitors, then this is likely to offer the best option (Figure 1.6). In this case the marketing focus will be on enhancing the customer relationships, both currently and for the future. Hamel and Prahalad use the term *'premier plus 10'* to describe those competencies which must be developed in order to retain existing customers for the next five or ten years.

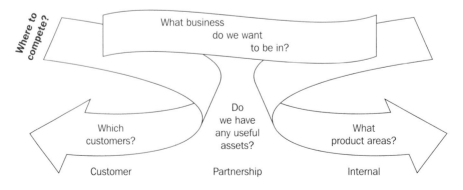

Fig 1.5 Where to compete?

If such a strategy based on building strong relationships with existing customers is selected then this will require an appropriate supporting culture throughout the organization. Gummesson (1997) stresses that relationship marketing is not just another add-on to a solid core of marketing, but it is a paradigm shift which requires a dramatic change in thinking and behaviour. Such issues are discussed more fully in Chapter 13.

So, in deciding where to compete, there must be an assessment of current trading and the advantages of 'sticking to our knitting'. Nevertheless, a good strategist should take an objective view of all opportunities and not be blinkered by the past.

The review of new opportunities leads into alternative strategies based on new markets, and/or new customers – Hamel's *'White spaces' and 'mega-opportunities'*. In such situations issues of market entry, customer creation and challenging established competitors are vital. Chapter 14 discusses issues of expeditionary marketing and the risks/rewards involved in such a strategy.

Following on from the 'where', an organization needs to decide how to compete.

Within any given battleground, strategy will involve the campaigns and manoeuvring necessary to achieve given objectives. This is all part of the decision on how to compete. The aim of marketing strategy is usually to achieve some level of competitive advantage so that a profitable exchange can take place with chosen customers, and, if possible, competitors can be kept out. Decisions on how to compete are the second element of marketing strategy.

We can again benefit by listening to the ancient Greeks. Xenophon suggests that a commander/strategist 'must be ingenious, energetic, careful, full of stamina and presence of mind, loving and tough, straightforward and crafty, alert and deceptive, ready to gamble everything and wishing to have everything, generous and greedy,

Core competencies (and capabilities)

	Existing/**strong**	New/**less certain**
Highly attractive Existing markets	*Penetration* *Fill the blanks*	**New product development** *Premier plus 10*
New markets **Unknown/white spaces**	**New market development** *White spaces*	**Diversification** *Expeditionary marketing*

Fig 1.6 Strategic decisions in existing and new markets: Ansoff matrix adapted to use dimension of competence suggested by Hamel and Prahalad

trusting and suspicious' – a list full of paradox but very relevant to the need to create a position where customer demand and competitive advantage both exist.

There are, of course, many other ways of differentiating an offering, for instance the whole issue of branding. It is perhaps helpful to read Ted Levitt's article, *'Differentiation of anything'* (1983). Levitt is a first-rate marketing thinker, beginning with his first classic, *'Marketing myopia'* in 1960. All of his articles are recommended to strategic marketers.

Customers buy those offerings which they perceive as the best value for them. However, value is not an easy economic measure. It can be derived from tangible product features, but even with these the comparison of the different features must be related to individual buyer requirements. When an offering is augmented by intangible service features then these elements can add value if they are relevant to customers. In this case the buyer's perception of the benefits from the service features becomes more important. The problem of intangibles is that they are much more difficult to measure in a direct fashion than tangibles. In addition to service features, there are intangibles that rely entirely on customer perception of such issues as company image, brand reputation or aesthetic quality. In this area the comparative value equation moves dramatically away from economic utility to psychological measures of value and perceived value.

Inputs to the value equation will come from the *position* that a supply company and its offering occupy in the minds of the buyers. For marketers positioning can be a misunderstood term as there are four distinct concepts, each masquerading under the same name.

- **Market positioning** is the choice of target market and it is related to the idea of strategy as a position. These policies often come from addressing the classic questions of 'What market/business are we in?' and 'What market/business do we want to be in?'. This will be discussed under the general topic of *'where to compete'*.
- **Company** or **competitive positioning** refers to the strategic choices such as specialist or volume producer, first to market or me-too, targeted or undifferentiated and the like. These are orientations of an organization and can be affected by the market positions available. A company might be a market leader and in this situation would probably try to defend a position of strength, but few organizations are so well placed. It is more likely that choices will have to be made about challenging or maybe adopting one of many other positions, perhaps as a *prospector* or *analyser* company as described by Miles and Snow (1978).
- Positioning of an offering (**product positioning**) is about assembling a total product/marketing mix to address coherently and cost effectively the wants and needs of a specific target market. Although the product positioning really needs

to be decided in the light of target market choices, it is an ideal which an organization wishes to achieve.

- This is measured by the perception that customers have rather than what companies think they are offering, so the fourth concept concerns **position as perception** – how customers rate the offering in relation to other products considered in a purchase decision. In contrast with the other three definitions, this is a *result* rather than a choice. However, it is this customer perception of a position which matters in the end because it is this which is critical in a purchase situation.

Positioning is a key issue in deciding how to compete; it should be approached by posing the questions:

- which position is best? (market, company, product)
- what position do we occupy currently?
- what must be done to achieve the chosen position?

These issues are discussed further in Chapter 7, and the relevance of customer perception is stressed throughout this book.

Two things that are vital to understand are:

- it can be very difficult to achieve a desired position
- it is a major task to change the perception of a product or an organization in the mind of a customer.

Competition can also go beyond products to endeavour to create market conditions favourable to a particular offering. Therefore *leverage* (using some instrument of power to gain control over a customer, e.g. reciprocal trading agreements) and *mega marketing* (achieving a competitive advantage by non-marketing external activities such as those described by Kotler (1986) are worth discussing (see Chapter 8). Such manoeuvrings in the external environment have the objective of reducing competition in a particular area, thus enhancing the position of those not disadvantaged.

There is, however, a final aspect of high-level strategy based on the nature of markets themselves. Markets are dynamic, and opportunities occur, but windows of opportunity both open and close. Derek Abell (1978) explored these windows and suggested that product offerings must be actively managed to take account of market changes, and marketers must not be afraid to delete as well as develop products. So the issue of *when to compete* is also critical.

At the highest level, strategic marketing covers three key decisions, which are shown in Table 1.1.

Table 1.1 The 'where', 'when' and 'how' of competition

Where to compete	
Issues regarding the selection of product/markets and choosing target customers, leading to a decision on	Which markets (customer groups) to trade with (who is to be satisfied).
the specific product areas in which to operate	Which customer needs/benefits to try to satisfy
How to compete	
Sustainable competitive advantage and those critical success factors that lead to it, such as branding, relationships and quality positions	What is the basis for our competitive offerings?
	Which technologies are we going to use?
	Which competitive position should we take?
	Are there any other ways to compete?
When to compete	

The basis on which decisions are taken involves:

- Analysis: structure and method for analysing external markets and internal 'assets'
- Evaluation: evaluating options in the light of company capacity and attitude to risk.

The role of analysis

To underpin effective strategic decisions it has been argued that a good audit must be undertaken, although there is limited empirical evidence to support this. One result of good analysis should be an identification of the really important issues. Without this the strategic choices will tend to be continuations of the past. The goal is competitive advantage, and good strategists understand their markets even if they try to move away from conformity with industry norms to achieve some form of sustainable competitive advantage. If a formal audit is to be undertaken then it must be done critically. The basic models are only useful if they help true understanding of the few critical success factors in the chosen market and the real strengths/weaknesses rather than produce a long menu. We must consider strategy as a response to external opportunities and threats as well as to internal strengths and weaknesses. Therefore, there is a need for a thorough understanding of customers, competitors and the decision to be made on what competitive stance to adopt. Analysis is discussed further in Chapter 3.

Evaluating strategy

Any resulting strategy must be evaluated from the viewpoint of the customer, who is the ultimate judge. However, such decisions as low price/high volume, heavy promotional spend, or maybe a follower strategy of slipstreaming a brand leader could have as much to do with organizational resources as with the wants of customers.

A useful framework for evaluating decisions is the one suggested by Johnson and Scholes (1997). Their interpretation of these three aspects considers them in relation to the objectives of an organization and its stakeholders on the basis of:

- Suitability to meet objectives
- Feasibility of achievement
- Acceptability to stakeholders in the organization.

In this text the test is being amended slightly and the tests of marketing strategy will be:

- Suitability to customers in a dynamic competitive environment
- Feasibility of achievement by the supply organization
- Acceptability to meet the needs/expectations of customers.

However, it is sometimes dangerous to rely on acronyms in order to remember issues. For instance the SFA acronym is also used in another way by the Federal Express Company to mean Survey → Feedback → Action. This is, of course, the core of the management process.

Strategic marketing management

As already suggested, it is important to separate the strategic marketing decision making from the marketing management necessary to put that strategy into operation and achieve effectiveness. The first covers the analysis and decision making; the second, the planning, implementation and control.

Analysis and decision making are the equivalent of the highest level of grand strategy. Planning, implementation and control are a second-level business strategy. Ansoff (1965) once said that 'strategy and objectives are interchangeable both at different points in time and different levels within the organization. Thus elements of strategy at a high level become objectives at a lower level'. However, both levels require an appreciation of the three key elements: customers, competitors and our own organization. In fact, it is necessary to consider each of these players separately within all levels of strategy. It is of course obvious that both good strategy and good implementation (tactics) are necessary for success (Bonoma, 1984).

So the real test of strategy and the involvement of marketing management comes at the second level of strategy.

- Planning
- Implementation and effectiveness issues
- Control.

Conclusions

The basic concept of marketing is that of a profitable exchange with customers. In order to achieve this it is necessary to understand the differences between *needs*, *wants* and *demands*. In fact, these can be considered as emerging from a customer activity cycle, and consideration of this will establish where a total offering fits in.

Customers receive the benefit from the supplier, but they also establish a relationship as a result of an exchange. The links do not have to be very deep, but there could be advantages in establishing strong relationships. Successful strategy is based on customer choice when faced with a range of different offerings and different suppliers. It is therefore based within the triad of customers, corporate capabilities and competition.

Strategy has many roles, but good marketing principles should underpin strategy in all trading organizations. Marketing strategy focuses on the *product/market/exchange* area, and will aim to achieve some form of competitive advantage to ensure exchanges take place. Some advantages derive from the assets that companies have as a result of past operations. These could be obtained by the networks and partnerships that exist, or be dependent on the perception that the customer organization has regarding the supplier. In all evaluations it is the customer perspective that is paramount, this being especially obvious where the costs of switching suppliers is low.

While it is necessary to evaluate from a customer perspective, the actual decisions are taken by the supplier with regards to where, how and when to compete. Such decisions have to be suitable, feasible and acceptable when considered within the overall strategy, and when judged against the dynamics of changing competitors and customer demands.

KEY POINTS

1.1 It is important to understand basic marketing issues such as the differences between needs, wants, desires and expectations, as well as the idea of the total product as embracing everything received by a customer when considering strategy.

1.2 It is crucial that marketers understand both their customers' activity cycles (how they operate in a wider frame than just the product being considered) and the critical success factors that energize those customers to make purchases in a specific product area.

1.3 While the choice of strategic direction is important in the strategy process, it is equally necessary to complement this with effective implementation.

1.4 Strategy has many facets, and all must be appreciated by strategists, not just the issue of strategy as a future plan.

1.5 Organizations can possess many strong marketing assets, which they should utilize. These can be divided into internal assets (competencies and capabilities) and partnership- and customer-based (perceived) assets.

1.6 Marketing (market oriented) strategy involves three major issues: where to compete, how to compete and when to compete.

1.7 Success is not always the result of good marketing – it can derive from external initiatives which lead to a strong competitive situation (mega marketing). The possibility of achieving market power over customers by such means must not be ignored.

QUESTIONS

1.1 How is it that, in spite of excellent marketing feedback through research, a product offered to a customer might still fail to meet that customer's basic needs?

1.2 CSF stands for critical success factors. Define the term (CSF) and give an example from an industry of your choice.

1.3 Porter suggests *differentiation* and *focus* strategies; similarly, Sun Tzu recommends looking for *areas with distinctive advantages* and *areas ignored by the enemy*.
Give an example of a successful company adopting each strategic position.

> **1.4** Companies have 'marketing' assets in the same way that they have 'balance sheet' assets. Define the three categories of 'marketing' assets and identify an example of each.

Bibliography

Aaker, D., *Strategic Market Management*, 5th Edn, Wiley, 1998.

Abell, D., Strategic Windows, *Journal of Marketing*, July, pp. 21–26, 1978.

Ansoff, H.I., *Corporate Strategy*, McGraw-Hill, 1965.

Bonoma, T., Making Your Marketing Strategy Work, *Harvard Business Review*, March/April 1984.

Brownlie, D. and Saren, M., The Four Ps of the Marketing Concept: Prescriptive; Polemical; Permanent; and Problematical, *European Journal of Marketing*, Vol. 26 No. 4, 1992.

Dibb, S. and Simkin, L., *Marketing*, 2nd European Edn, Houghton Mifflin, 1994.

Doyle, P., *Marketing Management and Strategy*, Prentice Hall, 1994.

Drucker, P., *Innovation and Entrepreneurship*, Heinemann, 1985.

Fifield, P., *Marketing Strategy*, Butterworth Heinemann, 1993.

Grönroos, C., The Rise and Fall of Modern Marketing, in S. Shaw and N. Hood (eds) *Marketing in Evolution*, Macmillan, 1996.

Gummesson, E., Relationship Marketing as a Paradigm Shift, Some Conclusions from the 30R Approach, *Management Decisions*, Vol. 35 No. 4, 1997.

Hamel, G. and Prahalad, C.K., *Competing for the Future*, HBS Press, 1994.

Hamel, G. and Prahalad, C.K., Strategy as Revolution, *Harvard Business Review*, July/Aug. 1996.

Hooley, G., Market Led Quality Management, *Journal of Marketing Management*, Vol. 9, 1993.

Hooley, G. and Saunders, J., *Competition Positioning*, Prentice Hall, 1993.

Johnson, G. and Scholes, D., *Exploring Corporate Strategy*, 4th Edn, Prentice Hall, 1997.

Kotler, P., Mega Marketing, *Harvard Business Review*, May/April 1986.

Kotler, P., *Marketing Management: Analysis, Planning, Implementation and Control*, 9th Edn, Prentice Hall, 1997.

Kotler, P., *On Marketing*, Simon & Schuster, 1999.

Levitt, T., Marketing Myopia, *Harvard Business Review*, July/Aug., pp. 45–56, 1960.

Levitt, T., Differentiation of Anything, in *The Marketing Imagination*, Free Press, 1983 (originally published in *Harvard Business Review*).

McDonald, M., *Marketing Plans*, Heinemann, 1997.

Miles, R.E. & Snow, C.C., *Organizational Strategy, Structure and Process*, McGraw-Hill, 1978.

Mintzberg, H., 5 P's of Strategy, *Californian Management Review*, Fall, 1987.

Murray J.A. and O'Driscoll, A., *Strategy and Process in Marketing*, Prentice Hall, 1996.

Porter, M., What is Strategy?, *Harvard Business Review*, Nov./Dec. 1996.

Sun Tzu, *The Art of War*, Wordsworth, 1993.

Vandermerwe, S., The Market Power is in the Service, Because the Value is in the Result, *European Management Journal*, Vol. 8 No. 4, 1990.

Vandermerwe, S. and Trisholl, M., SKF bearings; market orientation through services, IMD case no. M383, Switzerland, 1991.

Wensley, R., Another Oxymoron in Marketing – Marketing Strategy, in S. Shaw and N. Hood (eds) *Marketing in Evolution*, Macmillan, 1996.

Whittington, R., *What is Strategy and Does it Matter*, Routledge, 1993.

Wilson, I., *Marketing Interfaces*, Pitman, 1995.

CUSTOMERS, COMPANY CAPABILITIES AND COMPETITORS

2 CHAPTER

INTRODUCTION

The important triad of customers, company capabilities and competitors was intro-duced in the previous chapter. The 3 Cs of marketing are the components of what Ohmae (1983) calls the 'strategic triangle'. Each of these elements is a 'living entity with its own interests and objectives'. By considering the 'strategic triangle' it is possible to consider how any chosen strategy matches company capabilities with the needs of a specific customer group. It also facilitates the assessment of advan-tages in the key success factors when measured against competition. In order to achieve this it is necessary to identify who is a customer, who is a competitor and what are the implications of each player, as well as understanding what are the capabilities of the organization (Figure 2.1).

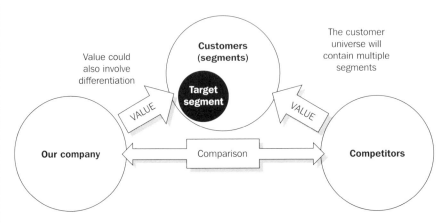

Fig 2.1 The strategic three Cs. *Source*: Adapted from Ohmae (1983)

This chapter will look at these elements in some detail to understand more deeply the varying make-up of each category. This is important because there are so many different ways of defining the scope of each grouping. The actual boundaries chosen can have a real effect when considering the complexities of strategic decisions, embracing both choice of customer and what to offer to those customers.

Marketing is, by its very nature, responsive to market conditions although it is important to act in a proactive way and not just be reactive. Nevertheless, all marketing strategists must appreciate their company resources and capabilities, and the limits these impose. This is not to restrict action where an organization stretches its capabilities and somehow overcomes a serious lack of competitive resource, but if it stretches itself too far, and is thus unable to satisfy all its customers in a highly competitive market, it could lose everything. In fact it is often better, and more profitable, to 'own' a small market niche where all activity is focused than it is to be too widely spread. Because of this it is stressed that all strategies must be *feasible* within the competencies of a particular organization, and this is a critical test of strategy. This must be remembered when considering the other 'actors' in the marketing triad of customers, company capabilies and competitors.

Customers

A customer is a 'person with whom one has dealings', according to a definition in the *Oxford English Dictionary*. For the purposes of strategic marketing the study of customers should be wider, including existing customers, potential new customers and lapsed (former) customers. A great deal can be learnt by such study, and much relevant information can be obtained from each distinct group.

In attempting to decide which customer groups to trade with, and what needs/benefits to satisfy, it is first necessary to realize that every organization has many distinct groups of customers, each with a different set of needs.

Organizations do not exist solely as a supplier or a customer in a dyadic relationship with another party. They are, firstly, part of a complex network of many suppliers and customers, and it might be necessary to map this network to understand fully the forces acting on any individual member or group. Within any network there are complex links involving different suppliers and customers, as well as suppliers to suppliers and the customers of customers (Figure 2.2). Nevertheless, it is often necessary to concentrate on one particular customer link in an attempt to make the consideration of decisions more manageable.

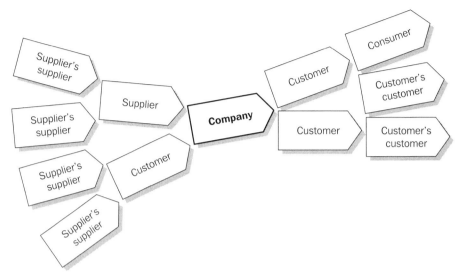

Fig 2.2 Marketing within networks

Secondly, there are strategic groupings of customers and other exchange partners, each of whom is following similar strategies or acting in similar ways. These groups can be considered as homogeneous entities if the common aspects of their behaviour patterns are relevant to their exchange decisions. But care must be exercised, as in the example below, where similarities in behaviour do not lead to identical needs.

Example: branded food products supplied to Sainsbury's and Tesco

> I once worked for Cadbury Schweppes. Sales of products through major supermarkets is of vital importance to this company. In negotiating with retailers such as Tesco and Sainsbury's, agreements are reached regarding the range of products to be stocked, the space to be allocated in store, and, of course, the buying and selling prices. Many years ago the manufacturer was able to dictate the final selling price, but this has been deemed illegal under competition legislation. Now the selling price is determined by the retailer, which calculates an acceptable level with reference to its sales objectives and its own costing situation. Although this price is not computed by a rigid formula, there is often a normal way of calculating it. Consumers do not know anything of these events. They see only the products on sale at a specific price in each store. For major brands such as Wispa and Dairy Milk in a crowded confectionery sector, no one retailer is happy to be any more expensive than its direct competitors. While Cadbury wants to maximize distribution and sales of Cadbury brands through all outlets, Tesco wants to achieve profitability from total sales of confectionery irrespective of the manufacturer. As profitability is a combination of

turnover and profit margin, if any brands are more expensive in Tesco stores than that same product in Sainsbury's there could be a problem affecting both volume of sales and consumer perception of the store. Consequently, any special deal that Cadbury might enter into with one retail group could have a negative effect on the relationship with other retail distributors.

Hence some strategic groups are made more complex due to the competitive relationships between specific suppliers as well as conflict between customers who are rivals in their own right.

Thirdly, there are different individual influences on any customer, industrial or consumer. The traditional industrial grouping of *users, influencers, deciders, advisers* and *gatekeepers* can equally well be considered in consumer markets, where family or peer influences can fulfil similar roles. It is therefore essential to identify the roles of different parties in the buying process to explore customer relationships. Each separate link is a two-way exchange, with both parties requiring a 'profitable' exchange to achieve satisfaction.

It is possible to use the term 'customer' for anyone with whom our organization has a relationship, and this leads to the consideration of a wider stakeholder group of 'customers'. Hunt and Morgan (1994) considered these exchanges between different stakeholder 'customers' and an organization. As can be seen from the double-headed arrows in Figure 2.3, each is a two-way exchange involving both giving and taking.

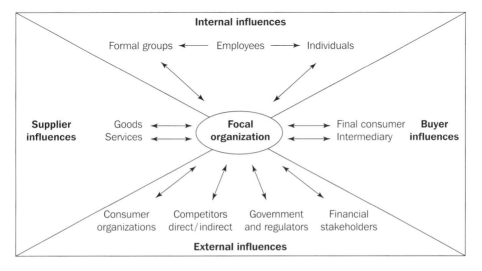

Fig 2.3 Influences on an organization. *Source*: Hunt and Morgan (1994)

While it is logical to suggest that 'customers' comprise all organizations or individuals involved in an exchange relationship with our organization, is the term 'customer' really appropriate and, anyway, who actually is the customer?

The term customer has now started to be applied in all sorts of areas. For instance, privatized rail companies often refer to passengers as customers, a term many resent, especially as customer care is perceived as poor in this market-place. Schools are also embracing a market focus, but who are their customers – parents or pupils? At a more basic level, considering this textbook, is the customer the library that purchased it, the lecturer who recommended purchase or the student who uses it?

It is not the term 'customer' that is important. In fact, there are often more appropriate words to use in specific situations, such as client, patient, passenger, visitor or voter. However, what is important is that an attitudinal shift is required by all employees to consider all *exchange partners* as important, and to seek ways of increasing satisfaction.

While the marketing focus will, usually, be on those customers who receive the planned output of an organization, exchanges with other stakeholders – employees, banks, suppliers of goods and services – cannot be ignored because requirements in one area for a profitable exchange can enhance or restrict efforts in another area.

Example

A particular investment bank has a policy of lending only to 'ethical' companies. This encompasses the way those companies operate internally, as well as the type of products they offer for sale and the markets which they serve. If such a company wishes to expand into areas considered unsuitable (unethical) then that company will either have to find a new source of finance or cancel the proposed expansion.

There are similar restrictions involving some licensed technology where the sale of products such as advanced computer systems to certain markets is prohibited by the terms of the licensing agreement.

Consistent with the consideration of influence and the concept of a profitable exchange, it is possible to consider suppliers as one type of 'customer'.

Some supplier/'customers' may, apparently, receive only a cash consideration as their payment for the exchange. However, this may not be the whole story. For example, being a 'Ford approved supplier' may be extremely beneficial for an automotive components company in that the status could be used as a mark of approval in dealings with other partners. In the same way, a holder of a 'Royal family warrant' can use the endorsement stating that a specific company is a supplier of particular goods to a member of the royal family. Other benefits that are not always obvious include access to specific technology, reciprocal trading or the security of knowing that a particular contract enables all company overheads to be covered so that other business can be pursued on a marginal costing basis. Therefore, the decision to deal with a particular 'customer' will involve consideration of a wide range of issues.

On the other hand, some suppliers of cash and technology might wish to restrict dealings to a limited number of organizations with which they prefer to trade. This goes further to the idea of exclusive distribution contracts operated by manufacturing companies. Such arrangements can be the cause of conflict when a distributor/ 'customer' feels unfairly excluded in a network. In the case of Tesco supermarkets and Levi jeans, the retailer actually bought jeans from small clothing stores across the USA to enable these to be sold in UK grocery outlets. There are now moves to find ways around the restrictions imposed on retailers by Adidas.

All of these issues focus on the question of defining as precisely as possible:

Who is or who might be a customer?

When considering strategic groups of existing customers it is behaviour, not characteristics, which is the appropriate area for study. One useful classification has four general categories. At one end of the scale there are the loyal 'advocates' who have built up a strong relationship and who do much more than trade in that they fully support and try to develop the partnership further. At the other end there are customers who can be considered as 'terrorists' – an extreme form of dissatisfied customer described by Jones and Sasser (1995) as 'customers who have had a bad experience and can't wait to tell others about their anger and frustration'. Customers will not be static in their views but will redefine attitudes based on each succeeding contact with an organization. All exchanges are judged on how they are perceived to meet the objectives of the participating parties. Jones and Sasser further suggest that 'the unreasonable demands of unhappy customers whose needs do not fit with the company's capabilities can devour excessive resources and wreak havoc on employee morale. For just this reason, such outstanding service organizations as Nordstrom department stores, and South West Airlines regularly "fire" customers they cannot properly serve. They recognise counter-productive efforts when they see them'.

In between are the 'mercenaries' who only deal if 'the price is right' or if they want a 'change of pace' from a more regular supplier. Such customers come and go but offer little commitment to developing relationships.

A fourth category, 'hostages', consists of customers who are trapped into dealing because of the lack of suitable alternatives currently available. Perhaps some of these hostages should be 'fired' as their lack of satisfaction could turn to 'terrorist' behaviour in time or when a more acceptable option appears.

These groups can be mapped on a loyalty/satisfaction matrix (Figure 2.4). There are differences in the strategies relevant to each of these groups. This again emphasizes the need for identification of the different customer groups, with different characteristics requiring distinct strategies. New 'advocates' could come from the conversion of 'mercenaries' into 'loyalists', by recovering 'defectors' (lost customers) or by identifying new potential customers who can also be considered as a relevant strategic customer group.

A great deal can be learnt by studying customers' motivations in depth. The customer activity cycle (CAC), introduced in Chapter 1, embraces the totality of customer actions and its study leads to a deeper knowledge of the reasons for such activities. This type of customer orientation is an ideal that is to be desired, but it is often not possible to get to the true motivations. Many suppliers rely on their belief, derived from long association or closeness to customers, that they *know* what their customers expect. This is dangerous unless such beliefs can be constantly checked and validated. Marketing research is the most common way of closing the market intelligence gap (gap 5, Figure 2.5). Such techniques are widely used when customers are remote, or when there are just too many to consider individually, but they often do not delve deeply enough, investigating only *expectations* rather than *wants* and more specifically *needs*. As shown in Figure 2.5, a large number of gaps can

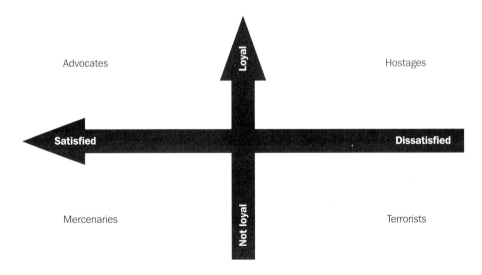

Fig 2.4 A matrix relating loyalty and satisfaction.
Source: Adapted from Jones and Sasser (1995)

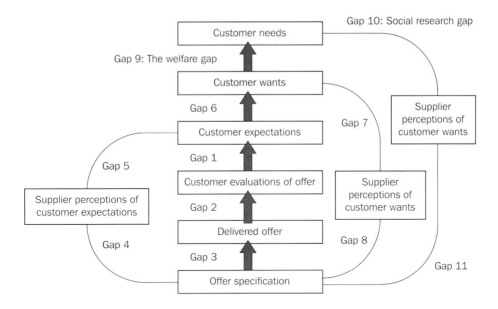

Fig 2.5 Market-led quality management. Professor Graham Hooley described 11 'gaps' that can occur in trying to meet customer needs (see also Figure 1.1). *Source*: Hooley (1993)

occur when evaluating customers' activities, and there is a risk of inadequate perceptions being assigned to customers.

Each strategic group of customers, and even many individual customers, must be studied and evaluated separately from every other group. Drucker (1968) suggested 'there is only one purpose for an organization, that is to create and retain a customer'. The retention of suitable existing customers is an activity quite distinct from the creation of new customers – it requires different skills and strategies.

It is possible to adapt the categories of the well-known Boston Consulting Group (BCG) matrix and apply them to Figure 2.5. Certainly the cash generating/cash requirement needs of the major groups are similar. By focusing on customers the emphasis becomes much more marketing oriented than the original Boston matrix (Figure 2.6). It is also possible to consider the development of customers, such as embryonic new customers who could become the loyalists of the future. The full range of 'wants' which such customers consider important should be established as these are the critical success factors that have such an influence on the buying decision in establishing which offerings are suitable.

Some of the criticism of the original Boston matrix must also be considered. For instance, not all 'cash cows' are available for continual milking, many longstanding loyal customers require continuous investment, and not all 'dogs' should be elimi-

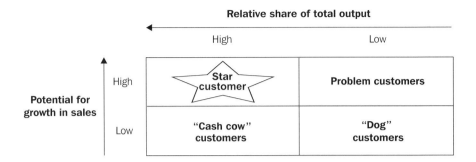

Fig 2.6 Adapting the Boston Consulting Group matrix to customer groupings

nated because some could be developed into satisfied customers with appropriate effort.

The issues regarding different customer groups and the various influences on them will be very important when trying to define a market and to segment a market effectively. Markets are discussed in Chapter 4; segmentation, which is covered in Chapter 6, is a strategic tool that all too frequently degenerates into a division of markets on the basis of easily accessed criteria such as age or location, without appreciating the range of different discriminators that should be chosen for useful 'customer-driven' segmentation.

Company capabilities

The study of customers will establish what makes an offer 'suitable' to satisfy the needs/wants of a particular segment or an individual customer. The achievement of a suitable output must be dictated by a study of what is 'feasible' in terms of the activities necessary to supply it. As mentioned above, some customers make demands that are excessive, and the attempt to fulfil such demands could lead either to a loss of profitability or to the creation of unhappy hostages or even terrorists among customers. It is therefore very important for an organization to 'know itself' and appreciate its assets, both tangible and intangible, so that a match can be achieved.

Porter (1987) has offered a framework in which to consider the activities of an organization in his value chain (Figure 2.7). He defined two types of activities:

- Primary activities: through which a company adds value to its inputs for those customers prepared to pay for the output.
- Support activities: those activities required to support the primary value-adding activities, both now and in the future.

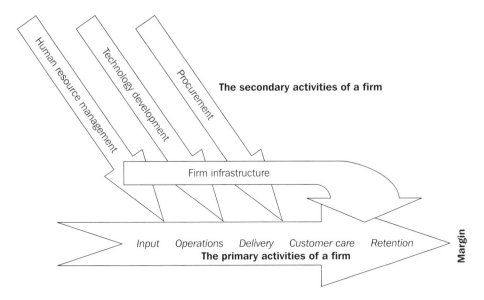

Fig 2.7 A firm's value chain activities. *Source:* Adapted from Porter (1985)

In order to offer 'products' to customers in an effective way, the 'chain' must exhibit strong linkages between each of the primary activities. However, when considering the margin achieved, the amount of added value can only be justified if the benefit from each action is more valued by customers than the cost of providing it.

The value chain does force questions about the internal processes, their role and their importance. When considering the support activities it is possible to address issues such as what must be *known* or *owned* in order to perform those primary activities necessary to fulfil strategy. That means those primary activities vital to market success with respect to the critical success factors that actually matter as they energize customers to make purchases.

This introduces the concepts of capabilities and competencies, which are now widely discussed by Hamel and others. Capabilities are rather more far reaching than Porter's concept of HRM as they include a study of the way things are done in an organization. Core competencies are defined by Hamel and Prahalad (1994) as 'a bundle of skills and technologies that enable a company to provide a particular benefit to customers'. As such, this concept embraces more than Porter's technological development. The consideration of the infrastructure should embrace the natural interaction between capabilities and competencies and how such activities should be organized. It is possible to widen this further to use techniques such as business process reengineering to assess whether there is a better way of doing things. The fourth Porter activity – procurement – can also be redefined and considered in terms of which resources are really available or could feasibly be obtained.

An amended value chain including these revised support factors could then be used to help the understanding and components of the internal company activities (Figure 2.8).

While the strategic concept of a 'fit' between an offer and a demand is a factor in a profitable exchange, there are a number of authors who warn against a static definition of organizational capabilities. Hamel suggests the separation of function (core benefit) and form (product/service being offered). He challenges an organization to distinguish between these two aspects and then reconsider the 'function' as defined by the chosen customer. It is then possible to ask if the 'form' (offering) is appropriate.

Three components of company capabilities require consideration:

1. The capabilities, competencies and resources that a company owns or could readily acquire.
2. The structural links that a company has established, its partnership-based assets.
3. The perception specific customers already have of a company and its offerings (customer-based assets).

In studying the first of these, Hamel and Prahalad looked at the stretching of resources to achieve more than the obvious. This is reminiscent of Robert Townsend's experience at Avis Rent-a-Car, when he drove the company to try harder because it was number 2 in that market.

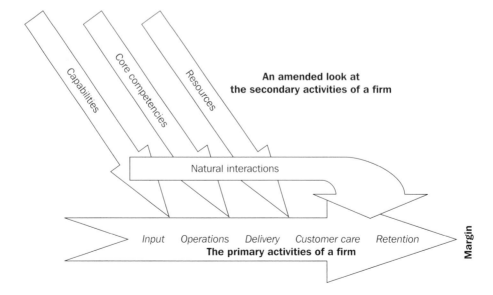

Fig 2.8 A revised value chain

The tangible resources of an organization are reasonably obvious and even the core competencies of skills can be identified. What is less easy to establish is how far these can be leveraged to create a greater level of capabilities than is apparent, and how the enhanced offering can be presented to customers.

The second component embraces the idea of a network with structural bonds or partnership-based assets coming from those links involving employees, suppliers and customers. Kay (1993) uses the term 'architecture' for these important sources of competitive advantage for a company. A strong architecture is built upon an established network of relationships, contracts or understandings between partners, which influence their behaviour towards each other. For instance, Marks & Spencer was able to offer high quality, good service and overall value for money because of its strong relationships with its suppliers. The recent events at Marks & Spencer, with a significant loss of sales and major reduction in profit, indicate that there are risks as well as rewards in long-term relationships if both parties lose touch with the changing demands in their immediate market-place.

Strong linkages will only result in a sustainable competitive advantage if the eventual customer in that market perceives one company's product offering to be superior to that of another company. This third component stresses the reality that customer beliefs are often more important than objective comparisons.

Customers have many beliefs about an organization, some positive, some negative. In considering capabilities both are relevant. They do not have to be true; it is enough that a customer perceives them to be true. Of course, if there is a gap between perception and reality in a critical area, e.g. quality or product performance, then action needs to be taken to ensure the gap is closed before such a difference becomes a strategic problem.

By comparing the requirements of the chosen customers with the available capabilities, the question of the suitability of an offering which it is feasible to offer can be established.

Adapting the Suitability–Feasibility–Acceptability test of strategy to the question of an offering, the only remaining question is whether that offering is 'suitable' when considered in a competitive context.

Competitors

Identifying current competitors must also be approached from a customer perspective. It can only be accomplished effectively after answering the question 'who are the customers we want to deal with?'.

Every one of our chosen customers will devise their own 'evoked set' or group of product/offerings which that customer considers as possible alternatives to meet a specific want. In considering the development of needs through wants to demands for particular offerings, there will be a stage when all those offerings which a customer believes could satisfy the deeper needs are evaluated either formally or instinctively. It is at this stage in the process that an evoked set is constructed. By adopting a customer perspective it will be possible to reflect the actual buying situation and so reveal whom the customer considers as the direct competition, and maybe also which substitute products are also relevant. By considering why a customer has placed certain organizations within or outside the 'evoked set' then it should be possible to assess why some competitor organizations are included while others could be surprisingly omitted. This could lead to a revised definition of the critical success factors present in that market.

The competitors from within the evoked set are today's current competition, and must be studied thoroughly. Beyond this group there are the 'potential entrants' as found in Porter's five-forces model. When considering competitors, a Porter analysis (see Chapter 3) may take us a little further in considering potential new entrants as well as direct competitors. These more distant competitors are often impossible to identify and hence are not always evaluated. Nevertheless, the analysis should try to generate competitors who fall into the categories shown in Figure 2.9.

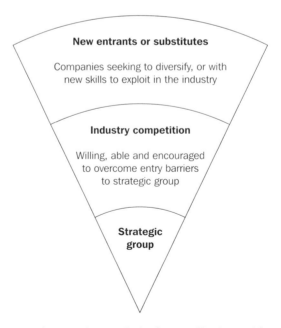

Fig 2.9 The targets of competitor analysis. *Source*: Hooley and Saunders (1993)

There will be both competitors who already have a relevant offering but for some reason are not yet included in the evoked set, as well as those who might overcome barriers to entry in the future. All such competitors should be included when assessing the future acceptability of an offering. Reference to the 'domain of marketing' (see Figure 1.3) will indicate that there could be competitors who are able to meet two out of the three necessary conditions of acceptability to customers, feasibility of being produced and suitability of their offering in a competitive market-place. All such companies could be considered as potential competitors, and thus evaluating the probability that they might overcome the limiting criteria can be an element in a competitor analysis.

The first aim of competitor analysis is to enable current offerings to be evaluated and so to judge the balance of competitive advantage that exists now and in the short-term future. A second role is to understand the constraints binding competitors and to predict competitive movements that could affect the market in the future. A third task is to build a 'response model', which can be used to consider how a competitor would react in response to changes in the strategy of others.

The overriding objective is to establish points of leverage that can be used at minimum cost against competitors to ensure the ongoing acceptability of an offering. It is necessary, therefore, to avoid ideological blinkers and to focus on the strategic essentials.

In the building of a response model, a lot can be discovered from public statements from competitors, what they say to explain their actions, as well as their obvious architecture. It is often worth holding a few shares in competitors for this purpose. However, many companies will try to confuse or at least be 'economical with the truth' and so the sort of market signals recommended by Porter are not always available or helpful. It is often more useful to study past patterns of actions as these can give a good guide to future responses. In this there are parallels with military strategy. For instance, the Duke of Wellington had studied all of Napoleon's campaigns and therefore expected an attempt to cut through his lines and attack *sur le derrière*. He chose his position and troop deployment at Waterloo to counter this and it played an important part in his victory.

Kotler (1997) identifies four roles that companies might adopt in competitive markets. These are market leaders, market challengers, market followers and market nichers. Miles and Snow (1978) suggested that companies could be defenders, prospectors, analysers or reactors. Each of these, except the Miles and Snow reactors, can be linked to the position of strength a firm holds in a particular market. Obviously, some roles are not appropriate for all players. If a firm is not the leader in a market the choice is often between challenging and following or prospecting new markets. A challenger will try to grow using aggressive marketing tactics aimed at gaining customers. These customers have to be acquired either from the leader or from less strong competitors. A follower will hope to benefit from a policy of slip-streaming the leader, not taking the initiative but picking up a modest level of sales without major investment. The position chosen will be obvious from past actions, and there is a good chance the same stance will continue into the future.

There are many examples of firms challenging and overtaking a market leader by leveraging their resources while the larger competitor failed to react. Hamel and Prahalad have studied a number of such cases: General Motors versus Toyota, Pan Am versus British Airways, RCA versus Sony and others. They suggest that it is the ambition of organizations as shown by their employees' actions rather than the corporate resources which dictate how well a company competes. Hamel and Prahalad discuss the managerial frame of reference – assumptions, premises and accepted wisdom – and suggest that this gives useful insight into why some leader companies have failed to react to meet challenges, and, equally, why some challengers have been able to succeed. It is one thing knowing who are our competitors, another having a realistic response model, but the critical third lies in the ability to react in the appropriate way.

Conclusions

There is no doubt that all strategic marketing decisions should be developed and evaluated within the triad of chosen customers, our organizational capabilities and the impact of potential competitors. However, as this chapter shows, it is not easy to define these components and it is difficult to assess the extent of the influence of any one group.

Within customer groups there are those who are very desirable advocates, loyal in action and profitable to serve. There are others who are awkward or even destructive, as well as some who receive our messages but react negatively without any other contact with our organization. Such behavioural patterns must be considered in any segmentation exercise.

In addition, all stakeholders are part of exchange relationships with a focal organization. There can be conflict in these relationships as the links with one stakeholder could directly impinge upon the development of a profitable exchange with another stakeholder/customer.

To achieve a profitable exchange requires the utilization of the appropriate capabilities by the supplier. These must reflect the critical success factors as developed from the actual way that the needs and wants of customers are met. The internal competence of a supplier depends partially on the physical resources available, but perhaps even more important is the way in which intangible elements are utilized. These might be reflected in extraordinary levels of service or in more appropriate offerings, which enhance the satisfaction felt by customers.

The satisfaction of customers is a comparative measure. It is determined by the individual customer within the framework of known offerings, although it is evaluated after a transaction has occurred. The ability of a supplier to identify relevant competitors and predict their future activities can be a major factor in achieving a position of strength when compared within the customer's evoked set, and may thus influence a purchase.

KEY POINTS

2.1 There are three key issues that interact in a market-place: customers, company capabilities and competitors.

2.2 Organizations do not operate solely as suppliers or customers in a dyadic relationship with another party. They are part of a complex network of many suppliers and customers.

2.3 Organizations should regard all their exchange partners as a form of customer with whom a profitable relationship can be developed.

2.4 Customer groups differ in particular with regard to their level of satisfaction from the exchange and their loyalty to the relationship.

2.5 Companies must identify and concentrate on a limited number of critical competencies which determine their ability to ensure a competitive offering (although they must endeavour to stretch these without extending them too far).

2.6 There are many competitors for all markets, and it is not always possible to identify the main threats. However, analysis of known competitors can both reduce suprise and identify points of leverage that can be used at minimum cost against a competitor.

QUESTIONS

2.1   When considering marketing strategy, is it more important to meet (satisfy) customer needs or to achieve a competitive advantage?

2.2   What is the specific problem with customers who are termed (a) mercenaries and (b) hostages? Suggest how these problems could be allowed for in a marketing strategy.

2.3   Why is it critical to understand a company's capabilities when developing strategy? Are these capabilities likely to limit strategic marketing options?

2.4   What are competitive points of leverage? How might identification of them contribute to an effective strategy?

Bibliography

Argenti, J., *Practical Corporate Planning*, Unwin, 1989.

Dibbs, S. and Simkin, L., *Marketing*, 2nd European Edn, Houghton Mifflin, 1994.

Doyle, P., *Marketing Management and Strategy*, Prentice Hall, 1994.

Drucker, P., *The Practice of Management*, Pan, 1968.

Hamel, G. and Prahalad, C.K., *Competing for the Future*, HBS Press, 1994.

Hamel, G. and Prahalad, C.K., Strategy as Stretch and Leverage, *Harvard Business Review*, March/Apr., pp. 75–84, 1996.

Hooley, G., Market-Led Quality Management, *Journal of Marketing Management*, Vol. 9, 1993.

Hooley, G. and Saunders, J., *Competition Positioning*, Prentice Hall, 1993.

Hunt, S. and Morgan, R.M., The Commitment–Trust Theory of Relationship Marketing, *Journal of Marketing*, Vol. 58, July, pp. 20–38, 1994.

Jones, T.O. and Sasser, W.E., Why Satisfied Customers Defect, *Harvard Business Review*, Nov./Dec., 1995.

Kay, J., *Foundations of Corporate Success*, Oxford University Press, 1993.

Kotler, P., *Marketing Management: Analysis, Planning, Implementation and Control*, 9th Edn, Prentice Hall, 1997.

Miles, R.E. and Snow, C.C., *Organizational Strategy, Structure and Process*, McGraw-Hill, 1978.

Murray, J.A. and O'Driscoll, A., *Strategy and Process in Marketing*, Prentice Hall, 1996.

Ohmae, K., *The Mind of the Strategist*, Penguin, 1983.

Porter, M., *Competitive Advantage*, The Free Press, 1985.

Porter, M., From Competitive Advantage to Corporate Strategy, *Harvard Business Review*, May/June, 1987.

Townsend, R., *Up the Organisation*, Michael Joseph, 1971.

ANALYSING EXTERNAL MARKETS AND INTERNAL ASSETS FOR STRATEGIC DECISIONS

CHAPTER 3

INTRODUCTION

The previous chapter emphasized that strategic decisions should be developed within a knowledge base of customers, our own organizational capabilities and competitors. Nilson (1995) wrote:

> The more chaotic the world is, the more important it becomes to have a well-founded view of what one should be doing. . . . The first step in effective marketing is to understand the total environment: the market place, the competition, the customers, the trends, etc. This is very basic but in a turbulent world it is more important than ever to have systems in place to monitor the behaviour of customers. It is also essential to have a good total understanding to be able to differentiate between real and what is only perceived change.

The role that ongoing information plays in the strategy is the subject of this chapter, in particular the use of analysis in the decision-making process.

The above quotation hints at two roles of analysis and research. The first is a formal review of all factors, which takes place as an *initial step* of any planning process. The second is the *ongoing monitoring* of trends and tracking of performance. So, on the one hand, analysis is the starting point of the marketing planning process, but on the other hand it should be part of the final act. At the end of the cycle it is the measure of whether previous strategic and tactical/operational decisions are really delivering against the objectives of the organization. Also, during regular ongoing analysis it should be possible to identify real changes taking place which could affect a business and thus avoid any risk of being caught unawares.

A formal review or situational analysis is often termed a *marketing audit*. Inevitably there are a number of different definitions of the scope and role of such an audit. Kotler (1997) refers to an audit as a control instrument used for periodic reviews of marketing effectiveness. This extends the audit into the second of the above roles. However, since strategic marketing is a continuous activity, the control review for the previous period can also be the foundation knowledge for future strategic decisions. Hence it can embrace both roles. But, as a formal review, it is necessary to ensure that the audit comprehensively covers all those areas that could affect future performance.

When audit data have been gathered, and integrated with information already available, then the next step in the strategy development process is to isolate those major factors that are really important to the future of the organization. These are the critical issues to be addressed in any subsequent marketing actions. One technique is to produce a SWOT (strengths, weaknesses, opportunities, threats) analysis. This is discussed later in the chapter, but it is absolutely essential that the SWOT is seen as a tool for critical analysis. It is *not* a convenient framework for listing issues, although it is all too often misused in this way.

A good SWOT is characterized by the rigorous process of analysis, which reduces the number of external and internal issues to those that are of paramount importance. The resulting factors, together with the reasons behind their choice and their potential impact, can then become a major consideration for future strategic options.

The aim of this type of analysis is to provide a basis for *future* decisions. The evaluation of strategic options is covered in Chapter 16. One interesting way of assessing future performance is to try to draw up a scenario of the most likely and the worst-case situation for the future. This is often done at the same time as a formal audit is taking place.

Author and marketing consultant Paul Fifield (1992) says that one of the most common questions he is asked is about how much research and analysis should be done before taking decisions. He suggests that 'This question is almost impossible to answer since it depends on so many different variables. Too little analysis and the organization can end up flying by the seat of its pants, producing products and services it knows nothing about and venturing into markets where it has no right to be. . . . On the other hand, too much analysis can also be a bad thing'. Marketing managers often have masses of marketing research data available, but this is not very useful unless they know how they are going to use it. Decisions should not be based on that information that happens to be available or on any that the manager just happens to know how to access; after all, the Internet gives unlimited scope in this respect. All information must have a purpose; its value is derived from the use to which it is to be applied, and the possibility of making a better decision by using that specific information. There is a dilemma between *paralysis by analysis* (an unhealthy obsession with numbers, analyses and reports) and *extinction by instinct* (stemming from ill-conceived, arbitrary decisions) (Langley, 1995). At best, information is like a jigsaw puzzle, each piece helping to make the overall picture clearer. Nevertheless, it is necessary to consider what information is required, and a marketing audit is one mechanism for acquiring this information.

Marketing audit

In the words of Malcolm McDonald (1994), 'there is no reason why marketing cannot be audited in the same way as accounts, in spite of its more innovative, subjective nature. A marketing audit is a systematic appraisal of all the external and internal factors that have affected a company's commercial performance over a defined period'.

A long list of the contents of a marketing audit can be found in many marketing texts. Kotler (1997) has grouped the components under six headings:

1. the macro-environment
2. the task environment (customers, competition and other stakeholders)
3. the current marketing strategy
4. the organization and systems
5. the link between marketing and productivity
6. the operational marketing mix currently in place.

Later this chapter will look briefly at the three major environments within the audit–macro, task and the internal environment. As part of the analysis stage it is usually necessary to study trends and extrapolate them, as it is the future impact of the factors that must be assessed. The few areas of greatest importance can then be explored by the gathering of relevant facts.

However, the problem with many audits is that they tend to be very mechanical and seem to demand a listing of the collected data. Raw data are not sufficient; data must be developed into useful marketing information, which can then be utilized in the marketing decision process. Linden Brown and Malcolm McDonald (1994) have researched many marketing plans, and their observation is that 'these include voluminous market data, but frequently little real interpretation for strategy'.

The general process of examining the external factors in order to identify threats and opportunities is often termed environmental scanning. Brownlie (1994) has reviewed a number of empirical studies from strategic management and suggests that they demonstrate 'a crude statistical link between environmental scanning behaviour and organizational performance'. But he also states that 'writers in the field of strategic management have added little to the basic notion, implicit to the marketing concept, that an *alertness* and *sensitivity* to the external environment is an essential ingredient of success and longevity'.

Almost three decades before the availability of vast quantities of online computer data, Aguilar (1967) warned that 'scanning is costly; information is boundless. In practice an organisation can attend to only a fraction of the information that keeps pouring in upon it from its environments. The rules of scanning must be framed with reference to the economics of this activity, and costs must be weighed against benefits'. These costs lie as much in the time and effort to study the data as in the cost of retrieval.

It is, therefore, necessary to deal with the problem of masses of data by having a framework for analysis that can assist in drawing out the vital issues. But since the gathering and analysis of data, especially external data, is expensive, it must be used effectively. It is for these reasons that this chapter emphasizes the need for relevant and valid information rather than the collection of the data.

Brownlie also writes 'Given that there are just too many environmental stimuli at any one time for the organization to pay adequate attention to all of them, environmental scanning could be described as *the process in which environmental stimuli are selected and organised into patterns which are meaningful to the organisation in the light of its current and future needs and interests*'.

To avoid unnecessary and irrelevant effort any study must decide which are the key topics before collecting data. The most important factors can be identified effectively by using a group brainstorming session involving operational managers drawn from a wider group than marketing alone. This technique should generate a list that will almost certainly include the specific areas of importance. The next step is to identify the few really key factors that could have a major effect on the business, either positively (opportunities) or negatively (threats). Environmental scanning does not occur at a single point in time, nor as a discrete act, but from a sequence of actions taking place all the time. However, the identification of key issues is often carried out as a single activity during the planning process. This is not always appropriate, and organizations should explore ways of considering issues on a more regular basis in order to evaluate significant changes as they occur, although there are risks in being over reactive in response to such changes.

For Pettigrew and Whipp (1991), environmental scanning is 'an uncertain process deeply conditioned by the industrial and organisational context from which it emerges'. Since the vital analytical task is to reveal the key issues, it is important that the people involved take an objective and externally oriented view, ignoring internal politics and not restricted by context. The task is also qualitative rather than quantitative, with a high premium on the opinions of a few managers.

Ansoff (1984) argues that the screening process that determines which data should be considered operates by means of three filters (Figure 3.1). Understanding these filters can help appreciation of some of the pitfalls that reduce the level of objectivity in many audits. The first, the *surveillance* filter, determines the width and strength of the scanning as it controls what is actually passed on to the decision makers. A second is the *mentality* filter, which is applied by those managers who receive the data and need to turn it into useful information. There will be considerable variation in the interpretative frameworks used and the way subjective

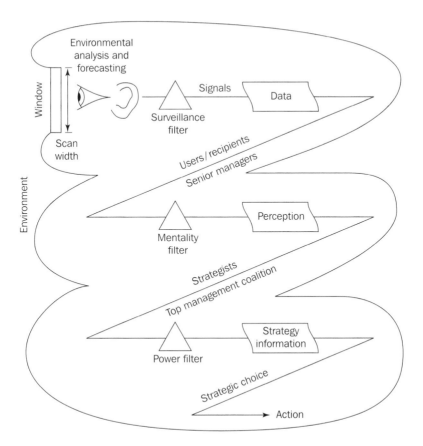

Fig 3.1 Selection, perception and attention in the firm. *Source*: Baker (1994)

opinions are introduced into any analysis of relevance. The third restriction comes from the *power* filter since there is a gap between the analysis itself and the power to convince the decision makers to consider the information in their future strategies.

Johnson and Scholes (1997) suggest that the process is a logical sequence funnelling down to the really big issues, although their model relates only to the external macro-environmental and competitive factors (Figure 3.2).

A marketing position audit should, in my opinion, go further, adding other aspects of customers and distributors to the external issues as well as reviewing the internal capabilities of an organization. The Johnson and Scholes model uses the terms 'opportunities' and 'threats'. These are part of the much used, but often misused, SWOT analysis, 'strengths' and 'weaknesses' being applied to internal issues, while 'opportunities' and 'threats' are considered externally.

The SWOT is widely used and recognized by managers as one of the most useful planning tools. This is, perhaps, due to its obvious simplicity in use, and because, as a broad general tool, it can be adapted to almost any situation. However, SWOT is too often badly used, resulting in indiscriminate, uncritical listings of many issues without any clear identification of the major factors of high importance. SWOT is

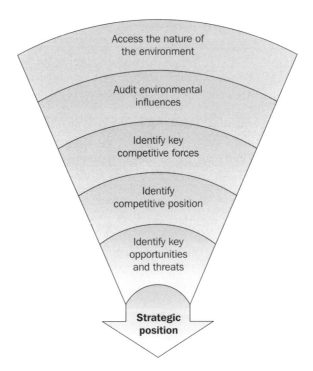

Fig 3.2 Steps in environmental analysis. *Source*: Johnson and Scholes (1997)

not the only technique available, but if it is properly thought through it can be one of the most effective. This is discussed later in this chapter.

Macro-environmental factors

First to be considered are those external factors affecting the wider environment. This step comes before focusing more closely on the actual organization and its operations. The range of macro factors is so diverse that it is very tempting to consider issues that have little impact on the business. Therefore an objective review of the factors is necessary to eliminate the irrelevant ones.

One traditional way of considering the external environment is to examine the four major component parts:

P   POLITICAL AND LEGAL FACTORS
E   ECONOMIC FACTORS
S   SOCIAL AND CULTURAL FACTORS
T   TECHNOLOGICAL FACTORS.

I usually add a fifth group – S, the structure of the market (or industry). This is consistent with Churchman's (1968) definition of the macro-environment as those factors that are not only outside the system's control, but which determine, in part, how the system performs.

The five groups make up the mnemonic PESTS. There are a number of equally good and widely used mnemonics, such as STEP, PCDENT and SLEPT, which are also used. However, it is not the identification of the issues but the evaluation of the impact they might have which is critical to future success.

Some organizations will build scenarios of the future – most likely or worst-case scenarios, for instance – so that strategy can be evaluated against different predictions of the future. Such analysis is particularly important with respect to political/legal, economic and social/cultural factors. These factors only become 'PESTS' if an organization fails to identify those that are likely to have a significant effect on future business. There is a difference between small, *evolutionary* changes, which can be accommodated within a developing strategy, and major, *revolutionary* changes, which require significant shifts to remain competitive.

With technological developments the changes are often more revolutionary. Aaker (1995), commenting on the effect of changing technology from outside the market or industry, which could affect strategy, suggests that it 'can represent an opportunity to those in a position to capitalise . . . [but] could also prove a significant threat'.

This is obvious, but he goes on to quote from research concerning the impact of new technology, finding:

1. 'sale of the old technology continued for a substantial period, in part because the firms involved continued to use it'.
2. 'it is relatively difficult to predict the outcome of new technology'.
3. 'the new technologies started by invading sub-markets, but they then tended to create new markets instead of simply encroaching on existing ones'.

With new technologies it is, perhaps, useful to proactively practise what Tom Peters (1988) calls 'creative swiping', stealing good ideas from other areas and adapting them to your market. This often leads to competitive, new products. However, it is all too easy to filter out 'novel signals and information' which are not consistent with a manager's previous experience – Ansoff's 'mentality' and 'power' filters. In order to avoid this in a technological sense, the type of scanning used must be radically revised away from a basic monitoring of the obvious environment to try to identify new ideas that could be of use. Then the evaluation needs to ask where we can use these novel ideas.

The structure of the market is included as a category within the macro factors because it forms the foundation for a more intense industry survey when analysing the task environment. Prior to the detailed consideration of close competition, customers and other stakeholders, it is useful to undertake a general market analysis. The content of such an analysis will usually include such factors as:

- definition of market boundaries
- market size – actual or predicted
- market growth
- number of organizations; concentration/fragmentation of the market
- economies of scale
- distribution channels.

The possibility of dynamic changes in any of these variables would have such a dramatic effect that any review must ask if such development is likely, the message being that careful evaluation of the impact rather than panic measures will usually be the best reaction.

Example Changing industry structure

Many retail-based industries have developed from specialist producers or craftsmen actually meeting customers in market-places, then through to locally based general stores, on to specialist high street retailers, only to be succeeded by large out-of-town superstores. These are now threatened by IT-based contact, which completely bypasses traditional outlets. Some elements of this can be seen in the historical development of grocery stores and the current experiments with television shopping. Of course, banks already offer well-established telephone banking, and the toy trade is now dominated by superstores such as Toys R Us, which have caused many smaller toyshops to cease trading.

There is a theory that retailers operate on a continuous 'wheel' of development with new competitors entering by utilizing new ways of reaching customers, improving services and reducing costs. These companies then start expanding their product ranges and their operations, but by doing so they fail to focus on future new developments. This leaves open opportunities for the next generation of retailers, who could change the industry structure and with it the way manufacturers/suppliers do business.

The task environment

The task environment refers to the immediate external market where interactions take place affecting our organization. In particular, these are:

- customers
- competitors
- distributors (could be considered as customers or partners)
- suppliers and other facilitators
- general stakeholders.

When auditing the task environment it is necessary to define those strategic groups of customers, competitors and distributors who operate within our existing market. The difficulty in defining customers and competitor groups means the boundaries in all cases need to be considered carefully to avoid being too restrictive. This will be apparent from the discussion in Chapter 2.

A detailed study of customer and competitor analysis can be found in specialized texts such as Lehmann and Winer (1997) or Hooley and Saunders (1993).

Analysis of the task environment will be based on the knowledge of the structure of the market and its potential changes as explored in the wider environment. There are a number of useful models that can provide a framework for analysing a given industry. Michael Porter's (1980) five-forces model is often a good starting point (Figure 3.3). However, models do not carry out the analysis; they only help by structuring the thought process. Wensley (1994) suggested that the basic analytical tools in orthodox strategic marketing consisted of '5 forces, 4 boxes, and 3 strategies'. Porter's five forces is an effective model which focuses on the threats of competitive

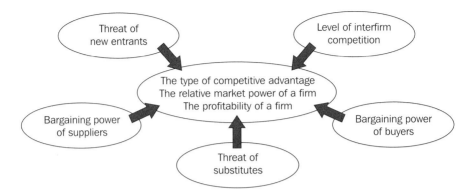

Fig 3.3 The five market forces proposed by Michael Porter. *Source:* Porter (1980)

offerings and the bargaining power of all types of customers. The four (BCG) boxes form one of several matrix models focusing on where to compete given cash flow requirements and availability, while the three generic strategies (also Porter) are relevant to how to compete.

One drawback of Porter's five-forces model is that it does not show opportunities within new sectors, nor gaps in the competition. I often find that UK managers are pessimistic when carrying out an analysis of their business, producing many more threats than opportunities. It has been suggested that no new products ever emerge from an analytical process. This obviously brings into question why we carry out such a process. The answer lies in the fear of missing some critical change that would make it difficult to defend a current position. In fact, the main purpose of a marketing audit is to support an existing position. If it is proposed to expand into a new area then a separate survey with a different focus will be required.

Although the audit studies where we are now, it is a basic foundation for the *future* strategic direction. Therefore it will be useful to answer the questions posed by Hamel and Prahalad (1994) in Table 3.1.

Although the usual output of such a study is a better understanding of the dynamics and linkages involving the various elements in the task environment, an analysis can lead to some unexpected conclusions. The former chief executive of the worldwide H.J. Heinz company, Tony O'Reilly, when researching for his PhD, analysed the impact on farm income in Ireland as a consequence of the Kerrygold brand of Irish butter. He states that 'the outcome was neither what I expected nor hoped. Objectivity forced me to acknowledge that plundering the unsuspecting European tax-payer by accumulating large farm surpluses was the quickest way to prosperity. Adding value at the farm gate through sound marketing was useful but less profitable'.

Table 3.1 Determining future strategic direction

Today	Five to ten years in the future
Which customers are you serving today?	Which customers will you be serving in the future?
Through what channels do you reach customers today?	Through what channels will you reach customers in the future?
Who are your competitors today?	Who will be your competitors in the future?
What is the basis for your competitive advantage today?	What will be the basis for competitive advantage in the future?

The above example may be the exception but it does reveal that there could be more than one way to achieve an objective, and marketing-based strategies are not always appropriate. Perhaps it also illustrates the need to continue to appreciate the wider context of strategy when conducting detailed analysis.

The internal environment: current strategy, organization and productivity links

When considering the internal components of the audit as proposed by Kotler, there are 12 areas where he suggests questions about the way the organization is operating. These cover:

- business mission
- marketing objectives and goals
- marketing strategies
- formal structures
- functional efficiencies
- interface efficiencies
- marketing information systems
- marketing planning systems
- marketing control systems
- new product development systems
- profitability analysis
- cost effectiveness analysis.

All of these areas are relevant to an audit of operations that seeks to ensure that our organization is working efficiently. However, these are part of a control programme rather than an input to strategy. The components of the revised 'value chain' as described in Chapter 2 could be probed in depth or, perhaps, the issues from a business process redesign exercise, which can sometimes propose radical new ways of operating in order to meet competitive requirements. Porter warns that strategy is not the same as operational efficiencies. For the future it is necessary to consider alternative ways of operating rather than just improve company efficiencies, therefore the questions should be 'what are we trying to achieve?' and 'are we approaching our objective in the most efficient way?'.

In fact, Hamel and Prahalad (1994) have some additional questions that could be applied at this stage (Table 3.2).

Tools for strategic analysis

The Porter five-forces model and value chain have already been introduced. There are many other relevant models that can assist both in analysis and in pointing towards options for future strategic direction.

New ideas for models and developments of old standards are proposed on a regular basis. A model is only as good as its ability to assist the thought process. Models are not sacrosanct: they can be amended and modified to meet new conditions or to address issues better. A good introduction to the more popular models listed below is given by McDonald and Brown (1994). Their review covers the strategic implications, limitations and practical significance of seven of the most widely used concepts, models and techniques used in strategy formulation. As can be discovered, none of the models is perfect, but each can work well in some situations provided it is applied critically. The models reviewed by McDonald and Brown are:

- the product life cycle
- the experience curve
- the growth/share portfolio model (BCG)
- attractiveness–competitiveness position model (GE matrix)

Table 3.2 Some further questions

Today	Five to ten years in the future
Where do your margins come from today?	Where will your margins come from in the future?
What skills or capabilities make you unique today?	What skills or capabilities will make you unique in the future?
In what end product markets do you participate today?	In what end product markets will you participate in the future?

- product–market growth model (Ansoff matrix)
- strategy experience models (PIMS)
- industry structure models and competitive strategy (Porter).

Effective SWOT analysis

The SWOT process is an effective way of identifying those issues that really matter: the major issues of high importance to the future which must be tackled in any strategy. SWOT is best seen as a useful framework which encourages a great deal of discussion as to the future impact of the factors identified. It takes place after the more specific analysis of parts of the marketing environment.

Raw material for a SWOT is generally drawn from the audit, although it may be supplemented by interviews with staff and customers. If such interviews are undertaken they ought to be non-attributable so that issues are revealed without any prejudice. This can be achieved by the use of independent researchers or consultants (see the Data column in Figure 3.4). The data are then analysed to identify a long list of actual issues, which are often listed under the relevant headings of strengths, weaknesses, opportunities and threats. The listing of the issues is not the end of the process, although many think it is. The critical activities are then analysed further to establish a small number of key *issues* and the future *impact* they are likely to have on an organization. The steps leading to a SWOT analysis are shown in Figure 3.4.

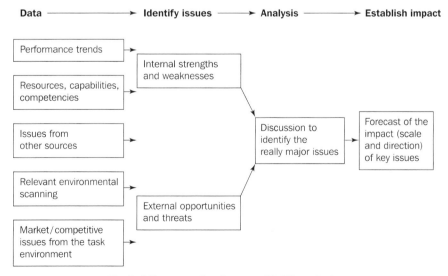

Fig 3.4 The steps leading to a SWOT analysis

The move from the listing of the issues in step 2, to the understanding of the impact of the most important strengths, weaknesses, opportunities and threats is a major task involving much discussion. In the SWOT process there is a gradual reduction of the list of issues to isolate the few key factors that will have a major impact in the future. Argenti (1989) describes the big issues as 'elephants'. He suggests that:

> in a few cases there will be only one elephant; more often there is a small herd, although [he] has never seen more than six. These key themes stand head and shoulders above all other issues in the company. . . . Either something is seen as plainly worthy of classification as a major strategic issue – an elephant – or it is plainly not.

Based on practical experience, Argenti suggests an 'elephant hunt'.

While all issues will require some consideration, it is those that are identified as having the greatest impact that must be reflected in strategic plans. However, only a few issues can be fully included – too many, and the strategy fails to focus on the things that really matter in the future.

It is all too easy to consider these issues from a subjective position when in fact they all need to be assessed in the light of a customer's perception of the comparative strengths and weaknesses. The analysis therefore requires an element of focused objectivity.

If a review was to consider Marks & Spencer, for example, then it is obvious that customers could have very different views from people who regularly shop at local markets and rarely go into Marks & Spencer stores. In fact, a separate SWOT can be completed for each strategic group of customers:

Marks & Spencer stores

Existing customers	**Regular/loyal**
	Occasional
Non-customers	**Never used**
	Former (lapsed) customers.

The strengths and weaknesses could show differences depending on the specific group of customers. Also, different opportunities and threats will be revealed. Such analysis can be critical in developing a targeted strategy for the future. Nevertheless, there will be a number of factors that will be common to all groups. These could be strengths like the 'quality' of Marks & Spencer merchandise, but even so there could still be differences in the importance each group gives to a specific factor. To a regular customer it could be of major importance while to a non-customer it could be of little relevance.

The analysis should take place in a structured way from the perspective of each group of customers. The factors could be ranked in terms of potential impact and consequences for the organization in an effort to highlight the key issues. Table 3.3 refers to a fictitious company.

Table 3.3 Analysis of loyal customers: strengths

Factor	Potential impact*	Consequences for future*	Overall rank
1. Comparative quality	4	5	20
2. Size of sales team	3	3	9
3. Effective R&D producing new products	5	3	15

*On a scale from 1 (low) to 5 (high).

In the fictitious example in Table 3.3 the comparative quality level will be more important as a strength to loyal customers than the sales team. The initial factor list is usually much longer than the three in the table, but it is to highlight no more than one or two issues of importance that the exercise is carried out.

In addition to an objective SWOT on our company, it is also possible to develop a SWOT on competitors. In this case it is still important to consider the perception of customers in evaluating the issues. It is the customer's perception of comparative offerings that is a critical determinant of customer buying behaviour. Issues such as quality are ones where perceptions can be more powerful than the actuality. Research considering food retailers and the 'retailer brand' products they offer as compared to 'manufacturers' brands' has regularly shown lower ratings for retailer brand quality among many segments of the population. The perception gap is gradually closing but it still lags a long way behind the actual quality comparisons.

McDonald (1989) suggests that a good SWOT will:

- be a summary emanating from the marketing audit;
- be brief, interesting and concise;
- focus on *key* factors only;
- list *differential* strengths and weaknesses *vis-à-vis* competitors, focusing on competitive advantage;
- list *key* external opportunities and threats only;
- identify and pin down the *real* issues – it should not be a list of unrelated points;
- enable a reader to grasp instantly the main thrust of the business, even to the point of being able to write marketing objectives;

- follow the implied question 'which means that . . .?' to get the real implications;
- not over-abbreviate.

In each SWOT with each customer group, the outcome should be a small number of 'elephants' in each category.

Davies (1995) suggests that 'At the end of the process there will be a clearer appreciation of how others see the business. . . . The conclusions should be validated by customer contact afterwards. In [his] experience this openness (checking with customers) is rarely abused and often produces insights which a wholly internal process cannot'.

Conclusions

Data on the business environment is readily available from many different sources. As such, it is relatively easy to monitor past performances. However, strategic decisions taken now will affect organizational performance in the future and there is no clear link to guarantee that data collected on the present or past state of a business will also predict the future. However, there is much conventional wisdom that good information will improve performance.

Many businesses prosper on the basis of managerial instinct, but it is possible to suggest that these instincts are founded on knowledge of the current situation, even when the decisions actually run counter to the known trends.

At the other extreme there is excessive analysis. It is always possible to calculate the *cost* of gathering and analysing data; this is a direct charge to a business and reduces profits. The *benefits* to be gained by gathering data can only come from enlightened analysis, which is focused on the transformation of data into useful information, which can then be used to try to predict future events. There are many ways of carrying out this analysis and many models that could be helpful. However, a model is only a way of structuring the data, and an analysis only produces information: it does not take decisions. There is a risk if an organization relies too heavily on analysis in that it is easy to reinforce ideas on conformity with industry norms and past experience. This could be acceptable in a slow changing market but could be very constricting in a dynamic one.

Although there will be risks associated with trying to forecast the future, it is appropriate for an organization to try to understand the market in which it operates. Knowledge about itself and comparative issues regarding competitors from the viewpoint of customers can be very strong stimuli for future directions. To fail to analyse the obvious elements of the environment is foolhardy, but to try to study every possible aspect is unrealistic, nor will a comprehensive analysis guarantee future success.

Every organization must decide for itself how much data on which aspects it should collect. The analysis should use structures with which the organization can feel comfortable, and this could involve modifications of well-known models to set them in the context of a particular organization. There is always a risk that some fact previously overlooked or excluded by the restrictions of a search could prove critical when hindsight is applied to past performances. This is a risk that all organizations should be prepared to accept. It is not an argument for comprehensive analysis; rather it emphasizes the need to deal with the chosen data within a disciplined structure containing enlightened filtering to highlight issues.

While it is not possible to be prescriptive about the process and contents of any analysis, what is critical is the objectivity of the participants and the need to include a customer perspective as a key measure of the issues. These issues should be fully probed and the resulting factors should be limited in number, revealing issues that really are critical to the future.

KEY POINTS

3.1 A marketing audit has two primary roles: (i) to provide a foundation from which future strategy can be developed and (ii) to act as a control/feedback process with regard to current/past activities.

3.2 There is *no* prescription as to the scope and precision of an audit. The dilemma facing marketing managers can be the choice between *paralysis by analysis* and *extinction by instinct*.

3.3 A marketing audit is a systematic appraisal of all the external and internal factors that have affected a company's commercial performance over a defined period. But the data gathered must be turned into useful information in order to underpin decisions.

3.4 Selecting what data is to be collected and screening that data can be very subjective, with a heavy dependence on the opinions of a few managers. Steps must be taken to try to achieve objectivity.

3.5 There are many different analytical models available to marketing managers. New ideas for models and developments of old standards are proposed on a regular basis. A model is only as good as its ability to assist the thought process. Models are not sacrosanct – they can be amended and modified to meet new conditions or to better address relevant issues.

3.6 The SWOT analysis should take place late in the process with the aim of isolating a few (three or four, perhaps) key issues of high importance to the future of the organization. Identifying a few really key issues, and the future impact they could have, should be the goal, not the sorting of a multitude of factors into four contrived categories.

3.7 It is important to appreciate Davies' view that 'At the end of the [analysis] process there will be a clearer appreciation of how others see the business.' The conclusions of a SWOT analysis should be validated by subsequent customer contact.

QUESTIONS

3.1 Are there any reasons why marketing cannot be audited in the same way as financial accounts?

3.2 Ansoff describes three filters that occur in the process of screening data and producing information. They are the surveillance filter, the mentality filter and the power filter. Explain the problems associated with each of these filters.

3.3 Analysis is too often backward looking, trying to understand problems of the past rather than opportunities for the future. Are there any ways of introducing a more future-oriented aspect to the process?

3.4 Suggest two models commonly utilized in marketing analysis. Describe the advantages and drawbacks of each.

Bibliography

Aaker, D., *Strategic Market Management*, Wiley, 1995.

Aguilar, F.J., *Scanning the Business Environment*, Macmillan, 1967.

Ansoff, I., *Implanting Strategic Management*, Prentice Hall, 1984.

Argenti, J. *Practical Corporate Planning*, Unwin, 1989.

Baker, M.J. (ed.) *The Marketing Book*, 3rd Edn, Butterworth Heinemann, 1994.

Brown, L. and McDonald, M., *Competitive Marketing Strategy for Europe*, Macmillan, 1994.

Brownlie, D., Environmental Scanning, in M. Baker (ed.) *The Marketing Book*, 3rd Edn, Butterworth Heinemann, 1994.

Churchman, C.W., *The Systems Approach*, Delacorte Press, 1968.

Davidson, H., *Even More Offensive Marketing*, Penguin, 1997.

Davies, A., *The Strategic Role of Marketing*, McGraw-Hill, 1995.

Fifield, P., *Marketing Strategy*, Butterworth Heinemann, 1992.

Hamel, G. and Prahalad, C.K., *Competing for the Future*, Harvard Business Press, 1994.

Hooley, G. and Saunders, J., *Competitive Positioning*, Prentice Hall, 1993.

Johnson, G. and Scholes, K., *Exploring Corporate Strategy*, 4th Edn, Prentice Hall, 1997.

Kotler, P. (ed.), *Marketing Management: Analysis, Planning, Implementation and Control*, 9th Edn, Prentice Hall, 1997.

Kotler, P., Gregor, W. and Rogers, W., Marketing Audit Comes of Age, *Sloan Management Review*, Vol. 18 No. 2, 1977.

Langley, A., Between Paralysis by Analysis and Extinction by Instinct, *Sloan Management Review*, Spring, 1995.

Lehmann, D.R. and Winer, R.S., *Analysis for Marketing Planning*, 4th Edn, Irwin, 1997.

McDonald, M.H.B., Ten Barriers to Marketing Planning, *Journal of Marketing Management*, Vol. 5 No. 1, 1989.

McDonald, M.H.B., Developing the Marketing Plan, in M. Baker (ed.) *The Marketing Book*, 3rd Edn, Butterworth Heinemann, 1994.

McDonald, M.H.B. and Brown, L., Strategic Marketing Planning, in M. Baker (ed.) *The Marketing Book*, 3rd Edn, Butterworth Heinemann, 1994.

Nilson, T., *Chaos Marketing*, McGraw-Hill, 1995.

Peters, T., *Thriving on Chaos*, Macmillan, 1988.

Pettigrew, A. and Whipp, R., *Managing Change for Corporate Success*, Blackwell, 1991.

Porter, M., *Competitive Strategy*, Free Press, 1980.

Porter, M., *What is Strategy?*, Harvard Business Review, Nov./Dec., 1996.

Stevenson, H.H., Defining Corporate Strengths and Weaknesses, in D. Asch and C. Bowman (eds) *Readings in Strategic Management*, Macmillan, 1989.

Wensley, R., Strategic Marketing: A Review, in M. Baker (ed.) *The Marketing Book*, 3rd Edn, Butterworth Heinemann, 1994.

WHERE TO COMPETE

PART

The two major issues in a dynamic market-place are *where* and *how* to compete. Many years ago, Peter Drucker wrote that the sole purpose of a business was to *create a customer*. However, the important issue for strategic marketers is to ensure that the business creates the *right* customers – that is, those with whom a profitable exchange can be achieved. In order to identify such customers it is necessary to consider the boundaries of existing available markets and the scope of potential new markets. Of course, all such investigations have to be carried out in the light of what is *feasible* given the capabilities of the organization. Part II seeks to explore the issues of customer selection and the breadth of markets to be considered.

Decisions about where to compete involve the two key dimensions of *product* and *market* brought together by Igor Ansoff in his famous matrix some 30 years ago. Since then many refinements have occurred. One of these stems from the debate on the degree of newness of both product and market, and this can lead to an enlarged matrix. Such a model is more able to reflect the precise levels of risk involved in moving away from the base of existing business areas. However, the most interesting recent refinement is probably the work of Hamel and Prahalad, who replaced the product dimension by one covering *organizational competence*. They explore strategies designed to retain existing customers, encouraging companies to develop relevant new business competencies which can be utilized to meet changing market requirements and thereby satisfy the needs of their customers for some time into the future. The issues of product/market scope and future competencies are discussed along with the various levels of new market opportunities in Chapter 4.

While marketing is about customer satisfaction, it must also consider the achievement of this in the light of the costs involved and other, perhaps conflicting, corporate objectives. The different attractions of globalization and the benefits of

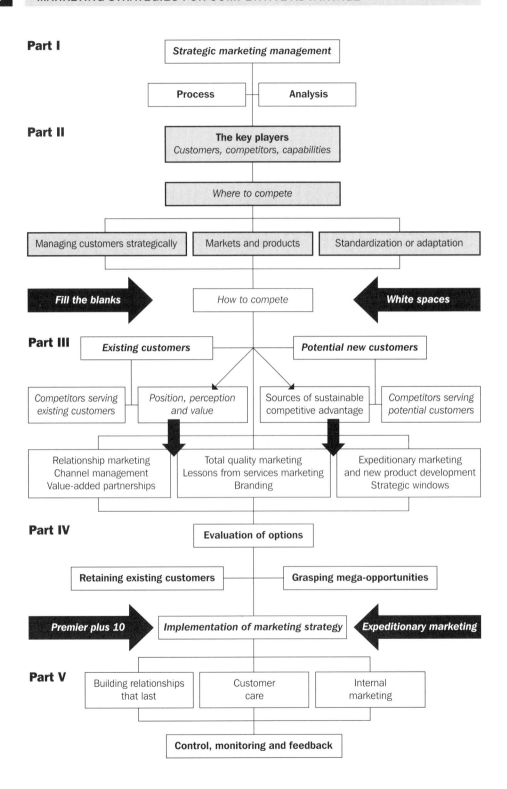

homogeneity of demand must be contrasted with the need for customization and issues of heterogeneity. In modern markets there is rarely a local market not affected by the global nature of competition. In the same way as the radius of competition is worldwide, so is the location of potential customers. Of course, few markets are truly global, although new technologies can lead to such a position, which can be exploited, as in the example of Microsoft. There are also a limited number of markets where American consumer imperialism has created a world standard of expectations, but even companies such as Coca Cola and McDonald's accept the need for some adaptability in their offerings. Generally cultural traditions, linked to the levels of technological and economic development of markets, mean that true globalization is an illusory target. Few companies can hope to control a diverse market-place without some adaptation, and the failure to meet specific needs obviously leads to the risk of markets being nibbled away on all sides by highly focused competitors. In any event, a product offering contains so many different elements, both tangible and intangible, that a degree of customization is easily accommodated. In addition, dramatic advances in manufacturing have allowed more economies of *scope* to be realized without sacrificing many of the economies of *scale*. Consideration of these issues must be seen from an organizational perspective, accepting the trade-offs that have to be made. This is the thrust of Chapter 5.

The final and crucial decision on where to compete comes down to the choice of specific individual customers or groups of customers. These customers must be managed in a strategic way over a long-term period, and this is the main issue in Chapter 6. Segmentation, as discussed in many marketing texts, still relies too heavily on the clear logic, but poor relevance, of the *easy-to-achieve* divisions often based on *readily available* demographic or psychographic data. The problem is that such groupings rarely lead to real advantage; they are more those that are convenient to the organization. By now all organizations have heard about segmentation and consequently utilize some of the thinking in their strategies. The real need is to use customer-driven segments and to utilize close customer links to manage the customer portfolio as effectively as possible. If decisions on where to compete are to lead to positive trading links then much more attention must be paid to better ways of segmentation and customer portfolio management.

WHERE AND WHEN TO COMPETE: MARKETS AND PRODUCTS

CHAPTER 4

INTRODUCTION

The problem of identifying competitive product–market combinations permeates all levels of marketing decisions. At the highest level marketing strategy involves the selection of where to compete and this must be expressed in terms of markets and products. The previous chapters have stressed the importance of considering issues from a marketing perspective, so that, when evaluating a specific customer group, all the key questions below should be answered from the customer's position rather than from the producer's point of view. If this is done then marketing strategy can be considered as an 'outside-in' process, with markets as the starting point followed by an assessment of those needs that can be satisfied, utilizing given capabilities.

The sequence of decisions starts with the identification of a customer segment or strategic customer group. This determines 'Who is to be satisfied?'. Although the presence of existing customers often determines the answer in practice, it is nevertheless important to review all potential groups. These need to be considered with respect to three basic questions:

1. What is to be satisfied?
   (demands and needs expressed in terms of benefits received)
   Identifying opportunities in terms of benefits to customers.
2. How are the customers to be satisfied? (capabilities and skills)
   Matching those opportunities to organizational capacity/capability.
3. Why should the chosen customers buy from us? (competitive advantage)
   Evaluating the outcome in a competitive sense.

These three questions can be illustrated as three overlapping circles, first introduced as Figure 1.3. Only where all three overlap is everything in place for our existing product market, although this is not a guarantee of ongoing future success (Figure 4.1).

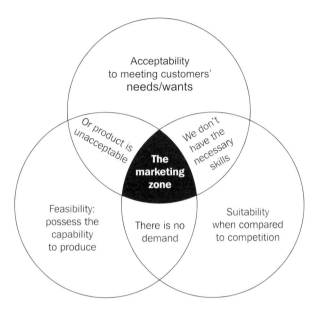

Acceptability to meeting customers' needs/wants

Or product is unacceptable

We don't have the necessary skills

The marketing zone

Feasibility: possess the capability to produce

There is no demand

Suitability when compared to competition

Fig 4.1 The marketing zone

In studying the areas where only two circles intersect it is possible to explore which element is missing and to decide on future action.

It could be that our offering is 'unsuitable' in that it fails the competitive test as the chosen customer perceives that their needs could be better met by a competitive product. This could be caused by incremental changes in the demand from previous customers or changes in competitive offerings, which have shifted the market and now require a response by the supplier.

Or perhaps there could be a lack of skills or other capability so that some existing needs of the chosen customers cannot 'feasibly' be satisfied by the current offerings of our organization. This is, of course, a new product opportunity. This could lead to entirely new product offerings but most marketing development concentrates in familiar areas where some products already exist and small changes are all that is required to become competitive.

Where there is no demand for current product offerings, it must be assumed that they are not 'acceptable' to the chosen customer group. This is an opportunity to reconsider both the segment and the offering. It is possible that although there is a capability, the offering is not considered relevant by particular customers. This could be the case with 'new to the world' products, and a programme of education and awareness might be required.

Alternatively, this process could identify new uses for existing products, capabilities and/or technologies. Also on a positive note, there could be new market opportunities with new users in a different segment that we are not currently reaching. But be aware that the presence of an opportunity does not mean that a market exists for the supplier.

Finally, there is the aspect of timing in a dynamic market. There are continuous developments by all companies as they try to establish some advantage for their offerings in the market-place. New products, new technologies and new ways of making offerings are all present as markets evolve over time. The interactions that customers have with the different supply organizations mean that their reference frame will constantly be changing as they become aware of new initiatives in the market. In addition, there are also changes in the macro-environment which can influence the behaviour of customers. It is therefore very important that market developments are studied to identify when is the best time and when an inappropriate time for introducing changes to any offering.

Marketing has been irreverently defined as:

> offering the *right* product, at the *right* price,
>> in the *right* place, at the *right* time.

Problems in defining a market

In order to define a market in marketing terms it is necessary to first consider the traditional meaning of it as a place where potential buyers and sellers meet. For a successful exchange to take place there must be both willing buyers and willing sellers with an appropriate offering – a degree of suitability, feasibility and acceptability.

In traditional market-places, many different offerings are made and each potential buyer will be interested in their own personal subset of these offers. So, in effect, a market-place is comprised of many different individual markets, each one focusing on a different grouping of potential buyers with a different set of multiple needs. In each separate 'need' category there are likely to be a number of suppliers who could satisfy such a need. But there is not necessarily any single one-to-one relationship between the same group of buyers and the suppliers of different need satisfiers.

Traditionally, markets are geographical locations where the trading takes place. These evolved because of the need for buyers physically to meet the sellers. However, marketing activities today are not restricted by this requirement – many different ways of linking buyers and sellers are now possible, especially with the application of modern technology. This then emphasizes that a key decision in marketing is how to reach, and interact with, all those potential customers with a particular need.

It is common for marketers to talk about the chocolate confectionery market or the car market or other descriptions drawn from the products they sell. Such definitions can be very misleading as they are not based on customer need but, rather, on the goods that the suppliers are offering. It is important to remember that people want the benefits that products provide rather than the product itself. Specific products represent the available combinations of benefits and costs.

It is far more appropriate to consider the demand–technology–product life cycle relationships described by Ansoff (1965) to see how product offerings come to meet demands (Figure 4.2). The demand life cycle is closely related to customers' needs. This should be seen as the pre-eminent life cycle. Within this all the technologies and different ways of meeting these needs can be represented. Each of the technologies can be further subdivided, and specific offerings can be seen at this level. All of these – demand, technology and specific products – follow separate individual life cycles. This ensures that the thinking is outside-in, starting with that need which is to be satisfied.

By considering overall customer needs, it is possible to focus on the competitive situation which will lead to the identification of the subsets of individual product/technologies, each of which is a possible way of satisfying a specific need.

However, we should not forget that one of the roles of marketing is to manage customer expectations in respect of the way needs are met. In a dynamic market it is possible to modify the components of the product and technology subsets which a customer perceives appropriate to meet a particular need.

Viewed from the customer's perspective, any purchase decision will consider a wide evoked set of product offerings, including some that can be described as indirect competition to some of the many products available at any one time, as well as the direct substitute products.

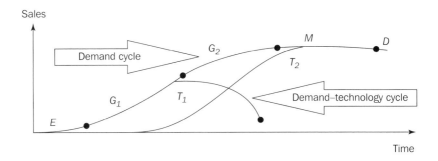

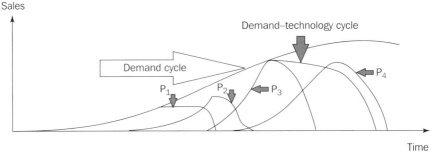

P_1; P_2; P_3; P_4 are all different products with life cycles

Fig 4.2 The demand–technology–product life cycle.
Source: Ansoff and McDonald (1990)

Over a quarter of a century ago William Moran (1973) suggested that:

> In our complex service society there are no more product classes; not in any meaning-ful sense, only as a figment of some file clerk's imagination. There are only use classes – users which are central to some products and peripheral to others – on a vast overlapping continuum. To some degree, in some circumstances almost any-thing can be a partial substitute for almost anything else.

George Day (1994) reinforced this by asking:

> Where does this leave the manager who relies on share of some (possibly ill-defined) market as a guide to performance evaluation and resource allocation?

Day suggests two issues as vital:

1. We must recognize that most markets do not have neat boundaries.
2. Different customers will have different perceptions of products and substi-tutes, thus making it difficult to describe a market in an absolute sense.

He also suggests that there may be a need to define separate markets for the same basic product by a link with the channels of distribution used. Here he gives the example of tyres which can be sold in bulk direct to car assemblers such as Ford or sold as a consumer product.

In spite of these writings and others since, there is still a dangerous tendency to rely on the 'myopic', obvious, product-centred classification of many markets. Reference to Levitt's (1960) classic research, 'Marketing myopia', will show how he stresses *benefits* rather than *products* as the basis for market definition. Of course there is also a risk of being too wide in the market definition and thus being unable to consider specific competition or to measure trends. Perhaps the best advice to marketers is to continually review the boundaries of any market in which they operate, including a careful watch on what might be included as a substitute product as described in Porter's five-forces model.

Ansoff is the originator of the best known matrix linking products and markets. First developed as a product/market expansion grid, it is still a valuable tool for an organization. It should be considered against the background of the low established potential for new products and known opportunities for existing offerings. Management writers are extremely fond of 2×2 matrices, and with a little adaptation there is an obvious link between the classic growth vector of Ansoff (1965) (Figure 4.3) and the matrix proposed by Hamal and Prahalad (1994) (Figure 4.4). Writing from the perspective of strategic management, the latter use the term 'competence' instead of product, although in other writing Hamel does consider 'product form' as a separate issue. The consideration of competencies does perhaps lead to a better understanding of the ways in which customers can be satisfied. This is a subject we will return to later.

Both these matrices use the term 'markets' – existing and new – but neither author is very clear about what is a market as distinct from a product offering. Ansoff refers to a company's mission, but most definitions of markets include all those customers sharing a particular set of needs. This is echoed in Hamel's use of the term 'function' to reflect the benefit received by customers. This description is useful but by

	Existing products	New products
Existing	Penetration Winning customers and expanding value-added partnerships	Product development especially new offerings
New	Market development White spaces	Diversification

(Markets)

Fig 4.3 The Ansoff directional matrix. *Source*: Ansoff (1965)

Market

	Existing	New
New	*Premier plus 10* What new core competencies will we need to build to protect and extend our franchise in current markets?	*Mega-opportunities* What new core competencies would we need to build to participate in the most exiting markets of the future?
Existing	*Fill in the blanks* What is the opportunity to improve our position in existing markets by better leveraging our existing core competencies?	*White spaces* What new products or services could we create by creatively redeploying or recombining our current core competencies?

Core competence (row label, left of table)

Fig 4.4 Establishing the core competence agenda. *Source*: Hamel and Prahalad (1994)

including specific benefits it does overlap with the product/competence dimension when considering the range of potential new products that could be evaluated. A combined matrix was shown in Figure 1.6 and is repeated as Figure 4.7.

Perhaps it is best to consider a market as all potential customers who have a common need. This total group is diverse and it is useful to subdivide it, especially when considering customers from the standpoint of a specific supply organization. Customers already trading are obviously our existing markets:

- Existing markets: customers currently trading with us buying our product offering.

This group can be subdivided by considering customer behaviour and the satisfaction received from existing trading. The following Jones and Sasser categories were referred to in Chapter 2:

- advocates
- mercenaries
- hostages
- terrorists.

It is obvious that different strategies are appropriate for each of these different market categories.

Those customer groups with whom we are not currently trading can be related to the areas within the overlapping circles from Figure 4.1. These form three groups of potential new markets:

Fig 4.5 New and existing markets

- Expanded markets: potential customers for our product offering, possibly buying from our competitors due to our lack of competitive advantage.
- Extended markets: customers with needs currently met by other technologies. The question is whether or not to develop/acquire such skills.
- Excluded markets: customers who are currently unavailable to our organization via existing channels of distribution.

There is one final group of potential customers who have unfulfilled needs due to their inability or unwillingness to purchase any current offerings. This group is much more difficult to develop. These *expeditionary markets* require special attention and often a radically new product offering (Figure 4.5).

An expanded product–market matrix should include all of the above categories. Further aspects of market subdivisions are considered in Chapter 6, which homes in on segmentation issues.

Product offerings

The term 'product' can be interpreted in a number of different ways. In one (operational) definition it is the end result of production; from another (marketing) viewpoint it is often the means by which consumers' needs are satisfied. Reference to two widely read marketing texts adds to the confusion, with Kotler *et al.* (1996) defining it as '*anything* that can be offered to a market to satisfy a need or want', and Dibb *et al.* (1997) suggesting it is '*everything*, both favourable and unfavourable, that is received in an exchange'. So is a product 'anything that . . .' or 'everything that . . .'? The use of the word 'offered' is perhaps useful as it leads to an enlargement of the term 'product'. Stephen King (1973) referred to a product as being 'naked' without the totality of an offering to surround it. He went on to conclude that '*prima facie*, the bias of both literature and practitioner towards the (*naked*) product as the principal constituent of the offer is misguided'. It is, therefore, useful to consider total product offerings, these being a complex mix of tangible and intangible attributes. This is closer to the idea of a product as 'everything that . . .' . This includes the naked product and many other additions. It does not exclude any unfavourable attributes which sometimes accompany an offering and devalue it by their very presence.

If we consider the levels of products suggested by Levitt, there are four distinct subdivisions of a total product offering (Figure 4.6):

1. The generic (core) product, which meets the basic needs of a chosen customer;
2. The expected product, which includes all the features and value necessary for the product to be considered by the chosen customers;
3. The augmented attributes, which differentiate, thereby separating one competitor's offering from another;
4. The potential features, which could be added at some time in the future.

The expected level of any product is that basic mix of goods and services that customers *expect* from *all* offerings. This is the collection of elements that are necessary in order to be considered in the evoked set of our customers, and are only the minimum entry requirements. These will depend upon a range of competencies but although *necessary* these will not be *sufficient* for success.

The augmentation of an offering by an individual supplier is the way to gain competitive advantage by adding value to a product. The competencies which support the augmented product are certainly 'core' in a competitive evaluation. The critical category of augmented features can be split, as suggested by MacMillan and McGrath, into two classes. Most obvious are those attributes which act as *discriminators*, demonstrating to customers how one company's offering stands apart from its competitors. The other group are the *energizers*, which not only discriminate but add

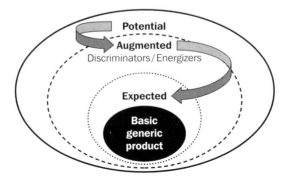

Fig 4.6 The total product concept: continuing migration of elements

value in a way that stimulates action by the chosen customers. Energizers are those features that attract customers and encourage them to purchase a particular product. These energizers are the factors that should be included as strengths in a SWOT analysis.

There is a great similarity between the way strengths are identified and the selection of core competencies. However, both are often carried out with insufficient thought when the real test is to focus attention on those factors that lie 'at the centre rather than the periphery of long term competitive success' (Macmillan and McGrath, 1996).

Potential product features are those that are potentially feasible 'to attract and hold customers' (Macmillan and McGrath, 1996). They comprise those additions that are possible but at present have not been offered.

In dynamic markets there is a constant migration of elements from potential to augmented, and from augmented to the expected level of a product offering. As competitors see some 'possible to copy' augmentation, then they will react to avoid being left behind.

Examples

> Most banks now open for extended hours, and supermarkets open on Sundays.
> Virtually all cars have enhanced warranty periods and increased service intervals.
> Many stores offer their own credit cards, although it is difficult to identify a real energizing advantage from them.

In most highly competitive markets any breakthrough or development is soon spotted and often copied quickly. Peters (1988) writes about the 'millisecond advantage' as many skills-based augmentations are easy for competitors to imitate. Therefore, many advantages last for only a very short period of time. This forms one of the challenges of marketing. As each advantage is nullified, what was once an augmentation by one supplier can become an expected feature demanded from all suppliers – hence one aspect of migration between the levels of a total product.

To recover an advantage, 'potential' features can be offered, so redefining the augmentation category. Thus a continuing migration takes place, with features moving in from the outer rings of Levitt's total product concept.

It is not all one way, however. There was a time when all supermarkets in the UK offered discount (Green Shield) trading stamps. To increase advantages a few even offered double and triple stamps on many purchases. In a mould-breaking move, Tesco decided to end offering stamps and concentrate on actual prices and value. This move was very successful and showed that the 'expected' category can be reduced, although obviously a compensating benefit was necessary to avoid an uncompetitive situation developing.

By considering the competencies that underlie existing products, it is possible to appreciate more fully what is being offered to our customers. It includes every customer-oriented action which adds to the tangible aspects of an offering.

A core competence is the sum of learning across individual skill sets and, as such, can include any primary activity of an organization. Hamel and Prahalad give specific examples of Motorola, with a core competence in fast cycle-time production (fulfilment of orders), and Federal Express, whose competence is in routing and delivery. Both of these offer benefits to customers which rely on a complex range of underlying activities. For marketers consideration of the benefit received by the customer is vital. However, an offering is an output from the integration of many activities, hence the concept of core competencies.

The word 'core' is a critical part of the description as it is important that a distinction is made between core and non-core competencies. All organizations have a very large number of competencies but only a few are absolutely vital for success. These are the core competencies – those skills and technologies that really contribute to profitable exchanges.

The tests proposed by Hamel and Prahalad for a core competence are:

1. customer value
2. competitive difference
3. extendability.

The first two categories are absolutely necessary for all competitive offerings. The last is more difficult in relation to existing products but is, of course, relevant when looking at potential products or new product offerings.

Degrees of newness of products

A study of competencies should enable an organization to consider the full scope for new offerings. There will be some potential products where new capabilities are necessary, and the products are possible only if it is feasible to acquire such assets. Other new offerings require a re-bundling of existing competencies, or maybe only a few small modifications are necessary.

The category of new products contains varying degrees of newness, ranging from product modifications to 'new to the world' products. In the classic Booz, Allen and Hamilton research (1982), the following six categories were identified:

- improvements in/revisions to existing products
- cost reductions
- repositioning
- additions to existing lines
- new product lines
- new-to-the-world products.

The first three categories, which account for almost half of all new products recorded in the study, are really only minor product and/or market modifications. Mercer (1996) suggests four types of modifications: features, quality, style and image. To these must be added issues of value including cost reductions. In most dynamic market-places this type of development takes place on a regular basis, providing incremental improvements.

Although such modifications do result in a change to the product offering, they are the low-risk *tweaks*, which are really attempts to keep existing products both competitive and relevant in the ever-changing market-place. Hence, this type of modification is not really a growth strategy; rather it is a prudent and regular review of an offering to avoid what Johnson and Scholes call strategic drift. Incremental changes are likely to include the migration of features and quality changes from the augmented product category into the expected product category described above, as well as from the potential product category (see Figure 4.6).

In contrast to the regular, low-risk tweaks, there are more substantive categories of new products. Additions to existing product lines are *twists* on current offerings, such as the launching of Ariel Colour alongside the well-established Ariel product. This type of addition is likely to extend a product line, probably utilizing the same umbrella brand name, and with the use of related technologies and existing competencies. It will involve some additional risk but is likely to offer high returns on the investment. These twists benefit from changes in the primary demand for an offering, which can then be exploited.

A more radical development comes from new product lines that could redefine an established market. These can be thought of as *twirls*, where a new way of offering a benefit gives an opportunity to enter that market. All the evidence on new product failures shows that me-too products with no real advantage over existing products have a very high failure rate. However, if a real benefit is offered, such as when CDs were launched, delivering superior sound when compared to vinyl records, then there is more chance of success.

Twinkles, or new-to-the-world products, are extremely rare – less than 10% of all new products. Typically, they are high-risk, high-cost, long development products. They may utilize a fundamental change in the basic technology but are likely to result in an unique offering which really moves into the area of expeditionary marketing. Here the example of CDs can be shown in respect of computer use and the now accepted CD-ROM, which has enhanced personal computing over recent years.

Tweaks, twists, twirls and twinkles represent four different categories of new products. They can be added to the product–market matrix to enlarge the NPD area and allow each of the various types of new product to be considered. These will be discussed further in Chapter 4.

Linking markets and products

The product–market growth vector (Ansoff matrix; see Figure 4.3) was devised as a way of structuring decisions on future direction. Bringing it together with the Hamel matrix helps to answer the question of where to compete (combined matrix; see Figure 4.7). The first and most certain area for consideration is the top-left corner of existing products and markets. This is the reference market that a company should fully understand and so is an area where the opportunities to penetrate can be effectively evaluated.

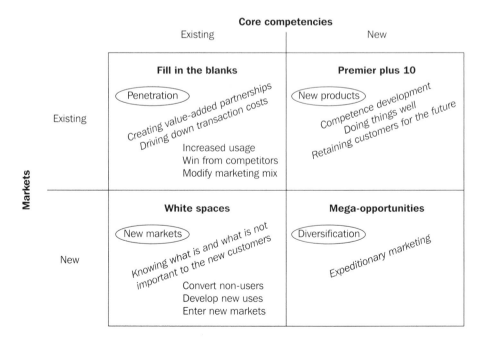

Fig 4.7 Revised direction matrix, after Ansoff (1965) and Hamel (1994)

If the decision is taken to continue to operate within the existing trading area, then one important action is to *defend* the current position in addition to building from strength. In this sector, developing strong relationships with customers and increasing the value added to the partnership can put an emphasis on driving down the costs of transactions. Hamel and Prahalad describe these actions as 'filling the blanks'.

Vandermerwe (1990) suggests that the gap between some producers and customers has narrowed over the past 50 years so that now many relationships are so close that suppliers come into the customer's activity cycle. The advantage of being within this cycle is that it is then possible to see when 'windows' are open and when closed. The customer's activity cycle is rather more focused on users and usage than on formal buying behaviour, and as such considers whether a customer is ready for a change in their regular buying patterns. Constructing a CAC for our chosen customers is a helpful exercise even if there is no intention of getting as closely involved as Vandermerwe would recommend. However, it is essential if the chosen objective is either filling the blanks or ensuring that the relationship continues well into the future.

Premier plus 10, the area of competence development, considers the expanded needs of existing customers. Hamel is more concerned with ensuring that our current offerings remain competitive in respect of future changes in customer requirements. New competencies are equally relevant where there is a lack of competitive advantage now, or where enhanced capabilities could lead to the development of a new product. Ansoff concentrates on those new opportunities with existing customers which could require new competencies, or at the very least a new application of existing competencies.

In new segments where we do not currently operate there are 'white spaces'. It may be necessary to creatively redeploy or recombine our current core competencies to reach new customers, but the key is knowing what is important to those groups expressed as the critical success factors to be mastered.

Ansoff (1965) suggested that 'The common thread in the first three alternatives is either marketing skills or product technology or both'. In the fourth quadrant (diversification) the common thread is less apparent and certainly weaker. The original text described it as 'distinctive in the fact that both products and missions are new to the firm'.

For Hamel and Prahalad (1994) this area offers mega-opportunities and requires 'expeditionary marketing' to capitalize on them. Over the years there have been many high-risk new-to-the-world products. Those that fail are soon forgotten. Those that succeed create a new market, and initially they control it. Examples of successful developments are Häagen-Dazs with adult ice cream, Sony Walkman and the personal stereo player and Psion electronic organizers.

	Existing	Tweaks (modified)	Twists (extended)	Twirls (related)	Twinkles (unrelated)
Existing	✔				
Expansion: new users					
Extension					
Excluded markets				☠	
Expeditionary markets					💣

Fig 4.8 A 2 × 2 matrix is very confining. Try a 25-cell matrix. The key is the diagonal distance from existing operations. *Source*: Ansoff (1965) and Hamel and Prahalad (1994)

The replacement of products with competencies should force a positive reassessment of what can be achieved by an organization. The integration of the two matrices should encourage more creative thinking about how to satisfy both existing and new markets.

Consideration of the components of both products and markets enables an enlarged matrix to be constructed (Figure 4.8).

As with the 2 × 2 matrix, this exploded one can be used to consider strategic opportunities. Similarly, the risk in pursuing a particular option is increased the further that cell is from the known safe haven of supplying existing products to existing advocates.

Different company typologies

In the late 1970s Miles and Snow (1978) identified a number of strategic company positions based on an organization's intentions with regard to product-market development. These categories are still valid and they are especially useful when considering the appropriate activities that a business can adopt. A firm could concentrate on the achievement of growth through developing new products and new markets. These pioneering companies are termed *prospectors*. Such companies are active in looking for new opportunities within a broad product or market domain. They are structured to respond quickly when they spot new openings, and they compete by stimulating new demand. However, they do not always build strong positions before moving on to yet more new ventures.

By contrast, there are the so-called *defender* businesses, which attempt to achieve and maintain a secure position in a relatively stable product-market. They pursue strategies which protect their business and concentrate on building strong value-added relationships with existing customers. While not usually at the forefront of technology, they concentrate on efficiency of operations and strong marketing offerings in order to increase the barriers to competitive entry.

A third typology is the *analyser*, which comes between the other two, maintaining strong existing positions while using investments carefully to consider developments into new, possibly closely related, areas. They are seldom pioneers or first movers with respect to new developments, but they often act as fast followers, the second or third entrant into a market area relating to their own competence base. They succeed by offering improvements in the form of higher value or lower cost than the pioneers.

A final group is the *reactor* business, which lacks any clear direction. It was once said that there are three types of companies:

1. those who make things happen;
2. those who watch things happening;
3. those who wondered what happened!

Reactors are likely to be in the last group. However, success comes to the companies in the other three categories that pursue effective competitive strategies.

Miles and Snow acknowledge other typologies, but theirs has become a standard, which has been robust enough to survive for over twenty years. Table 4.1 gives further details about these different possible positions for an organization.

Strategic decisions

The product-market growth vector can also be studied in association with a planning model such as one of the attractiveness/competitiveness models. Several of these have been developed in response to criticism of the simplistic and two-dimensional nature of the BCG matrix. Both Shell, with the directional policy matrix, and General Electric, with its nine-cell business screen, have developed useful models. These have been merged in Figure 4.9. In this representation, 'Industry/market future attractiveness' has been placed on the vertical axis, so increasing the common links with the Ansoff/Hamel models. It is likely that existing markets are high on attractiveness for many organizations and hence it is possible to see even closer links between the models. The converse is that unknown markets can often be rated rather less attractive, especially in terms of the potential risks.

Table 4.1 Defenders, prospectors, analysers and reactors

1. *Defenders* are organizations which have narrow product-market domains. Top managers in this type of organization are highly expert in their organization's limited area of operation but do not tend to search outside of their domains for new opportunities. As a result of this narrow focus, these organizations seldom need to make major adjustments in their technology, structure, or methods of operation. Instead, they devote primary attention to improving the efficiency of their existing operations.

2. *Prospectors* are organizations which almost continually search for market opportunities, and they regularly experiment with potential responses to emerging environmental trends. Thus, these organizations often are the creators of change and uncertainty to which their competitors must respond. However, because of their strong concern for product and market innovation, these organizations usually are not completely efficient.

3. *Analysers* are organizations which operate in two types of product-market domains, one relatively stable, the other changing. In their stable areas, these organizations operate routinely and efficiently through use of formalized structures and processes. In their more turbulent areas, top managers watch their competitors closely for new ideas, and then they rapidly adopt those which appear to be the most promising.

4. *Reactors* are organizations in which top managers frequently perceive change and uncertainty occurring in their organizational environments but are unable to respond effectively. Because this type of organization lacks a consistent strategy–structure relationship, it seldom makes adjustment of any sort until forced to do so by environmental pressures.

Source: Miles & Snow (1978).

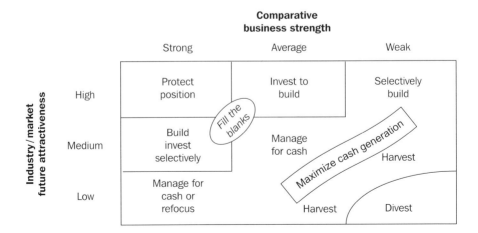

Fig 4.9 Industry attractiveness/business strength matrix, derived from the General Electric and Shell Directional Policy matrices

Similarly, successful existing products should offer a strong competitive position, whereas new products and new categories are likely to be weaker initially as the markets will usually need time before they accept such developments.

The links between the models must not be overdone. However, the warnings and strategic advice indicated in the nine-cell matrix illustrated do highlight the risks when choosing to venture into a new area. When developing new markets and new products within an organization, there is a risk that the internal enthusiasm for and excitement about the new development will obscure an objective view of market attractiveness and competitive strengths. The low success rate of new launches and the reasons for failure are testament to this.

The Shell and General Electric matrices are, primarily, a way of reviewing existing offerings rather than a predictor for new developments. All existing offerings can be studied to determine whether they are really in attractive markets with a good level of competitive advantage. If so, building from strength is an obvious strategy. If the position is considered weaker then there is a need to look towards new opportunities. But it ought to be remembered that it is not always the new, fast developing markets that are attractive. Many a fortune has been made out of mature, or declining markets by establishing a position of strength. Consider the success of Hanson Trust with such unattractive products as building bricks, aggregates and waste management.

By contrast many organizations have been bankrupted in fast-growing IT markets, including hardware suppliers, software houses and retailers. The developments in these markets have been so erratic that it is sometimes impossible to predict the next development.

Strategic windows

Returning to the problems and opportunities caused by the constant changes that are taking place in dynamic markets, if a supplier (defender or analyser) really understands its customers and their activity cycles, then it will continually be updating its offerings with appropriate enhancements in order to secure ongoing business. But some market changes can also give rise to new opportunities for prospector companies. These opportunities come about because of structural changes, actual or perceived, in the market, which create an opening and thus increase the chances of success for a new product offering. It is sometimes forgotten that any decision regarding where to compete *in the future* should also include the vitally important dimension of timing. To be too early with a new product is just as bad as being too late.

Example

> I remember launching a high fruit/low sugar conserve when working as a product manager for Chivers-Hartley in the mid-1970s. It researched well and showed every sign of success. The product failed to meet target and was withdrawn. The same product is a success in the 1990s as consumer taste and other market factors have developed to change the market conditions.

Within companies there is a danger of a self-fulfilling prophesy when considering previous activity. Past experience and the resultant mindset of managers sometimes link to constrict strategic options, and thus reject some developments on the basis that they have already been tried and failed. If this had been the case, then Hartley's high fruit jam would never have been launched. Steps must be taken to avoid this 'collective myopia' where effects, not causes, are remembered. However, this is not to reject the concept of a *learning organization*, where collective experiences are brought to the fore as part of future decisions. The risk comes about because of the failure to understand all the factors, including the importance of timing with any new initiative, thus introducing some element of 'groupthink', whereby inappropriate norms are accepted without challenge.

In Chapter 1 the terms 'foresight', 'advantage', 'enterprise' and 'resolution' were taken from ancient military strategy and applied to marketing. Strategic marketing is about anticipating and responding in an effective way in those market-places where it has been decided to operate. Abell (1978) coined the term 'strategic windows' to focus attention on the fact that:

> there are only limited periods during which the 'fit' between the key requirements of a market and the particular competencies of a firm in that market is at an optimum.

The concept suggests that these strategic windows of opportunity both *open* and *close*. New developments are only appropriate when a window is open, and disinvestment should be considered if a window of opportunity closes.

Of course, the proactive role of marketing communications will allow for some manipulation of the windows. If it is necessary to try to change attitudes or give information to certain customers in order to create the right climate prior to a new product launch then this is an obvious marketing activity. Such actions could ensure a window is open when required. However, while the opening of a window is not entirely outside the control of marketers, it is more usual for the cause to be external due to some environmental shift.

Strategic windows are, therefore, more likely to be opened due to major revolutionary changes when it is possible to move dramatically away from existing trading and capitalize on important new opportunities. In these situations it could be helpful to consider the four major categories of market evolution that, Abell suggests, open strategic windows:

1. development of new primary demand
2. redefinition of markets
3. availability of new competing technology
4. channel changes.

The first, development of new primary demand, often comes when new markets are in the growth stage. The market norms may not be firmly established and not all potential customers will have fully adopted a product. In spite of the advantages often enjoyed by pioneering companies (see PIMS data below), there are real opportunities for later entrants to revise their offerings and build on the work of the pioneers to create new primary demand.

The PIMS (Profit Impact on Marketing Strategy) research programme was an ambitious study of over 3000 strategic business units over a 14-year period. While mainly US companies were involved, the international aspect covered some 19% of the sample. The study concentrated on averages across the industries and this can always be challenged when one organization is far from average. However, the data (Figure 4.10) on the average market share achieved at a time of maturity by firms pursuing different market entry strategies are very revealing. The advantages of being a successful pioneer are obvious, but must be balanced by the high risk of failure if the market conditions or the market entry strategies prove inappropriate. In such circumstances the opportunities for the follower firms are obviously greater.

In fact, redefining a market can take place at any time, although it is more difficult in an established market. However, the second of Abell's windows is present when there is such a redefinition. It could be the move to total solutions (turnkey systems)

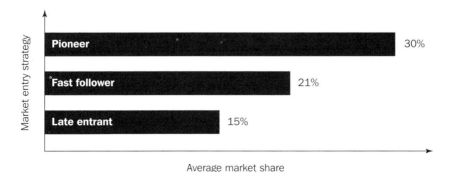

Average market share

Fig 4.10 Average market share at industry maturity of firms pursuing different market entry strategies

by a computer company wishing to move away from hardware alone and to enhance its offering. Another example is development of complete design and build contracts in the construction industry, which have changed the way business is done.

Many examples involve the introduction of elements from the 'potential' product category in an effort to move far enough away from existing offerings to make it difficult for some competitors to respond. However, decisions are not always ones where additions need to be made; for example, Canon was able to redefine photocopier requirements by providing *less* than Xerox.

New technologies do provide opportunities, but the warning in Chapter 3 still applies. Often the new technology leads to a completely new market rather than a redefining of an existing one.

Changes in the channels of distribution can have far-reaching consequences. They might enable an organization to reach customers previously excluded. Telephone banking is an example that combines new technology and new channels. However, the move by grocery supermarkets to sell books, records and even gardening equipment is only a channel change but it has certainly widened the user groups for these categories.

It is possible to overlay the product-market growth vector with the potential windows of opportunity and so illustrate the likely requirements for specific developments (Figure 4.11). The actual catalyst in creating an open window could still be a proactive marketer taking appropriate decisions, but opportunities also arise from external stimuli.

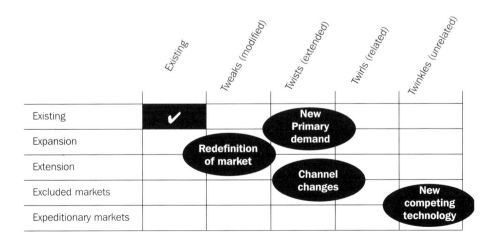

Fig 4.11 Strategic windows and product/market matrices

Conclusions

The highest level of marketing strategy involves decisions on where and when to compete. In considering the question of where, the link between markets and products is paramount. There are two areas that need to be assessed:

1. the existing product/market area
2. new areas.

Within the first it is possible to subdivide the customer group by a measure of satisfaction and loyalty, thereby considering how strong an organization is in its relationship with particular existing customers. It is not enough to consider all existing customers as fully satisfied, therefore different strategies are necessary. As markets are dynamic, attention must be given to constant improvements in the offering, 'tweaking' so as to remain competitive and possibly benefiting from low-cost modifications which could help to strengthen an existing position.

Ansoff used the term 'penetration' and for Hamel it was 'filling the blanks' when developing strategies for existing business. These activities lead to the building of closer relationships and the reducing of transaction costs, which make it more difficult for challengers to attack, and possibly assist in stealing some business from close competitors.

The second category is more varied, with a large number of options that must be evaluated. Entering new product-markets usually involves taking business from some other organization, so it is important that customers are offered real added value in order to persuade them to switch.

There are three basic directions available, irrespective of whether a 2×2 matrix is used or an expanded one.

If the first consideration is new markets, these can be seen on the vertical axis in the directional vector. These markets have been described as *expanded*, *extended* and possibly *excluded*. The reasons why such customers are not currently buying from our organization will be obvious from these categorizations. It will therefore follow that each group must be approached differently in a specific way relevant to the potential that there is to switch that customer onto our offering.

Any consideration of product developments can be seen on the horizontal axis, which moves to the right into Ansoff's new product quadrant. Here it is the strength of an existing supplier's reputation that is relevant. New product offerings are unlikely to be a valid strategy if those existing customers are already dissatisfied, like the hostage or terrorist categories described earlier. However, if existing loyal advocates are targeted, then it is to be hoped that they have enough confidence to consider the new offerings against a background of strong trading links. Even so, this may not be enough if the new product involves displacing another strong supplier, but at least there will be some added value in the form of reputation on which to develop a new offering.

Both of these directions can be evaluated by considering the cells of an expansion matrix. Using an enlarged matrix allows a more careful study of some developments, including those which move into new markets and new products. For instance, a minor product modification that adds value to an offering and so gives a competitive advantage, making it suitable for an expanded market, is a rather less risky move than a total diversification into a new product form offered to previously unknown customers. The smaller Ansoff/Hamel matrices do not highlight these various levels of risk.

The enlarged matrix can be used to indicate the risk as consideration is given to cells remote from the home of existing trading, such as Hamel's white spaces and mega-opportunities. These developments will be possible but only if all the factors are positive. Not only have new customers to be receptive to new offerings, but the new offerings must offer real advantages to the customers. But this is not enough as the dynamics of the market demands that the timing must be considered so that the strategic windows are open sufficiently for the developments to stand a chance of success. This is the importance of always considering the additional strategic question of when to compete.

KEY POINTS

4.1 Marketing offerings can be evaluated by the test of suitability, feasibility and acceptability. Only where all three are met is an exchange possible.

4.2 Market definitions should be based on customer use (use classifications) – e.g. flexible travel – rather than the products offered – car market. The Ansoff 'demand–technology–product' life cycle can be used to demonstrate the subsidiary role of the product.

4.3 It is important to recognize that most markets do not have neat boundaries, and different customers will have different perceptions of products and substitutes, thus making it difficult to describe a market in an absolute sense.

4.4 There are several categories of new markets: terms used here could be expansions, extensions, exclusions and expeditions.

4.5 There are advantages in considering internal competencies (as proposed by Hamel) rather than the product output of an organization with respect to both new and existing products.

4.6 Products should be viewed as 'everything', both favourable and unfavourable, that is received in an exchange. Attention should be focused on the 'expected' elements of a product offering, which must be present as a necessity, and the 'energizers', which actually encourage customers to buy.

4.7 New products can be split between those that modify an offering incrementally (tweaks), those that are new to a particular organization, allowing it to enter new markets (twists and twirls), and those that are new to the whole market-place (twinkles).

4.8 The different categories of products (existing and new) and markets (existing and new) can be shown on an enlarged matrix. As with the original Ansoff matrix, the level of risk increases the further a development is from the existing base in the top left corner.

4.9 Organizations adopt different ways of operating within product-markets. The orientation of a company could determine the appropriate area in which to operate (e.g. prospector or defender).

4.10 There are many different matrices that can be used in considering product-market decisions. Many of these can be shown to exhibit similarities, and they can be very useful in suggesting future strategic direction. However, care must be taken when considering new initiatives as some seemingly attractive markets offer no real opportunity for successful trading.

4.11 New product development is risky. Most markets are already serviced by existing offerings (from competitors). There are limited periods of opportunities during which the fit between the key requirements of a market and the particular competencies of a firm in that market is at an optimum. These are sometimes termed strategic windows.

QUESTIONS

4.1 Market share is generally considered a key measure of marketing success. In view of the problems involved in defining a market, and its boundaries, is market share really an acceptable measure?

4.2 What is the difference between the augmented elements of a product offering that are termed 'energizers' and other discriminators? Suggest examples of each category.

4.3 Many new product offerings are really only 'tweaks' designed to maintain competitiveness by incremental improvements. Suggest five categories of modifications which could be suitable for regular 'tweaking'.

4.4 A strategic window is described as that limited period when an opportunity exists to enter a new market. Describe the four windows suggested by Abell, and give examples of each.

Bibliography

Abell, D., Strategic Windows, *Journal of Marketing*, July, 1978.

Ansoff, H.I., *Corporate Strategy*, McGraw-Hill, 1965.

Ansoff, H.I. and McDonnell, E., *Implanting Strategic Management*, 2nd Edn, Prentice Hall, 1990.

Booz, Allen and Hamilton, *New Product Management for the 1980s*, Booz, Allen & Hamilton Inc., 1982.

Buzzell, R.D. and Gale, B.T. *The PIMS Principle: Linking Strategy to Performance*, Free Press, 1987.

Day, G.S., The Capabilities of Market Driven Organizations, *Journal of Marketing*, Oct., 1994.

Dibb, S., Simkin, L., Pride, W.M. and Ferrell, O.C., *Marketing Concepts and Strategy*, 3rd European Edn, Houghton Mifflin, 1997.

Hamel, G. and Prahalad, C.K., *Competing for the Future*, HBS Press, 1994.

Hamel, G. and Prahalad, C.K., Strategy as Revolution, *Harvard Business Review*, July/Aug., 1996.

Johnson, G. and Scholes, K., *Exploring Corporate Strategy*, 4th Edn, Prentice Hall, 1997.

King, S., *Developing New Brands*, Pitman, 1973.

Kotler, P., Armstrong, G., Saunders, J. and Wong, V., *Principles of Marketing*, European Edn, Prentice Hall, 1996.

Levitt, T., Marketing Myopia, *Harvard Business Review*, July/Aug., pp. 45–56, 1960.

Levitt, T., Differentiation of Anything, in *The Marketing Imagination*, Free Press, 1983.

MacMillan, I.C. and McGrath, R.G., Discover your Products' Hidden Potential, *Harvard Business Review*, May/June, 1996.

Mercer, D., *Marketing*, 2nd Edn, Blackwell, 1996.

Miles, R.E. and Snow, C.C., *Organizational Strategy, Structure and Process*, McGraw-Hill, 1978.

Moran, W.R., Why New Products Fail, *Journal of Advertising Research*, April, 1973.

Peters, T., *Thriving on Chaos*, Macmillan, 1988.

Vandermerwe, S., The Market Power is in the Services; because the Value is in the Result, *European Journal of Management*, Vol. 8 No. 40, 1990.

STANDARDIZATION VERSUS ADAPTATION OF OFFERINGS: GLOBAL ISSUES IN MARKETING COMPARED TO CUSTOMIZATION

5

CHAPTER

INTRODUCTION

The marketing concept emphasizes the matching of customer needs with specific suppliers offerings to facilitate a profitable exchange. An offering is that complex mixture of products and other elements, tangible and intangible, that together are passed from a supplier to a customer. Marketing thinking considers that the exchange is affected by the strength of the relationship that exists between the two parties, although it is judged in comparison to all other competitive offerings seen by the customer. Adherence to marketing principles may suggest that the most successful companies will be those that achieve the closest links and develop the best-matched offerings.

There are some markets where every offering is individually constructed, and each customer can be considered separately, a segment of one! These are, usually, markets where the orders are of relatively high value, e.g. capital plant and equipment, but there are also markets where there is obviously no room for standardization, for example prescription spectacles. Then there are other markets where it is possible to identify strategic groups of customers, and in these cases each resulting segment is treated as a homogeneous whole and can be offered a standard product at an attractive price. In fact, there are many examples of organizations that have transformed fragmented and heterogeneous markets into unified industries typified by mass production, mass distribution and standardized products. Globalization is the extension of standardization to a worldwide market-place. By making a uniform offering to a global market, the benefits of scale are thought to be even greater.

There is a risk, however, that a particular group might not have absolutely similar needs in all respects. This gives rise to a paradox where the advantages of standard-ization are directly opposed to the customer focus within the marketing concept. Accepting some form of compromise, as can be seen in many companies, can solve it. Once the Ford Motor Company offered 'any colour as long as it was black'; now it offers so many variations on a basic car that the total of different products is enor-mous, although Ford can still benefit from mass production. The past success of companies like Ford illustrates that the problems are not insurmountable.

The degree of adaptation that is necessary if a particular offering is to satisfy a wide group (global) of potential customers will be specific to each particular situation. It is most often achieved by offering a standard 'core' product adapted by modifica-tions to the expected and augmented levels of the same product. For instance, the expected service level might differ for two airline passengers although both wish to travel from London to New York. At a crude level the presence of First Class, Club Class and Economy reflect these differences, although this is really the use of differ-entiated marketing to satisfy three specific segments.

It is possible to offer a more precise adaptation of the offer, especially in the aug-mented category. Maybe one passenger could receive transport to and from the airport, while another could enjoy accelerated check-in, and a third might be provided with an 'office in the air' (fax and other requirements) to allow that person to work while travelling. Each of these packages must be viewed from the perspective of meeting each individual customer's need rather than as a series of promotional additions intro-duced for general competitive reasons. At present few airlines have actually personalized their offerings to this extent, and there is no evidence of such a develop-ment. If there were to be such mass customization then the supplier would need to take a specific strategic decision to provide flexible resources, and, before providing them, there is likely to be an evaluation of the cost of adapting parts of the offering when compared to the additional returns that can be achieved. Toyota certainly thinks it is beneficial to be able to produce basic cars with additional features incorporated to reflect individual customer orders. For other marques, the car dealer can add pack-ages of optional extras, but this level of adaptation is at a very low level.

From a production perspective it is the difference between economies of scale (standardization driving down costs) and economies of scope (adaptation to demands). Adaptation may be limited to a few product features or may embrace all the elements in the marketing mix. Figure 5.1 gives some idea of how this could apply across the mix.

There are some marketers who reject any adaptation, suggesting, in the words of a

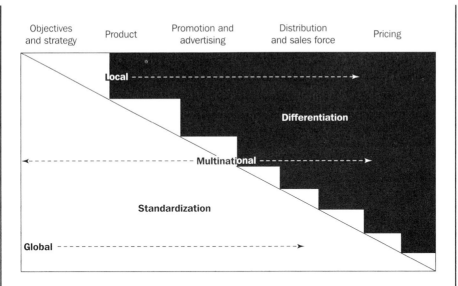

Fig 5.1 Standardization versus adaptation

UK advertising executive, that 'it is best to allow brands and businesses to be themselves, letting consumers come to them by self selection'. It could be argued that such a product-oriented approach is outdated, but it still takes place.

Any decision as to the orientation of an organization and the degree of adaptation or standardization to be utilized is a key aspect in deciding the strategic marketing question of *how to compete*.

The dilemma regarding individual customization is present in all market locations, but it becomes more obvious when considering global markets. In such markets, the differences in the environment, the cost structure, customers' cultural activities, and degrees and scope of competition reach a more acute level, and consequently the debate about the need to adapt an offering is much more intense.

Global marketing

Global marketing is marketing in an unbounded geographic market. It is the most extreme development of international marketing and is applicable to products or services that have similarities stretching across national boundaries, and for which a unified strategy is feasible. It is a logical extension to the process of standardization that took place in the US some 70 years ago. In this respect it is interesting to study Kimball's essays on new and old industries written in 1929. He reports from a US government survey that there were some 23 560 custom shoe-making operations in 1900. Just twenty years later only a few hundred remained, with most replaced by mass production facilities producing the now familiar standard sized shoes. It is hard to believe that shoes were once all custom made; now we are used to knowing our approximate shoe size, leaving only a handful of hand-made shoe makers. Shoe production is now part of a global industry with much of the production taking place in Brazil and Italy, but there are still national differences in shoe sizes; for instance is a 43 on the European continent the same as a size 9 in the UK? In another industry a manager has been reported as saying 'over a period of years of experience with builders and architects, as well as homeowners, we have found that the five-foot tub is on average an adequate size bath for the average size person'. Standardization means average. In some product areas customers are happy to be average and benefit from the production economies that should accompany mass production.

The issue of globalization was highlighted by Levitt's classic article in 1983. In this he suggests

1. The world's needs and desires have been irrevocably homogenized.
2. Everything gets more and more like everything else.
3. National and multinational companies that do not 'go global' have little chance of survival.

In fact, Levitt admits he exaggerated the issues in order to make his points, but there is a degree of truth in all the statements. Now, a decade and a half later, there are a number of markets where these statements are patently valid, as well as others where they still do not apply. Therefore, it is important to look at each market individually to assess the impact of the particular dynamic. In new technology markets such as computers and electronics there is a high degree of homogeneity. In more traditional markets, such as food products, there has been some migration of tastes across national boundaries over time, but far more variability remains in respect of many of the products offered.

Study of different markets could also reveal variability regarding the requirements, such as those in developing countries as opposed to industrialized countries; rural-based communities different from urban-based communities; equatorial areas with different needs from more temperate climates, and many others. There are also some markets where the averaged standard product fails to meet any requirement properly.

Differences are particularly apparent in the European market-place. Here wide cultural variations must be considered, whether it is in the way we shop and the resulting different specifications for freezers, or the differences in washing machine requirements. Both of these have been studied in the widely quoted case study on the Electrolux company. In this situation there is a case for a strategy that combines both global and domestic marketing activities: the phrase 'think globally – act locally' could be rephrased as *Eurobalization*.

Levitt's original article failed to differentiate between product function and product form. Although the same product may be sold in several different countries it does not follow that its branding, positioning, promotion or pricing are also identical. They *may* be, but this is a decision for the marketing strategists. In order to decide on the level of adaptation, it is necessary to examine the similarities in customer needs as well as the differences that exist in the various market-places.

There are a number of enabling conditions that are necessary, but not sufficient, for global marketing to be possible. Doz and Prahalad (1994) suggest these are:

• homogeneity of markets
• decreasing costs of transport and communications
• reducing trade barriers
• competitive pressures from new competition.

The first of these categories derives from Levitt's predictions. Of course some geographic markets are being drawn closer by the media (international television), travel and activities of multinational corporations. Such markets include cars, electronics, fast food and popular drinks. However, it has been said that there are enough different models of the Ford Escort car that if each were placed bumper to bumper they would stretch most of the way around the globe. This illustrates the level of adaptation and modification that does actually take place in seemingly global markets.

Lower costs, in terms of both reaching customers and reducing fiscal barriers, have helped to facilitate competition by leading to more consistency in prices, but, as many marketers know, there are many situations where cost/price is not a major determinant in the buying process. Premium-priced luxury goods have always had the opportunity to be global brands because image and status are far more important as criteria in purchase decisions. Even for regular priced items there have always been ways in which multinational corporations have overcome cost barriers by arranging local production or licensing deals. For instance, many car assemblers use production plants throughout the world.

In the lager market, I was involved when a decision was taken to sell Red Stripe lager (from Jamaica) in the UK. Brewmasters from the Caribbean company Desnoes and Geddes came to the UK to work with Charles Wells' Bedford Brewery. When the product was produced to the correct standard it was launched in parallel with a cricket tour by the West Indian team sponsored by Red Stripe. HP Bulmer, the cider company, undertook the UK off-licence distribution. At the same time Bulmer acquired the UK rights to distribute Perrier mineral water as part of a diversification of its portfolio of products. While Red Stripe was produced in the UK, Perrier continued to be bottled at source at Vergeze in France. With Perrier the magic of the product lies in its origins as a 'natural' sparkling water. In this case the imagery has been important in overcoming any cost disadvantage incurred by transportation of bottled water over long distances. Perrier might be a standard core product but its position is certainly not standardized.

When studying a product like Perrier it is useful to appreciate the different traditions in markets that are geographically close like France and Britain, as they diverge when other factors are considered. Mineral water consumption is much higher in France and the product has been a popular drink in that country for many years. In the UK, Perrier was a specialized product sold to the London hotel and restaurant trade up to 1979. Of course its appeal has widened in the past twenty years, but even so it still has a different position in the minds of British customers from the way it is perceived in France.

Reducing trade barriers can be seen both in the development of the European Union and in the agreements that underpin the GATT (General Agreement on Tariffs and Trade). An international agreement can allow access to a new marketplace; however, changing the entrenched attitudes of the customers in that market and persuading them to change established purchasing patterns usually take a lot longer. In particular, new competition cannot succeed unless it can effectively reach the customers. In many markets there are traditional channels of distribution already in existence and committed to existing offerings. Unless the new competition can enter these channels it must find alternative ways of reaching customers. This is not as easy as it might sound, hence it is the final enabling condition.

Universal/global offerings

At the basic level a universal offering will be the standard core product that meets the needs in the homogeneous markets and fits Levitt's model. There are other concepts for global products which avoid total standardization while taking account of market differences. Ohmae (1989) described one option using a relevant example:

> Market data collected by Nissan showed that there was no single 'global' car that could solve all the problems in their world-wide markets. America, Europe, and Japan are quite different markets with quite different mixes of needs and preferences. It seemed that they should design four dozen different models in order to develop sepa-

rate cars for each distinct segment of their global market. But they didn't have enough world class engineers to design so many models; nor have enough managerial talent; nor enough money. No company does. Worse still, Nissan felt that they could not write off any of these markets, as a global company they knew that they simply had to be in every market – and with first class successful products.

The solution for Nissan was to first look region by region, and identify each market's dominant requirements. These were then developed into each core *standardised* product, allowing add-on features to produce the required adaption.

Ohmae described the process, saying:

In the UK, tax policies make it essential that you develop a car suitable for corporate fleet sales. In the US you need a sporty 'Z' model as well as a four wheel drive family vehicle. Each of these is described as a 'lead country' model – a product carefully tailored to the dominant and distinct needs of individual national markets. Once you have your short list of 'lead country' models in hand, you can ask your managers in other markets whether minor changes can make them suitable for local sales. But you start with the 'lead country' model. With this kind of thinking Nissan have been able to halve the number of basic models needed to cover global markets and, at the same time, cover 80% of the requirements with cars designed for specific national markets.

Of course this process is a compromise but it offers a better match of product than trying to produce a standard product that is not derived from a specific market requirement. For many companies the core product is that which is promoted in their home market. Obviously, this can be a relevant starting place for a 'lead' model. The difference between this way of thinking and in the Nissan example it is the global perspective and resulting attitude throughout the organization. If the starting point is global then local issues will have less influence on strategic thinking in the future. If the starting point is domestic then there is a high risk of failing to track future changes in the wider global markets.

Mass customization

In the past few years there has been an increasing level of debate on the subject of customizing offerings. This has focused on new technologies, increased levels and radius of competition, and more assertive customers, which are combining to make many organizations look at ways of customizing their offerings. Prior to the industrial era, which led to standardized products such as the model T Ford (any colour as long as it is black), most products were individual. Today, individual tastes can still be met with interior design or hand-made clothes, but both of these involve a premium price. The issue now is whether it is possible to offer a customized product without the cost penalty. There are now a number of companies that are proving that this is possible. They achieve it by rethinking the production process. Westbrook and Williamson (1993) describe the Japanese tailoring company Melbo, which offers a 'ready made order system', which guarantees a suit designed by Givenchy, Daniel Hecter or Nina Ricci, but individually cut and sewn to fit the customer. There is a choice of over 100 fabrics, and it will be made in less than a week at a price which reflects the automated production utilized. These authors also studied the personal bicycle, made to measure for the specific size of the customer by National Panasonic. They report that the availability of such a machine has also stimulated sales of the standard National Panasonic products available at the same stores. To enable the customized bicycle to become a reality National Panasonic has had to 'select and train (and equip) 15,000 dealers with the kind of facilities and staff necessary to communicate the advantages of customisation'. The effect on the choice of distributors is obvious. See Chapter 12.

In a follow-up to *The Machine that Changed the World*, Womack and Jones (1996) argued against the 'sins of batch production mentality'. They show flaws in the theories of economy of scale and economic order quantities if application of such thinking leads to extra costs of warehousing and handling items that may never be sold because they are not quite right in specification. Most 'make to sell' production systems can be shown to be economically senseless when considered in the context of the total supply chain and the flexibility available from utilizing modern technology. Nevertheless, there are advantages in creating a basic *standardized* core that can be augmented to come closer to individual customer requirements.

Gilmore and Pine (1997) suggest that organizations should consider trying to become 'mass customizers', which they suggest as a way of offering many of the benefits of individual customized offerings while retaining some control on the costs and complexity of such programmes. They state that 'altering the product itself for individual customers provides the most clear-cut means of customization. But adept mass customizers realize that customizing the actual product is only one way to create unique value'. There are four approaches to mass customization suggested: adaptive, transparent, collaborative and cosmetic (Figure 5.2). These are similar to, but they extend, the four generic strategies suggested by Mathur (1997). He suggested the dimensions of merchandise (product) and support (service) as part of the total offering in the retail industry, which he was studying (Figure 5.3). The objective is to move from the undifferentiated product/service – commodity – into an area where an element of differentiation provides a competitive advantage, whether in global markets or in more narrow geographic areas. Mathur suggested

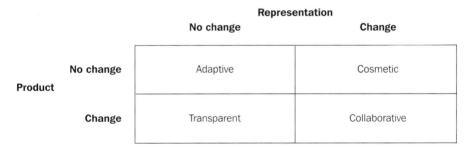

	Representation	
	No change	**Change**
No change	Adaptive	Cosmetic
Change	Transparent	Collaborative

Product (row label, spanning No change / Change rows)

Fig 5.2 The four faces of mass customization. *Source*: Gilmore and Pine (1997)

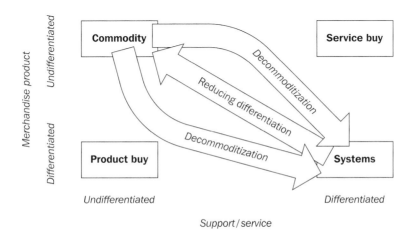

Fig 5.3 Adaptation of Mathur's generic strategies and transaction cycle.
Source: Adapted from Mathur (1997)

that the evolving of markets can be seen in a cycle (the *transaction life cycle*) that sees constant movement from commodity type products via some additional differentiation into *product-buy* or *service-buy*. The process then moves into *system-buy* as the other dimension is differentiated. However, there are then moves in the market that reduce the advantages, or deliberate attempts by suppliers as customer needs change and pressure develops to return to the commodity status again. These movements are present in every competitive market and are reflected in the migration of product features from augmented to expected and from potential to augmented discussed in Chapter 4.

Gilmore and Pine (1997) argue that an undifferentiated offering could be designed in such a way that customers could customize it for themselves. Perhaps this could involve additions but just as easily it could reflect the way the product is used. This is their *adaptive* category. It is not the same as the *commodity* in Mathur's model in that conscious efforts are made to allowing adaptation. But in many commodity markets there are customer inputs which determine why one offering is purchased and not another.

Differentiated merchandise, add-on features, can be obvious but Gilmore and Pine suggest that it is possible to provide individual customers with unique goods without letting those customers know explicitly that the product they receive has been customized. They offer an example of an industrial soap company which ensures that its offerings are each tailor-made to meet the needs of the various customers, including car wash companies and floor cleaners. They suggest that the buyers 'only know – or care – that the soap works and is always delivered when needed'. This is an interesting development within the automatic rebuy purchase behaviour shown by the customers in this market. Gilmore and Pine term this *transparent* customization.

Collaborative customizing, or Mathur's *system* offering, is present when an interaction takes place between supplier and individual customer to identify and supply a customized product made to satisfy an individual need such as in the 'made to measure' bicycle example.

The final category is *cosmetic*. This is where the presentation is varied in order to appeal to different individual customers. This might involve one or more of the elements in the marketing mix and can be considered against the balance of these shown in Figures 5.1 and 5.4.

Customized standardization

When considering product offerings the choice is not between pure customization and pure standardization, but rather the position is chosen on a continuum stretching between the two extremes, as shown in Figure 5.4.

It is interesting to note the similarities between Figure 5.4 and Figure 5.1. However, the earlier diagram looks at the continuum from an internal strategic content perspective, and Figure 5.4 is seen from a customer position. The five categories across the model, taken from the work of Lampel and Mintzberg (1996), are:

- Pure standardization
- Segmented standardization
- Customized standardization
- Tailored customization
- Pure customization.

Pure standardization is the model T Ford – a universal product aimed at the widest possible group of customers, distributed widely and produced to gain the maximum

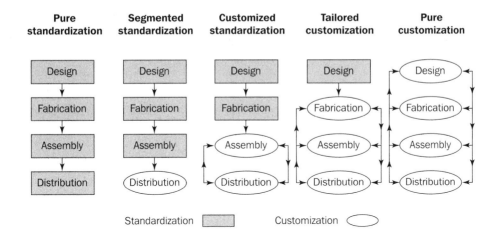

Fig 5.4 A continuum of strategies. *Source*: Lampel and Mintzberg (1996)

economies of scale. Standardization is often present with new high-tech products launched into the global market-place. An example could be the Nintendo Super Mario products. However, there are already developments in the delivery, which in Japan can take place through the Nintendo Computer Communication Network. This pioneering channel is now moving to the US and, if successful, will be rolled out into other countries, but such consistency is not always the case.

Sometimes historical study of major products will reveal that they originally were offered in a standardized format such as Coca Cola in the first part of the 20th century. Later it was adapted as sales were extended into new areas and it was considered appropriate to try to meet an even wider audience through different packages, flavours and modified promotional messages.

There is an ongoing cycle of new competition and developing customer tastes that can require a strategy offering limited customization. In 1980 Michael Porter suggested that there were three generic strategy options for any organization – cost, focus and differentiation. The justification for pure standardization could be based on the attainment of a cost leadership position. If this is not achievable then focus (segmented standardization) could be a viable alternative.

Targeting specific segments with standardized products, each of which has been aimed directly to the needs of a specific cluster of customers, is a form of focus strategy. Thus the airlines that ensure that their first-class travel product differs from the economy offering and that both are consistent in form and promotion to the relevant separate segments are adopting a policy of segmented standardization. However, the adaptation might only affect the distribution and promotion of an unchanged core product; for instance, a calculator sold in bulk through an office supplier compared to one sold direct to a student, or the tyres sold direct to the Ford Motor company when the same product is also sold as a consumer product through Tyresales or Kwikfit. In Chapter 4 this example from George Day was given to illustrate his contention that two separate markets exist. In fact a segmented standardization strategy will involve operating in distinct and different markets. Segmented standardization can be considered as increasing the well-matched choices available to target customers without those buyers having any direct influence over the design or production decisions.

Increased satisfaction often comes from the presence of optional extras available to buyers if those extras help to create an offering that is better matched to individual customer needs. This is customized standardization of an offering. It might be a sunroof or a CD player for car buyers, or even the ketchup or sauce available in a McDonald's restaurant. In this category each buyer receives a product of their own choice selected from within the constraints of the available additions.

The fourth category is the tailored customization of an offering, which links customer choice into the production operation. This is the Toyota car made to order, although there are still limits to the available choices of colours and finishes. The result is that the offering is not totally customized.

Total or pure customization is the ultimate – an individually painted portrait or designer clothes made from a specially woven fabric. The distinction between the customized categories can be a little blurred as even when designing and producing an individual product, maybe an architect-designed house, there could still be some cost benefits in using a number of standard components and utilizing these in appropriate ways.

Conclusions

While the marketing concept is focused on customer needs, the operation of supplier organizations does benefit from some level of standardization. This dilemma contrasts effectiveness (measured by the way an output achieves its purpose) and efficiency (measured by the internal costs of achieving an output) (Figure 5.5).

The problem facing marketing strategists is to find the best compromise between a customized offering and one that is more standardized within a given area of trading. The pressures become intense because of the way the world is gradually shrinking as global trends reveal homogenization of needs in an increasing number of geographic markets. This is matched by increases in the radius of competition of multinational companies.

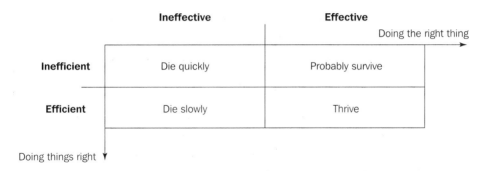

Fig 5.5 The efficiency/effectiveness matrix. *Source*: Adapted from Brown (1987)

The global debate in marketing is about how to respond, in particular how to adapt offerings to each of the national markets in which a company chooses to operate. They can use either a pure standardized strategy at one extreme, or a customized one at the other. Many possibilities for modification exist between these two extremes.

Most organizations will adapt their offerings, even if it is only slightly to meet local preferences, e.g. Coca Cola is less sweet or less fizzy in some countries, McDonald's offers different foods, such as salads in warmer climates. Labelling will often have to be adapted to cater for the different languages and legal requirements. Packaging may have to be altered as in some cultures colours can mean different things, e.g. white signifies death in Japan but it is a colour of purity, health and cleanliness in Europe. Price is also likely to be different although the decreasing costs due to transportation and fiscal barriers lessen the cost pressures. Of course, all marketers know that price is about affordability and demand and should not be driven by costs.

Promotions are another element of the offering that can be adapted, especially as messages do not always translate or could fail to appeal in some markets. This has to be managed carefully because the international positioning of a brand in the minds of highly mobile customers has to be consistent, not confused. Renault promotes cars successfully in the UK as 'fun to drive', in France as 'little supercars' and in Germany as safe, comfortable and reliable. Other issues could concern brand names. The decision by Mars a few years ago to rename the Marathon bar in the UK as Snickers was a move to benefit from brand image standardization. When Vauxhall renamed its Nova cars as Corsa it chose the name used in Spain because literally translated the word *nova* in Spanish means 'it doesn't go' – hardly the best way of describing a car.

These levels of adaptation are all possible and the benefits/costs of each must be fully evaluated by the strategists. The fact remains that pure customization is really the application of marketing; any compromise will leave opportunities open for adventurous competitors to exploit.

KEY POINTS

5.1 Successful marketing involves meeting customer needs at a profit. There is a paradox, however, in that the financial and efficiency advantages to the supplier of standardized products are directly opposed to the benefits a buyer seeks from a customized offering.

5.2 Companies must be aware of global activities in their markets, but while *thinking globally* should *act locally*.

5.3 While some markets have become more homogeneous, others have retained their variety, giving great scope for marketing activities.

5.4 In mass markets individual products are not always possible. But there are many ways of customizing an offering and thus getting as close as possible to the desires of customers.

5.5 Decisions regarding the offer of a standardized product, or moving along the continuum to create some form of customized offering involve a trade-off between cost (efficiency) and satisfaction of customers (effectiveness). There is no right answer, but the decision is likely to influence the company culture (orientation) and to have a significant impact on company performance.

QUESTIONS

5.1 Do you agree with Levitt's (1983) statement that the world's needs and desires have been irrevocably homogenized?

5.2 In the attempt to act locally in a global market, which parts of the marketing mix are likely to be the easiest to vary for different countries or market areas?

5.3 Suggest two ways in which a standard core product could be customized. Give some relevant examples of each.

5.4 Define customized standardization and suggest which type of offering could be suitable, and which unsuitable, for such an approach.

Bibliography

Doz, Y. and Prahalad, C.K., *Competing for the Future*, HBS Press, 1994.

Gilmore, J.H. and Pine, B.J. The Four Faces of Mass Customization, *Harvard Business Review*, Jan./Feb., 1997.

Kimball, D.S., *Recent changes in the United States*, McGraw-Hill, 1929.

Levitt, T., Globalisation of Markets, in *The Marketing Imagination*, Free Press, 1983.

Mathur, S.S., Talking Straight about Competitive Strategy, *Journal of Marketing Management*, Vol. 8, p. 17, 1992.

Mathur, S.S., *Creating Value: Shaping Tomorrow's Businesses*, Butterworth Heinemann, 1997.

Lampel, J. and Mintzberg, H., Customizing Customization, *Sloan Management Review*, Fall, pp. 21–30, 1996.

Ohmae, K., Managing in a Borderless World, *Harvard Business Review*, May/June, 1989.

Porter, M., *Competitive Strategy*, Free Press, 1980.

Westbrook, R. and Williamson, P., Mass Customization – Japan's New Frontier, *European Management Journal*, Vol. 11 No. 1, pp. 38–45, 1993.

Womack, J.P. and Jones, D.T., *Lean Thinking*, Simon & Schuster, 1996.

CHAPTER 6

SEGMENTATION AS A STRATEGIC TOOL

INTRODUCTION

A market is simply a collection of customers with similar needs. Within any market there will be subgroups that have more in common with respect to those needs and therefore could form a homogeneous segment.

Most marketing texts give a precise definition of segmentation, such as Kotler (1997), who suggests:

> Market segmentation is the subdividing of a market into homogeneous subgroups of customers where any subgroup may conceivably be selected as a market target to be reached with a distinct marketing mix.

Segmentation is also necessary in order to pursue a 'focus' strategy for competitive advantage, as proposed by Michael Porter (1986) and others. But remember that it will lead to an advantage only if it reduces the 'distance' between a supplier and the customers, *distance* being a measure of the gap between an offering and the needs of chosen customers.

The idea of identifying the different user subgroups and targeting a marketing offering at a particular segment is credited to Wendell Smith (1956). The justification for segmentation is usually based on a view that targeting a specific group will enable the offering to be modified so that it is a better match for the precise needs of chosen customers. This can be difficult to sustain as it is, at best, something of a compromise between a *customized* offering (perfect match to established needs) and a *standardized* product in a wider, perhaps global, market-place. The concept of segmented standardization was described in the previous chapter.

Targeting an offer to a defined segment can also be justified on the basis that it allows the efficient concentration of limited resources because if an organization cannot afford to operate individually with each separate customer then it must deal in a composite manner with a cluster or segment instead. However, the reasons for segmenting a market are more likely to be linked to achieving competitive advantage than they are to any need for operational efficiency. These competitive pressures should also ensure that marketing investment is not being wasted on those people who are not interested in the particular offering.

Smith was, in part, reacting against the mass standardization of the previous 40 years and was bringing marketing closer to its basic principle of evaluating and satisfying each individual customer's needs. Segmentation has been described as one of the most fundamental concepts in marketing. I would dispute this, but would stress that it is a very important aspect of effective marketing practice. However it is not a basic requirement, although it can be a profitable balance between pure customization and operational efficiency.

The logic of segmenting markets is attractive and appeals to hard-pressed managers who cannot offer everything to everyone. The problem is that there is no best way to segment markets, each approach having some advantages, but the practice of segmentation more often relates to available data than to finding an effective way of targeting activity to gain maximum effect, and thus to really benefit from the process.

Segmentation is a great deal more than the collection of dull demographics. It is not an operation where an organization attempts to find ways of describing its existing or potential customers. It is rather a process to be followed which could lead to a more appropriate marketing offering that achieves a real advantage over the competition. At key stages in the process it is necessary to ask if the focus on a given customer group will really offer such advantages while still being possible within the constraints of organizational capabilities and objectives.

Paul Fifield (1994) has summed up segmentation by saying:

> Market segmentation, dealing as it does with people as its raw material, cannot and should not be approached in a purely scientific manner. The only workable long term segmentation basis comes from the market place, not from our own wishful planning. No matter how well your organization is versed in the 'science of marketing', it is only by getting closer and closer to the target market place that real market segments can be identified.

> The process, like marketing itself, is necessarily long, messy, intuitive and fraught with danger for the logically minded.
>
> When most organizations approach segmentation they tend to rely on past actions and the development of correlations between past purchase behaviour and marketing activity. The real test, however, must be future oriented, and should encompass the flexibility to react to changes in customer motivations. These changes should be evaluated in the segmentation process so that the bases used are continually reappraised to maintain their relevance.

The segmentation process

Mapping the market

The first stage of the process involves mapping the market. A market map or flow chart should show all the competitors operating in a particular product class, and it will track their channels of distribution right through to the eventual consumers (Figure 6.1). It will be redrawn as a succession of variables are considered that highlight the differences within customer groups, which are then subdivided for a revised map.

By compiling a map that tracks products from suppliers through to eventual consumers, a detailed picture of the market will emerge. It will include various

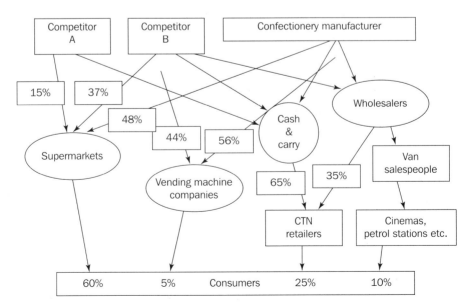

Fig 6.1 A simple market map for a confectionery manufacturer

intermediaries as well as all relevant competitors. For each customer group it could show geodemographic and psychosociological characteristics. It could also highlight high-profit customers, growth potential customers, loyal customers and mercenaries (switchers), who show little loyalty to any supplier. These could form the basis of effective segments for future action.

Actually, it is sometimes easier to compile the map in reverse order, starting with the customers and their needs then backtracking to the various suppliers. This technique produces a more complete picture of competitive offerings than the alternative method. The risk of this reverse technique is that it reinforces any established groupings as segments instead of developing new, more relevant, groupings for the future.

> I keep six honest serving men, they taught me all I knew;
> Their names are What and Why and When, And How and Where and Who.

The above ditty is one that should appeal to all marketing researchers. However, there is a serious point in quoting it as the six adverbs (What, Why, When, How, Where and Who) indicate the key questions to be asked in composing a detailed map. As more questions are asked, the answers are included in the map, leading to differences that must be represented separately. The revised map could become very fragmented as each subgroup is further subdivided to accommodate these differences in attitude or behaviour. The resulting micro-segments will need to be evaluated to decide if they are sustainable or if they are too small for marketing action. If a customized offering can be efficiently supplied then the micro-segment could be utilized, but it is often appropriate to link several of the small groups together. The clustering together of micro-segments is the next step in the process of developing relevant segments. However, before any attempt to consolidate them, they must be studied to reveal future motivations of members, as well as to determine any major influences on the buying process within each group.

This detailed analysis, which leads to a fragmented map of the market, is the raw material from which new macro-segments can be developed by the clustering of similar groupings.

It will be obvious that there is a difference between segmenting a market *prior* to the launch of a new offering, when compared with the market-based groupings that will emerge for an established market for an existing product class. The former is an *a priori forecast*, where an organization will attempt to predict segment boundaries that can then help in the targeting of the initial promotional effort. The other is *post hoc*, reflecting established market trends and the actual determinants of buyer behaviour. However, most new products are launched into existing need-markets with existing competitors supplying those needs. Therefore, even in an *a priori* situation it should be possible to map the relationships and exchanges in the proposed market and to identify current groupings of customers. Hence a degree of *post hoc* review is necessary even for apparently new markets, and this should lead to a better understanding of the market as it currently exists. While existing clusters can be identified at an early point in the mapping exercise, the real need is to forecast future groupings based on future intentions and motivations of future potential customers. Redefining segments could lead to a decision to try to deal with the market in a different way in the future, and it might offer real competitive advantages.

Clustering

When attempting to build new homogeneous segments from the micro-segments developed through market mapping and analysis, it is always necessary to keep checking how similar each cluster really is to others. In particular, the links should arise from a consistency in the way each member of any proposed segment reacts in specific buying situations. It is, therefore, important to identify what McDonald and Dunbar (1995) call the *critical purchase influences* (CPI), which are those factors that stimulate customers to buy. The term 'energizers' was used in Chapter 4. These are derived from the results of the 'What' questions, with the responses arranged in some rank order reflecting the varying importance of different factors in the buying process. This must be done for each distinct micro-segment. The objective is to separate those factors that play a key role in a particular group's purchase decisions from those that are only secondary. The former are the CPIs and there are a number of statistical research techniques that can be used alongside good judgement in identifying such factors. When these CPIs are identified, they can then be matched by the specific product features. In particular, it is the features that really 'energize' a potential buyer which are critical. These are the attributes of a product that will attract the chosen customers and stimulate them to purchase.

Clustering is the process of bringing together micro-segments with similar CPIs. The clusters must then be described in terms that can be used to develop marketing programmes. These could include traditional factors such as age, sex and other geo-demographic or psychographic characteristics, but they could equally be based on behavioural patterns or attitudes and responses of customers. The problem with traditional demographics is that, in many markets, they fail to discriminate effectively.

Abell (1982) suggested three categories of variables to be considered when segmenting a market: customer group descriptors, customer behaviour and technology. The last category could affect the ability of an organization to interact with a particular customer group. In fact, the segment descriptors will usually comprise a mixture of types of variables which together help to identify smaller, better defined, target groups. Each cluster can then be profiled in terms of specific CPIs as well as the key discriminators, perhaps extended to other factors such as media viewing and preferred marketing channels. These profiles will be used in developing a differentiated strategy for each particular cluster/segment.

Strategies based on the subdivision of a market using segmentation techniques in order to target specific customers assume a high degree of discrimination by the potential consumers. They often assume that customers will always loyally select the same one brand from the choices available. However, detailed analysis of consumer panel data by Hammond *et al.* (1996) has suggested that this does not always occur. In a study covering 23 grocery markets in the UK, USA, Germany and Japan it was found that there was no general pattern of strong segmentation between individual brands. The researchers tested the hypothesis that there is little brand segmentation; in other words, competitive brands will not be bought by notably different kinds of customers. The conclusion reached is that while there is some general evidence of segmentation due to appeal, usage benefits, seasonality or other factors, these are elements of product type segmentation that applies equally to the different brands in each market. Nevertheless, there are different brand preferences, but these are not distinguishable using available data. This emphasizes the need for a test of relevance when considering possible segments and their characteristics.

Tests of effective segmentation

When an organization has identified the clusters, it then needs to evaluate each one again, specifically focusing on how appropriate each is as a usable segment. Most marketing texts ask questions about *measurability, sustainability* and *exclusivity* as there is no doubt that if a segment is too small it is unlikely to offer the desired returns. However, the key tests really are:

1. Is the segment homogeneous? It is most important that every member of a segment responds in a similar way to marketing inputs. Fifield (1994) says that if they do not act in a uniform manner you have a 'classification', not a segment. He also asks if the segment is recognized by the members themselves and by channel intermediaries so that they will also understand or identify with promotions and communications aimed at them.
2. Is the segment accessible? Can the segment be effectively reached by our communication and distribution channels? If not then it is impractical for marketing purposes.
3. Is the segment actionable? Can a competitive target marketing programme,

which is likely to achieve the desired levels of profit, be formulated? Some marketers even demand above average returns on the basis that if they are to deal with a smaller overall market then it must offer real benefits in terms of greater returns than is possible from undifferentiated marketing.

Segmentation and resegmentation: dynamic segmentation

Market segments, the descriptors used and the CPIs are not static; they are continually changing as competitors and customers react to new opportunities and new developments. Also, changing technology and organizational capabilities can lead to new ways of interacting with some customers or groups of customers. Therefore, segmentation must be reviewed and revised on a periodic basis to ensure maximum benefit.

There is no rule about when to reconsider the segmentation bases, but all segments can be reassessed as to whether they retain the necessary homogeneity whenever the marketing strategy is reconsidered. However, a review should go deeper than just revisiting the basic tests of usable segments, and reach into a full revision of the market map and the CPIs for each segment. This could lead to an opportunity to introduce new criteria such as the 'cost to serve' a particular customer, or maybe a base of customer profitability, which has been shown as a way to focus on high profit areas in mature markets. Most changes in the structure of segments require equal changes in the marketing offerings.

The downside of segment changes can be illustrated by the analogy of ecological niches in biology, as described by Reynolds (1965). He writes that 'certain plants and animals have managed to adapt themselves to environments hostile or even lethal to other organisms. They thus avoid competition from other forms of life. This kind of adaption can be highly successful as long as the extreme conditions to which the organism is adapted do not change. In the event of change, however, the specialized organism – unfitted to survive in other environments – is most likely to perish'. The moral is obvious.

Target marketing

The natural extension of segmentation is target marketing. The first step is to prioritize the segments according to their attractiveness, as mentioned earlier. An organization then has to decide if it is to focus on a single segment or develop differentiated programmes for a number of segments. This depends as much on organizational resources as on the opportunities and threats relating to each specific market segment.

Marketing strategy is concerned with competitive decisions about products and markets. The two dimensions of market attractiveness and competitive organizational strength must be evaluated in respect of each segment, highlighting the opportunities and threats of dealing with that specific group. Not all segments will be equally attractive, and, in addition, limited organizational resources could constrain the scope of operations. Therefore, it will be necessary to prioritize the segments that are to be attacked. The greatest opportunities will not necessarily be in the largest segments. It is important, therefore, to identify the ones where competitive marketing capabilities offer the best chance of success. The largest and most lucrative segments often attract the greatest level of competition, and so entering such a segment must be carefully evaluated on the basis of comparative organizational strengths and competencies. However, it might be important to have a presence in a specific major segment to ensure a degree of credibility and to increase customer awareness, so the decision about *where to compete* is not always purely financial. Nevertheless, the benefits from using segmentation are based on focus and concentration; if these are dissipated by operating in too many segments, the advantages of strong target marketing will obviously reduce.

It is vital to select the segment carefully. This is why well thought out bases for segmentation are necessary. Slywotzky and Shapiro (1993) warn 'A popular way to lose money is to plunge into an established category and take on three or four leaders that have already built substantial customer loyalty – and to do so with an undifferentiated product'. They do suggest that with careful and creative targeting it is possible to break into such a market. The recommendations for this rely on focusing on the three groups of customers that create maximum value for the marketing investor:

1. Those who have low acquisition costs: 'switchables'
2. Those generating the most returns: 'high-profit customers'
3. Those contributing to long-term growth: 'share determinators'.

The identification of such characteristics is part of segmentation and will derive from a full and detailed understanding of individual customers. However, it is as well to remember the Pareto effect when considering which customers to target with increased effort in order to gain increased sales: 80% of business will typically come from 20% of the customer base. This grouping of existing customers forms a key segment of high-profit customers who should be identified. They should receive maximum attention aimed at retaining them as customers into the future

('Premier plus 10' in the Hamel matrix), and developing the strongest possible relationships with them to deter competitors. Retention strategies are discussed
further in Chapter 13. A key issue of building long-term relationships is the enhancing of the mutual benefits by increasing the *value* perceived as received by both
parties from their continuing links. This is likely to involve some form of augmentation to a product or, maybe even a customized offering.

When considering customized products, or *service additions* to augment a product,
then those that 'energize' the key, high-potential customers are critical. Identifying
segments of specific existing customers to be retained, or particular new customers
to be attracted, is extremely worth while. In studying the activity cycles of these customer segments it should be possible to identify the different energizers for each
different segment and thus improve the future target marketing to these strategically important groups.

All these elements of an offering must be designed specifically for the chosen segment, and the energizers must be tested to ensure they offer real competitive
advantages. Of course, the delivery of any competitive offering will involve the
whole of the supply organization; it is far more than a bolt-on to the sales/marketing
effort.

A lot of what passes for differentiated target marketing is really what could be
termed a 'variety' strategy. A characteristic common to some consumers is that they
switch from one brand to another, possibly for a 'change of pace' or because of the
attraction of a competitive or a new offering. Certainly persistent brand-switchers
should be considered as a completely different segment from loyal advocates. It
could be instructive to consider the classification suggested by Jones and Sasser
(1995), which was derived from the links between satisfaction and loyalty. Their categories of *loyalists*, *mercenaries*, *hostages* and *terrorists* form a useful group of behavioural
clusters.

Marketing and its discontents

Target marketing is more than identifying the needs and wants of customer segments in terms of product attributes. It is devising a total offering that promises the
benefits derived from these attributes and particularly emphasizing how the offering fulfils the critical purchase influences within a chosen grouping. Apart from the
product exchange with customers there are other interactions involving media
communications and contact with distributors. One of the requirements of a
focused strategy is to try to ensure accurate targeting of *all* the exchanges between
supplier and customer.

It is usually possible to define a segment in terms of characteristics and behaviour. However, available media and channels of distribution often do not precisely reflect the boundaries of a segment described. There will be some segment members who fail to receive messages from the supplier, others for whom the offering is unavailable, and those outside the segment who do actually come into contact with an offering. Even with well-maintained databases and using direct micro-marketing techniques, this can still, unfortunately, be a problem. Of course marketers acknowledge a lack of precision as they strive to develop implementation programmes that coincide as closely as possible with the chosen targets.

That subgroup of potential customers who fail to be aware of an offering or where it is unavailable are lost customers. When marketing managers are measuring the coverage of their chosen segment achieved by a media campaign, or the level of distribution availability of the product, the extent of this 'lost' trade can be calculated and other ways of reaching these customers can be explored.

However, there is another group who are exposed to the marketing programme even though they are not part of the chosen segment. These might be people who really have no interest in the offering. Of course they could ignore the communication – after all, most consumers receive thousands of messages every day and selectively filter these contacts. However, Star (1989) suggests there could be a problem with some recipients becoming frustrated, distracted or irritated by the highly specialized messages they happen to see. He looks at the trade-off between functional and dysfunctional effects, although he eschews a deep venture into welfare economics. Nevertheless, the warning is appropriate since the effect on those outside the segment will create an image of the offering and the supply organization that could influence its other activities. These are the discontents.

Example

Top Shop, the fashion retail part of the Burton Group, is targeted at young people and has created an in-store atmosphere supported by other messages which does not appeal to the older or more conservative customers. This group is more likely to visit Principles, also part of the Burton Group. When both Top Shop and Principles are located together in the same retail outlet it is important that the older customers are not put off by having to fight their way through Top Shop first. Alternatively, the younger clients want the excitement of a Top Shop. To ensure the benefits from an effective segmentation policy, many Burton developments separate the different outlets.

Organizational issues in segmentation

Successful strategic marketing exists where organizational capabilities are matched with market opportunities. Actionable segments must be evaluated in the knowledge of any restrictions that organizational structure can impose. Plank (1985) has taken this further, suggesting 'conventional segmentation theory has been founded on conceptual evidence on how organizations *should* segment their markets. . . . Such frameworks are of undoubted value, but have been criticised for failing to consider the practical issues of how these concepts are implemented in practice within organisations'. In fact, it is often the case that organizational issues drive segmentation rather than the segments emerging from the market. For instance, a well-known food company has three divisions – grocery retail, cash and carry, and catering outlets. It organizes all its activities around three distinct sales forces even though product decisions would benefit from a different arrangement.

The problems can be placed within the wider context of the link between structure and strategy, which is part of a debate in strategic management. In the marketing literature Piercy and Morgan (1993) have suggested that implicit perspectives which derive from internal paradigms, cultures, processes and structures have a far greater part in defining and segmenting a market than is apparent. This contrasts with the explicit view of market segments as clusters of external customers who form their own groups. The problem of internal structures affecting the construction of segments has been described by Jenkins and McDonald (1997) as a form of marketing myopia leading to market drift. The results can be similar to those suggested by Levitt (1960) when companies fail to answer the traditional question of 'what business are we in?'.

Jenkins and McDonald suggest a four-cell matrix based on two key organizational factors. The first is customer orientation, or the way an organization is driven to serve its customers. The ubiquitous customer care programmes are sometimes an outward sign of the emphasis placed on achieving customer satisfaction as a key component of strategy. The problem is that this is not sufficient unless the organization also understands the relevant groupings and their CPIs, and structures its operations accordingly. Therefore, the second dimension is organizational integration, or the way organizational structures reflect chosen market segments.

The matrix in Figure 6.2 illustrates a range of structures. These start with the superficial sales-based segmentation, where only that function really reflects usable clusters and there is little attempt to apply target marketing. The 'bolt-on segmentation' organization does try to respond to different customer needs in the total offering, but suffers from an organizational straightjacket. However, it is no use

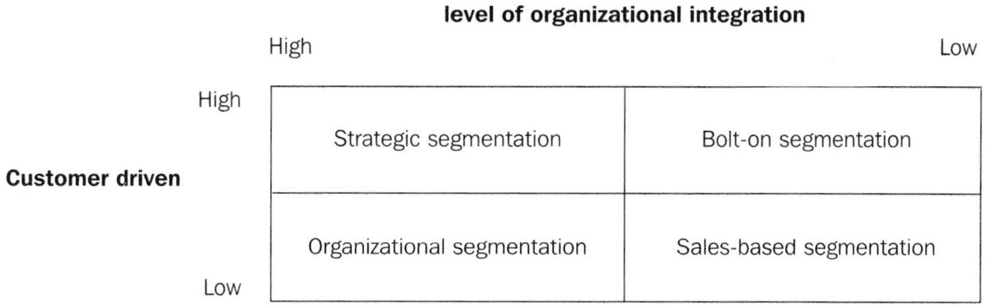

level of organizational integration

	High	Low
High	Strategic segmentation	Bolt-on segmentation
Low	Organizational segmentation	Sales-based segmentation

Customer driven

Fig 6.2 Segmentation archetypes in companies. *Source*: Jenkins and McDonald (1994)

correcting just the structural issues if the offering is not accurately matched with the precise needs of customers in the chosen market segment. The combination of a customer orientation and organizational integration is the only option where the process of segmentation is fully reflected in a way that encourages strategies that really do deliver the focused benefits that a target marketing strategy should offer.

Conclusions

It is very important for marketers to remember that segmentation is about improving the effectiveness of their marketing activity. If it fails to reduce the emotional distance between customer and supplier, and thus strengthen the relationship, enhancing the benefits to both parties, there is no point in pursuing a focused strategy. Segmentation is, at best, a compromise between customization and manageable marketing activity. It is therefore appropriate in those markets where combining customers into clusters can make the marketing operation more effective. This means it should deliver better penetration of the chosen target market, and higher profits.

Companies too often allow segmentation to be driven by the available data. This is wrong – it should be the result of a detailed understanding of the market, and the highlighting of the CPIs or energizers that are the real drivers of purchaser choice. Full understanding of customer motivation is a time-consuming exercise, but the time will be well spent for any marketing manager as this underpins the basic marketing concept.

Although markets throw up their own segments, outstanding organizations can help to create innovative segments by identifying clusters of benefits and needs based on motivations, not descriptions. It is the causal link between the stimuli from the suppliers and the reactions of the segment members which is critical, and not some dubious correlation based on past activities. By understanding the various groupings in a particular market and the motivations and reactions, it is possible to produce innovative segments that react in a consistent way to specific offers. This is the basis of effective target marketing.

It is necessary to continually test segments for relevance, but also to remember that market-places are dynamic and so changes must be expected and embraced. If an organization can move with the market to develop better segments, such as homogeneous clusters which are cheaper to serve, it will reap the benefits. Remember that competitors will not necessarily segment the market in the same way; there is no right way of segmenting a market. The process of developing segments will necessarily lead to grouping the key characteristics of a particular cluster; from these the marketing programmes should follow naturally.

However, it is not only the marketing mix which gives a focus to the target marketing, it is the way the whole supply organization structures itself to reflect the segmentation strategy. Structure must not be allowed to restrict competitive strategy. Of course the wider marketing mix of Booms and Bitner (1981) does include 'people and processes', and this goes some way towards the reflection of wider organizational issues.

One final consideration for firms adopting a segmented approach to their markets is the need to assess how much of their marketing effort is misdirected, and possibly wasted. The accuracy of the targeting determines, in part, the effectiveness of the strategy. There will be lost sales from customers who are not reached by distribution or communication. They could be considered a separate segment. There are also groups that fall outside the specific cluster by virtue of different characteristics but do receive some communication. These groups must be assessed and their likely reaction included in any evaluation of a target marketing programme.

KEY POINTS

6.1 Segmentation is often seen as an important marketing *technique*. The proposal here is that it is, at best, a realistic compromise between customization (a segment of one) and standardization.

6.2 Segmentation is appropriate only if it reduces the 'distance' between a supplier and the target customers.

6.3 While segmentation of new markets is often done on an *a priori* basis with preliminary views on that market, the use of *post hoc* behavioural divisions is often more valid as long as it is remembered that it is the *new* future and not the past that should be the focus of target marketing strategies.

6.4 The process of segmentation involves *mapping* the market to identify micro-segments, *clustering* those micro-segments into cohesive/consistent groups, *testing* those groups for homogeneity, accessibility and use (actionability), then *repeating* the process to *revise* segment groupings as markets develop.

6.5 Competitive marketing is about targeting the most likely segments, and realizing these are *not* always the largest groups.

6.6 Even in an age of direct marketing and new media, many offerings will be inefficiently targeted. In part offerings can be seen by inappropriate customers, in part not seen by some within the chosen market segment. The various effects (good or bad) of any marketing programme on every segment should be studied and assessed.

6.7 To implement segmentation and target marketing strategies it is necessary to consider the structure and orientation of the supply organization. Segmentation is not an add-on at salesperson level – it should be a way of operating, and a perspective on the marketing task that pervades every aspect and every department in an organization.

QUESTIONS

6.1 Explain why Fifield states that 'the only workable long term segmentation basis comes from the market place, not from our own wishful planning'?

6.2 What is the difference between *a priori* and *post hoc* segmentation, and what are the appropriate uses and risks associated with each?

6.3 Three key tests of an effective segment are proposed in this chapter. What are they, and would you agree (with reasons) that they are the most important criteria to be considered?

6.4 'High-profit customers' describes one segment where strategic benefits might accrue if such a group were identified in the segmentation process. Describe another such group, and give examples from an industry of your choice.

Bibliography

Abell, D.F., *Defining the Business: The Starting Point of Strategic Planning*, Prentice Hall, 1982.

Booms, B. and Bitner, M.J., Marketing Strategies and Organizational Structures for Service Firms, in J. Donelly and W. George (Eds) *The Marketing of Services*, American Marketing Association, 1981.

Croft, M.J., *Market Segmentation*, Routledge, 1994.

Day, G.S., Strategic Market Analysis and Definition: An Integrated Approach, *Strategic Management Journal*, Vol. 2, pp. 281–299, 1981.

Fifield, P., Market Segmentation, Standpoint No. 2, occasional paper, Winchester Management Resources Group, 1994.

Hammond, K., Ehrenberg, A.S.C. and Goodhardt, G.J., Market Segmentation for Competitive Brands, *European Journal of Marketing*, Vol. 30 No. 12, pp. 39–49, 1996.

Jenkins, M. and McDonald, M., Market Segmentation: Organizational Archetypes and Research Agendas, *European Journal of Marketing*, Vol. 31 No. 1, pp. 17–32, 1997.

Jones, T. O. and Sasser, W. E., Why Satisfied Customers Defect, *Harvard Business Review*, Nov./Dec., 1995.

Kotler, P., *Marketing Management: Analysis, Planning, Implementation and Control*, 9th Edn, Prentice Hall, 1997.

Levitt, T., Marketing Myopia, *Harvard Business Review*, July/Aug., pp. 45–56, 1960.

McDonald, M. and Dunbar, I., *Market Segmentation*, Macmillan, 1995.

Piercy, N.F. and Morgan, N.A., Operational Market Segmentation: A Managerial Analysis, *Journal of Strategic Marketing*, Vol. 1, pp. 123–140, 1993.

Plank, R.E., A Critical Review of Industrial Market Segmentation, *Industrial Marketing Management*, Vol. 14, pp. 79–91, 1985.

Porter, M., *Competitive Advantage*, Free Press, 1986.

Rangan, V.K., Moriarty, R.T. and Swartz, G.S., Segmenting Customers in Mature Industrial Markets, *Journal of Marketing*, Vol. 56, 1992.

Reynolds, W.H., More Sense about Market Segmentation, *Harvard Business Review*, Sept./Oct., 1965.

Slywotzky, A.J. and Shapiro, B., Leveraging to Beat the Odds: The New Marketing Mind-Set, *Harvard Business Review*, Sept./Oct., pp. 97–107, 1993.

Smith, W.R., Product Differentiation and Market Segmentation as Alternative Marketing Strategies, *Journal of Marketing*, Vol. 21, pp. 3–8, 1956.

Star, S.H., Marketing and its Discontents, *Harvard Business Review*, Nov./Dec., pp. 148–154, 1989.

HOW TO COMPETE

PART

This is the major section of this book, covering nine chapters. It starts with a general discussion of *positioning* and *perception of value* from a customer perspective in Chapter 7. This builds on the foundation of competitive positioning from Chapter 1. The next six chapters are then designed to dissect the sources of competitiveness, and especially sustainable advantage, by exploring the various issues in depth. All these apply to *all* product offerings, old and new. However, *new products*, *expeditionary marketing* and *strategic windows of opportunity* form a particular area that involves much marketing activity and where the future hopes of many organizations are either realized or destroyed. Therefore, in order to deal with the specific nature of competing by moving into new market areas, these topics are considered in two separate chapters, 14 and 15.

Professor Graham Hooley once suggested that 'you don't do marketing; you create positions'. In some ways he was correct as all external marketing activity is aimed at achieving a strong image in the minds of potential customers. However, it is the customers who construct such an image from their perception of what is being offered; it is the customers who compare the positions of competitive suppliers when considering purchases; and it is the customers who evaluate the various offerings in order to make buying decisions. Therefore the creation of a good competitive position involves issues of perception and understanding of how customers behave. The controllable variables, tools of marketing, are focused first on the total product and its *attributes*; these are then considered in the light of the *benefits* they offer to customers; they are brought together by the *claims* made by suppliers about their offerings. These three form what is termed the ABC of positioning (attributes, benefits, claims). *Value* arises in the interaction between supplier and customer, coming from a combination of economic and non-economic benefits. These benefits are reduced by the sacrifices a customer has to make in order to obtain them. Chapter 7

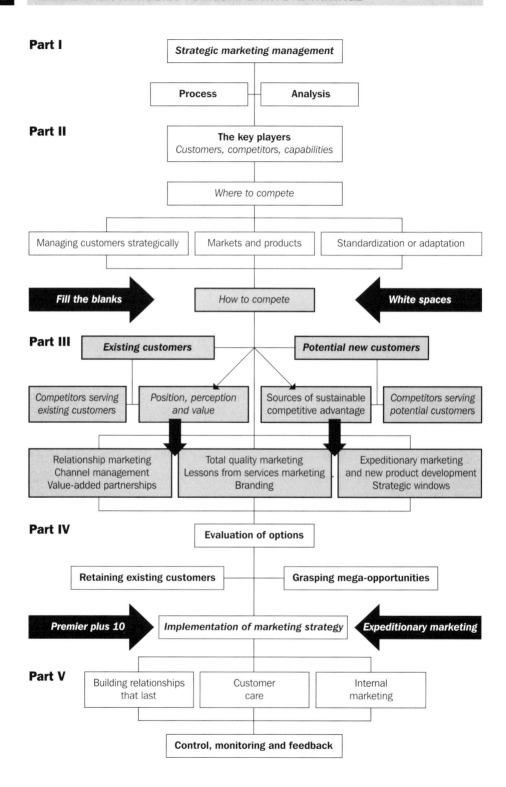

is an attempt to bring these issues together so that the sources of *competitive advantage* can then be discussed in the subsequent chapters.

Chapters 8-13 consider competitive advantage based on the two key dimensions of *high perceived value* and *low delivered costs*. The issue of perception is again present here, and it is important as the more quantifiable dimensions of value in such concepts as *quality, intangible service features* and *brand image*. These are three sources of competitive advantage covered in Chapters 8-11. However, it is also possible to gain advantage by obtaining *power* over customers as an alternative to manipulating *perceptions*. This is referred to before the end of Chapter 8.

Chapter 9 is dedicated to *quality*, a topic that should be of interest to all functions within an organization. The history of the modern quality movement shows it began with no marketing involvement, although it has now evolved to include a strong focus on customer satisfaction. It must therefore be of concern in all marketing operations. Nevertheless, there are still many areas of conflict between the view of quality as understood inside an organization and what can be termed a marketing orientation. These have to be faced in order to achieve what could be seen as true *total quality marketing*. Also important is the exploration of the many 'gaps' possible between what could satisfy actual customer needs and the offering developed by a supplier. It is possible to identify many of these gaps, which occur because of compromises made by suppliers or from some misunderstanding in the evaluation of the differences between needs, wants and expectations of customers. All affect the achievement of a quality offering, making it more difficult than ever, but, in the end, it is the ability to satisfy customers fully that determines quality.

The special nature of *services* marketing is included in Chapter 10 because so many real sustainable advantages come from the *intangible features* of an offering. Good strategies will emphasize the benefits of such features, and in order to do this it is necessary that the particular aspects of services marketing are understood.

Branding, which is covered in Chapter 11, is an extension of *positioning*, and there are many parallels with the development of strong positions. Some academics, such as Cowley, criticize the terms *image* and *positioning* as 'fat words with a multitude of meanings', allowing that brands, while a paradox, are more specific. The marketing task of 'decommoditizing' a product, creating advantage through non-economic reason for purchase, can be seen more precisely from a study of branding and the development of *'naked' products into personalities*. Hence this chapter touches on many aspects of competitive advantage.

Channel management is very different from quality, service marketing and branding. However, creating and exploiting *distribution 'assets'* is just as important as a source of sustainable competitive advantage. Chapter 12 attempts to widen the traditional issue of *channel choice* into the more beneficial area of *adding value by creating channel partnerships*. Achieving strong networks, distribution assets, requires consideration of power and conflict as well as other issues in building strong relationships with organizations that have relevant complementary competencies.

Chapter 13 is a logical continuation of value-added partnerships. *Relationship marketing*, where appropriate, is not an add-on to traditional marketing; as Gummesson says, it is a paradigm shift. A great deal has been written about relationships in the past few years, but surprisingly little has been done to integrate relationship marketing into strategic marketing and the building of competitive advantage. This chapter discusses different types and levels of relationships, providing a framework so that the *cultural changes* and *investment required* can be put into a strategic context. Relationship marketing is a critical area of attention for companies operating with existing customers and existing competencies that wish to protect their markets by 'filling the blanks' in those relationships.

The final two chapters, 14 and 15, cover *new product development and launch*. Professor Gary Hamel used the term 'expeditionary marketing' for the revolutionary new opportunities, this being the opposite of his category of 'filling the blanks'. If competitors already have strong relationships with potential customers it is often better to undertake some form of product-market development, a by-pass attack strategy, than to put resources into direct competitive activity. In any case, new product development is a key element of strategic marketing and is a potential source of future competitive advantage. It is linked to strategic windows in Chapter 15 because the timing of new developments, and the enabling conditions for entry, are so much part of the success of such initiatives.

Part III is not to be seen as offering an exhaustive coverage of every source of sustainable competitive advantage; rather, it explores the key aspects from a strategic marketing point of view. Advantage can come from product/service attributes, perceptions of value and quality, image dimensions like positions and brand, better availability or more acceptable partnerships, or just uniqueness due to lack of direct competition. All of these offer ways of competing; they are not exclusive of one another, but the prime consideration in achieving *advantage* must be *relevance* and *consistency* of the elements.

POSITIONING, PERCEPTION AND VALUE

INTRODUCTION

The key issues in strategic marketing are:

- Where to compete
- How to compete
- When to compete.

The first issue relates to products and markets, and involves questions about the scope of activities, such as whether to offer an undifferentiated product or service to a broad group of potential customers (maybe even global standardization), or perhaps whether the organization should focus specifically on a chosen segment. These options have already been discussed in previous chapters. The evaluation of such options will be influenced by what is possible given the organization's capabilities and competencies. The resulting decisions are likely to describe the desired market positioning for a particular company.

The issue of how to compete is equally important. An organization succeeds only if it is able to achieve a satisfactory competitive (product-market) position in its chosen market. It has to decide the best way to achieve a comparative advantage when evaluated by customers. In a book about strategic marketing and competitive advantage, the terms *positioning*, *perception* and *value* are certain to be widely used. They have already been mentioned in this text. This part of the book looks specifically at issues of how to compete, and the issues that must be considered if an organization is to establish an advantageous position in its chosen marketplace.

The position selected needs to be both different from competitors and sufficiently attractive to enough customers to be commercially viable. Differentiation alone is not enough, this just distinguishes one competing product or service from others. The total offer must 'energize' customers so that they are drawn to the specific offering. The way an offering is portrayed and the way it energizes customers is a statement of position. Such a position must also be one that the organization is able to sustain given the available resources and skills (company capabilities) and any constraints that may exist.

These requirements can be considered by using the SFA test introduced in Chapter 4, which suggested an offering should be:

- Acceptable (to meet the needs of the customers of the organization)
- Feasible (within available capabilities and constraints)
- Suitable (i.e. advantageous when set in a competitive market-place).

Achieving a distinct and well-chosen position is a key objective which will give direction to an organization and will guide any decisions relating to its marketing activity. Positioning is generally referred to as a process of finding and establishing a distinct place in a market, which will be judged by the customer's view of the offering when compared to competitive offerings.

As mentioned in Chapter 1, there are four distinct aspects of positioning:

- Market positioning
- Company positioning
- Product positioning
- Positioning as perceived by customers.

Market positioning has already been covered in previous chapters – it relates to the question of which markets are to be targeted or 'where to compete'. This chapter will look briefly at company issues but its emphasis will be on product positioning and perception and how they affect customer evaluation.

Market, company and product positioning are ideals that organizations wish to achieve. They are all important as the objectives within a marketing strategy, but they are measured by the perception that customers have about an organization and its products, rather than what those companies think they are offering. This is why it is necessary to consider the situation from a customer viewpoint, and to look at the influence of psychological factors on the evaluation of offerings.

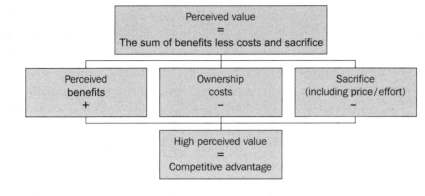

Fig 7.1 Perceived value

Customers will base their consideration of an offering on some personal set of evaluation criteria, including the perceived benefits and costs. In general, *value* is the computation of the perceived benefits of ownership when reduced by both the cost of acquiring a product and the cost of ownership (Figure 7.1).

Company positioning

Company positioning or competitive positioning covers the chosen attitude of an organization in its competitive arena. All marketing managers will aspire to an orientation that puts the customer first; however, this is not enough as companies must also position themselves against competitors. For this, an organization will need to decide the basis on which it is going to compete. Porter (1980) suggested three generic strategies – cost leadership, differentiation and focus – as the basis for competitive advantage.

The first, cost leadership, is not a marketing strategy as internal costs and efficiencies are about supply and have nothing to do with prices charged, competitive value or customer satisfaction. A cost leader does, however, have more choices in deciding how to utilize its *cost-based* advantage while still delivering an acceptable profit from its operations. However, competitive advantage comes from a valuable marketing offering made to, and judged by, prospective customers. It will be helped by cost-efficient operations, but it is the effectiveness of the output in the competitive market-place that is ultimately critical. The link between efficient companies and effective ones was neatly summarized by Rik Brown (1987), and his effectiveness/efficiency matrix was shown in Figure 5.5 following the discussion of standardization versus adaptation in Chapter 5.

Porter's second generic strategy, differentiation, is obviously important. Differentiation by itself will not be sufficient to attract (energize) customers. The factors leading to effective differentiation must be offered in a way that produces real value for customers. Mathur (1992) suggested 'decommoditization' by differentiating either the service or the product or both (his systems-buy; see Chapter 5). But since the ultimate judge of any offering is the customer, the various elements of differentiation will be considered in relation to the way they offer either *high perceived value* or *low delivered cost* to those customers. A company can therefore position itself as a differentiator offering either high value or low costs to its customers. These two categories are at the heart of effective differentiated strategic marketing and will be discussed in the following chapters.

The comparative positioning could be directly against another offering by highlighting the different features of each, or it could be away from competitors. One way of achieving a unique defensible position is the final generic strategy focus. This could apply to both efficient and effective companies. It is the proper application of segmentation and, as stated in Chapter 6, results in the reduction of the distance between supplier and customer. If this can lead to stronger relationships with customers then it is a relevant position for a company.

Another way of considering company positioning is to describe it in terms of the marketing objectives within a given market-place. Kotler (1997) suggested the categories of market leader, market challengers, market followers and nichers. Obviously all organizations will fall into one of these categories. Whether they are considered a leader or a follower/challenger could depend on how broadly or narrowly the market is defined. For instance, a nicher is likely to be a market leader in a small market segment.

Companies will adopt a different strategy depending upon their starting positions and the activity of their competitors. The objectives that could be adopted are to defend a market position, to attack a competitor, or some other strategy. The followers have most choice as they could choose to challenge the leader with an aggressive marketing campaign or decide to try to hold a subordinate position while benefiting from the work of the market leader.

An alternative categorization can be drawn from the work of Miles and Snow (1978) mentioned in Chapter 4. They consider companies as prospectors, defenders, analysers or reactors. Success comes from developing new competitive positions and/or defending an existing profitable relationship. Positive strategy involves the first three types of company; the last, reactors, fail to achieve a market position and therefore can lose out in a competitive market-place.

The actual position chosen will start with the question 'which competitive position is best for our organization?'. A company which chooses a defender position will utilize a different type of strategy, require a different range of capabilities and show a different orientation from one that is attempting to achieve one of the other company positions.

A number of defence and attack strategies developed from military thinking were popularized in the 1980s by Kotler and Singh (1981), Ries and Trout (1981, 1986), and Barrie James (1984). These are worth studying, but are a little stereotyped. Each individual company context is unique and requires a strategy specifically tailored to the situation.

Product positioning

Product positioning is the creation, by a supplier, of a total product offering aimed at meeting the wants and needs of a specific target market. It can also be closely related to the company position as a provider of high perceived value products or perhaps a supplier offering low delivered costs to customers. In order to be included in the evoked set, it will have to contain those features expected by customers. However, the general features expected, which are met by all competitive offerings, are only a basic requirement. An individual offering should include the differentiation of that total product offering from competitors in order to achieve a possible competitive advantage. This gives another form of expectation linked to a particular product. This is the expectation of what that specific product will offer and it comes directly from the consumer interpretation of the product position.

It is possible to position a product in a number of ways by the appropriate emphasis in the claims made about the offering. These could include some or all of:

1. the product/service features
2. the benefits that it offers
3. the relevance to specific usage occasions
4. the suitability for particular users or uses
5. positive associations with complementary products
6. the comparison with competing products.

The first five categories do not consider competitive issues overtly, although some advantages will need to be present if the product is to succeed. In the last category the differentiation of an offering is stressed by positioning it against competition.

Differentiation usually derives from the augmented elements of the total product but, by itself, differentiation does not automatically lead to competitive advantage. This is achieved only if the features which give rise to the differentiation are valued by customers. Such features have been described as energizers to identify them as the type of feature that actually stimulates customers to purchase. Any other discriminators simply separate one offering from alternative competitive ones without actually presenting the customers with any benefits perceived to be of value.

Since it is the evaluation of the benefits less the costs of a differentiated offering that will be included in any customer assessment of competitive values, only those energizing features that offer real benefits will enhance value. Although it is important to win the competitive battle, the product positioning really needs to be decided in the light of target market requirements, and specifically the elements of a total offering valued by those customers.

Lautman (1993) addressed the problem of defining product positioning, suggesting that it can be broken down into three major components:

- Attributes
- Benefits
- Claims.

The attributes and claims are both controllable variables and as such are part of the operational marketing mix. Benefits derive from attributes but they are experienced by customers, and so are a key element in a customer's perception of a position. Attributes can be tangible or intangible; they are the features that make up a total 'augmented' product or service. The actual product position, however, is more likely to reflect, to a greater extent, those particular attributes that augment a product, differentiating it from competitors, rather than those expected elements that many offerings contain.

Customers obtain products in order to experience the benefits offered, whether functional, physical, psychological or sociological. There should be a direct relationship between benefits and attributes, but it is the benefits that actually satisfy customer needs and wants. Consumers and customers are, therefore, more likely to define a product position by reference to the benefits received, rather than by describing attributes.

The communication of the attributes and the relevant benefits to potential customers will result in claims being made. These claims or promises will then be interpreted by customers, leading to an expectation about that offering as perceived in the mind of those customers. The offering will thus achieve a position and acquire a level of expectation that needs to be satisfied when a purchase exchange finally takes place. Claims can also include issues of usage occasions, uses or users as well as the comparison with other products where this is appropriate. They will be an input influencing customer expectations and it is the way that expectations are met that determines satisfaction.

Of course, after a purchase the customer has the additional input from the experi-ence of ownership with which to judge satisfaction. This will be set against the expectations that existed prior to buying. A positive gap where experience exceeds expectations will be a measure of satisfaction with the offering received. A negative gap will indicate dissatisfaction.

When reviewing a product or service position it is useful to establish how that offer-ing and directly competitive brands are used by customers. This is usually done together with research into customers' attitude towards the product class by a regu-lar 'usage and attitude' survey. This is a form of market research which, if similar questions are repeated over time, can track the position and identify trends that require strategic action.

The product position can be modified over the life cycle of a product. Most market-ing theory recommends that regular product modifications should take place to ensure continued relevance to the changing needs of customers. However, less is said about the associated modifications necessary in the position adopted in the minds of customers. Obviously a major change in product features will lead to a change in the promises made about a product, but even if no features are changed it could be beneficial to develop the claims that are being made and thus ensure that any messages about the current position are the most appropriate in relation to the demands of the existing market (Figure 7.2). For instance, for many years Volvo positioned its cars on a strong safety image. More recently this has not been stressed, and performance and style are now being promoted.

It has been suggested that in the introduction stage of a product's life the task is to establish an image for the product. In the growth phase of the life cycle this can be

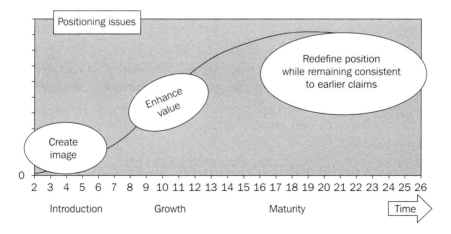

Fig 7.2 Positioning as a product moves through its life cycle

elaborated to enhance the value of the benefits offered. As a product reaches maturity the need is to redefine the established position to current customers while still accommodating the relevance of all the previous claims that have been made.

Ries and Trout (1981) have suggested that successful companies need to have the 'guts to stick to one position'. There is some merit in this dictum, especially over the shorter term, as consistency is necessary to avoid confusion about a product position. However, as long as the progressive claims made are complementary then a development over time could be desirable. There could be a situation where one position is so firmly established that it can be accepted as a real intangible asset, such as Volvo cars with respect to safety. In this situation it was both possible and appropriate to move on with other non-conflicting claims to develop an image for a Volvo as a more stylish and performance-driven car. But to return to Ries and Trout, who have approached positioning from the perspective of advertising, they warn that it is very difficult to get an effective message across to customers if it makes more than one claim at a time. It is therefore necessary to consider how many messages a customer can properly receive, and then to put stress on the key ones relating to a desired position.

While it is possible and appropriate to develop a product position over the life cycle with changes that do not conflict with previous claims, it is very difficult to alter a position radically. Classic cases such as Lucozade, which was successfully redefined as a high-performance sports drink, in contrast to its previous position, are not common. Currently efforts are being made by the Volkswagen group to dramatically improve the image of the Skoda car range but this is still some way from success in the UK.

Positioning and perception

The final aspect of position is the consideration of it as *perception*. This involves an element of judgement, and is sometimes seen as irrational. It is how customers themselves rate the offering in relation to other products or services considered in a purchase decision. In contrast with the other aspects, this is a *result* rather than a choice, but it is, after all, the customer perception of a position that is critical in a purchase situation.

Customer perception is, of course, influenced by all the cognitive appeals made by a supplier, which makes claims and offers information about an offering. Such actions are the explicit and implicit promises made, but customers will evaluate them alongside other clues from previous experience and knowledge gained from a variety of sources. It is not the actual claims from a supplier that matter but the perception customers have about the offering. In practice, the existence of a strong position in the minds of the customer can be a major intangible success factor leading to a purchase decision.

When Grönroos (1990) suggested a redefinition of marketing he emphasized the concept of *promises* made to customers. Although this was developed out of work in services and industrial marketing in Europe, the concept can be applied to any marketing offering or situation. Customer expectations are developed from the promises made about a particular offering. Prior to a purchase a customer will judge competitive offerings on the basis of the different expectations and costs of each. This will constitute the value equation for each offering.

If the prior customer expectations of a particular offering fall below what is actually offered then that supplier will be at a competitive disadvantage in the customer's decision making. If the expectations are too high compared to the actual then there is a serious risk of customer dissatisfaction after the purchase. Therefore the managing of expectations is critical to both competitive success and to customer satisfaction.

Of course this highlights the vital relationship between promises and the total product actually offered. Any competitive advantage enshrined in the promises must be reflected in the product. This will involve issues of total quality of an offering as well as delivering those aspects of high perceived value and low delivered cost (see Chapter 8) that form the key success factors energizing customers to purchase.

The value concept

Value arises in the interaction between suppliers and customers. It is derived from the interrelated primary business activities of the supplier, which connect inputs through decision making and operations to an output for a customer. However, comparative value is evaluated by the customer, who is likely to include reference to some measures of the utility that he or she receives. A competitive advantage is created when an offering gives something of value that is not available from other sources. In industrial markets calculations based on the comparative level of economic value to the customer are perhaps more important than in consumer markets, where such evaluations are more difficult. The concepts of value and utility are well established in economics, but were not widely used in marketing until the development of services marketing as a distinct area of study in the 1980s. This perhaps highlights how much positive consumer value actually derives from the intangible service elements of an offering, rather than the tangible features. There is obviously some value experienced from those tangible aspects of a product that meet the needs and wants of customers but the final evaluation will be based upon the total product as received, and this will also include the intangible features.

A useful marketing definition of value comes from Monroe (1991), who in writing about price has suggested that value, as perceived by customers, is the difference between the perceived benefits and the perceived sacrifice necessary to obtain those benefits. He was trying to put pricing into the context of customer perception and to move the evaluation of price accordingly. This echoes the famous quotation from Oscar Wilde, suggesting that a cynic is someone 'who knows the price of everything, but the value of nothing'. But price is an input into the calculation of value. Obviously it is a measure of the sacrifice made, but it can also be an indicator of the benefits. For instance, most people know of the price charged for Nike running shoes and so when someone is seen with the famous 'swoosh' trade mark there is a social benefit received as the wearer is seen to be a person who can afford the price for that brand.

It is important for a supplier to consider both the benefits received by each of its customers and all the costs involved when assessing value. The cost incurred by a customer will often be more than the basic price paid as it should include the costs of searching and evaluating an offering, together with any other economic cost related to the transaction. The 18th century philosopher and economist Adam Smith wrote that the 'real price of anything is the trial and trouble of acquiring it'. The costs could go further, involving also the opportunity value (benefit less cost) of other purchases not undertaken as a result of a particular purchase. In some situations, especially business to business marketing, total lifetime costs of ownership are often calculated so that an item of capital equipment, for instance, will be evaluated in a way that includes running costs, maintenance costs, anticipated useful life and the eventual scrap value when the item needs replacing. One of the effects of the typical organizational buying unit is to involve a wider group in purchase decisions, and it is often suggested that this leads to rational economic evaluations, but even in this situation there can be non-economic pressures.

A few years ago there was a purchasing philosophy that 'no one ever got fired by buying IBM'. Although it is less true today, the 'safe' albeit more expensive option to buy from IBM, the dominant hardware company at that time, was acceptable in many business situations where a buyer did not want to let down his or her colleagues by taking a risk in purchasing from a less well established computer company. Sometimes the industry benchmark company sets the standards against which others are judged, and if buying IBM was a no-risk decision with the benefits found in the status of the manufacturer, then the decision has a non-economic dimension which cannot be overlooked when considering such business markets. In consumer markets there are obviously non-economic factors involved, so both psychological and social dimensions must be considered when assessing value.

As a trading relationship develops over time it is necessary for both the supplier and the customer to feel that there is an increase in the perceived value received as a result of continuing the links. In part this comes from an increase in the mutual benefits, especially the non-economic factors present in a satisfying partnership. It can also derive from reductions in the costs of trading since there should be scope for efficiencies as both parties gain experience of each other. A great deal has been written about the gains to a supplier from retaining customers due to both the lower costs of dealing with existing customers and the fact that the high initial costs of obtaining that customer have been absorbed. However, the customer will also review the benefits of a continuing relationship and will usually expect some increase in the value received as a reward for continuing loyalty. Suppliers will need to develop strategies to satisfy such customer demands and this could involve utilizing some of the economic savings to augment their offering with additional added-value features over time. If there are any areas of weakness that could be exploited by a competitor, these need to be tackled. This is what Hamel calls 'filling the blanks' with respect to building stronger relationships with existing offerings to existing customers. Such actions are typical of strategies utilized to defend existing partnerships. These were introduced in Chapter 4 within the discussion of the Ansoff and Hamel matrices.

Value is a very personal measure and is probably different for each individual customer. Also, the value delivered can be seen to have a number of different levels (Figure 7.3). The most basic is the *expected value*, which should correspond to the expected product benefits (see Chapter 4). Above this is a *desired* level of value, which is an ideal level that a particular customer would like to receive. This is not

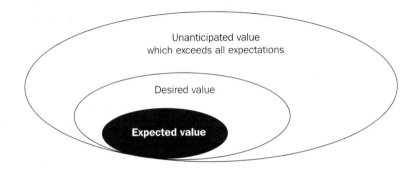

Fig 7.3 The three levels of value

necessarily the same as that delivered by the augmented product as the *desired value* reflects customer desires, while the augmented product is based on the specifications that a supplier decides to offer. If there is a close match here then there is a greater chance of fully satisfying the customers. Over and above the desired level is the *unanticipated value*, which exceeds customer expectations. Some extra, unexpected service that is added, perhaps at the point of delivery, could enhance an offering in an unforeseen, but wholly acceptable, way, thus increasing value and satisfaction for the recipient.

It must be remembered that the evaluation of both the benefits received and the costs incurred are specific to the individual purchaser. They are dependent on the particular resources available to each specific buyer, as well as the comparative value ascribed by that potential customer to the many other activities that require similar resources.

Concentration on the actual transaction ignores how satisfaction derived from the use of a product can increase the perceived value during the post-transaction period. It is said that the 'quality of a product is remembered long after the price is forgotten'. Of course the opposite is also true and a poor quality experience will decrease any value. There are many opportunities to continue contact with a customer after a sale. These are important both in building relationships and in trying to achieve repeat purchase, and all businesses have to decide the role and level of such contacts. It could involve a formal after-sales contract (maybe a guarantee or maintenance deal) or some needed service such as installation, but it might be restricted to a single communication which asks if everything is working as expected. The level and effectiveness of the after-sales service can dramatically affect the value as seen by customers. Kotler (1997) suggests that:

> most companies operate customer service departments. The quality of these varies greatly. At one extreme are customer service departments that simply turn over customer calls to the appropriate person or department for action, with little follow-up as to whether the customer's request was satisfied. At the other extreme are departments eager to receive customer requests, suggestions, and even complaints and handle them expeditiously.

The fact that value is multidimensional and that it also is variable over time means that it is a difficult concept to measure. The inclusion of non-economic factors such as psychological and social benefits makes its evaluation even more a matter for judgement than of precise calculation. However, these difficulties do not alter the fact that value is a vital component in the comparison of competitive offerings and as an input into the purchase decisions made by customers.

Most studies concentrate on the provision of more benefits as a way to increase value provided to customers. However, it is equally valid to try to reduce the necessary sacrifice made by those customers. Ravald and Grönroos (1996) discuss this, suggesting that:

> this approach forces the company to look at things from the customer's perspective, which is a central aspect in relationship marketing. In order to be able to reduce the customer-perceived sacrifice, the company needs a thorough understanding of the customer's value chain. The company has to get close to the customer to be able to understand his needs, preferences and all the activities which constitute his value chain. Such a commitment from a company is a prerequisite for survival in the 1990s.

From a study of the customer's value chain it should be possible to identify relevant actions which can increase the convenience of a purchase such as the changing of opening hours for a shop or bank. Alternatively, there could be actions that result in a reduction in the exchange transactional costs. In business marketing, costs can be reduced in many ways, such as minimizing stock holding by utilizing JIT delivery, or improving speed of response by linking suppliers' and customers' production planning systems. Any creative way of driving down transaction costs will help to build value-added partnerships, and the actions involved must be considered as part of the total marketing offering in that they contribute to customer satisfaction and value.

It is easier to find examples of reducing transaction (delivered) costs in business marketing, but the process is just as important in building relationships in consumer markets. Examples such as 'no hassle exchanges' from Marks & Spencer, 'no waiting checkout' for holders of the Trust House hotel loyalty cards and the system of shopping at Safeway where selected customers are able to calculate the cost of their own shopping trolley and thus avoid long queues are all current in consumer service industries.

But to reiterate some key points, customers in most purchase situations use value as a reference when they consider the comparative attractiveness of competing offerings. Value can be increased by relevant additional benefits or by a reduction in the necessary sacrifice. In fact, Monroe (1991) claims that more customers value a reduction in costs in preference to an equivalent increase in benefits.

However, both costs and benefits are complex and have many elements, some of which are qualitative in nature and thus difficult to evaluate. If a decision is taken to add value to an offering then it is vital that the additions are directly related to the actual needs of the chosen customers.

Conclusions

For a business to be successful in its chosen market-place it has to know how to compete effectively. Because competitive offerings will be considered against one another, the specific criteria on which a customer makes such a comparison must be understood in order to develop the most appropriate combination of products and services. However, most customers – consumer and industrial – come to a purchase situation with some level of prior knowledge and with preconceived ideas about competing offerings. The perceptions that a customer has in this respect are the most important interpretation of the 'position' of that offering in the eyes of the purchase decision maker. While there are other meanings given to the term marketing position, all these others are based on an ideal that an organization would wish to be true. There may be a distinct difference between what a supplier believes about its total product and the perception of the customer about the same offering.

Nevertheless, a supplier has to work with the controllable variables of the marketing mix, using these to try to create a suitable position in the minds of the customer. The attributes of a total product that are communicated to a customer are part of an implied contract with that customer. They come in the form of a number of promises, which encapsulate the claims made about what that product can do to create benefits for a customer. A key marketing task is to manage customer expectations so that there is a satisfactory relationship between what is promised and what is actually received.

All offerings comprise a number of different elements. Some are the ones that are expected by customers from all competing products, and others are ones that discriminate between competing brands. As to the expected elements, these have to be included as a necessity in order to be considered by customers. The discriminators, which distinguish individual offerings, are only relevant if they are valued by the chosen customers. Those that are valued become the energizers, which actually stimulate customers to purchase one specific product.

The concept of value is also critical when considering competitive advantage. Value comes from a combination of economic and non-economic benefits when set against the sacrifice a customer has to make to obtain those benefits. While it is difficult to measure value, and it is a very personal issue with different individual criteria and perceptions, attempts must be made to understand this, perhaps in terms of a customer's value chain.

The perceived factors of value can change over time. As trading links develop between a buyer and a seller, the non-economic factors can increase in response to the commitment of the parties to the relationship, and the trust they develop in each other. In fact, the increase in perceived value over time is a major reason why long-established relationships are an effective defence strategy, acting as a real barrier to entry for competitors.

KEY POINTS

7.1 There are four distinct aspects of positioning:

1. Market positioning
2. Company positioning
3. Product positioning
4. Positioning as perceived by customers.

7.2 The way an offering is portrayed and the way it energizes customers is a statement of position. Such a position must also be one which the organization is able to sustain given the available resources and skills (company capabilities) and any constraints that may exist.

7.3 Market, company and product positioning are ideals that organizations wish to achieve. They are all important as the objectives within a marketing strategy, but they are measured by the perception that customers have about an organization and its products, rather than what those companies think they are offering.

7.4 Product positioning is the creation, by a supplier, of a total product offering which is aimed at meeting the wants and needs of a specific target market.

7.5 Product positioning involves three major components:

1. Attributes
2. Benefits
3. Claims.

The attributes and claims are both controllable variables and as such are part of the operational marketing mix. *Benefits* derive from attributes but they are experienced by customers.

7.6 The product position can be modified over the life cycle of a product.

7.7 There may be a considerable difference between what a supplier believes about its total product and the perception of the customer about the same offering

7.8 Value arises in the interaction between suppliers and customers. Value, as perceived by customers, is the difference between the perceived benefits and the perceived sacrifice necessary to obtain those benefits.

QUESTIONS

7.1 What is the difference between market positioning and product positioning?

7.2 Company positioning describes where a company is and how it competes in its market. Give an example of a company positioned as (a) a market leader, (b) a market challenger, (c) a market follower and (d) a nicher.

7.3 What is the ABC of product positioning? Explain which of these factors can be controllable variables within the marketing mix.

7.4 How might a potential customer assess the value of an offering he or she is considering for purchase?

Bibliography

Brown, R., Marketing – A Function and Philosophy, *Quarterly Review of Marketing*, Spring, 1987.

Dibb, S. and Simkin, L., *Marketing*, 2nd European Edn, Houghton Mifflin, 1994.

Doyle, P., *Marketing Management and Strategy*, 2nd Edn, Prentice Hall, 1997.

Fifield, P., *Marketing Strategy*, Butterworth Heinemann, 1993.

Grönroos, C., Marketing Redefined, *Management Decisions*, Vol. 28 No. 8, pp. 5–9, 1990.

Grönroos, C., The Rise and Fall of Modern Marketing, in S. Shaw and N. Hood (Eds) *Marketing in Evolution*, Macmillan, 1996.

Hooley, G., Market Led Quality Management, *Journal of Marketing Management*, Vol. 9, 1993.

Hooley, G. and Saunders, J., *Competition Positioning*, Prentice Hall, 1993.

James, B.G., *Business Wargames*, Penguin, 1984.

Johnson, G. and Scholes, K., *Exploring Corporate Strategy*, 4th Edn, Prentice Hall, 1997.

Kotler, P., *Marketing Management: Analysis, Planning, Implementation and Control*, 9th Edn, Prentice Hall, 1997.

Kotler, P. and Singh, J., Marketing Warfare in the 1980s, *Journal of Business Strategy*, Winter, 1981.

Lautman, M.R., The ABCs of Positioning, *Marketing Research*, Winter, pp. 12–18, 1993.

Levitt, T., Differentiation of Anything, in *The Marketing Imagination*, Free Press, 1983.

Levitt, T., *The Marketing Imagination*, Free Press, 1983.

Levitt, T., Marketing Myopia, *Harvard Business Review*, July/Aug., pp. 45–56, 1960.

Mathur, S.S., Talking Straight about Competitive Strategy, *Journal of Marketing Management*, Vol. 8, pp. 199–217, 1992.

Miles, R.E. and Snow, C.C., *Organizational Strategy, Structure and Process*, McGraw-Hill, 1978.

Mintzberg, H., 5 Ps of Strategy, *Californian Management Review*, Fall, 1987.

Monroe, K.B., *Pricing – Making Profitable Decisions*, McGraw-Hill, 1991.

Murray, J.A. and O'Driscoll, A., *Strategy and Process in Marketing*, Prentice Hall, 1996.

Porter, M., *Competitive Strategy*, Free Press, 1980.

Ravald, A. and Grönroos, C., The Value Concept and Relationship Marketing, *European Journal of Marketing*, Vol. 30 No. 2, pp. 19–30, 1996.

Ries, A. and Trout, J., *Positioning the Battle for your Mind*, McGraw-Hill, 1981.

Ries, A. and Trout, J., *Marketing Warfare*, McGraw-Hill, 1986.

Smith, A., *The Wealth of Nations*, 1779.

SOURCES OF SUSTAINABLE COMPETITIVE ADVANTAGE

CHAPTER 8

INTRODUCTION

The basis of both marketing and business success is the creation and retention of profitable customers. Kotler (1999) reflected on this when he suggested that 'customers are attracted by promises and retained through satisfaction'. In both cases, the promises made and the ongoing satisfaction, the ultimate judge is the customer. Customers evaluate *promises* in comparison to other competitive offerings, and measure *satisfaction* in relation to the benefits received and the way these satisfy basic needs. Because all offerings are judged by such comparisons, *competitive advantage* must be considered from this same, customer-based, perspective. It can, however, be defined as one or more element of an offering that competitors cannot or will not match.

Analysis of the large PIMS (Profit Impact of Market Strategy) database at the Boston-based Strategic Planning Institute suggested that 'In the long run, the most important single factor affecting a business unit's performance is the quality of its products and services relative to those of competitors' (Buzzell and Gale, 1987). Certainly quality products are vital to long-term satisfaction and resulting profit, but at the point of sale it is the accessibility of the offering and the value of the total package of benefits when compared to other offerings that are really critical to achieving a sale.

Competitive advantage could arise from some demonstrably superior value of an offering or it could be achieved simply through the competitive weakness of other organizations. However, it is not prudent to rely on your competitors being incompetent for all time. Positive advantages derive from an organization's specific capabilities, but an offering is considered by customers in terms of perceived value and satisfaction. When sustained over a period of time these advantages lead to repeat business and profit.

Nevertheless, it is as well to heed the warning given by Brookes (1990) when considering whether an advantage can be sustained over time. He says 'where there are markets – especially mature ones – with many very capable adversaries, short term gains by one are usually costly to achieve, and are almost invariably countered by the swift, and even more costly, reactions of others. The end result is often some form of stalemate, with only small changes in market shares'. It is therefore critical to try to establish advantages in areas that are difficult for competitors to copy easily.

Because comparative offerings are evaluated by customers, market knowledge must underpin any quest for competitive advantage. The way such knowledge is used can make an enormous difference to the achievement of a competitive offering. However, the advantage is achieved by the offering, not the knowledge, although knowledge will assist in predicting the way a customer might react.

From a customer perspective there are three key dimensions of competitive advantage:

1. The *product/service itself* judged by its quality and by how acceptable it seems to be with regards to the needs and wants of a customer. In addition to the quality aspects this could include 'better' service, continuous product improvement or more product innovation.
2. The *perceived value*. The value derives from the benefits expected less the cost. This cost will include such issues as the relative price of an offering but it will be modified by the perceived cost of obtaining and cost of ownership. The way components of value are assessed and compared could vary from one customer to another. However, it is often possible to 'delight' customers by exceeding their expectations. The problem with this is that those purchasers will have much higher expectations in the future.
3. The *convenience of obtaining* a product/service in terms of its availability and the support that is offered to increase accessibility.

There is a fourth issue that follows from the availability, which is the *degree of influence* that a supplier might achieve over a customer to restrict choice to one or a limited number of alternative offerings. The creation of a near monopoly situation by manipulating the market could lead to a situation where customers have little choice in the matter. Kotler (1986) termed this *mega marketing*.

While the first three relate to the evaluation of the offering by customers, the last covers any factors that encourage or compel a customer to purchase from a specific source. The influences could come from within a strong satisfactory relationship but more restrictive conditions could derive from some way that a controlling influence is utilized to reduce a customer's free choice. Issues of persuasion and power are discussed later in this chapter.

It is necessary to include all these four dimensions in any study of competitive advantage. However competitive advantage does not usually derive from a single factor but from a combination, which could include elements from any of the four dimensions. Therefore this chapter will consider the interactions of elements rather than each separate category.

Customer types and the 'total' product offering

In Chapter 2, four classifications of customers were introduced based on the work of Jones and Sasser (1995), which looked at customers against the dimensions of satisfaction and loyalty. These are loyalists/advocates, mercenaries, hostages and terrorists.

Excluding the latter category, who are neither loyal customers nor satisfied with our offering, the other three groups are each attracted to purchase, but competitive advantage is achieved in very different ways.

The *loyalists* are those loyal and satisfied existing customers who consider that both a supplier and their offering are so superior to the competition that they continue to buy on a regular basis. The reasons will be based on the nature of the total product, including many intangibles derived from the quality of the relationship between the supplier and the customer. Loyal repeat buying by this group is always being reinforced by the way the offering continues to meet the customer's needs and wants over a long period of time. Loyalists are likely to exhibit a high degree of involvement, and this closeness becomes a powerful source of sustainable competitive advantage.

Mercenaries, on the other hand, exhibit no loyalty; they consider each exchange as a separate event, and they re-evaluate the potential suppliers on every purchase occurrence. They have a free choice and utilize it, deciding between competitive offerings and buying from that organization which they perceive as the best match for their current requirements within their affordable limits at every separate occasion. Customers who act in this way tend to value tangible product attributes more highly.

In fact, with both the above groups the final decision will usually be made on the basis of some measure of perceived value, which involves the expected benefits of ownership less the cost of acquiring and owning. However, loyalists are likely to be committed to a particular supplier, hence they will include different components when assessing value. There may be situations where free choice is not available. This is the *hostage* situation, where the customer feels trapped to deal with a particular supplier, perhaps because no suitable alternative is available. These loyal but dissatisfied customers are retained by a different type of competitive advantage.

Perceived value for both loyalist and mercenary customers will derive from a comparative evaluation of the dimensions of acceptability and accessibility mentioned in the introduction. These are related to the total product offering and can be based on either *high perceived value or low delivered cost*.

The third advantage can come from some measure of uniqueness based on a *specific focus* which enables the supplier and customer to be close – the reducing of distance discussed in segmentation.

From the customer's perspective each of these groups of advantages will be assessed in comparison to other available competitive offerings. Each will involve non-price benefits as well as price-specific factors that help evaluation of the value of an offering. If too much emphasis is placed on price as a differentiator the effect will be a 'price war' and extreme pressure on profit levels. Price changes can be implemented and communicated very quickly, but it usually takes a lot longer to modify the non-price factors and such changes require planning ahead. Mathur (1992) suggests 'Price differentials largely reflect the remoteness of substitutes. [Non-price] differentiation is the more significant dimension of (competitive) positioning ... Differentiation and positioning can be regarded as virtually interchangeable terms'.

Marketing should attempt to achieve both added value to the customer as well as an added return to the supplier in a profitable exchange (Figure 8.1). To do this it is necessary to move an offering as far away as possible from the economist's concept of 'perfect competition'. This is sometimes difficult when dealing with mercenaries. Levitt's total product concept, introduced in Chapter 4, is a valuable model when considering competitive advantage. The four levels of the model are shown in Figure 4.7. The categories covered are:

- Basic product
- Expected product
- Augmented product
- Potential product.

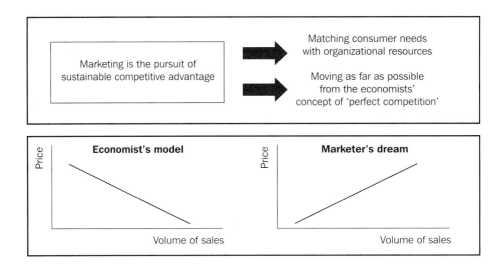

Fig 8.1 The marketer's dream

The categories are not fixed but in dynamic markets there is a continuous migration from one to another, as described previously.

The expected level of an offering covers those elements that are currently necessary to participate in a market. Far from being factors leading to competitive advantage, they are what Varadajan (1985) calls 'failure preventers'. While these factors may act as 'barriers to entry by new competitors, these minimum expected standards do no more than get an organization to the starting line. To achieve competitive success a product has first to meet the basic and the expected levels but then to offer something extra. The augmentation level covers those factors that lead to competitive advantage.

The sustainability of the augmented features is a measure of long-term competitiveness, and those that are most difficult to copy are obviously the most valuable. Those that are copied very soon move from the augmented category into the expected level of the offering.

It has been suggested that an offering is usually a combination of both product and service elements and that there are four different combinations of tangible product with intangible service that could be present:

- Pure product
- Product with service element
- Service with some tangible features
- Pure service.

However, this belies the fact that there is actually a continuum stretching from pure service to commodity product, and each offering can be placed on this scale at a point that reflects the balance between the different components. Study of the sources of competitive advantage later in this chapter will reveal both product (tangible) and service (intangible) features. Very often it is the service element that provides the sustainable advantage in a way that competitors cannot match. It is perhaps better to consider the categories of expected and augmented product and to include in each category a combination of both tangible and intangible factors. Levitt (1983) rightly states that 'there is no such thing as a commodity, all goods and services can be differentiated'. He considers many well-known companies, suggesting that it is their ability to differentiate the most commodity-like product that contributes to their success.

It is not the act of differentiating an offering that leads to success but, rather, the type of differentiation when judged by how well it attracts a customer. Differentiation is, as the name suggests, only a way of making one offering distinct when compared to a competitive offering.

The augmented level of an offering has been divided into those features that *discriminate* – separating it from competitors – and those that *energize* – attract and stimulate customers these should reflect critical influencers.

The marketing task is to develop some level of competitive advantage for an offering. This will be achieved by emphasis on the energizing aspects of the augmented offering, which will link to the critical purchase influences (CPIs) of the customers. A revised product diagram should help to illustrate this (Figure 8.2).

Marketing advantage and generic strategies

The three sources of marketing advantage, based on high perceived value, low delivered cost and specific focus, are not too dissimilar to Michael Porter's generic

Product attributes	Positive	Neutral	Negative
Basic			
Discriminator			
Energizer			

Fig 8.2 Analysing attributes within a product offering.
Source: MacMillan and McGrath (1996)

	High perceived value	Low delivered cost
Broad focus	Adding value through energizing features or reductions in price	Driving down delivered costs through increased availability and low-cost distribution channels
Narrow focus	Adding value through focused differentiation and building individual relationships with specific customers	Driving down delivered costs by JIT programmes and other relationship links with specific groups of customers

Fig 8.3 A matrix of competitive advantage

corporate strategies, the main difference being that low delivered cost has more to do with transactional cost than internal costings. However, in a similar way to Porter, these three sources of advantage can be extended into a four-cell matrix reflecting the narrow or broad scope of the focus dimension (Figure 8.3).

Porter's advice was not to get 'stuck in the middle' by confusing strategic positions, although this has been challenged, such as the example of 'Good food costs less at Sainsbury's'. With the matrix in Figure 8.3 it is also important to consider which position to adopt. Although there may be a position combining low cost and high value, there should be no confusion as to what is offered to customers and how the benefits reflect the CPIs in a positive way.

The high perceived value advantage can be considered as differentiation, but the elements of this must be evaluated from a comparative *customer* perspective. The word 'perceived' is used to emphasize the fact that value is a subjective evaluation rather than a direct measure of utility. The ability to include such factors in an offering is a positive advantage which enhances the supplier's image and hence its competitive advantage. When established, these advantages will fall into the category of better acceptability linked to greater affordability. Hooley *et al.* (1998) suggest these are customer-based assets, which they define as those factors, both tangible and intangible, that are valued by potential customers.

An indication of some of these types of competitive advantage is set out in Table 8.1.

Low delivered cost advantages are not the same as Porter's low cost. The problem with the Porter generic strategy is that there can only be one lowest cost producer in any market, and to achieve this the organization tends to focus too much on internal operational matters. This often involves significant capital investment, which relies on a period of relative stability in order to get a full return on such investment. The

Table 8.1 Factors leading to competitive advantage

Factors leading to better acceptability

Superior product benefits
- Better end result
- Greater convenience
- Superior service

Better in-use characteristics
- Longer lasting
- More features
- Superior design
- Complete product range

Intangible advantages
- Imagery rather than function
- Market position
- Brand strength

Relationship advantages
- Key customer relationships
- Joint venture partners
- Counter trading
- Sales force contacts

Factors leading to greater affordability

- Lower prices
- Better credit terms
- Cost in use
- Generous trade-in deals

major risk is that the company could lose touch in a dynamic market-place, especially one where technology is changing. An example of this is NCR investing to produce electromechanical cash registers while Canon was rolling out an electronic machine. The total investment of $500 million had to be written off. Lowest cost does not mean lowest price. Costs are about supply and production; prices are about market demand. The only marketing advantage for a (Porter-style) cost leader is that it can obtain higher margins by matching competitive prices or, alternatively, it could be the strongest firm in a price war.

Of course, it is possible to break down the primary activities of a firm using Porter's value chain. If a firm concentrates on those activities that are really important in the link between producer and supplier then it is possible to see a link between lowest delivered cost and a cost leadership strategy (Figure 8.4).

When transactional exchange costs are driven down then the real advantages are felt by both supplier and customer. These costs are located within the distribution

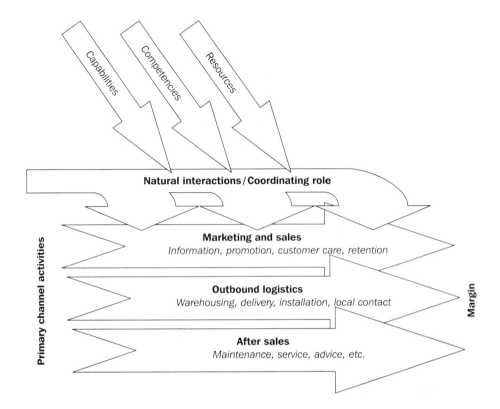

Fig 8.4 Value chain of channel management issues

links and can include more than basic delivery. For instance installation and service may be important, but it could be equally beneficial to integrate production planning as in a just-in-time system which meets very specific needs. This strategic stance can be considered as providing better availability together with greater affordability. Where established these links are some of the partnership-based assets, introduced in Chapter 1, which derive from the way the product or service is made accessible to customers. They are attractive to customers only when experienced directly in use. Some of them are listed below:

- easier availability
- delivery lead times
- security of supply
- skills of intermediaries
- after-sales support
- network linkages
- lowest total cost
- low cost distribution channels
- flexibility/speed of response.

However, both customer-based assets and partnership-based assets also derive from the closeness of the supplier–customer relationship. This leads into the third dimension of value and its associated competitive advantage, which is the scope of an offering based upon intense *focusing* on a niche position. Such a position derives from a strong appeal made to a specific cluster of chosen customers. These customers have to experience the advantages of specialization by the supplier in a way that offers real value. Such value usually comes in a non-economic form due to a customer valuing the attention or specialized knowledge of the supplier. In order to achieve such a position it is essential to understand the activity cycle of cluster members exceptionally well (see the discussion of customer activity cycles in Chapters 1 and 2), and to complement this by promoting specifically to the chosen group. This requires a focus of internal structure involving processes, systems, R&D and often the superior allocation of resources to close the gap between customers and supplier. These issues were discussed in the organizational aspects of segmentation in Chapter 6.

The 4Ps of competitive marketing

The much maligned traditional 4P framework is of course McCarthy's *product, price, place, promotion* dimensions of an offering (McCarthy and Perrault, 1964). Back in 1967 Kotler wrote 'McCarthy's classification is especially useful from a pedagogical point of view. Nevertheless, the feeling remains that some other classification, still to be born, will develop better conceptual distinctions among the large variety of marketing decision variables'. Thirty years on we are still waiting! However, it is important to distinguish between tactical and strategic marketing. The traditional 4Ps refer to the controllable decision variables that constitute the *tactical* outcome – they are not the *strategic* marketing process. Too many practitioners and others in business still equate marketing with the 4Ps, or sometimes the expanded Booms and Bitner 7Ps.

Criticism of the traditional 4Ps is based on the restrictive nature of the elements and the naive application, which can lead to real strategic problems. Nevertheless, many of the outcomes of an organization can be categorized using the traditional framework of 4Ps. This can be useful but it does not highlight the role of strategic marketing and it does not involve a customer perspective. In fact the traditional framework can foster a production orientation. An alternative view of the marketing task could be seen as:

1. Striving for a *position* in the minds of customers (and evaluating the actual achievement).

2. Making *promises* to potential customers as to what to expect with regard to an offering.
3. *Persuading* customers as to the merit of a particular offering.
4. Exerting *power* over markets to achieve customer loyalty with regard to future exchanges.

While this alternate 4P framework is not likely to achieve universal appeal as a prescription for marketing, it does include those aspects of external marketing that are both regularly practised and critical to success. The first two are the result of market-based actions as judged by customers; the others cover the role of marketing in attempting to attract customers or to gain some degree of influence over them.

Kotler (1991) once suggested his own variation of the 4Ps for the strategic marketing process, which he admitted was 'just renaming a lot of things'.

- Probe: researching the market
- Partition: segmenting the market
- Prioritize: specifying markets to target
- Position: deciding a role with respect to the target market.

The analysis (probe) and segmentation (partition) aspects have already been discussed in previous chapters, and, of course, decisions that lead to the choice of the markets to serve (prioritizing) are necessary preliminaries to the achievement of competitive trading.

Positioning appears in both lists so putting the two lists together gives a new 7Ps framework specific to marketing activities (Figure 8.5).

Four distinct aspects of positioning were introduced in Chapter 7. When seen as part of the strategic marketing activities, it is the attainment of a product position which is the objective of any marketing activity and this will be reflected in the promises made to customers. Grönroos (1990) explores the importance of promises, both made and kept, to the development of long-term relationships. He also suggests that it is not only the supplier but also the customer who has to promise commitment to a relationship if it is to flourish in the future. Such relation-

Fig 8.5 An alternative 7P framework for marketing

ships are very powerful sources of advantage, which may be more important than short-term issues of price and promotion.

It is, of course, possible to go further than simply making promises to customers. Strategies can be developed with the specific aim of changing the behaviour of a target group. Such persuasion will be achieved by placing appropriate emphasis on different aspects of the offering in the attempt to get customers to revise their perceptions. While this is certain to involve the communication components of the marketing mix, all other elements must be consistent in supporting any claims made, the objective being to change the perception held by a customer as to how their particular need could be satisfied in a different way by a different offering, thus trying to alter what is demanded by the customer.

Hooley (1993) studied the gaps between customer evaluations of an offer, customer expectations, customer wants and customer needs as part of a wider study of market-led quality. He defined the first as the *satisfaction gap*, leading through to a *customer delight gap*, and what he then describes as a *welfare gap*. This work highlights that customers do not have a perfect understanding of how a particular underlying need is able to be satisfied. In fact, Hooley suggests in his welfare gap that sometimes 'customers don't know what they need' and hence their wants do not always satisfy those needs. It is in this imprecise area that persuasion can be applied (Figure 8.6).

Marketing has to develop a balance to ensure that while any promises made are not exaggerated, as this will lead to dissatisfaction, any comparative evaluations made by customers are as well inclined as possible in favour of a particular offering.

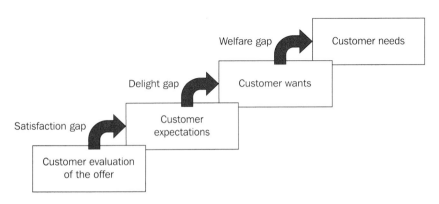

Fig 8.6 The gaps between customers' evaluation of an offer and their actual needs.
Source: Adapted from Hooley (1993)

Persuasion

Persuasion has always been part of marketing. This dimension of the marketing task recognizes the fact that customers are not a fixed group with known demands, but are people who can be influenced to try alternatives or to modify some existing attitude. Of course, persuasion brings with it all the undertones of unethical behaviour and confidence tricks, as well as subliminal activities, all of which have led to criticism of marketing. However, such considerations mask the realities as listed by O'Shaughnessy (1984) that:

consumers in general are open to persuasion because:

Shopping is a learning experience and consumers can learn right up to the point of sale.

Consumers are rarely experts but simply collect enough product/ brand information to state a preference. This does not mean that they would not like to be experts but sacrifices are involved. However, not being experts, consumers have less confidence in their judgements.

Where buying involves deliberation, consumers are uneasy about trade-offs as there is no objective way of doing the weighting.

Even when satisfied with past choices, consumers recognise that things could have changed.

New facts, new appeals that bring the consumer's attention to the potential of the product may swing the sale right up to the point of buying.

Until people have tried all brands, they cannot be absolutely convinced about their preferences.

In marketing situations persuasion is the attempt to influence customers by use of the full range of selling, communication, PR and promotional tools. It is through these that customers are informed about an offering and promises are made about it. The role of persuasion is important in the dynamics of customer needs, wants and demands since there may be several alternate ways of satisfying a basic need. If a supplier can *persuade* a customer that a particular offering will meet their needs in a superior way then the resulting demand will of course be worth while. Marketers should never forget that they can influence the demand in their markets, but it must also be remembered that there are limits to such influence. The ultimate test is customer satisfaction and that depends exclusively on how customer expectations are perceived to have been met.

Power

In studying buyer–seller relationships it is possible to utilize the concept of power reflecting the different ways one party can gain influence over another. The classic work categorizing the different sources of power was produced by French and Raven (1959), who suggest five typologies:

1. *Reward power* This is the result of attractive financial benefits which bind a customer to a particular supplier. These benefits could come from use of loyalty discount schemes or increased rewards for increased orders. In the case of loyalty schemes these have to offer real competitive benefits. However, the supermarket card schemes introduced by Tesco, Safeway and Sainsbury's do not qualify as they do not offer any incentive to encourage increased levels of loyalty in return for the discount points. In fact, many people participate in several supermarket schemes, benefiting from discounts but not changing their shopping habits.

2. *Legitimate power* This is the most obvious power, where a supplier holds legal advantages such as patent protection or copyright. It also exists where trading is defined by a formal or an implicit contract between buyer and seller. In this case there are obligations on both parties and each can use its legitimate power to modify the behaviour of others. This source of power could also be present in situations where no contract is involved if the customer accepts a position of subordination to a supplier. Such a situation could exist in a distribution channel, maybe where there is an exclusive right to stock a specific brand.

3. *Expert power* This exists when one party has specific skills necessary to the other, such as a special after-sales service or maintenance for some equipment. There may not be any alternative but to deal with the expert supplier, which can exert a monopoly position as a result of its expertise. The issues of patents included in legitimate power can also extend into this category. It is also possible to visualize the hostage type of customer being compelled to deal with an expert supplier in spite of a lack of satisfaction from the total offering.

4. *Coercive power* This is where a customer feels trapped by the power of suppliers – a classic hostage situation. For instance, a supplier might own a strong brand and use it to demand specific activities from a customer. It could be backed by a threat of withholding supplies in some situations. An example of this was the attempt by a Scotch whisky producer to stop supplying a supermarket that was using the product as a loss leader (selling below cost to build store traffic). Another was the insistence by Microsoft that its Windows product is sold together with an Internet browser. Both these high-profile cases ended up in litigation as the Office of Fair Trading in the UK and the equivalent in the US

sought to stop monopolistic behaviour based on coercive power. Another example is the way Walls Ice Cream has supplied freezers to convenience stores but restricted their use for competitive products.

However, coercive power is often present in situations that are less apparent but just as manipulative. This could be power over a small distributor; it could exist in reverse, where a powerful customer uses its position to demand actions by suppliers. This can be seen in some instances of approved-supplier status to major car companies or own-label suppliers to a major supermarket.

5. *Referent power* This is where customers admire the supplier, or perhaps identify with a brand so that they want that particular one above all others. Obviously, a strong brand is a major competitive resource and one that it is impossible for competitors to match.

Power is best seen within a direct dyadic relationship, perhaps a distribution channel or within a business to business situation. Porter's famous five-forces model emphasizes the bargaining power of both buyers and sellers. Kotler (1997) suggests that suppliers will gain cooperation best if they resort to *referent power*, *expert power*, *legitimate power* and *reward power*, in that order, and generally avoid using *coercive power*. Remember, hostage customers are loyal but dissatisfied and will move to a new supplier as soon as a suitable opportunity arises.

In the mid-1980s Kotler defined the term mega marketing as 'The strategic co-ordination of economic, psychological, political, and public relations skills to gain the co-operation of a number of parties in order to enter and/or operate in a given market'. The influences can also be used to alter demand in a market or to reduce levels of competition. Of course, it must be legal – activities that result in a cartel are illegal. Also, unofficial payments to government officials are not allowed although there are some countries where this is a normal practice. Mega marketing covers all types of third-party cooperation aimed at creating a protected market or a partial monopoly.

Example

The British poultry industry tried to persuade the UK government to ban subsidized European chickens and turkeys for a time. In the US the recovery of Harley Davidson was assisted by the protection given by a short-term ban on the imports of motorcycles, and there are many other examples. Mega marketing can work in the opposite way, opening up markets that are difficult to enter. The various attempts by European and US authorities in respect of the Japanese market, where there is a large adverse balance of trade, is an example.

However, mega marketing is not confined to government actions; it includes any influence or application of such power. An example could be a trading directive in a major multinational corporation specifying purchase from other group companies in preference to external suppliers even if the deal is not the most financially attractive. This is an obvious hostage situation.

Conclusions

The marketing concept emphasizes the meeting of customer needs. However, commercial success comes from creating and retaining customers. To do this the customer's needs have to be met in a way that is superior to competitors. This is the basis of competitive advantage. Customers who have a free choice will purchase from those suppliers that they perceive as offering the best value, and that value will be judged in a number of ways which interact with each other.

The acceptability of an offering (product/service) can be considered as giving high (or low) perceived value based on the attributes of that offering and how the resulting benefits meet basic needs. Of course, it is the high value that is the competitive advantage. The actual assessment of perceived value will depend to some extent on customer expectations and the promises made by suppliers. Customers will evaluate both tangible and intangible features, but their evaluation frame will depend upon their customer activity cycle and will include previous experience with the supplier. The high perceived value features can be considered as customer-based assets (strengths existing in the minds of customers).

Availability and accessibility are also ways of achieving a competitive advantage. These are the distribution or partnership-based assets which focus on the components of low delivered cost. Such costs include the costs of acquisition as well as the ownership costs experienced by the customer. They can be reduced by effective networks and attention to after-sales support and service.

In both categories it is important to separate those factors that merely discriminate between offerings from those energizers that really stimulate customer actions. Advantage comes from the energizers, not the discriminators. However, customers are usually in a situation where they are not absolutely certain as to all competitive offerings. They often rely on limited product/brand information and make their decisions based on incomplete knowledge. Because of this they are more open to persuasion, although the real test of satisfaction comes from experience after purchase. While it is possible to persuade, it is also possible to go further and achieve a powerful position of influence over a customer. This could come from free choice, where a customer is loyal to a supplier that seems to meet their needs precisely; it could also come from the use of mega-marketing strategies, which reduce choice. It is, of course, far better to achieve a customer base that is both loyal and satisfied, rather than hostages who feel trapped into a relationship.

KEY POINTS

8.1 Competitive advantage must be considered from a customer-based perspective. It can, however, be defined as one or more elements of an offering that competitors cannot or will not match.

8.2 From a customer perspective there are three key dimensions of competitive advantage: the product/service itself, the perceived value, and the convenience of obtaining a product/service in terms of its availability.

There is a fourth issue that follows from the availability, which is the degree of influence that a supplier might achieve over a customer to restrict choice to one or a limited number of alternative offerings. The creation of a near monopoly situation by manipulating the market could lead to a situation where customers have little choice in the matter. Kotler termed this mega marketing.

8.3 Different customer segments will value different factors when assessing competitive advantage.

8.4 There are many product features that contribute towards sustainable competitive advantage. Some categories are listed in the text but the key issue is that they should energize customers by offering 'better' acceptability, affordability and availability.

8.5 Few competitive advantages are sustainable because in a highly competitive market any breakthrough is soon copied.

8.6 If marketing is to be irrevocably linked to a 4Ps framework, then the factors of strategic importance – position, promises, persuasion and power – are the ones to be considered.

QUESTIONS

8.1 Where a customer's expectation has been exceeded then that customer could be rightly delighted. Would this situation offer the supplier a sustainable competitive advantage?

8.2 Suggest specific ways in which a supplier might achieve a competitive advantage through the general strategy of offering high perceived value.

8.3 Availability and accessibility are ways of achieving a competitive advantage. These utilize the distribution or partnership-based assets which focus on the components of low delivered cost. Such costs include the costs of acquisition as well as the ownership costs experienced by the customer. Suggest an example of this type of competitive advantage from your own research.

8.4 It is possible to gain power over customers by reducing competition and utilizing the techniques of mega marketing. What forms of power might a supplier employ and are there any risks involved in following this type of strategy?

Bibliography

Brookes, R., *The New Marketing*, Gower, 1990.

Buzzell, R.D. and Gale, B.T., *PIMS Principles Linking Strategy and Performance*, Free Press, 1987.

Calonius, H., The Promise Concept, Research report, Swedish School of Economics, Helsinki, 1987.

French, J.R.P. and Raven, B., The Bases of Social Power, in D. Cartwright (Ed.) *Studies in Social Power*, University of Michigan, 1959.

Grönroos, C., Marketing Redefined, *Management Decisions*, Vol. 28 No. 8, pp. 5–9, 1990.

Hooley, G., Market Led Quality Management, *Journal of Marketing Management*, Vol. 9, pp. 315–335, 1993.

Hooley, G., Saunders, J. and Piercy, N., *Strategic Marketing and Competitive Positioning*, 2nd Edn, Prentice Hall, 1998.

Jones, T.O. and Sasser, W.E., Why Satisfied Customers Defect, *Harvard Business Review*, Nov./Dec. 1995.

Kotler, P., *Marketing Management, Analysis, Planning and Control*, Prentice Hall, 1967.

Kotler, P., Mega Marketing, *Harvard Business Review*, March/April 1986.

Kotler, P., Kotler on . . ., *Management Decisions*, Vol. 29 No. 2, pp. 44–47, 1991.

Kotler, P., *Marketing Management – Analysis, Planning, Implementation and Control*, 9th Edn, Prentice Hall, 1997.

Kotler, P., *Kotler on Marketing*, Free Press, 1999.

Levitt, T., *The Marketing Imagination*, Free Press, 1983.

Mathur, S.S., Talking Straight about Competitive Strategy, *Journal of Marketing Management*, Vol. 8, pp. 199–217, 1992.

McCarthy, J.E. and Perrault, W.D., *Basic Marketing*, 2nd Edn, Irwin, 1964.

Millman, T., The Emerging Concept of Relationship Marketing, paper presented at the 9th IMP Conference, Bath, 23 September 1993.

Murray, J.A. and O'Driscoll, A., *Strategy and Process in Marketing*, Prentice Hall, 1996.

O'Shaughnessy, J., *Competitive Marketing – A Strategic Approach*, Allen & Unwin, 1984.

Porter, M., *Competitive Strategy*, Free Press, 1980.

Varadajan, P.R., A Two Factor Classification of Competitive Strategy Variables, *Strategic Management Journal*, Vol. 6, pp. 357–375, 1985.

TOTAL QUALITY – TOTAL MARKETING

9

CHAPTER

INTRODUCTION

There is no doubting that the most important aspect in achieving marketing success is the meeting of the requirements of a chosen customer better than competitors. These customers will be drawn to a product or service that either best matches their needs or offers them greatest value. This should lead an organization to consider offerings against these measures. For the customer any 'offer' will be assessed in terms of utility and value. For the supplier the measure is one of *quality* – product quality, service quality, relationship quality, all defined in terms of how well the different elements of the offering deliver value to customers.

Quality is a widely used, and misused, term in management and, as a result, has been defined in many different ways. It is often considered as a measure of excellence. Alternatively, it could relate to some distinctive attribute in an offering. Sometimes quality can be a comparative evaluation of one product when set against another. However, the best definition of quality is that it is everything that leads to customer satisfaction. This chapter will look at some of these aspects, in particular the qualitative and quantitative components involved. However, it seems illogical for quality to be considered in any non-*qualitative* way, so perhaps it is best to talk about the perceived and the measurable components of quality.

It is generally accepted that the modern quality management movement had its beginnings in post-War Japan with the application of the work of W. Edward Deeming and Joseph Juran, followed by the introduction of quality circles, which is credited to Kaoru Ishikawa. However, the history of quality is as old as trading itself, whether through standards for weights and measures, which Hooley (1993) traces back to ancient China in 210 BC, or as the simple application of quality checks by customers who inspect an item prior to purchase. Of course such checking assumes those customers are able to judge quality, but, as has been seen with the consideration of the value concept, this is not as obvious or as easy as it might be supposed.

An interesting example of the problems associated with the assessment of quality occurred when I worked with a group of Soviet managers a few years ago. I asked what they would do if they purchased a radio, then, on getting it home and putting in the batteries found that it did not work properly. I expected that they would suggest taking it back to the retailer. However, the response was unexpected. They suggested the only answer was to sell it to an unsuspecting third party. When asked why they would not return to the retailer, they argued that 'the shop won't want it back because they know it doesn't work!'. As to the re-selling, 'the new customer won't know it doesn't work'. This conjures up a bizarre picture of many faulty radios being sold on throughout the former Soviet bloc.

The problem in the above example is that these Soviet managers considered that the sale was more important than satisfying the customer – not a very good recipe for future sales! However, it does also reflect the difficulty in determining quality even with respect to the simple fact of whether a product works properly or not. This can be easily understood by anyone who has bought goods at a car-boot sale and realized there is a substantial risk in such a purchase. In this type of situation it may be necessary for the seller to find a way of reassuring the customer by a guarantee, or in some other way, that the product being considered will actually meet their needs in an effective manner.

Of course there is a distinct difference between a one-off sale occasion where the objective is to dispose of an unwanted item, and the marketing of products over an extended period of time with the necessity of repeat purchases and the hope of developing a positive reputation from which the selling organization can benefit in the future.

Quality management initially revolved around the operations process with an emphasis on quality control (control measures during production and after processing that aim to prevent the release of defective goods) and later quality assurance (the activities aimed at achieving specific standards by eliminating the basic causes and preventing problems occurring). However, both these initiatives rely entirely on the knowledge of what is required by customers as it is necessary to have a standard against which to check. It is only then that controls can be developed and work can be undertaken to ensure minimum acceptable defects (or even zero defects). In the early development of total quality management there was too much emphasis on how to meet standards within the operations process. The question of what those standards should be and the study of actual customer needs were given less emphasis although it is getting these things right that moves the focus from a type of *production orientation* to a *marketing orientation.*

Even in 1993 Kordupleski *et al.* were asking why improving quality doesn't improve quality, and answering their question in terms of not understanding customers. They commented that 'there is considerable participation by quality control engineers, manufacturing people, operations managers, human resource people and organizational experts. A group notable by its absence is the function closest to the customer – namely marketing. *Whatever happened to marketing?'*. Unfortunately, there are still many organizations where this remains true. Obviously, marketing has to ensure it plays its part in defining the standards that have to be attained and monitoring the effect on customer satisfaction, but quality as a whole should be a strategic business concern, integrating marketing activities with all the other primary functions.

There is a real distinction to be made between a standards-based approach to quality as compared to one founded upon an organizational culture in which employees commit themselves to values that will deliver high levels of quality. The latter is a true marketing orientation if these quality levels are the actual demands of customers.

The different dimensions of quality

The quality standards that can be measured – such as performance levels, reliability, conformance to established norms and the durability (technical life of a product) – are sometimes described as the 'intrinsic' measures of the quality of an offering. These four aspects form half of the eight dimensions of quality suggested by Garvin (1987). His seminal article was able to consider the different aspects of quality and separate them from the unhelpful view of quality as some kind of superior specification (Figure 9.1).

It might be that a hard cover book will last longer than a paperback novel, but for many readers who do not intend to read the book more than once, nor require to display the novel in a library, the cheaper binding and the less durable product will be perfectly acceptable. It will thereby meet the required quality standards. Of course, things could go a little too far: some years ago, Gerald Ratner, head of a large chain of jewellers, said in a widely reported, but off-the-cuff, remark that his low-priced

Fig 9.1 Eight dimensions of quality. *Source:* Garvin (1987)

jewellery 'was cheaper than a Marks & Spencer sandwich, and didn't last as long'. This made many people stop and think about the quality of the cheap costume jewellery in Mr Ratner's stores, and that remark is said to have cost him his business as the trade collapsed dramatically.

In quality terms 'extrinsic' factors form a group even more important than the 'intrinsic' ones. Two of Garvin's dimensions – aesthetics and perceived quality – have an 'extrinsic' bias. These are generally qualitative measures, relying on personal opinions, and they relate to how well a product or service delivers against the customer's specification.

Two more of Garvin's dimensions have not yet been considered. One of these, serviceability, he described as 'speed, courtesy, competence and ease of repair', suggesting that in addition to any worries about a product breaking down, consumers are 'concerned about the time before service is restored, the timeliness with which service appointments are kept, the nature of dealings with service personnel, and the frequency with which service calls or repairs fail to correct outstanding problems'. This dimension has elements of both an intrinsic and an extrinsic nature.

The final dimension of quality is the added features (Garvin's 'bells and whistles' of product augmentation), which is essentially intrinsic in that most added features are decided by the supplier. However, some of these could be viewed as inessential or of little value when assessed by consumers. For instance it could be said that a Mercedes or a Rolls-Royce is a quality car in terms of features and specifications, but these models may not be suitable for someone who lives in a crowded city where a motorcycle or a small Fiat is more appropriate to their daily needs. Similarly, a customer might not value the extra features available to first-class airline passengers. This leads back to the concept of value, and the links between value and quality.

It is this link with customer value that is the key to any discussion of quality. Juran's famous statement that 'Quality is *Fitness for use*' (1989), and Deeming's view that

Marketing = Quality benefits to customers

Quality = Implementing marketing

Fig 9.2 Marketing and quality

'Quality should be aimed at the needs of the consumer in the future' both illustrate the role of the customer in setting any quality standards. Hooley (1993) suggested that in defining quality it is possible to start with a classic definition, used in Chapter 4, that marketing is 'having the right product, in the right place, at the right time, for the right price' and then replace the word marketing with the word quality. This gives a good definition of quality in terms of the acceptability, availability and affordability of a product or service offering. It is therefore possible to view one role of marketing as ensuring the delivery of quality benefits to customers. Quality could then be defined as the implementation of marketing within an organization (Figure 9.2).

These definitions seem to suggest that *marketing is quality* and *quality is marketing*. What is really at stake is the application of the marketing concept and a customer focus to the quality process, and the need to appreciate the different dimensions of quality within all marketing activities, and perhaps even applying measures of quality control and quality assurance specifically to the marketing department.

These links can also be seen in the extravagantly titled article 'Marketing is everything' by Regis McKenna (1991), who suggests 'Marketing today is not a function, it is a way of doing business. Marketing is not a new ad campaign or this month's promotion. Marketing has to be all-pervasive, part of everyone's job description, from the receptionist to the Board of Directors'. The same applies to quality. Garvin sums it up as 'Quality means pleasing consumers, not just protecting them from annoyances'.

Quality gaps

Quality, or pleasing customers, can be considered a vital issue in any discussion about achieving satisfaction. In simple terms, *satisfaction* occurs when expectations are either met or exceeded, but the real situation is more complex in that the critical question is whether a customer's *perception* of what was received actually met his or her expectations. It is not the actual products offered but the customer's evaluation of what is received which is compared at this stage, and these could be very different. It may be that the evaluation is based on criteria that are not properly understood by the supplier. Alternatively, it could be when some part of the offering stands out and affects the perception of the total product – for instance when the instructions supplied with a product are so complex that the customer cannot understand them and hence reassesses his or her opinion of the whole offering. Another example could be when the evaluation of a well-designed item is overshadowed by poor service levels given at the point of purchase.

Whether the evaluation criteria are not properly understood or some other issue affects the perception, there will obviously be a resulting effect on the levels of satisfaction. The difference between what the seller offers and what the customer perceives that he or she has received is an important consideration in assessing satisfaction. Hooley called this the *perceptual gap* (Figure 9.3). This contrasts with the *satisfaction gap*, which is situated completely in the customer's domain and compares the perception of an offer with expectations (Figure 9.4). As shown, there is a direct relationship between satisfaction and perceived quality. Study of the satisfaction gap will help the determination of specific marketing programmes aimed at customers and designed to influence attitudes and perceptions. It is one of the roles of 'persuasion' marketing to help develop positive perceptions and to try to influence expectations. If these can be brought closer together, then perceived quality can be increased. But it must be remembered that the evaluation of both expectations and what was received will be personal to every individual customer.

While it is obviously important that the satisfaction gap is closed, a greater task is to ensure that expectations and perception are as close as possible to the reality of the

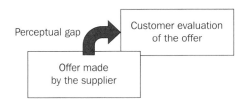

Fig 9.3 The perceptual gaps between customers' evaluation of an offer and the actual offer. *Source*: Hooley (1993)

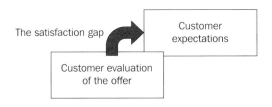

Fig 9.4 The satisfaction gap. *Source*: Adapted from Hooley (1993)

offering. This requires the closing of both gaps and avoiding an untenable position developing. To do this marketing actions must provide the right cues to a customer, and while perception is critical there must be a level of reality in the influencing of expectations. A sensible approach is necessary with regard to the 'hyping' of an offering, which may raise the perception of a potential customer too far above the offering that can be delivered.

A delivered offering will usually be a combination of tangible product and intangible features, but the evaluation is likely to be biased towards the *people*, *process* and *physical evidence* elements from the enlarged marketing mix (Booms and Bitner, 1981). In evaluating the perceptual gap, and assessing satisfaction in relation to quality, all the categories in the SERVQUAL model should be considered. SERVQUAL, which is discussed in Chapter 10, is a widely used measure of delivered service quality. The five most important dimensions of service quality emerging from the use of factor analysis techniques are:

1. Tangible aspects, e.g. facilities, appearance and equipment
2. Assurance, e.g. knowledge, security and professional credibility
3. Reliability, e.g. ability to perform dependably and accurately
4. Responsiveness, e.g. willingness to help and promptness
5. Empathy, e.g. care, courtesy and attention as perceived.

It is necessary to study both the perceptual and the satisfaction gaps when considering the customer role in setting the quality standards to be met and in order to assess quality from a marketing perspective. Placing these two gaps together gives a simple model linking the offering made, through the customer evaluation of that offer, to a comparison with expectation. Hooley (1993) builds on this core to extend the links forward to customer wants and needs as in Figure 8.6. For the supply organization he develops the model backwards to the original specifications from which the marketing offer was developed. His enlarged model highlights several links where problems could occur, each one having an effect on the quality of an offer as perceived by the customer (Figure 9.5). Such a model shows the complexity of achieving total quality in meeting customer needs.

By further study of the ways in which information about customer needs, wants and expectations are used as input to the design of an offering, Hooley came up with 11 so-called gaps that require attention if the aim of satisfying the needs of customers is to be achieved. Perhaps the most important of these gaps to consider in relation to the basic marketing concept are the three design gaps (Figure 9.6). These all revolve around the perception of a supplier regarding needs, wants and expectations.

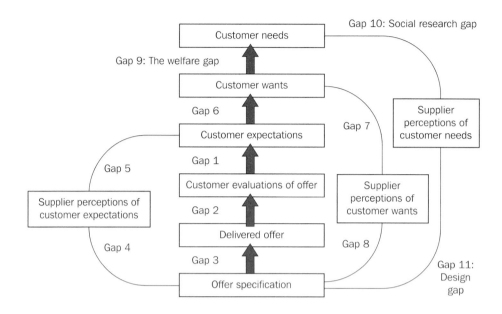

Fig 9.5 Market-led quality management. *Source*: Hooley (1993)

As was described in Chapter 8, there are many reasons why needs do not match wants, and equally why wants do not match expectations. In the classic article 'Marketing Myopia', the problem of not identifying basic needs as opposed to wants or expectations was exposed by Levitt (1960). However, marketing research into needs, wants and expectations is usually the starting point for developing the specifications for designing an offering. If the research undertaken does not embrace all three aspects then it is likely that any resulting offer will not be entirely satisfactory. In fact, inadequate marketing research is said to be a major cause of new product failure (Cooper and Kleinschmidt (1993) claim this accounts for 15% of all failures). If research does find a lack of congruence between the different aspects of needs, wants and expectations, then marketing activities can be planned and decisions taken as to the most appropriate design specifications for an offering.

Total quality management

There are a number of important issues that are well covered in TQM literature. In general four of these dominate:

1. Quality must focus on customer needs.
2. Everything is a process that can contribute to quality.
3. Quality requires universal participation from everyone in the organization.

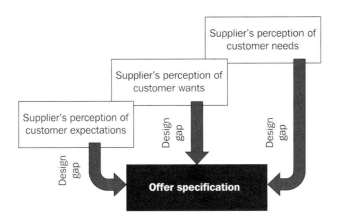

Fig 9.6 The three design gaps – compromises between a supplier's perception of needs and wants and the offer specification. *Source*: Adapted from Hooley (1993)

4. Quality is a journey, not a destination – there should be continuous quality improvement.

The first should now be obvious; quality, like marketing, must focus on satisfying customers. However, marketing activities go further in that they embrace communication and persuasion in the hope of bringing about changes in both customer expectations and perceptions. Marketing techniques can be utilized to clarify and influence the criteria on which satisfaction is judged. In particular, strategic marketing is aimed at all the issues that could affect any future trading exchanges. There is an interesting story, now part of quality folklore. Apparently IBM's Ontario company placed an order for some components with a Japanese firm. They specified that an acceptable quality level was that the delivered items should have no more than 3 defective components per 10 000 parts. When the order was delivered there was a covering letter from the supplier which read 'We Japanese have a hard time understanding North American business practices. However the three defective parts have been included with the order, but they are wrapped separately. We hope this pleases'. This is an interesting interpretation of the quality needs of the customer.

In terms of process, every part of a company's operations should be assessed to see how each can enhance the quality of the final output. Again, marketing extends further than quality management in that it studies the total marketing network – a channel which stretches from a supplier, through distributors and other intermediaries, and onto the final consumer. The actions of this final consumer will affect, through the derived demand, all the separate parts of the distribution network. Therefore, all the activities, whether carried out wholly by a particular organization or by another member of the network, can affect the quality as received. It is appropriate for marketing actions to be taken with a view to influencing quality levels throughout the entire network.

Most quality management is usually seen as applicable to the ongoing output of an organization through the operations process. It therefore has a short-term horizon related to current production. But it is not only within the activities of the *operations process* where quality is necessary, it is also in the *innovation process* where the application of quality assurance techniques, and the inclusion of appropriate standards, can eliminate many future quality problems in production. This can dramatically increase the chances of satisfying future customers.

Quality requires everyone to be involved. This is a form of marketing orientation, affecting the total culture of an organization. Interaction with customers is dependent on people, both the front-line contact people and the support personnel. Gummesson (1991) described the contact staff as 'part-time marketers'; that is, people whose prime job is not marketing, but who, because of their interaction with customers, have an influence on the delivery of an offering. Carlzon (1987), the former Chief Executive of SAS Airlines, writing on service contacts between employees and customers, described the 'moments of truth' as the actual contacts, often lasting only a few seconds, that take place between a customer and an employee of the supplier organization. He suggests these actually determine a company's success or failure. They are certainly very important in delivering a quality experience. Carlzon says that for SAS in a year 'each of our 10 million customers came into contact with approximately five (SAS) employees, and this contact lasted an average 15 seconds each time. These 50 million "moments of truth" are when [SAS] must prove to its customers that it is the best alternative for their needs'. This leads on to what is sometimes termed 'internal marketing', which is the use of marketing skills and techniques within an organization, treating employees as internal customers, and company plans, linked to a positive attitude to external customers, as the product.

Such an orientation is of more benefit to marketing than the bureaucratic systems that sometimes pass for quality management. In fact, there are debates still running as to the economic value of TQM. Powell (1995) reported that 'TQM can produce economic value to firms, but it has not done so for all TQM adopters. TQM success appears to depend critically on executive commitment, open organisation, and employee empowerment, and less upon such TQM staples as benchmarking, training, flexible manufacturing, and improved measurement'. His study goes on to ask 'Is TQM necessary for success?', answering that 'although TQM can produce competitive advantage, adopting the vocabularies, ideologies, and tools promoted by the TQM gurus matters less than developing the underlying intangible resources that make TQM implementation successful'. These could be seen as a *learning culture* and a *marketing orientation*.

As far as the quality journey is concerned, nearly every market-place is dynamic, and customers receive many new influences, which can affect expectations, perceptions and even wants. It is because of this that no organization can ever feel that it has reached the end of its quest for quality. It is not the achievement of ISO 9000 or some other quality standard that matters, but the continued relevance of an offering. This is TQM, total quality *marketing* as distinct from total quality management. The comparative benchmarking of performance is a continuous activity. As competitors improve their offerings so programmes can be implemented with the aim of keeping ahead in the key components which 'energize' customers. Such activities involve more than basic product developments, incorporating everything that affects the output, including the processes and procedures used as well as issues related to the people who are the key to all service delivery.

Quality improvements can help to build strong relationships by developing additional benefits for both buyers and sellers. This follows Hamel's dictum of 'filling in the blanks' (see Chapter 4), which should ensure a strengthening of a position in an existing market. The journey is also necessary to achieve the 'premier plus 10' state, this being the necessary development of a modified offering suitable for the future. Hamel and Prahalad (1994) ask 'what new core competencies must we be building today to ensure that we are regarded as the premier provider by our customers in five or ten years' time?'. While they talk about new competencies, it is just as important to consider new quality developments. Such improvements sometimes require a quantum leap, or a full business process reengineering, rather than tighter specifications and closer monitoring of tolerances. For this reason I would prefer to see TQM standing for the *total quality – total marketing* concept. This contrasts with some applications of total quality management, and attitudes that sometimes exist within operations management, that quality is an end in itself.

The benefits of total quality marketing

It is possible to reflect the four issues from the previous section on total quality management directly in the writings of Tom Peters (1987) on the benefits of a quality orientation. He states that his 'unequivocal findings' are:

- Customers – individual or industrial, high tech or low, science trained or untrained – will pay a lot for better, and especially the *best*, quality.
- Firms that provide that quality will thrive.
- Workers in all parts of the organization will become energized by the opportunity to provide a top-quality product or service.
- No product has a safe quality lead, since new entrants are constantly redefining, for the customer, what's possible.

While Peters does not actually define quality, he does aggressively promote it in all its dimensions. He also reflects the message of the quality gurus that:

- Higher quality yields lower costs.
- Higher quality comes with fewer inspectors.
- More products (with shorter production runs) does not mean lower quality.

Perhaps the greatest benefit from a quality culture is the intangible virtuous circle that results from the mutually supportive achievements of strong employee motivation and a positive customer focus. While customers are far *less* likely to praise good service than they are to complain about a poor offering, it is always more satisfying for employees to work in an atmosphere where plaudits are more common than criticism. This applies equally to the satisfying of internal customers as it does to the exchanges with external customers. The positive attitude that can develop within a company from the satisfaction of the internal customers will eventually extend down the line to affect the output to the external consumer.

Is quality enough?

For a marketing person it will be obvious that quality (satisfying customers needs) is a *necessary* objective, but it may not be *sufficient* to gain a sale or ensure repeat business. There will be certain levels of quality that are expected as 'order qualifying'. These have to be met in order to be considered in the market-place, but this is the minimum acceptable level and it does nothing to contribute towards achieving a competitive advantage. As discussed in previous chapters, customers will assess the comparative value of competitive offerings and will decide based on their own perceptions and personal frames of reference.

Quality programmes that lead towards the delivery of 'superior' customer value are the only ones that really count. These could be the result of including real tangible and intangible features that enhance the benefits of the offering. The ultimate test, however, is the perception by a customer that an offering not only meets their needs, but does so in a way that offers the greatest *added* value to them.

It is also important to remember that a quality programme of service delivery cannot save a poor product. While the activities that surround the promotion of an offering can sometimes dominate at the point of sale, the true test is whether the product/service meets the customer's basic needs, both current and over the life of the product. This will be the ultimate test and will be remembered long after the clever advertising or the low price is forgotten.

Philip Crosby (1979) has suggested that 'quality is free' based on the relative cost of eliminating the causes of quality problems when compared to the real costs of defective products, quality control checks and the negative effects of customer complaints. As Crosby said, 'the true cost of quality is the cost of doing things wrong'. These costs should be considered both in the short term with respect to the effects of dissatisfaction, and in the longer term, with respect to the effect on the organization's image and the perception of future potential customers.

Achieving quality

There are two distinct approaches to achieving a quality output from an organization. The first is standards based, the second culture based (Figure 9.7). Albrecht (1990) has argued that a standards-based approach is rather 'authoritarian' and 'management led', and therefore more suitable for organizations offering more tangible products. A culture-based approach is necessary where an organization is involved in less tangible offerings with a strong service element. In fact both approaches have advantages and problems, and it could be argued that there are benefits from merging the two. After all, standards are best applied in a receptive culture, and a culture of quality still requires standards as targets.

Linking the two approaches will be the organizational structure that allows a quality culture to thrive while accommodating the systems and standards based on feedback from customers. If all are brought together then a true *marketing orientation* will be achieved within the company, leading to a quality output founded upon:

Standards-based approaches	
Advantages	Criticisms
• Simple to define • Clear logical framework • Suitable for tangible products • Less susceptible to leadership changes	• Management-led • Authoritarian • Less suitable for intangible services • Preoccupied with internal measures
Culture-based approaches	
Advantages	Criticisms
• Suitable for intangible services • Instil values that drive actions • Employee ownership • Autonomous efforts beyond specified standards	• Hard to define • Measurement is obscure • Very difficult to implement • Leadership changes and subcultures can derail the new culture

Fig 9.7 Two approaches to quality

- a quality *culture*
- an appropriate *structure*
- effective quality *systems*.

Such a culture and structure should encourage the sharing of information between functional areas, openness in dealings with customer relationships, and flexibility in considering future requirements – in short, a marketing oriented learning organization. Information, especially information about customer needs and wants, should be seen as a positive input and not a component of departmental power. While functional conflicts will inevitably occur, in the right culture such conflict will lead to constructive developments, not destructive, dysfunctional friction.

Everyone in every organization has a responsibility to help build quality relationships with the chosen customers. These activities will range from achieving satisfaction through quality delivery and service, to effective dealing with any complaints and ensuring corrective action. Consideration of a quality culture and comparing it to both a marketing orientation and a learning organization will demonstrate how important the softer issues of business are to the implementation of marketing and the achievement of a strong competitive position.

Conclusions

The first issue to be tackled with respect to quality is 'what exactly is quality?'. The eight dimensions suggested by Garvin do help to show that quality can have many faces, each dependent on a particular context and a relevant interpretation of customer needs. In general, as Stauss (1994) shows, TQM is the inclusion of a customer perspective within all the various business processes and functions. Good TQM programmes will be based upon a deep understanding of the needs and expectations of chosen customers, and will be able to deliver the *quality* and *value* that these customers require: If Total Quality Management efforts become everybody's duty – customer satisfaction is everybody's business. In fact, 'total quality' and 'customer first' programmes generate real employee involvement and focus. From another perspective, Davies (1995) reported that 'We all know many tales of marketing departments that have laboured to create customer bonds and have been betrayed by the inadequacies of other functions. Customers do not distinguish between departments; a promise from any employee is a promise from the company. Whether the promise was rash or even misunderstood, the customer looks to the whole company to redeem it'.

The link with customer needs, wants and expectations is not as easy as it first seems, and this is a critical area for the marketing role of reflecting customers within the company. Satisfaction comes from the meeting of needs, and quality is really the achievement of customer satisfaction. However, as Hooley (1993) demonstrated, there are many gaps between needs, wants, expectations and perception of an offering. There are also gaps between the supplier's interpretation of these and the actual design specifications used to construct the offering. Standards-based quality relies on the effective specifying of those standards, therefore, when trying to understand customers, all the potential gaps must be studied and efforts made to close them, thus ensuring the best possible match. Such actions are necessary to achieve quality and the resulting competitive advantage.

The answer to the question 'is quality enough?' is that the only quality that matters is that which leads to superior customer value and relevant competitive advantage. Total quality management programmes are widespread, and the techniques of TQM are easy to imitate. Competitive advantage does not come from application of programmes but from a real change in the underlying culture of an organization and the competencies of employees. As Powell (1995) says, 'these [competencies] appear to produce success with or without a formal TQM adoption – TQM firms that lack them do not succeed and non-TQM firms that have them do succeed'. This can be interpreted as suggesting that it is not total quality management but *total quality* able to deliver *total customer satisfaction* that is a key component of sustainable competitive advantage in a market-place.

KEY POINTS

9.1 Quality is a widely misused term that has been defined in many different ways. Although it is often considered as a measure of excellence, this is very misleading as quality is really a comparative evaluation of one product when considered against another.

9.2 The best way to approach quality is to understand that it is everything that leads to customer satisfaction.

9.3 Quality has many dimensions; Garvin identified eight key aspects. He also suggested that 'Quality means pleasing consumers, not just protecting them from annoyances'.

9.4 Marketing is quality and quality is marketing. But what is really important is the merging of the marketing concept and a customer focus with the quality process and quality culture.

9.5 Quality as the link between a supplier's 'offering' and the customer's 'needs' is simple in abstract, but as Figures 9.3–9.6 show, there are many opportunities for gaps to appear.

9.6 The four dominant issues of the TQM literature are all relevant to the marketing role. These are:

1. Quality must focus on customer needs.
2. Everything is a process that can contribute to quality.
3. Quality requires universal participation from everyone in the organization.
4. Quality is a journey, not a destination – there should be continuous quality improvement.

9.7 While quality (satisfying customers needs) is a *necessary* objective, it may not be *sufficient* to gain a sale or ensure repeat business. Expected quality can be an 'order qualifier' but to energize customers requires something more.

9.8 There are two approaches to achieving a quality output from an organization: (i) standards-based and (ii) culture-based. They can be used in a complementary way.

9.9 There are obvious links between a true marketing orientation and a quality output founded upon:

- a quality culture
- an appropriate structure
- effective quality systems.

QUESTIONS

9.1 In what way might an efficient quality programme, which meets all the expected performance standards, fail to create a sufficient level of sales?

9.2 Garvin suggested eight dimensions of quality. Two of these – aesthetics and perceived quality – have an extrinsic bias. Do you consider that marketing managers should be particularly concerned about these two aspects? From a marketing perspective do you think they are more important than the other six dimensions?

9.3 Both quality and marketing require universal participation from everyone in an organization. Are there any other similarities between them which strengthen the maxim that 'marketing is quality and quality is marketing'?

9.4 Give an example of the quality dimension of (a) product quality, (b) service quality and (c) relationship quality as they relate to marketing. Then identify where potential problems might occur.

Bibliography

Albrecht, K., *Service Within*, Irwin, 1990.

Booms, B.H. and Bitner, M.J., Marketing Strategies and Organizational Structures for Service Firms, in J. Donelly & W. George (Eds) *The Marketing of Services*, American Marketing Association, 1981.

Calantone, R.J. and Cooper, R.G., New Product Scenarios – Prospect for Success, *Journal of Product Innovation*, No. 45, Spring, 1981.

Carlzon, J., *The Moments of Truth*, Ballinger, 1987.

Cooper, R.G. and Kleinschmidt, E.J. Screening New Products for Potential Winners, *Long Range Planning*, Vol. 26, 1993.

Davies, A., *The Strategic Role of Marketing*, McGraw-Hill, 1995.

Deeming, W.E., *Out of Crisis – Quality, Productivity, and Competitive Positioning*, MIT Press, 1986.

Crosby, P.B., *Quality is Free*, McGraw-Hill, 1979.

Garvin, D.A., Competing on the Eight Dimensions of Quality, *Harvard Business Review*, Nov./Dec., pp. 101–109, 1987.

Grönroos, C., Marketing Redefined, *Management Decisions*, Vol. 28 No. 8, pp. 5–9, 1990.

Gummesson, E., Marketing Orientation Re-visited, the Crucial Role of the Part Time Marketer, *European Journal of Marketing*, Vol. 25 No. 2, pp. 60–75, 1991.

Hamel, G. and Prahalad, C.K., *Competing for the Future*, HBS Press, 1994.

Hooley, G., Market Led Quality Management, *Journal of Marketing Management*, Vol. 9, pp. 315–335, 1993.

Hooley, G. and Saunders, J., *Competitive Positioning*, Prentice Hall, 1994.

Jones, T.O. and Sasser, W.E., Why Satisfied Customers Defect, *Harvard Business Review*, Nov./Dec., 1995.

Juran, J.M., *On Leadership for Quality*, Free Press, 1989.

Kordupleski, R.E., Rust, R.T. and Zahorik, A.J., Why Improving Quality doesn't Improve Quality, *Californian Business Review*, July/Aug., 1993.

Kotler, P., *Marketing Management, Analysis, Planning and Control*, Prentice Hall, 1997.

Levitt, T., Marketing Myopia, *Harvard Business Review*, July/Aug., pp. 45–56, 1960.

Levitt, T., *The Marketing Imagination*, Free Press, 1983.

Mathur, S.S., Talking Straight about Competitive Strategy, *Journal of Marketing Management*, Vol. 8, 1992.

McKenna, R., Marketing is Everything, *Harvard Business Review*, Vol. 69 No. 1, p. 65, 1991.

Murray, J.A. and O'Driscoll, A., *Strategy and Process in Marketing*, Prentice Hall, 1996.

Parasuraman, A., Zeithmal, V.A. and Berry, L.L., SERVQUAL scale for measuring consumer perceptions of service quality, *Journal of Retailing*, Vol. 64 No. 1, 1988.

Peters, T., *Thriving on Chaos*, Macmillan, 1987.

Powell, T.C., Total Quality Management as Competitive Advantage: A Review and Empirical Study, *Strategic Management Journal*, Vol. 16, pp. 15–37, 1995.

Stauss, B., *Total Quality Management: Customer Orientation without Marketing*, Working Paper No. 43, Universitat Eichstatt, 1994.

LESSONS FROM SERVICES MARKETING

10

CHAPTER

INTRODUCTION

A decade ago J.B. Quinn, with others, wrote that:

> thanks to new technology, executives can divide up their company's value chains, handle the key strategic elements internally, outsource others advantageously . . ., and yet coordinate all essential activities more effectively to meet customers' needs. . . . Companies that understand this build their strategies not around products but around deep knowledge of a few highly developed core skills. . . . To rethink strategies objectively, managements need to break out of the mind-set that considers manufacturing (for goods production) as separate from (and somehow superior to) the service activities that make such production possible and effective.

There are three messages in this quotation, all very relevant to strategic marketing. First is that an organization does not have to provide everything itself in an attempt to satisfy the needs of its customers. It can work together with other complementary providers to produce a competitive offering. But to do this effectively it is necessary to integrate activities to ensure the customer sees a unified, consistent and relevant offering. At the simplest this could be a partnership between a manufacturer and a distributor, with the latter enhancing the tangible product by offering purchase advice, high levels of availability close to the customers, and efficient after-sales service. Obviously Quinn also looked at more complex alliances.

The second issue follows on from the first. It is the need of a business to focus on the areas of its core competencies, specifically those where it can deliver a real competitive advantage. It should be able to identify and accommodate other companies, which can contribute their capabilities to ensure value for customers.

The third point is that every offering is likely to include a mix of tangible goods together with intangibles such as services, and these intangibles are equally important to the total offering. The combination of tangible and intangibles can be seen on a continuum stretching from commodity product to pure service. This idea was introduced in Chapter 8 with respect to the sources of sustainable competitive advantage, and the discussion went on to suggest that each offering can be placed on this scale at a point which reflects the balance between the different components, and in many cases the real advantage comes from the intangible elements. It is possible to see many industrial companies as service providers, for instance major car assemblers such as Ford, or the examples of Honda, Apple and Merck, which are described in the article by Quinn *et al*.

The initial development of services marketing came about because of the rapid post-war growth in industries closer to the pure service end of the continuum, such as travel, hospitality, leisure, financial services and communications. As a result efforts were made to identify what was similar, and what different, in these industries. Attempts to apply marketing techniques to 'service products' has brought about a rethinking of what is important in the marketing concept. When in 1981 Levitt wrote his seminal article on intangibles he asked, 'Is the marketing of *services* different from the marketing of *goods*?'. His answer was equivocal: 'the principles may be the same, but the translation into practice may be profoundly different'. Focusing on the differences has enabled four important characteristics of services to be considered:

- intangibility
- inseparability
- perishability
- heterogeneity.

Understanding these different aspects has led to a re-examination of the basic operational marketing mix, with *people*, *processes*, and *physical evidence* being added to the traditional 4Ps.

From a strategic perspective, an alternative enlarged 7P framework has already been proposed in Chapter 8, with *positioning* and *promises* as key components. It will be obvious, both in respect of the promises made and the achievement of a desired position, that the interactions with customers reflected in the *people*, *processes* and *physical evidence* issues play an important role. Consideration of these additional elements as part of the marketing mix is a major lesson from the study of service products.

It is during the interactions with customers – the *moments of truth* – when the service components of an offering are most apparent. The perception created by the service experience is central to the customer evaluation of satisfaction. The *inseparability* dimension whereby services are 'produced' at the same time as the delivery of the service benefits illustrates the importance of considering the role of services in achieving customer satisfaction and competitive advantage. It does not matter if the offering is a pure service, or a tangible product with accompanying services, detailed marketing attention must be given to all aspects of the service component.

In fact, the intangible nature of an offering goes further than the service encounter. As Murray and O'Driscoll (1996) suggest, 'all marketers must remember to design and deliver the non-tangible product benefits that customers inevitably demand. Excellent physical and service characteristics alone are seldom enough to guarantee customer satisfaction and competitive effectiveness, achieving a seamless balance of these product components is a complex but ultimately rewarding endeavour'. This raises two separate aspects requiring attention from marketing. First is the need to widen the management of intangibles beyond the direct service encounter. This should embrace all other contacts between supplier and customer at any level; it will also include the *processes* as well as the *people*, and should extend to the management of customer satisfaction through relevant, non-direct, intangible components of the total offering such as guarantees or helplines. The second requirement is for consistency between all the elements of the offering so that each is mutually supportive and leads to a seamless balance from everything that is done.

Mathur (1992) suggested that differentiation, as a means of achieving competitive advantage, could come from either the tangible or the intangible parts of an offering. He went further in suggesting that while the merchandise (core offering) could be tangible or intangible, it is important to separate this core offering from the support (advice, instructions or assistance) given to augment the total product. His 2 × 2 matrix (Figure 10.1) illustrates how it is possible to move away from a pure commodity – that is, the 'expected' state, where both the product and the support are undifferentiated and no competitive advantage exists – and develop an offering that has real additional benefits for customers. The process was shown in Figure 5.3 which illustrates the transaction life cycle.

Fig 10.1 Four main competitive strategies from two main dimensions.
Source: Mathur (1997)

If the differentiation is to be through the intangible features, then it is important that the other characteristics of a service such as *inseparability* and *perishability* are fully appreciated. The issue of *heterogeneity* is wider, as will be seen from Chapter 9. Obviously there is a greater likelihood of variability with a service, but the whole purpose of quality control and quality assurance is to ensure that there is a consistent output, whether it is a product or a service.

It is vital that efforts are made to benefit from the distinct aspect of a service, rather than suffer because of the real problems of maintaining consistent quality. All marketing is aimed at creating and keeping customers, which leads onto the development of relationships. Levitt (1981) writes that 'the relationship with customers must be managed much more carefully and continuously in the case of intangibles'. In this he is particularly worried about their inherent variable (*heterogenetic*) nature, and this again leads through to issues of the quality of services. Levitt also highlights the need for developing 'risk-reducing reassurances' for customers to counteract the difficulties brought about by the intangibility of parts of the offering.

The dimensions of competitive advantage

In Chapter 8 three major components of sustainable competitive advantage were discussed, these being *high perceived value, low delivered cost* and *focus*. Focus is really an application of tangible and intangible features to deliver value specifically to a small group of chosen customers. All the above components will be part of the input that customers will use when they evaluate the perceived competitive position of an offering. Mathur (1992) suggests that 'positions can unconsciously emerge, but competitive strategies (plans about future positions) cannot'.

Elements of high perceived value, low delivered cost and focus will be included in a competitive strategy, but the specific components will change over time as circumstances, events and opportunities develop. The strategy itself will need to be formulated and reformulated accordingly. The proposed tests of marketing are whether the product/service is *acceptable* in satisfying the customers' needs or expectations, whether the strategy itself is *feasible* of achievement, and whether the offering is *suitable* in a competitive market-place. In assessing these it will need to be determined if the strategy will lead to an appropriate sustainable competitive advantage. Judged from a customer perspective, competitive offerings are evaluated by the value, perceived or previously received, and this value comes from either non-price benefits or lower costs, or both. The non-price benefits that matter are, first, those that are 'expected' as part of every offering considered, second, those features which differentiate the basic offering, changing its nature and maybe even moving it into another product/market area, and, third, those features that 'augment' the offering, adding additional support over and above what is expected by a purchaser. These last are the ones that must be perceived as relevant and valuable by the customers (energizers).

Examples of the first could be extra features or a longer guarantee. These enhance the basic offering. Examples of support will include point-of-sale advice, installation packages and easy payment schemes. In both cases it is possible to use intangible features to move an offering away from the expected (Mathur's commodity-buy) into a differentiated category. However, in considering the intangibles, it is useful to separate those that enhance the offering by delivering additional core benefits of value from those that make the purchase decision easier, supporting the selling activity.

The way each is treated by customers will be different. Augmenting the core product will affect the positioning of the offering; differentiating the support will reflect back onto the supply organization. If there is a supply chain involved, then the support is likely to be delivered by a downstream partner or distributor rather than the basic producer. This applies equally to the marketing of an intangible, say life assurance, as it does to more tangible products such as food and drink. However, by understanding the characteristics of intangibles and the lessons of services marketing, an organization can better develop total offerings that achieve real competitive advantage along either of Mathur's dimensions.

Intangible features

A competitive advantage exists when a customer perceives one offering as meeting their needs better than any other. Customer satisfaction goes further in that it comes from needs being fully met. Often it is the intangible benefits, not the tangible product, which define the meeting of a need. For instance thirst is quenched by a drink. The thirst quenching is an intangible benefit, the drink a tangible consumer product. Levitt's classic research published under the title of 'Marketing Myopia' some 40 years ago led to the call for all companies to define what business they were really in. Levitt's answer was that it was transport, not railways, for American rail companies, and entertainment, not film making, in Hollywood. When set against the definition of intangibility as something 'that cannot be touched', these answers are intangible benefits received by consumers. Levitt's examples are, of course, predominantly from the service sector; the surprising thing is that even with the producers of goods rather than services, a business can still be defined in terms of its intangible consumer benefits. Thirst quenching, as in the above example, and not the tangible drink; cosmetics giving 'hope', as in the famous quotation from Charles Revlon, which illustrated the intangible benefit of his products; basic clothing offering the benefit of protection while designer labels give status are other examples; even capital industrial plant can be seen as a facilitator of production. In fact in a retrospective 15 years after 'Marketing Myopia', Levitt (1975) suggested that his original article had 'had more impact on industrial companies than consumer ones'.

Levitt warned against defining benefits by 'looking into a mirror rather than looking out of a window'. By this he meant that a company should ensure that it avoids reflecting the internal organizational view of what is to be provided, and instead looks at the issues and desired benefits from a customer perspective. The product examples given above are tangible – drinks, clothing and industrial plant. Each can be touched, measured and assessed, but the customer benefits that they deliver are intangible. It is often these aspects which will be stressed when promoting the product, but these benefits will be discovered only if suppliers look out of the window.

The idea of stressing intangible benefits should be extended into composite offerings, where there are both obvious tangible and intangible elements. Fast food in a McDonald's or Burger King might be perceived and promoted as an enjoyable experience alongside the nutritional benefits; maybe a supermarket group would develop its image rather than the fact that it stocks several thousand actual products. Another example is the way Cadbury's associates chocolate with love, romance and caring.

A warning from the early writing of Levitt (1975) that is still often ignored is that 'companies have attempted to serve customers by creating complex and beautifully efficient product/service packages which buyers are either too risk-adverse to adopt or incapable of learning how to employ – in fact there are now steam shovels for people who haven't yet learned to use spades!'. His examples from the financial services and computer-based services sectors are as fresh today as when they were originally published.

Intangibility presents both opportunities and problems for a marketer. From the strategic perspective of designing a competitive offering, the advantages are in the use of intangible benefits to develop a unique position in the minds of chosen customers. Claims made about these benefits are one element; the level of positive feelings perceived and valued by the customer are another. Such positions, once developed, are powerful stimuli, which will directly affect purchase decisions. As stated in Chapter 7, strong positions are difficult to establish and equally difficult to change should customer attitudes move on.

The problems with intangibles are not just ones of ensuring consistent quality. There are also difficulties in trying to avoid the worst extremes of uncertainty that customers sometimes feel in relation to an intangible offering. The purchase of an intangible can be seen as a risk because, by its very nature, it cannot be touched or measured before receipt. Therefore, as a distinct contrast to the use of intangible benefits to enhance tangible features, there is an opposite momentum to provide tangible cues in order to reassure customers and as a tactic in risk reduction as applied to services. These tangible cues are the basis of Booms and Bitner's (1981) enlarged marketing mix leading to the three categories of people, processes and physical evidence being included. All tangible cues should be designed to add to the credence properties of the total offering.

Some of the 'evidence' as evaluated by Lynn Shostack (1977) can 'seem trivial until one recognises how great their impact can be on perception. Correspondence is one example. Letters, statements and the like are sometimes the main conveyors of the "reality" of a service to its market, yet often these are treated as peripheral to any marketing plan. From the grade of paper to the choice of colours, correspondence is visible evidence that conveys a unique message. A photocopied, non-personalised, cheaply produced letter contradicts any words about service quality that may appear in the text of that letter. Conversely, engraved parchment from the local dry cleaners might make one wonder about their prices'. This example covers both the way tangible evidence is used with regard to intangible offerings, and the effect it can have either to reassure or pose questions in the minds of customers.

The intangible aspects of an offering are difficult for competitors to copy, and therefore present major opportunities for sustainable competitive advantage. However, because purchase decisions are made on the basis of a customer's perception as to what is likely to be received, together with confidence in the supply organization, it is necessary to present the intangible aspects in a way that can be judged favourably by potential customers. The types of questions used in the SERVQUAL survey are helpful in considering this. They include:

> Has the Company got modern looking equipment?
> Are the Company's physical facilities visually appealing?
> Do the Company's employees appear neat in appearance?
> Is the Company literature and material visually appealing?
> Does the Company have convenient business hours?
> Does the behaviour of employees instil confidence?
> Do you feel safe in transactions with the Company?
> Do the employees have the knowledge to answer your questions?

All of these questions are aimed at establishing whether customers have confidence in the supply company. It is perhaps useful for the supplier to try to answer such questions in an objective way when they are designing or evaluating an offering. This will lead to study of the perceptual gap (see Chapter 9) and the other categories of the SERVQUAL model which will be required in order to identify appropriate service strategies that deliver both customer satisfaction and competitive advantage.

Those inseparable 'moments of truth'

When discussing quality in Chapter 9 it was suggested that the experience of a customer during the short 'moments of truth' contacts was a critical determinant of success or failure. A powerful argument can be constructed to this effect as it is during interactions with any part of an organization that opinions are formed about the wider capacity of that supplier. Although not all of these meetings are with the primary supply functions, every encounter will influence attitudes beyond the actual point of contact. In an ideal situation all such meetings will lead to positive reinforcement, but this can only be a goal, although it is the key objective of effective customer care programmes. Certainly every employee should be viewed as a part-time marketer (someone whose actions can affect customers directly even though their prime job is not specifically marketing) if there is any chance of direct interaction with a customer.

Moments of truth are usually thought of as direct personal contacts, but they could be remote, such as a telephone call, or even impersonal, maybe a letter or an invoice. Therefore the interactions between a supplier and a customer can have many different forms; in addition, they can occur on several different levels. There have been revealing stories of a salesperson entertaining a customer to a long lunch, while the accounts department is telephoning about an unpaid invoice; perhaps the Managing Directors of a buyer and a seller company attending the same conference discuss future cooperation, while the buyer's works manager is trying to resolve a problem with a recent delivery. Obviously such problems can occur in any buyer–seller relationship but they are more apparent due to the multi-level contact that is a feature in business to business markets. Whether business markets or consumer markets are considered, the 'defining moments' in the building of buyer–seller relationships are the actual 'service exchanges' between the parties. The development of a strong relationship requires mutual trust and commitment from both parties, which will help to overcome any difficulties that might arise. The 'moments of truth' contacts must be seen in their widest form as covering all exchanges, whether planned or informal. They are all part of the total marketing offering, and these interactions are distinguished by the inseparable nature of the production and the consumption.

The marketing implications of simultaneous production and consumption according to Zeithaml and Bitner (1996) are that:

- mass production is difficult if not impossible;
- there are not any significant economies of scale;
- the customer is involved, both observing the process and affecting the outcome;
- the quality of service and customer satisfaction will be highly dependent on what happens in 'real time', including actions of employees and the interactions between employees and customers.

Consistent positive exchanges will occur only if all employees understand and are committed to the marketing strategy. Every part-time marketer must interpret their role in a way that is consistent with other employees towards the same customer. Structures and systems help, as does training, but in the end it is the *people* who determine the outcome.

Relationships go through several stages as they develop from exploratory initial contacts to a mature, stable and deeply involved connectedness. Of course some do not achieve the full interdependency, although trading might still continue between the two parties. However, it will be obvious that the effects of a good or a bad 'moment of truth' will be very different, depending on the depth of relationship that exists. In a new association, one poor experience could destroy everything; in a stronger relationship there could be more opportunity to recover the situation.

When the ways of doing business, and the values and objectives of both supplier and customer, show some congruency, then there is a reduction in the 'distance' between the two parties. This is important if strong relationships are to develop with mutual trust and understanding. There are two specific dimensions of a relationship that can be considered as important in this respect:

1. Social and cultural differences between supplier and customer
2. Technological differences.

Both need to be understood as it is possible that they each will develop in different ways and at varying speeds over time.

Social aspects relate to the direct links, whereby buyers and sellers come to understand each other and are comfortable dealing together. This can extend to the differences in cultural norms and values and the effect these have on interactions. The social distance between parties does influence their ability to interact efficiently. In particular, a focus strategy, based on effective segmentation, needs to consider how to reduce any social or cultural barriers. This is much more difficult than just identifying attractive segments, since it demands actions to ensure that all activities of a supplier can be viewed as sympathetic and complementary to the norms and values of a customer. However, the inseparable nature of service interactions can be used in a positive way to bring about greater understanding and thereby reduce the distance involved.

Technological considerations refer to the similarities or divergences in the processes, and the degree of fit that exists between buyer's and seller's technologies. For instance, a major car assembler will have more in common with a high tech component supplier than with a small jobbing welding shop. The mutual understanding in the first should lead to a different context for any contacts when compared to that appropriate to the greater technological distances present in the second case.

Effective moments of truth, like any communication, need to be built from the differences that exist between the parties. However, because of the joint involvement of buyer and seller, it is possible to use such interactions as a means of closing any gaps that might be identified.

The absence of mass production and the lack of economies of scale which exist with the inseparable elements of the total offering, do have the advantage of forcing a degree of customization. When, through employee training, attempts are made to standardize 'service encounters', there are a number of problems that can arise.

Pre-planned uniform standards can become oversimplified and incomplete in what they offer for a particular situation. They also risk subjectivity and biased interpretation by employees as to their roles. This is often the case when there is a reliance on words and off-the-job training for a particular service activity. These issues will be explored further when considering the *heterogeneity* of services and the problems of consistent service quality.

Here today, gone tomorrow: the perishable nature of services

There should be no doubting that a total marketing offering can have both tangible and intangible components. The intangible could be the benefits as perceived by customers, but they might also derive from specific services deliberately included as part of the total offering. Examples could be the checkout and packing service in a supermarket, or technical advice from a knowledgeable service engineer, or an all-inclusive carpet fitting offered free as an inducement to purchase. Looking beyond the composite category of 'goods with additional services' towards 'pure services', it is possible to identify an inherent problem which is just as important for composite offerings as it is for pure services.

Services exist in 'real time'. If no checkout is free at the supermarket you have to wait; equally, if the carpet fitter is fully booked or the doctor's surgery full then there is more waiting. Waiting for a service, or for the service element of a total offer, could reduce the level of satisfaction, or, at the extreme, make the service unacceptable to the customer. This would be the situation when the customer considered the total package as a complete entity and the problems with the service element were seen as devaluing the whole. In fact it is often the case that the service is not an event by itself but is an integral part of a total offering. If the service component is inadequate then so is the whole offering.

The various, and ever increasing, writings on the marketing of services all give suggestions on how to approach the different characteristics of a service, and how to put together a marketing plan for service products. They also accept that most offerings are a combination of elements, tangible and intangible. The real marketing task is to integrate all parts of an offering into a seamless and balanced whole which satisfies chosen customers. Therefore, attention must be given to all aspects of an offering with the aim of achieving the right balance for each consumer. This could mean offering a different combination of elements to each and every customer.

The real-time nature of services brings about two problems that need to be addressed. First, and most obvious, is demand management. The second is the perishable nature, which means that once 'lost' the service cannot be resurrected.

It is apparent that a service cannot be stored until required: there has to be enough capacity to deal with current demand such as supermarket checkouts and carpet fitters. This demand fluctuates and forecasting is an imprecise activity. It is possible that a little flexibility could exist. Customers are prepared to queue or wait for a short time without detracting from the satisfaction level; they understand some situations and modify their expectations accordingly. However, there will be a range of acceptable waiting times for each service and every customer. There are also tactics that can make the wait more acceptable. One of the roles of marketing is to understand what boundaries exist and to manage the customer expectations accordingly.

An example of a good marketing initiative is the employment of street entertainers to entertain the queues waiting to enter Madame Tussaud's waxwork museum in London. This makes waiting part of the total experience and it diffuses frustration. Another example is National Breakdown's guarantee of a one-hour maximum response time. If the call is not answered within the time, the company pays £10 compensation, thus recompensing the customer.

An example of poor demand management of customer expectations comes from a well-known supplier of hardware products sold through major department stores. A new MD took over at a time when sales and market share were declining. His first, and highly commended, act was to go out to speak to existing retailers (customers) about the problems as they saw them. The major complaint was that orders were always delivered late, an average 10 weeks after the order was placed, and were often incomplete. This seems like an operational problem but from the retailers' perspective the lack of stock when required was a direct cause of lost sales. Anyway, the operations department were aware of the problem and proposed several improvements, suggesting these could halve the delays. These were agreed. However, the MD decided to set a target maximum of 4 weeks for delays and he rightly insisted that complete orders must be met. He sent a personal letter to all existing and lapsed customers to this effect and backed up his promise by asking anyone who was dissatisfied to telephone him. The operational changes did significantly reduce delays, but only to 6 weeks. This was a considerable improvement on the previous situation but it failed to match the new expectations and new promises. The result was many irate telephone calls, continued (in fact, increased) dissatisfaction, and the MD had a breakdown and resigned. This company still trades but at a very reduced level compared to previously.

There are other ways of managing demand. The first is shifting demand to match capacity; variable pricing including off-peak discounts is an example. Second is the provision of flexible levels of capacity to meet variations in demand, such as increasing part-time staff at peak times to ensure all checkouts are open when required. These and other examples are well presented in specialist texts. When discussing levels of service, conventional wisdom warns against over-provision; after all, if service staff are idle then costs increase. This is, of course, a relevant efficiency issue, but when considering the problems from a strategic marketing perspective it will be seen that some customers are more valuable than others. Strategies must be designed to ensure loyal regular customers are properly looked after, and even given priority in times of high demand. These customers represent the most significant segment as far as future profitable sales are concerned. They are the customers that would cost most to replace, and programmes which increase benefits as relationships develop are strategically important.

An example of this occurred when growth of new demand linked to production constrictions led to a major shortage of glass jar and bottle making capacity in the UK during the 1970s. One supplier, Rockware Glass, made extreme efforts to ensure that existing loyal customers were given priority. They set up additional service links with chosen customers, which were valued by those customers and remembered after the short-term crisis, leading to even stronger relationships.

Other examples of a more frequent nature are the fast, no-waiting, checkout facilities in some hotels for loyalty card holders. There are also special arrangements made by banks for certain selected customers. A major US manufacturing company processes bills electronically with regular suppliers, instead of waiting for invoices. With 4% of its suppliers (accounting for much more of the actual supplies) it does not use purchase orders; instead, the internal production and inventory systems computers of both supplier and customer are linked. Automatic replenishment takes place and the key customer benefits not only from the JIT advantages, but by guaranteed supplies. There are other examples of similar systems.

These positive actions are in direct contrast to the average UK supermarket. Although with the increased use of loyalty cards it is possible to identify high-spending regular shoppers, in most supermarkets they have no special privileges, having to queue alongside everyone else. The only priority shoppers seem to be low spenders, who can often utilize an 'eight-item maximum' fast checkout. This rewards low-value casual shoppers but does nothing for more valuable customers. Safeway is experimenting with a fast checkout 'Shop & Go' system for a limited group, and this shows good strategic thinking with regard to both demand management and loyal customer benefits.

There is another issue relating to the perishability of services. This is the fact that a poor service, once experienced, is possibly more difficult to replace. If a pair of trainers is defective, maybe the sole comes off the first time they are worn, then it is easy to replace them with another pair from stock. It is not so easy if a haircut goes wrong; the customer has to wait for the hair to regrow. Restitution is impossible if a train arrives late. The only option is to compensate passengers in some other way. While in many situations a service can be repeated, the repeat service is in fact a new offering, it is not a clone of the original, nor is it a ready-made 'service product' taken out of stock to replace a defective experience. Hopefully any repeat service will be more satisfactory, thus recovering the situation, but the variability of services is the fourth of the important characteristics of services, and there are lessons to be applied to the total offering from considering this aspect in detail.

Heterogeneous services: the need for quality assurance

Every service experience is a new event, and for the customer it is the people who are delivering that service who are usually thought of as the 'supply company'. Every service depends on the context in which it is delivered – time, place and participants. All of these are subject to variability and this inevitably leads to heterogeneity in the service as received by the customer.

At one level this can be a positive opportunity to deliver the most relevant service elements designed to meet a particular combination of circumstances. Adaptation of this sort can be very effective. On another level the variability means that the satisfaction experienced is also variable, with the service delivery sometimes falling short of what is required.

The problem inherent with the first is that it relies entirely on the actual person (front-line employee) providing the service to assess the situation and adapt accordingly. This can be seen in so far as a competent salesperson, perhaps offering financial advice on pensions or life assurance, could have the skills to listen to a customer, identify needs in detail, then deliver a customized response consistent with those needs. This is a situation where the skills and training of the service staff are of a high level, and the supply organization puts full trust in such staff in respect of such variations. There are only a limited number of such skilled personnel.

For the other perspective, many complaints and customer defections are directly blamed on the service experience and the unhelpful attitude of staff. Studies of service industries have shown that in retail, catering, hotel and other such businesses, over 90% of service staff are in so-called 'dead-end' jobs. These are jobs with low basic wages and little prospect of promotion. It is in these areas that it is necessary to try to achieve tight standards covering the levels of reproducible quality for every service occasion. By designing the service with a careful appreciation of its effect on customers, a level of quality assurance can be built in. Often this will involve standardization of actions, and activities aimed at increasing the productivity of the service workers. This is what Levitt (1976) terms the 'industrialization of the service'. In his 1976 article, Levitt explores the British attitude to service, contrasting it with other advanced economies such as the US. He suggests that 'in Britain, to serve is encrusted with master–servant pretensions which block the path to efficiency . . . one person's labour for the benefit of another . . . as long as we think of service as being next to servility; of serving as a synonym for thoughtless obedience; of service as a lower occupation (when it comes to work – butlers, cooks, etc.) or a higher occupation (when it comes to elite professions like the military where the premium is on marshal obedience not on thought or independence) . . . none of the applied rationality that has produced efficiencies in the industrial system will be brought to bear on the retarded maze of inefficiencies in the service sector'.

Of course, much has changed in the last quarter of the 20th century; service provision is more efficient and attitudes have changed. But there is still room for more improvement if the service component of an offering is really to provide both a quality experience and a level of desired customization able to contribute to a real competitive advantage for a particular supplier.

The problem of how to provide an effective service that meets customer needs, but does it in an efficient way, is a major dilemma for all supply organizations. There needs to be a balance between what Drucker (1991) calls qualitative and quantitative activities, and the measures of a service worker will be a mixture of both. Obviously, for a skilled doctor the emphasis will be on customization and effectiveness of their service, for a supermarket checker there is standardization and efficiency. Most jobs fall between these two extremes. The understanding of the variable nature of services, and the appreciation of how a customized service can contribute to the competitive advantage of an offering will be important marketing issues in developing a total product. It is this which moves the consideration of the role of service marketing from the implementation issues of strategy to the earlier strategic planning stage where means of achieving competitive advantage are critical.

It may be possible to offer different levels of service to different categories of customers deliberately. Key prospects, where long-term relationships and greater volume of repeat trade are the aim, could be offered extra services or higher calibre staff with more authority to negotiate and deliver any additional services. However, deliberate planned variability in the actual service activities delivered to each specific customer is a very different thing from the heterogeneity in the way a particular service is performed on each service occasion. The first is positive quality as defined by individually meeting the needs of each and every specific customer or group. The second is negative quality in allowing some service encounters to fall below the best standards. It is the second that is the subject of quality assurance, quality control and measurement such as that using the SERVQUAL survey.

Service quality measurement

SERVQUAL was first mentioned in Chapter 9. It is a multidimensional scale, developed in the 1980s, to measure customer perceptions and evaluations of service offerings. The scale was based on empirical studies within four industries, and the emerging categories have now been reduced to the five most important dimensions:

1. Tangible aspects, e.g. facilities, appearance and equipment
2. Assurance, e.g. knowledge, security, professional credibility
3. Reliability, e.g. ability to perform dependably and accurately
4. Responsiveness, e.g. willingness to help and promptness
5. Empathy, e.g. care, courtesy and attention as perceived.

Two of these, *tangibility* and *assurance*, are elements of an offering that can be considered prior to purchase. They have already been discussed in this chapter. The others, *reliability*, *responsiveness* and *empathy*, are all high in what is termed 'experience properties', attributes that can be judged only after a purchase, or during receipt of a service. This is a major determinant of satisfaction, but because these elements cannot be evaluated before purchase there is a greater need for attention to these properties and their resultant effect. Before a purchase customers might have some views based on their own prior experiences and the evaluation of others, but they are certain to reassess the factors after every experience. This will be done by comparing the expectations with the perceived receipt, as discussed in earlier chapters. The actual model achieves this by using a battery of questions about these two aspects, expectation and perception, within each of the five SERVQUAL categories. It then allows for the results to be compared to a zone of tolerance, which is the acceptable range for each dimension. As a marketing research tool it is an effective measure of satisfaction in each individual category, and it also will highlight possible trade-offs, allowing the exceeding of expectations in one category to be set against a failure to achieve satisfaction in another.

This type of continuous tracking research is an important part of satisfaction measurement. In smaller firms key managers might have regular contact with customers and the first-hand knowledge on which to base future developments. In larger organizations research is needed, together with the internal dissemination of such information. In this way improvements can be planned and implemented.

Experience properties and relationship building

Establishing long-term relationships with chosen customers is, rightly, seen as an important aim of strategic marketing. There will be more discussion of the benefits and costs of relationships in later chapters, but it will be apparent from this chapter that the special characteristics of intangibles require careful and continuous attention if strong links are to evolve. Key to any partnership is the commitment of both parties to develop a relationship, and demonstrating this is an important aspect of building trust in each other for the future. Every contact between supplier and customer is part of this process, and hence any failure to deliver benefits could put a strain on the relationship. The experience properties of an intangible offering, reliability, responsiveness and empathy, are obvious areas where such a strain could arise.

Experience properties are not restricted to services; they can also be identified in many tangible offerings that can only be properly assessed after purchase, but the qualitative nature of intangibles makes both the delivery and the quality control of these attributes more challenging. By accepting the holistic nature of any offering, with both tangible and intangible elements, and realizing that satisfaction is a consumer measure based on experience, it will be seen that attention to service delivery can enhance overall satisfaction, trust and relationships.

Studies underpinning the SERVQUAL work have shown that reliability is the most important aspect in the perception of service quality. It is the ability of a company to deliver against the promises made which is critical; customers want to do business with suppliers who keep their promises, especially the promises about delivery and service, as well as the resulting performance of a total product. In evaluating an offering prior to purchase these promises are vital; after purchase most complaints are based around the failure to deliver as promised. Hence, all organizations must understand the expectations of customers, in particular the way promises are interpreted and reliability is perceived. Customers are not very tolerant of failures regarding promises, and even one slip-up will have an immediate effect on future relationships. A company can build a strong and highly competitive position based on reliability. The example often quoted in this respect is Federal Express. There has to be real achievement if a position is to be attained; it is not much good claiming, as in the case of the UK Royal Mail, that 93% of all first-class letters arrive the next day. Customers are always wondering if their letter will be the one (out of every fourteen) that won't get the service!

It is suggested by Tom Peters (1987) that Federal Express thrives because of its great 'people orientation, matched by equally great support systems'. Failures of reliability can sometimes be traced to poor systems and operations, but in many cases the delivery of promises is totally in the hands of contact employees – the part-time marketers who, during the moments of truth, are so critical to customer satisfaction and marketing success.

This is particularly true with respect to the responsiveness and empathy properties. Contact employees are seen as the supply company, and often relationships are effectively determined by the moments of truth experiences between them and a customer. If the employees pay attention, listen and adapt to the needs of customers, showing a personal willingness to help, then the experience is positive and a relationship can develop and strengthen.

Conclusions

Many lessons have emerged from the development of services marketing over the past decade. However, it is important that these are integrated within, and not seen as a separate part of, strategic marketing. Most offerings are a combination of tangible and intangible features, and customers will evaluate a 'total product' including all the elements involved. The greatest need is for consistency in achieving a seamless balance between all components.

Competitive advantage can come from any of the parts of an offering, but if a synergy exists, the combination will be stronger than the individual parts. In achieving this a study of the intangible, inseparable, perishable and variable aspects of a total offering is necessary.

There is no reason why specific customers cannot be offered individual packages with different levels of support or perhaps with modified or customized elements as part of the basic product. It is easier to modify the service element of an offering because the flexibility can be based on the heterogeneity possible and the inseparability of production and delivery. By evaluating the needs of each chosen customer, or segment, a differentiated offering can be designed which will both reduce the 'distance' between supplier and customer and reflect the differing potential of specific customers. The utilization of intangible components of an offering can enable a greater focus to occur, as well as enabling more of the costly long-term relationship building activities to be targeted at the more attractive (profitable) prospects.

Because of the perishable nature of services, each new service offering is, effectively, a new product. Of course good aspects can and should be retained, but, over time, experience will allow new relevant features to be added and redundant ones to be scrapped. This can be more accurately done with intangibles than with most tangible products, although it requires careful monitoring and effective understanding of customers. Continuous redesigning of an offering means that it can be kept much more up-to-date and appropriate to needs. Long production runs and economies of scale, while financially attractive, can bring about a production orientation into marketing thinking. While it is possible to industrialize a routine service, because of the very nature of an intangible, inseparable offering, it is likely that service components will remain more relevant than mass produced goods.

When customers are dissatisfied with a purchase they could focus on the direct supplier (retailer), indirect supplier (manufacturer) or, sometimes, themselves (buyers). For tangible goods the customer's most direct involvement is in the making of the 'buy/no buy' decision. In this instance the problem is that either the product did not perform as expected, or maybe the purchaser made a poor decision. Sometimes the decision to buy a cheaper, but inferior, product is viewed in this way after the event. However, with services the customer actually has a role in production. Direct influence due to the inseparability could actually result in a poor experience. For instance a haircut or an installation could go wrong because of poor specification by the customer during the delivery of the service. Here it is more likely that a purchaser could feel partially responsible for the problem, and it is noticeable that in these circumstances there are fewer complaints registered. The dilemma for the supplier is that they need to maintain a dialogue with customers, especially in situations where there is some dissatisfaction. In fact, it is good practice to encourage complaints, and by keeping contact to recover the situation. If the customer does not complain, due in part to some feeling of personal guilt, then there is a high probability that they will not return to buy and all further contact will be lost. This makes the quality of the inseparable elements of an offering so critical to an exchange.

Customer satisfaction is determined by promises made and kept, and this requires attention to quality. It is the nature of intangibles which makes their quality more difficult to control. There are many ideas from research of service quality, and in particular the SERVQUAL studies, that are directly relevant to the strategic marketing of all offerings. It is only as a result of good quality experiences that trust is developed between customers and suppliers. Trust leads on to the development of strong relationships, and therefore an understanding of the totality of an offering, including all components, and the application of the lessons from services marketing are crucial to overall competitive success.

KEY POINTS

10.1 An organization does not have to provide everything itself in an attempt to satisfy the needs of its customers. It can work together with other complementary providers to produce a competitive offering. But to do this effectively it is necessary to integrate activities to ensure the customer sees a unified, consistent and relevant offering.

10.2 Every offering is likely to include a mix of tangible goods together with intangibles such as services, and these intangibles are equally important to the total offering. The combination of tangibles and intangibles can be seen on a continuum stretching from commodity product to pure service.

10.3 Four important characteristics of services need to be considered:

- intangibility
- inseparability
- perishability
- heterogeneity.

10.4 Intangibility presents both opportunities and problems for a marketer from the strategic perspective of designing a competitive offering. The advantages are in the use of intangible benefits to develop a unique position in the minds of chosen customers.

10.5 It is the inseparable interactions with customers – the moments of truth – where the service components of an offering are most apparent. The perception created by the service experience is central to the customer evaluation of satisfaction of the whole offering.

10.6   Services exist in 'real time', and are therefore perishable. This brings about two problems. First, and most obvious, is demand management. The second is that once 'lost', the service cannot be resurrected.

10.7   Every service experience is a new event, and, for the customer, it is the people who are delivering that service who are usually thought of as the 'supply company'. Every service depends on the context in which it is delivered – time, place and participants. All of these are subject to variability, and this inevitably leads to heterogeneity in the service as received by the customer.

10.8   It is vital that efforts are made to benefit from the distinct aspect of a service, rather than suffer because of the real problems of maintaining consistent quality. All marketing is aimed at creating and keeping customers, which leads on to the development of relationships.

10.9   Service quality can be measured, and continuous tracking is an important part of satisfaction measurement.

10.10 Studies underpinning the SERVQUAL work have shown that reliability is the most important aspect in the perception of service quality. It is the ability of a company to deliver against the promises made which is critical; customers want to do business with suppliers who keep their promises, especially the promises about delivery and service, as well as the resulting performance of a total product. In evaluating an offering prior to purchase these promises are vital. After purchase most complaints are based around the failure to deliver as promised. Hence all organizations must understand the expectations of customers, in particular the way promises are interpreted and reliability is perceived.

QUESTIONS

10.1   In what ways can the service elements of a product offering contribute towards a *sustainable competitive advantage* for that offering?

10.2   Reliability has been shown to be the most important aspect of service quality. How might a supplier ensure that it keeps its service promises?

10.3   What is a *'moment of truth'*? Why are such moments vital to successful marketing?

10.4   How can the use of *tangible* cues help to reassure customers and thus remove some of the risks inherent with the purchase of services?

Bibliography

Bitner, M.J., Managing the Evidence of Service, in E.E. Scheuing and W.F. Christopher (Eds) *The Service Quality Handbook*, AMACOM Press, pp. 358–370, 1993.

Booms, B.H. and Bitner, M.J., Marketing Strategies and Organisational Structures, in J. Donnelly and W. George (Eds) *The Marketing of Services*, American Marketing Association, 1981.

Carlzon, J., *The Moments of Truth*, Ballinger, 1987.

Cooper, R.G. and Kleinschmidt, E.J., Screening New Products for Potential Winners, *Long Range Planning*, Vol. 26, 1993.

Davies, A., *The Strategic Role of Marketing*, McGraw-Hill, 1995.

Grönroos, C., Marketing Redefined, *Management Decisions*, Vol. 28 No. 8, pp. 5–9, 1990.

Gummesson, E., Marketing Orientation Re-visited, the Crucial Role of the Part Time Marketer, *European Journal of Marketing*, Vol. 25 No. 2, pp. 60–75, 1991.

Hamel, G. and Prahalad, C.K., *Competing for the Future*, HBS Press, 1994.

Hooley, G. and Saunders, J., *Competitive Positioning*, Prentice Hall, 1993.

Jones, T.O. and Sasser, W.E., Why Satisfied Customers Defect, *Harvard Business Review*, Nov./Dec., 1995.

Kotler, P., *Marketing Management: Analysis, Planning and Control*, Prentice Hall, 1997.

Levitt, T., Marketing Myopia, *Harvard Business Review*, July/Aug., No. 4, 1969.

Levitt, T., Marketing Myopia 1975: Retrospective Commentary, *Harvard Business Review*, Sept./Oct., No. 5, 1975.

Levitt, T., The Industrialization of Services, *Harvard Business Review*, Sept./Oct., No. 5, 1976.

Levitt, T., Marketing Intangibles and Product Intangibles, *Harvard Business Review*, May/June, No. 3, 1981.

Mathur, S.S., Talking Straight about Competitive Strategy, *Journal of Marketing Management*, Vol. 8, pp. 199–217, 1997.

Murray, J.A. and O'Driscoll, A., *Strategy and Process in Marketing*, Prentice Hall, 1996.

Parasuraman, A., Zeithmal, V.A. and Berry, L.L., SERVQUAL Scale for Measuring Consumer Perceptions of Service Quality, *Journal of Retailing*, Vol. 64 No. 1, 1988.

Peters, T., *Thriving on Chaos*, Macmillan, 1987.

Quinn, J.B., Doorley, T.L. and Paquette, P.C., Beyond Products: Service Based Strategy, *Harvard Business Review*, March/Apr., No. 2, 1990.

Shostack, G.L., Breaking Free from Product Marketing, *Journal of Marketing*, Vol. 41, April, pp. 73–80, 1977.

Zeithaml, V.A. and Bitner, M.J., *Services Marketing*, McGraw-Hill, 1996.

BUILDING STRONG BRANDS

CHAPTER 11

INTRODUCTION

Strategic marketing is about where, how and when to compete. Having decided upon a target group of customers it is important to give them reasons for the choice of a specific company's product offering. If an offering is perceived as similar to competitive products then, logic suggests, people are likely to choose the cheapest. However, there are many examples of two apparently identical products where buyers are willing to pay considerably more for one offering. An example of this from the US, reported by Bird (1998), tells of the Mitsubishi Eclipse and the Plymouth Laser, made in the same factory and identical except for the badges. The Eclipse outsold the Laser fivefold and even when the Laser was reduced in price it still didn't sell well. In fact the UK market for 'people carriers' shows a similar phenomenon with the production similarities between the VW Sharan and the Ford Galaxy, and between the Peugeot 806 and Fiat's Ulysses, where similarity in product contrasts with differences in image.

Of course there are many differences that can be exploited, such as the addition of desirable service features, or the closeness of links between supplier and customer, or even the perception of quality with respect to customer expectations. The value of these is dependent upon their importance to the customer.

It is quite common to hear marketing managers ask 'what does the customer think?' but they often go further when attempting to understand the particular points of leverage by trying to establish the image or position of their offering, or, more specifically, which Unique Selling Proposition (USP) will give the greatest advantage.

Don Cowley (1996) suggests that image and position are 'fat' words covering a multitude of meanings. The terms can be made to mean whatever the speaker wants them to mean. He criticizes the lack of precision in such concepts. This does not negate the usefulness of debate on these topics as marketing is a qualitative function and competitive advantage often relies on psychological rather than hard economic factors. It could be argued that marketing is about moving a purchase evaluation away from the rational economic base – what Doyle (1994) described as decommoditizing, that is creating non-economic reasons for purchase.

The total offering was defined in Chapter 4 as 'everything, both favourable and unfavourable, that is received in an exchange'. The offering is, therefore, a multidimensional concept and should not be confused with a simple commodity. The idea of a 'product' as being *naked*, without the totality of an offering, is also useful, especially if it is understood that much of the *clothing* will be provided by the customer. Image and positioning are outcomes of customer perception, and alongside these there is the complementary concept of a brand, which is derived from customers' attitudes towards specific products offerings and the values they ascribe to them.

The term 'brand' is used in many ways. So what is, and is not, a brand? A brand is not a product that just happens to have a high awareness, nor is it even a recognizable name or logo, although both of these are often present. A brand is so much more; it is a powerful stimulus that conjures up a complex image and level of expectation about itself, and what it can do for a consumer. Bird (1998) described a brand as 'intangible, magic, mysterious – but enormously powerful'. When compared to a 'product' we can see the contrasts listed in Table 11.1.

Table 11.1 Brand and product compared

The brand	The product
Emotional	Phlegmatic
Irrational	Rational
Intangible	Tangible
Values, attitudes, beliefs	Feature, benefits, advantages
Symbolic	Functional

The brand is the link which Cowley claims 'patrols the boundary between people (consumers) and the world outside'. Kotler (1997) suggests a brand is 'A name, term, sign, symbol, or design, or a combination of them, intended to identify the goods or services of one seller or group of sellers and to differentiate them from those of competitors'. This definition covers the more tangible attributes of the brand, and also refers to the brand's purpose as a means of differentiation. But it is too mechanistic to uncover the brand's complexity, as an intangible, largely irrational and emotional influence.

Brands do not have a physical presence; they are a paradox. As Paul Feldwick (1996) affirms 'a brand may have a personality but it is not a person. You cannot talk to it and it cannot answer back. In fact it has no absolute or objective existence'. So what is a brand? I would suggest it is effectively a mass of values, images, promises and attitudes all brought together, but perceived in terms of a meaningful whole rather than in elements or parts. The resulting integration is then considered by consumers against a background of individual experience, knowledge, prejudice and, importantly, the marketing input aimed at enhancing the attributes of a specific offering.

Brands are not confined to consumer markets but are equally important in business to business and service markets. A strategy based on a strong brand is likely to be sustainable because it creates competition barriers impossible for others to copy. However, the actual brand is shaped by the customer's mind, by the environment and perhaps by society in general, although no universally accepted definition has yet been agreed. In comparison with human psychology, the study of what makes a brand tick is in its infancy. John Murphy (1988), founder of Interbrand, refers to the work of Gestalt psychologists who argue that:

> nothing is simply the sum of its individual parts . . . A baby does not initially understand that the shapes it sees around it are people. Once it does, however, it is able to take scraps of information (a brief glimpse of a hand, or the smell of a particular fragrance) and conjure up . . . an overall form (a gestalt) . . . A brand acts as a gestalt in that it is a concept which is more than the sum of its parts and which takes a long time to establish in the minds of consumers.

[The German word *Gestalt* is sometimes translated as configuration, pattern or form.]

When considering the development of brands and any ensuing brand loyalty, a similarly complex relationship emerges. Brand equity builds up slowly over time and comes to fruition only when all conditions are complementary, and all components are perceived by a customer as mutually supportive within an overall entity. There are classic examples of brands that have become generic, synonymous with their product class, but there are even more where the brand seems to be hardly anything greater than a name without any accompanying personality. In both of these situations there is a problem with the 'brand name' failing to offer real benefits to either supplier or customer. A name is not enough to add excitement and value to a product, nor can it help buyers to easily identify with a particular offering that could be relied upon to meet their defined needs.

In the first case, generic brands such as Hoover, Thermos and Walkman have developed beyond a single brand and now are synonymous with the total product class. We don't hear of a Hoover hoover, or the original (and still the best) vacuum cleaner, but we might hear an Electrolux called a Hoover! The Hoover brand values have been dissipated so that now the identification of particular products (models) with specific attributes is extremely weak. This is, perhaps, more worrying for the owners of generic brands than in the second case where no personality has yet emerged. It is possible that there could be opportunities to build the levels of *awareness* and the strength of *image* for an anonymous brand. This will move it through the stages of *recognition* to a *strong devotion/loyalty*. Such developments can be seen on a basic brand life cycle diagram, which is similar, but not identical in time, to the much abused product life cycle (Figure 11.1).

A brand follows a life cycle, intrinsically linked to other cycles such as the demand–technology–product life cycles in Chapter 4 (see Figure 4.2).

When a brand reaches the 'acceptance' stage it is likely to have achieved high awareness and, probably, has become the preferred choice for some purchasers. At

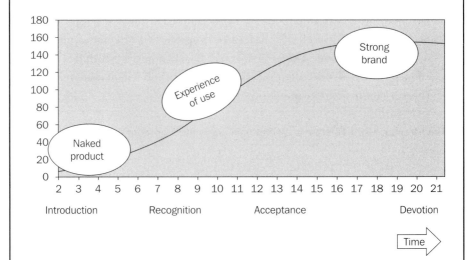

Fig 11.1 The brand development life cycle

the 'devotion' stage loyalty has developed. A major role of competitive marketing must be to help to develop acceptance and loyalty for a given brand, because if customers perceive that a brand offers greater benefits then it is more likely they will buy it and, perhaps, they may pay more for it. This depends upon the *emotional distance* between a consumer and an offering, and the intensity of feelings that determine the power of the brand as a valuable motivator in the purchase situation.

Returning briefly to psychology, there has been much debate between the Gestalt school and others on the so-called stimulus–response theory of behaviour. Traditional transactional marketing relies on the use of stimuli, but in marketing, as in psychology, this is a simplistic view of a situation. Of course there are situations where a powerful promotional marketing stimulus can trigger a purchase response. There is a role for this at one end of the marketing spectrum. It is at the other extreme where branding operates; this is where customers provide their own motivations, seeking out offerings which they perceive as relevant to their needs, and in which they have real confidence. Consideration of this leads on to the study of the importance of the emotional values that can be part of a brand.

The most common measures of brand strength are *brand awareness, brand image, brand loyalty* and *brand values.* The first, awareness, is a relevant but simplistic measure. If a chosen customer is unaware of the brand, either prompted or after some prompting, then there is a basic opportunity to inform, build knowledge and maybe then to capitalize on a widening of the potential customer base. However, this measure is of little value when used in connection with well-established brands with high awareness ratings. In these situations the basic fact that customers know our brand is taken for granted; what is important is what they know, what they think about the brand, and how they behave in a purchase situation.

The components of brand image, and a consideration of how loyalty and value occur, will be discussed in later sections of the chapter, as will some of the actions required to build a strong brand.

The benefits of branding

There is a feeling among many managers that the ability of most companies to copy the tangible aspects of competitors' actions, such as production methods or application of technology, and to replicate service levels will mean that these areas offer little in the way of sustainable competitive advantage. A brand, however, is an intangible which develops out of exchanges with customers, and is impossible for competitors to copy. It is therefore able to distinguish a specific offer, separating it from others in the same product class.

Most studies of branding consider the benefits from the position of the brand owner. There is often an assumption that a well-established brand will produce loyal regular purchases, generating a desirable revenue stream. However, a brand is an identifier and a differentiator, not a guarantee of loyal customers. It is necessary to separate successful brands, ones which have high customer demand, from less successful ones. Success can be measured crudely by the level of customer demand, or more qualitatively by dimensions such as *salience*, which is a term used to describe the level of importance of a brand for a chosen group of customers. Salience is more than any single measure; it relies on all the different aspects of performance and brand strength.

If branding is considered from the position of a potential customer it can be seen as a way of helping buyers to choose between different offerings, and to determine those that best meet given needs. The ability to identify a particular brand thus makes the purchase decision quicker and easier, and it gives some reassurance by reducing the risk of an unfamiliar selection. To quote again from Bird, 'a brand and its image come about as a result of countless tiny things – from what your stationery looks like to the language you use in your recruitment ads'. The perceived attributes of a brand are brought together to form a pattern in the mind of a customer, the Gestalt, and are then utilized to assist that customer in a purchase situation. In some circumstances the benefits go further by offering psychological rewards to buyers in the post-purchase period. These come from the outward statements such as the ownership of a VW Golf car, or the wearing of some designer label clothing, or being seen consuming a recognizable brand of drink.

Brands are particularly useful to customers when considering many of the low-involvement purchases made on a regular basis. In these situations the brand acts as a reassuring 'shorthand' about an offering, often based on satisfactory past experience. This relates to straight rebuy purchases, including many fast-moving consumer goods, which meet specific needs, but which do not warrant a detailed search/evaluation on every purchase occasion.

Brands can also act as a major encouragement for more expensive *shopping* purchases due to the perceptions that develop about them. A brand could have developed an image based on many inputs over an extended time period. This image cannot be ignored by the customer and it will subjectively affect the evaluation of any offering even if it is not an entirely accurate view of the particular product. A positive image is of course a major competitive advantage. Wendy Gordon (1996) tackled the complexity of developing brand image, suggesting:

> It may seem strange to think of brands as existing *only* in consumers' heads. . . . Although the manufacturer or service company is able to change the nature of the product itself, its distribution and presentation, the *added value* the brand has (functional and non-functional) are built in the minds of consumers. New entrants to established product categories require an enormous financial investment to build these values, which ensure that a target group of consumers are able to share a similar pattern of specific belief systems about a brand.

Of course the brand as a barrier to entry depends on positive attributes and associations. There are examples of brands that have achieved high levels of awareness but suffer from unwanted reputations or unappealing images. These *negative* brands are a liability, deterring customers and adversely affecting sales.

The long-term effect of a good or bad brand image can influence potential purchasers over a considerable period of time. Many young people aspire to the positive image of a Porsche or a Jaguar well before they can afford such a purchase. They perceive the positive or negative benefits from ownership, including psychological benefits. When they reach a position where such a product is affordable there is a strong bias towards a given attractive brand, and against a less desirable one.

In the UK it was considered very brave, if not foolhardy, for the Volkswagen company to maintain the Skoda brand name when it bought the Czech car company. Neil Denny (1995) described Skoda as 'the brand from Hell!'. However, if the total potential market were explored it would be discovered that in much of mainland Europe Skoda has quite a good image based on engineering, which is not affected by the negative associations prevalent in Britain. In this case a decision was taken that considered all possible market opportunities and not one based on a small specific group of customers. (To be fair, it was also a condition set in the original purchase agreement because the Czech government wished to maintain a branded car business and did not want to be a subcontract manufacturer to a powerful Western operation.)

The benefits to a supplier derived from ownership of a strong brand are obvious; if it is valued by their customers then this is an asset that can be exploited. The exploitation could come from the ability to charge higher prices, or from one of two other ways of utilizing the leverage in the brand. The first requires building on the resulting loyalty to achieve higher sales and higher market share. The second involves the appropriate extension of the brand name across other offerings, and including new products, thus using the positive attributes to extend into new product/market areas.

Brand extension is the use of a strong brand name for other product offerings. The major advantage is that it transfers the positive attributes to the new offering, thus developing customer confidence and achieving early recognition. Achieving *aware-ness* and then *trial* are critical to the success of a new consumer product and there is no doubt that utilizing an established, strong and relevant brand name helps in this respect. It can also assist in obtaining entry to distribution channels and in produc-ing some economies of scale in promotion and advertising. However, there are risks involved. One is that it might confuse customers as to the important attributes of the brand image, another that a poor product could, by association, damage the original offering. There is a link between the pros and cons of brand extension and the role and use of 'umbrella' brand names which encompass a range of prod-ucts. This is considered in the next section.

Returning to the issues of loyalty and market share, these are measures of sales per-formance and not intrinsic elements of a brand. Ehrenberg *et al.* (1990) warn of what is termed the 'double jeopardy' effect, which links awareness and loyalty with mar-ket share. Their research shows that brands with lower levels of awareness tend also to suffer because they often have lower rates of repeat purchase too. The combina-tion of these two results in a dramatic drop in market share. The converse is also true, with high scores giving rise to very high market share. Achieving small improvements in each of the measures will have a very significant effect on sales lev-els. Evidence from the massive PIMS database shows that higher share means disproportionately greater returns on investments (ROI). Buzzell and Gale (1987) report that a brand with a dominant 40% share generates an ROI some three times higher compared to one with a 10% share. The absolute level of profit is, on average, some six to eight times larger, showing the benefit of reaching such a large critical mass of sales in one market. If this profitability evidence is linked to the low share, double jeopardy, effect then an even greater imbalance occurs.

This evaluation shows the benefit of focusing on a target market, and practising niche branding. A brand with a strong presence, and high share of a small market might have lower total sales than one with a small share of a much larger market. However, the niche operator is usually considerably more profitable in the short term, and more able to defend its market position in the long term. The outcome is also reflected in a strong brand image closely associated with the target market. This compares with a weaker image and position for the offering with a low share of a large market.

For a brand to be considered as an asset it must have a high level of awareness in the chosen target market, and must offer buyers relevant product attributes together with some form of added value which is perceived as desirable in meeting the psy-chological needs of these customers.

There is a dilemma for multinational companies relating to the advantages of global brands as compared to local ones. A global brand would typically have an identical formula, packaging and positioning *everywhere*. Some of these globalization issues have already been considered in Chapter 5. A short while ago it was reported that the Unilever group had a different product shape for its Walls Cornetto ice cream in each of the 15 European countries. It did, however, have a consistent position in these markets. Usually global brands are most appropriate in either:

- Mass markets: typified by high volume, basic quality and low margins
- Niche markets: where geographic factors are irrelevant, but which have high added value and high margins, though usually medium volume.

With increasing international travel and communications, global brands must be as near standard as possible. Confusion in product specification, or in brand name, will always be found out and any inconsistencies punished by customers. Local brands are ones tailored to specific or regional tastes. While local brands may not obtain the economies of scale or achieve the high recognition of global offerings, it is easy for them to benefit from a high awareness within a specific local target market.

Levels of branding and brand image

When a strong brand exists it is best encapsulated as a 'name, term, sign, symbol, or design' as defined by Kotler. It is this that acts as a focus for customers, and easy identification is a distinct advantage. Frequently an individual brand name is linked with another name or symbol such as a company logo or range name. Linking two such identifiers together is effective if both enjoy similar images, and if the additional name does not bring any undesirable associations with it.

While I was the marketing manager for the Chivers and Hartley range of jam and marmalade, then owned by Cadbury Schweppes, there was a move to bring all products together under the umbrella Cadbury brand. Research was undertaken on 'Cadbury's New Jam' and 'Cadbury's Olde English Marmalade' (replacing Chivers). The results were extremely negative in spite of the good associations of the Cadbury name. It was seen as a chocolate heritage, which spoilt, rather than enhanced, jams and marmalade. The association with the Cadbury name would have harmed the established brands and, sensibly, no change was undertaken.

There are three levels of brand names that have to be considered.

1. Individual brand names, such as Ariel, Persil, Snickers or Flora.
2. Range branding, such as Weight Watchers or Panasonic
3. Company/corporate brands, such as Ford, Black & Decker or Tesco.

The last two, range and company (or house brands), can be seen as interchangeable umbrellas for groups of brands if there is only one company range, but they can be combined in considering, say, the range of Ford Fiestas.

The choice of name, or names, is a key marketing decision for a supplier. While the brand develops in the mind of the customer, the actual name is supplied to them. Therefore great care is necessary when trying to obtain the maximum benefits from the branding. If an umbrella brand name is to be used it is important to consider all other offerings which share that name. An umbrella branding strategy works if all products within the range share some attribute or image as this provides a logical link between members, thus giving a reason for the existence and a promotional focus for the whole group.

Brand image is a composite, made up of a number of elements. The most obvious are *brand personality*, *usage occasion* and *user image*. Each of these can provide a logical basis to integrate a range of products. A range based on complementary brand personalities will include offerings sharing images that support each other, thus reinforcing the overall grouping. The range can then be developed on the basis of similar psychological benefits for customers. Any offering that does not fit will stand out, and its presence will harm the whole range. Examples are high-performance cars such as the BMW series benefiting from the BMW umbrella, or Cadbury's Dairy Milk and Cadbury's Drinking Chocolate enhancing the range, whereas Cadbury's New Jam has no similar advantage.

A related dimension of brand image is the occasion when a product or range is used. Kelloggs breakfast cereals are an obvious example. This range includes products for all types of users from children through to healthy-eating adults. Both personality and usage occasion can be considered as a basis of brand image differentiation and it is important that none of the individual brands in an umbrella range show such differences.

The final element of a brand's image relates to the consumer. This can also be exploited with an umbrella branding strategy which includes a number of offerings each aimed at a similar target group, for instance De Walt professional power tools for construction workers or St Ivel Shape for calorie counting consumers. For a range based on the user there is often a heavy emphasis on the umbrella name and its personality rather than the individual offering. The specific products could be identified by a generic description, e.g. Shape yogurt and Shape cottage cheese, thus allowing the promotional emphasis to focus on the common benefits of the overall range.

Brand extension is a controversial subject with uncertainty over the benefits to the new offering and the risks to the basic brand. Of course the extending of a strong brand name to a new offering does help in building awareness and trial, but only in those areas where knowledge of the host brand is already established. For a new offering to *existing* customers (same target market) there is experience through use. The original brand might also be known, although with fewer positive attributes, to the *expanded* market currently buying from our competitors. When *extending* into new segments there is no guarantee that the host brand name is known and, even if it is, it will be necessary to research the image and associations, both positive and negative, before any decision to widen the use of that name.

It was recently reported that the Virgin Group of companies has decided not to put its familiar red logo onto jeans and other clothing, an area where it is planning to expand, competing with Levi and Wrangler. A spokesperson for Virgin said 'It was clear when we did our research that the garish Virgin logo would not appeal. It was inappropriate in a fashion environment. People didn't want it in your face all over the place'. In fact, the extending of the Virgin Group has been one of the success stories of the past two decades, but it is now being asked whether the Group has extended too far, with poor performances from Virgin cola and Virgin vodka, as well as bad publicity for Virgin trains.

It will be obvious that many brand extensions are best handled within a strategy of umbrella/range branding which allows the similarities or differences in both personality and target market to be accommodated. The problems come when moving beyond the reasonable limits of a range or company name. Marks & Spencer has successfully entered the financial services market; it will be interesting to watch the progress of Sainsbury's, BMW and Virgin in their expansion into this market.

Researching a brand's personality could reveal unusual opportunities for developments. An example is qualitative research, using projective techniques, conducted by HP Bulmer, the largest cider maker in the UK, into the personality of the Bulmer company brand. The description of 'Mr Bulmer' as an honest countryman who offered good quality traditional products was seen as consistent with extensions into such products as garden centres and English country holidays. These could have been interesting but were considered outside the competence of the company, where the Board of Directors were looking to increase the portfolio of alcoholic drinks. The only positive association with a new alcoholic product was fruit wines, but it was decided to restrict developments to the traditional cider. A number of new ciders were developed and launched, including Bulmer's Original Cider (established 1887), which was actually launched much more recently, but borrowed from traditions and the image of 'Mr Bulmer'. At the same time moves were made into other alcoholic products, but all used separate branding. More recently new, modern, cider brands such as Strongbow Ice have been successfully launched into new market segments. One product, White Lightning, is associated with a subsidiary company, Inch's, rejecting the traditional Bulmer house name.

Creating successful brands

The possibility for new brand extensions is only one issue within the effective management of individual brands and umbrella ranges. The central question is how to build and sustain strong positive brand image, and how to translate this 'asset' into profitable sales. If a brand already has a strong image this will continue over a long period of time, even after changes have taken place, because past associations decay very slowly. Generally this is an advantage if it leads to a strong reason energizing a customer to buy. It can also be a problem when a negative image has to be improved or dispelled.

The salient features of a brand, positive or negative, are those that are important to the chosen customer. They develop over time from the complex interactions of past and present experience and messages, and expectations as to future developments. It is the combination of these that is represented by the brand, and which should make it the primary source of competitive advantage. These aspects of the brand should form the basis for communication between supplier and customer. Aaker (1995) argues that 'too often the brand message is weak, confused, irrelevant or worst of all indistinguishable from competitive offerings'.

The brand message is much wider than advertising. It includes everything a customer experiences related to a brand. Doyle (1994) states that 'Brands are rarely created by advertising. This is often misunderstood because the advertising is generally much more visible than the factors which create the differential advantage'. Advertising boss Gary Duckworth (1996) explains this, suggesting 'Once you understand a brand as a collection of meanings commonly held by human beings, and that these meanings affect people's purchasing behaviour, the part that advertising can play in the fortunes of a brand becomes clear. The role of advertising is to *manipulate* the meanings connected with the brand to the brand owner's advantage'. This illustrates the role of advertising in informing, persuading and perhaps reinforcing attitudes and beliefs.

A brand will develop as a result of direct and indirect input from the brand owner/supplier, together with input from the customers themselves. If a brand is considered over time these inputs and the influence they have can be studied. Figure 11.2 describes the development from a *naked product* to a *brand*.

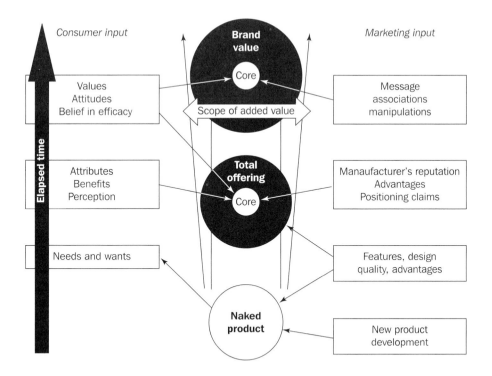

Fig 11.2 Brand development.
Source: Adapted from de Chernatony and McDonald (1994)

This diagram gives clues about how to build a successful brand, one where con-sumers believe in its efficacy and customers will purchase it in preference to competition. At the development stage it is essential to understand fully customers' needs and wants, then to build these into the features and design of the naked prod-uct. Selnes (1993) looked at the links between product performance, brand reputation and loyalty. He found direct links in all areas and this emphasizes the need for attention to the different dimensions of quality (see Chapter 9), which is vital at the design stage.

Following the initial trial of an offering, every customer will shape their own percep-tions, but these can be influenced by the addition of added-value features, tangible or intangible, developed to augment the offering. Any claims as to the brand posi-tioning will be evaluated by the customer but it is important that the supplier ensures this assessment is made with all the appropriate facts available in order to help its case. Joachimsthaler and Aaker (1997) go further, suggesting the direct involvement of customers in various brand-building activities. They look at creating brands without mass media but with the creation of relationship activities such as the Cadbury World theme attraction in Birmingham. Marketing input will be based on measurements of customer satisfaction and then creating and communicating added benefits which meet or exceed expectations. Effective achievement in this respect enhances the developing reputation of a brand.

As time goes on customers will evaluate their experiences when using an offering, together with any new claims, and they will form even stronger views about the brand. In this dynamic situation, brand owners must manage all the messages, or, as Duckworth (1996) suggests, manipulate them to achieve the best input. Manipulation has all sorts of unethical undertones and, even the new in-word 'spin' seems a little problematic. The task is to assess what really matters to customers and consumers and then to ensure a high level of consistency in every action. Messages must be strong, simple, relevant and distinguishable from competitors, thus meeting Aaker's criticism of some marketing effort.

If these messages are consistent with customers' experience, then the reputation of a brand will increase, and, as shown by Selnes (1993), a good brand reputation has a positive effect on purchase loyalty.

The seven golden rules of brand development are:

1. Understand the customer's activities
2. Offer a quality product
3. Maintain a relevant, distinctive position with appropriate added-value
4. Utilize powerful and influential communication
5. Consider all ways of involving customers
6. Be consistent in *all* messages and actions
7. Allow time for developments.

Conclusions

A brand can be identified by a recognizable name or symbol but it is far more than that as a name alone cannot energize the emotions of customers nor stimulate them to buy. Every mature brand is built from a mass of values, promises and experiences which customers bring together as a Gestalt or whole, but while it still has many facets it never develops a physical presence. It remains an intangible image 'gifted' to a company by its consumers, and exists only because it fulfils a need to give substance to a distinctive position. But while a brand is a complex outcome of customer assessments, the marketing input that offers some of the critical components of a brand is supplied by the brand owner and requires careful management and promotion to achieve the maximum value possible.

If a brand develops a strong, positive image then there is evidence that its reputation will have a real effect on the customer's decision to buy that offering. Negative images have the opposite effect, deterring purchases. In addition to the benefits that customers receive from their attitude and knowledge of a brand during a buying occasion, they can also achieve extra psychological enjoyment after a purchase from the actual ownership and use of a specific, desirable brand.

For a supplier the benefits of owning a strong brand are now being calculated so that the 'asset' can be added to the company balance sheet. Obviously, brands are major assets because they are symbols of future sales potential and they reflect the powerful emotional links between an offering and potential customers.

The role of marketing is to manage a company's input into the brand development process so that new brands are nurtured and established brands continue to be relevant in dynamic markets. Every action of a supplier and all the messages received are seen by their customers as an input to the process, and these customers are not selective between planned events and unplanned contacts. One of the most important marketing tasks is to try to ensure consistency in all exchanges, but it is possible to go a little further by using communications and relationship-building activity to influence (manipulate) attitudes, the objective being to develop a naked product into a competitive brand offering.

Often the first decision made involves the name, or combination of names, to be used. If an umbrella name is utilized then the whole range will profit from internal consistency and the mutual support from other brands in the same range. This same thinking can also be applied to the debate on brand extensions. Where similarities exist either with the basis of competitive advantage or the target market then range names are appropriate for the new offerings because of the need to achieve initial awareness and trial. If no such similarities are present then there is a real risk that extending the range will dilute the salience of the original brand by dissipating its core values.

An established brand is such a valuable asset that it requires extraordinary marketing care in its maintenance and development. There are examples of once great brands that have now lost much of their meaning to customers. For example it is often thought that Pierre Cardin extended its range too far. It is crucial that a brand's personality should be fully understood so that careful additions of new offerings can be made to actually reinforce the meanings and associations that are at the heart of brand values.

KEY POINTS

11.1   If we start thinking of a product as being *naked*, without any discernible image, it is then possible to see it as being *clothed* – with much of that clothing being supplied by the customers, who make a major contribution towards the brand image.

11.2   A brand is a powerful stimulus that conjures up a complex image and level of expectation about itself, and what it can do for a consumer. It is not a product that just happens to have a high awareness, nor is it even a recognizable name or logo, although both of these are often present.

11.3   A brand is the link which 'patrols the boundary between people (consumers) and the world outside'. But although a brand may have a personality 'it is not a person. You cannot talk to it and it cannot answer back. In fact it has no absolute or objective existence'.

11.4   Brand development follows a type of life cycle:

introduction–recognition–acceptance–devotion. But it is a function of both marketing and customer input.

11.5   Strong brands are a source of sustainable competitive advantage. They are important as a way of helping buyers choose and they can offer real intangible benefits to customers.

11.6   Brands are (customer-based) assets which can be 'exploited' by the brand owner, both to further develop existing products and as a basis for assisting entry into new areas.

11.7   There are three levels of brand names that have to be considered: individual brand names, range brands and company/corporate branding.

11.8   Brand building requires a *quality* product, *consistency* in input and *time* for development.

QUESTIONS

11.1 Explain why brand development requires input from both marketers and consumers.

11.2 Are there any disadvantages in having a well-known brand name?

11.3 What is salience? How is this important in measuring a brand's value?

11.4 A brand is an asset for a brand owner. It might even figure on the balance sheet. How can a brand owner obtain a 'return' on this asset?

Bibliography

Aaker, D.A., *Strategic Market Management*, 4th Edn, Wiley, 1995.

Bird, D., Direct Mail Can Build a Brand, *Marketing Business*, May, 1998.

Buzzell, R.D. and Gale, B.T., *The PIMS Principles: Linking Strategy to Performance*, Macmillan, 1987.

Cowley, D. (Ed.) *Understanding Brands*, Kogan Page, 1996.

de Chernatony, L. and McDonald, M.H.B., Creating Powerful Brands, Butterworth Heinemann, 1994.

Denny, N., Could Skoda Still Have the Last Laugh?, *Marketing*, 4 May, 1995.

Doyle, P., Branding, in M.J. Baker (Ed.) *The Marketing Book*, Butterworth Heinemann/CIM, 1994.

Doyle, P., *Marketing Management and Strategy*, 2nd Edn, Prentice Hall, 1998.

Duckworth, G., in Cowley, D. (Ed.) *Understanding Brands*, Kogan Page, 1996.

Ehrenberg, A.S.C., Goodhart, G.J. and Barwise, T.P., Double Jeopardy Revisited, *Journal of Marketing*, July, 1990.

Feldwick, P., in Cowley, D. (Ed.) *Understanding Brands*, Kogan Page, 1996.

Gordon, W., in Cowley, D. (Ed.) *Understanding Brands*, Kogan Page, 1996.

Joachimsthaler, E. and Aaker, D.A., Building Brands without Mass Media, *Harvard Business Review*, Jan./Feb., 1997.

Kotler, P., *Marketing Management: Analysis, Planning, Implementation and Control*, Prentice Hall, 1997.

Levitt, T., Differentiation – of Anything, in *The Marketing Imagination*, Free Press, 1983.

Murphy, J., Branding, *Marketing Intelligence and Planning*, Vol. 6 No. 4, pp. 4–8, 1988.

Murphy, J., *Branding: A Key Marketing Tool*, Macmillan, 1992.

Selnes, F., An Examination of the Effect of Product Performance on Brand Reputation, Satisfaction and Loyalty, *European Journal of Marketing*, Vol. 27 No. 9, pp. 19–35, 1993.

CHANNEL MANAGEMENT AND VALUE-ADDED RELATIONSHIPS

CHAPTER

12

INTRODUCTION

The search for competitive advantage involves offering superior value to customers. In Chapter 8 three routes leading to advantage were suggested:

- high perceived value
- low delivered costs
- specific focus.

The perceived value will come from the basic offering, its quality and, particularly, the intangible additions of the support activities. Customers will bring all these aspects together when evaluating the positioning of an offering, and one of the outputs could be a brand perceived by those customers as having both attractive and desirable characteristics.

In addition to the attributes that make an offering acceptable to customers, value can also come as a result of the way it is made accessible to the selected segment. Obviously this includes the customer's expenses in acquiring a product, in particular the exchange delivery costs, where low direct costs lead to enhanced value. These benefits can also be increased by the addition of services offered at the distribution point from which the product is received. Such support could be provided by an independent distributor or a local outlet of the production company or, in the case of service products, the actual service deliverer. It is quite common with physical goods for a local base to be established close to the actual customers and to be used to provide a specialist service. In the case of intangibles, it will be obvious from Chapter 10 that closeness to customers and, usually, a degree of direct personal interaction has to exist. In fact the prime role of good distribution should be to enhance the focus felt by customers by reducing the emotional and physical distance between supplier and customer, as well as achieving advantage by lowering the delivered costs. This is consistent with the traditional view of channel management as the control of the conduit through which a product is offered on to the eventual consumer. However, a reappraisal of the role will recognize the real benefits to all parties that can accrue from effective channel linkages. In some instances it is still correct to consider distributors as customers, but it can be a great deal more rewarding to work with them as partners.

A product that is sold to a wholesaler may have some core similarities to that sold on to a retailer and that bought by a consumer, but in reality they are very different offerings. In building strong distribution partnerships it is important to appreciate these differences. Consider a food product, say a jar of coffee, maybe from a well-known supplier. Wholesalers, such as Spar, will buy in large quantities. They require a brand which will create a fast stock turnover in the warehouse, and which also comes in full containers from the manufacturer but is conveniently packed for the wholesaler's specialist role of breaking bulk and sorting stock. The benefits sought by Spar have nothing to do with the coffee except as a component in a complex range aimed at maximizing profit through the skills of a wholesale operator in handling and dividing shipments. These benefits are delivered through efficient logistics and can be increased by the supplier paying attention to the ease of handling of the outer packaging. As an independent organization, Spar requires some means of achieving its corporate objectives; Spar does not view itself simply as a link between manufacturer and final consumer.

A small independent retailer, say one committed voluntarily to purchase from Spar, will put priorities on some alternative benefits, and will want to receive them from both manufacturer and distributor. Attractive packs that fit well on the shelves are important as this helps to maximize the use of shelf space achieved through regular sales and replenishment of successful fast-moving consumer goods.

Prior to reaching the retailer the offering is not really a consumer product; rather, it is more akin to an industrial component with service activities designed to support that role. The first time the coffee itself, its taste and the quality of the roasting process, become important is with the customer who purchases from the retail shop and who will have direct personal contact with, or actually be, the final consumer.

All of the above exchanges are irrevocably linked, and the effect of consumer demand creating a volatile, derived, demand further up the distribution channel does illustrate why close relationships involving all channel members are better than a series of remote transactions. Of course it will be necessary for a supplier to work with all relevant routes to the chosen consumer groups. In the example of the coffee market these will include the major, powerful, supermarket groups as well as wholesalers such as Spar. It might be that some channel members are more predisposed towards close relationships than others. This often depends on some degree of congruence between the objectives of the parties. Of course the ideal situation allows companies to choose such receptive organizations as their partners after careful consideration of the total network required to reach consumers, but in practice compromises have to be made.

In the area of international marketing there is much greater emphasis on the strategic and long-term nature of these decisions. The care required with the choice of overseas agents and distributors is stressed to an extent that is not present in domestic channel theory. Channels can, and should, be reviewed and, if required, changed. There should be an openness to reject as well as to accept distribution partners. Of course one advantage of well-established distribution links is to 'lock out' new entrants from particular markets, but such situations are not fixed forever. This is another lesson from international marketing, which relates to the so-called immutable nature of distribution channels. The classic cases of Canon achieving entry to the UK photocopier market by using local independent distributors to break the Xerox control, or the similar case of Komatsu achieving entry into the US for farm machinery with new channels, or Honda utilizing non-standard motorcycle outlets show that there are often alternatives available to creative managers. Interestingly, all these examples are of Japanese companies who overcame domestic competition. The choices of new distribution channels should not be compromises undertaken in the absence of traditional openings; rather, they should be opportunities to rethink all components of an offering. This could be termed 'reengineering', in this case *distribution process reengineering.* In making channel decisions it must be remembered how they both depend upon and are determined by other complementary parts of the marketing mix utilized at each step in the chain.

For some product classes, such as specialized farm machinery, there will always be a preference for exclusive or selective distribution. For others, such as branded coffee, more intensive coverage is appropriate and other options are never likely to achieve objectives. It is much easier to form strong partnerships where exclusive arrangements are utilized than, as in the case of a product such as coffee, where intensive coverage is required in a highly competitive consumer market. Most grocery products are displayed alongside several competing brands within the same generic classification. In such situations there is rivalry between different manufacturers to 'push' products into traditional distribution channels and to support this by activities aimed at stimulating demand by 'pulling' consumers to buy. In this competitive market the retailer has the power to give greater support to one brand/manufacturer as compared to another. In fact the retailer usually takes the lead in deciding which products/brands should be stocked and which will not be made available. If a retailer takes such decisions solely on financial grounds then there is a high probability of short-term thinking and a destructive price war between the suppliers to that retailer. While this is good for the consumers, and is sometimes thought to be good for the retailer, there are many indirect 'costs' which, if ignored, could affect the performance and the image of the retailer. For instance, it is accepted that most shoppers like to have some excitement in their buying, but many consumer segments also have dominant preferences and desires and these are not necessarily satisfied when presented with an ever-changing range of brands, even if they are obviously low priced. If a retailer is to undertake a 'leadership' role, then it will do this by virtue of the 'power' it acquires from a closeness to, and understanding of, the customers.

For other products, such as farm machinery, the leadership in constructing a channel to reach the users will most likely come from the manufacturer. For this type of product a key requirement is for the manufacturer to utilize its technical capabilities in producing a suitable quality offering. It will then want a distribution partner that has experience and credibility with the target market, and is capable of supporting, or creating, a differential advantage for the product close to the point of sale.

Effective channel choice

There are four basic elements, identified by Jones and Sasser (1995), which affect customer satisfaction:

- The basic quality of the product or service
- The support service such as customer assistance
- The recovery process for counteracting bad experiences
- Extraordinary service which appeals to customers' personal preferences and values to the extent that the product/service feels customized.

Of these the last three are best delivered by that part of the distribution network closest to the final consumer. Michael Porter's value chain was introduced in Chapter 2 (see Figure 2.7) to emphasize the links between the various discrete activities present in any business unit. Porter considered the issues from the perspective of an industrial economist, considering the activities within diversified corporations. He suggests that at Procter & Gamble the sharing of common physical distribution for many of its separate business units offers financial benefits. He does, however, warn that such sharing must not take place if compromises by the individual business units are necessary, especially if these erode the effectiveness of that unit. The value chain is a powerful model, which illustrates how value is added at the activity level, and it can be used to demonstrate where competitive advantage can, and cannot, be achieved.

In Chapter 2 the discussion of the value chain focused on the four support activities that provide an infrastructure to allow primary activities to take place. Consideration will now be given to some of the *primary activities*. There are three primary activities which take place within that part of the network linking the prime producers to their customers. A value chain giving emphasis to these key channel activities was illustrated in Figure 8.4. The three are:

1. *Outbound logistics*, which includes physical distribution, collection, storage and delivery. This obviously is focused on tangible goods rather than services.
2. *Marketing and sales*, specifically the short-term promotional and selling necessary for established product lines. This concentrates on the dialogue between a supplier and customers.
3. *Services* such as customer assistance, installation, maintenance and repair, which are all aimed at ensuring the benefits expected by a customer are met or even enhanced. This category can cover many of the elements of satisfaction as identified by Jones and Sasser.

If these activities are considered with reference to the capabilities and competencies of a single organization it will soon become obvious where there could be problems in undertaking all roles necessary to satisfy the final consumer in an appropriate way. There is no reason why every primary activity should be undertaken within the same corporate grouping. In fact, a great deal of value could be generated by allowing some roles to be performed by specialist suppliers with relevant capabilities, although if this happens it can be seen that the key support requirement of a suitable 'infrastructure' must be designed so that it is possible to coordinate all the specialist activities.

Organizations seeking to achieve a competitive advantage should consider whether it might be effective for a particular activity to be performed by an external provider. There are actually two decisions that have to be made. The first relates to choice of channel structure, the other to the level of corporate activity within the channel. To illustrate this the value chain has been represented with an important change in scope which recognizes its extension from a single corporation to a complete supply chain (Figure 12.1). This requires a 'business unit' to be redefined as a

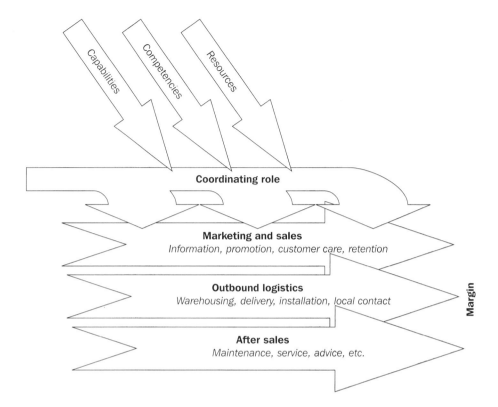

Fig 12.1 A revised value chain. An amended look at the primary channel activities within a network

'business network', linking prime suppliers through to final consumers. Each of the primary activities could involve a number of independent organizations brought together in a coordinated marketing and delivery system, which is considered as most effective by the channel leader.

When considering the structure the key decision is whether to undertake *direct* distribution, or to use intermediaries in an *indirect* channel link.

Direct channels are by definition ones with no intermediary organizations between producer and ultimate consumer. Of course there could be a company-owned sales force or maybe a direct marketing department. This structure is generally thought to offer greater control for the producer, who assumes responsibility for all the activities involved. However, it also involves all the risks, and in many cases it is the most expensive structure. Direct selling is the usual method in many industrial, business to business, markets. Direct marketing involves high delivery and promotional costs, and requires good management processes. It is appropriate for a range of consumer and industrial products.

Indirect channels can be short, with a single intermediary level, or long, with two or three steps between producer and customer. The advantages are that this structure can lead to closer contact with customers, perhaps enabling a larger geographic area to be covered. It also introduces distribution partners with complementary skills who can increase the effectiveness of the channel. Sometimes the choice of indirect channels is justified on the basis of reductions in transportation costs, but the choice of channel structure is a long-term decision and this reason alone is rarely sufficient when set against the reduction of control.

There is, in fact, a middle way, a mixture of direct and indirect links sometimes referred to as a *hybrid channel* structure. It might be that for financial or marketing reasons an organization wishes to benefit from both structures and the combination could enable them to reach different segments more efficiently and effectively. Perhaps large local customers can be served through direct channels, and more remote customers through indirect links. This mixed structure works only if the target segments are clearly delineated, and it does not work if the intermediaries feel they are being exploited for short-term gain. The golden rules are *harmony* between the channels and *loyalty* towards partners. It can be difficult if the different channels feel they are competing with each other and that one channel has an unfair advantage in reaching the target markets. This has to be carefully managed where such competition can reduce an individual member's performance, such as magazine publishers that offer subscription deals alongside sales through traditional newsagents, or computer hardware suppliers that require the support of retail outlets. In the clothing market, companies such as Next and Marks & Spencer offer mail order in parallel to their retail outlets, but these work because the common ownership of both channels eliminates the basic reasons for channel rivalry. In fact in these cases the use of mixed channels increases the effectiveness of the total network.

The most commonly used separation of channels is based on either product type, or customer definition. For instance the Viglen computer company operates a direct channel for sales to universities and colleges, but indirect for general consumers. Cespedes and Corey (1990) describe this as a *pluralistic* system which seeks to focus different channel members on different product/markets and thus minimize potential conflicts by distinct separation. They also offer an alternate model, which integrates individual channel members' strengths by utilizing one member to cover 'outbound logistics', another for 'sales', and maybe a third to deal with the other primary activity of 'servicing'. This is given the ugly name of a *monolithic* system. They offer an example of a company which uses its direct salesforce to educate and create awareness with the target market, while relying on indirect distribution for the administration and fulfilment of sales orders. Hybrid channels, if carefully managed, integrate the best features of differing structures together in the attempt to balance customer needs and company capabilities. If poorly organized they lead to conflict and major problems.

There is no prescription for effective channel choice, but to get maximum benefit from any arrangement requires a forward looking view to be taken. The chosen structure is likely to be in place for a long time and the importance of effective availability of an offering is crucial to marketing success. Issues such as cost and control are very emotive within organizations, but the ultimate test of a distribution channel is whether it delivers appropriate benefits to the final customers.

With regard to the level of corporate activity within a channel, even if the direct route is chosen, an external provider, perhaps a specialist in delivery logistics, could be employed as a subcontractor. So supply companies will face a kind of 'make or buy' dilemma over whether to acquire the necessary capability in order to undertake all aspects of direct distribution within a corporation, or to rely in part on external specialists. The decision should not be purely financial as it ought to include an objective evaluation of the competencies of potential partners in meeting customer needs in the most effective way.

The decision as to the level of corporate provision is also relevant within indirect channels. Some can be integrated and administered as though they were part of overall corporate activity; alternatively, they might be entirely independent arrangements. What must be remembered is that the final customer sees an offering as a totality, and all components, positive or negative, will be evaluated by the customer making a purchase decision.

Recently the term *vertical marketing system* has been used to describe a coordinated indirect channel where all the participants work together to achieve maximum marketing impact for the channel as a whole in its contact with customers. There is a continuum of the corporate involvement in indirect channels which ranges from full corporate ownership of all intermediaries, distributors, agents and others, through to entirely separate independent operations at all levels (Figure 12.2).

The advantages suggested from full corporate ownership are supposed to come from better coordination of vertical marketing activities. Experience does not always support this. There are many examples of other structures achieving greater impact and increased customer responsiveness. For example, compare the performance of a vertically integrated clothes design, manufacturing and retailing company such as Laura Ashley with the results achieved by some of their more dynamic competitors that do not own any retail outlets. Typically, three models of coordinated vertical systems are described. These are corporate, contractual, and

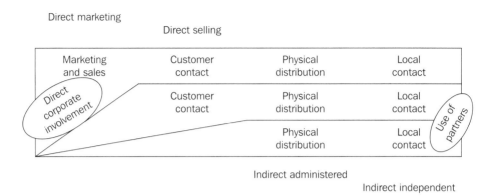

Fig 12.2 Channel options

administered. Corporate is full ownership of all channel members within the same, diversified, organization. Contractual includes external providers but with legal contracts to specify their roles. A good example of a contractual channel is one where franchise arrangements are used for retail outlets. Administered systems are less formal, without legal agreements. They usually rely on the 'power' of one channel member to determine and control the activities of the others. In the conventional independent structure, each channel member behaves autonomously, aiming to achieve its own objectives even if they are at the expense of the overall effectiveness of the total channel.

There is often a need for considerable investment to be made within a distribution network in both stock holding and specific facilities as well as commitment to developing the business. At each level the members must achieve close working relationships and the development must be allowed a long enough time scale in order for the full benefits to emerge.

In trying to decide on whether direct or indirect channels offer the best option, a number of factors will need to be considered. Lambin (1996) groups these into the categories of:

- market/customer factors
- product characteristics
- company variables.

A matrix can be constructed in order to assess the effect of each factor, and the importance/desirability of a particular channel design (Figure 12.3). The example in the figure is not definitive, but merely indicates the likely preferences based on a few chosen attributes.

In using this decision matrix a great deal of thought needs to go into the choice of influencing factors, expanding the list in Figure 12.3, and even more attention should be applied to the relative importance of each factor. In making any channel choice it will soon become obvious that the number of suitable partners, distributers or retailers is limited. This both restricts the initial choices available and makes any changes difficult. In fact, where a company wishes to change its channel structure or channel members such changes not only affect the immediate partners but have knock-on effects throughout the total network. Distribution changes are a key 'strategic window' of opportunity for entering a previously blocked market, as the earlier examples of Cannon and Komatsu demonstrate.

Returning to the three primary activities that take place within distribution channels, it will be seen that these are directed towards the final customers. However, if an *indirect* channel is chosen it will be necessary to consider the appropriate sales and services required at each level of the distribution chain and aimed at each spe-

	Direct	**Indirect**	**Indirect**	**Indirect**	**Indirect**
Influencing factors	Corporate	Corporate (VMS)	Contractual (VMS)	Administered (VMS)	Independent
Market/ customer					
Number of buyers	Small	Large	Large	Large	Large
Geographical spread	Limited	Widespread	Widespread	Widespread	Widespread
Order quantity	Large	Small	Small	Small	Small
Product characteristics					
Technology	Complex	Complex	Complex	Simple	Simple
Value	Higher	Higher			Higher
Handling	Complex	Complex	Complex		Easy
Variability	Customized				Standardized
Perishability	Perishable	Able to be stored	Able to be stored	Able to be stored	Able to be stored
Company variables					
Financial resources	Many	Many	Fewer	Fewer	Fewer
Desire for control	High	High	High	Low	Low

Fig 12.3 Channel design

cific intermediary. The emphasis will be different in a highly fragmented independent network as compared to a coordinated vertical marketing system. In fact, independent channel members are still best considered as 'customers' and treated accordingly by the exchange partners.

Distributors as customers or partners

It is not enough for organizations to view channel management solely as a way to gain access to a chosen market segment, even if it makes an offering conveniently available for customers and the delivery cost effective for suppliers. There are other measures of effectiveness, and competitive advantage comes from the customer's evaluation of a *total* offering rather than a comparison of the basic costs of acquisition. Consideration of total offerings leads to key decisions on the level of support service, and the addition of *extraordinary* service, based on a comparison of the benefit to a customer against the cost of provision. Extraordinary service is only valuable if it reaches the final customer. In an independent, and uncoordinated, channel it will be left to the ultimate provider, maybe the retailer, to facilitate appropriate support activity. In this case, others further upstream in the channel can, at best, offer resources such as demonstrators, merchandisers or service personnel. More commonly they can only attempt to influence such activities and, as the coffee example shows, a retailer might be very promiscuous in dealing with suppliers.

A distribution network is only as strong as its weakest link and even if a retailer is extremely competent in dealing with the target market customers, it might not operate as effectively with its supply company. Additionally, many suppliers assume that when their product has been 'sold' into a distributor the supplier's role is finished. This was a mistake made by the large UK confectionary company, Cadbury in the early 1980s. In trying to build in the US market they sold well into wholesalers via an American sales force, but encountered problems when traditional British chocolate failed to move in sufficient quantity through those channels to the final consumer. A few years later Cadbury sold its US confectionery interests to the US market leader, Hershey, having failed to gain a sufficiently strong business base.

Where an independent indirect channel exists, each link must be considered as a separate buyer–seller exchange. In this case the buyer is a 'customer' who requires to be motivated, first to purchase and then to actively 'sell on' the offering, delivering an appropriate level of service to the next intermediary or the final consumer. Czinkota *et al*. (1997) suggest 'it is difficult enough to motivate employees to provide the necessary sales and service support; motivating the owners and employees of an independent organisation in a distribution chain requires even greater effort'. All too often financial incentives are seen as the only option, but these are so easily copied by competitors that they provide only a short-term tactical advantage. A more strategic way of ensuring the extraordinary support at the final point of sale is by adopting policies that lead to the integration of channel activities, and the building of channel partnerships.

Martin Christopher (1994) wrote:

> Much of the recent focus on customer service has been towards what might be termed 'the people dimension'. It is often not difficult for competitors to imitate technologies, product features, emotional appeals and conventional marketing strategies. What they cannot imitate is the inherent corporate culture and shared values which distinguish the customer service-orientated business. . . . However, whilst it is clearly paramount that every business has motivated employees who share common values about the importance of customer satisfaction, it is also essential to have in place the systems that can ensure consistent reliable 'delivery of the service package. . . . Service has to be tailored to the needs of specific customers if it is to be a true source of differentiation.

If the focus is to be on providing extraordinary service to the final customer, then some form of coordination is necessary throughout the whole distribution chain. Christopher's comments seem to relate to a single corporate supplier but in a multi-level channel, systems must be in place to ensure 'consistent reliable delivery' from all the independent members of that channel. In fact extraordinary service requires the links to be even greater. As Narus and Anderson (1996) claim, 'Flawless distribution can seem an impossible goal. No matter how much inventory a wholesaler carries, when a customer places a rush order, the essential item is often out of stock. No matter how broad a range of services a dealer provides, what a customer desperately needs is often some out-of-the-ordinary service that the dealer has never supplied. And no matter how much effort a distributor expends to beef up its capabilities, when a customer has an emergency, the distributor often lacks the critical skills to respond'. They suggest a concept of *adaptive* channels, which views distribution networks as 'webs of capabilities embedded in an extended enterprise' and suggest that by sharing 'resources and capabilities they can take advantage of profit-making opportunities that they could not exploit alone. . . . The nature of such assistance, the procedures for providing it, and the appropriate remuneration are all defined in advance'. In these adaptive channels there is a high degree of cooperation and, more importantly, a wide appreciation of each other's capability. They offer real advantages from cooperation and avoid duplication of resources. It is necessary for the members of such channels to try to identify the unusual, infrequent, but important customer requirements that might be demanded and then work out cost effective systems to provide those seen as significant.

In this way distribution partners can work together to enhance their capabilities and so achieve a greater degree of customer satisfaction and competitive advantage. Stability in the channel membership is necessary for such improvements to be made. However, the search for greater efficiency and effectiveness could involve more substantive changes especially as technological advances make new arrangements possible. Because of the high investments and strong relationships within established channels, changes in the structure, or of membership, should not be considered unless large potential benefits are anticipated. However, as in all business areas, it is important to review the arrangements objectively on a regular basis. The review of the total channel structure is what I have termed *distribution process reengineering*, a chance to rethink issues without the constraints of existing arrangements. Long-term stable relationships without change have many advantages but they must not become fixed through inertia and habit; rather, the lack of changes should demonstrate that the arrangements are still considered the most effective way available to reach customers.

Narus and Anderson also recommend that the actual membership of a channel could be changed over time. They suggest improving the 'quality' of channel members by replacing some by others with superior capabilities in order to increase the total scope of the adaptive network. However, if a channel leader undertakes such actions it could adversely affect the relationship that is so important between partners. It might be that a manufacturer such as BMW substitutes one local car dealer with another, or a retailer such as Marks & Spencer changes the supplier for one of their St Michael branded products. Uncertainty is not conducive to good relationships; it is far better if advice and assistance are given to the weaker partners to help them improve their operations. In fact both BMW and Marks & Spencer offer such help, and thus they develop stronger links because of this involvement. Many of Marks & Spencer's suppliers have grown as the retailer developed, and many long-term relationships have survived over many years. Recently changes have been made. Therefore it might be prudent for an organization to avoid too great a dependence on an uncertain partner because if a change occurs then a major part of a business could be lost.

Within every network it is possible to identify an organization that can be considered to occupy a leadership role. Often it has been the pioneer that inaugurated the network, say a car manufacturer. It could be that it has developed a position of strength over time such as a major food retailer. Leadership is said to rely on four factors:

1. economic power over the network
2. non-economic power over the network

3. dependency of other channel members

4. the willingness to lead.

A channel leader will exert control over other members, thus helping to achieve efficient achievement of all the primary distribution activities. They should also be able to use their influence to increase the effectiveness of a channel by initiating actions to improve the capabilities and competencies of individual members, and of the network as a whole.

The sources of power exerted by channel leaders can come from economic dominance or from any of those identified by French and Raven (1959) in their classic study of social power (see Chapter 8). In particular, *reward power* is the ability to grant additional benefits to channel members. *Expert power* can be applied by a channel member with specific and valuable skills or knowledge, and *referent power* is said to be present when a channel member is so highly respected that others are proud to be associated with it, for instance a Marks & Spencer supplier or a Bang & Olufsen retail stockist. A less pleasant source is *coercive power*, where a channel member uses its strength to force actions on others. This does not lead to harmony and channel members can feel trapped so they will continually be looking for a way out. This is unlikely to produce added value for customers.

The role of a distributor in adding value is particularly crucial for a new product at the introductory stage and through the market growth period when new users are considering adoption. Distributors play a key role in contact with early adopters and in the education of target customers. The handling of volume and delivery of services then increases as a product moves into its growth phase. This poses a difficulty for a company requiring new distribution channels to reach customers. If the supplier has no established links then the relationship with distributive partners will be new at the same time as the product is new. Yet it is this period when distributors can really influence the building of awareness and trial of the new product. Positive impact at this time can account for some additional degree of success when a new product is launched through established distribution links.

Later, when a product has reached maturity, the quest for additional competitive value is sometimes achieved by looking for lower-cost channel members. However, this should not be a quick 'fire and hire' opportunity; channel relationships are long-term and working with a partner should lead to economies in the transactional costs through mutual experience of each other. In addition, the channel partners who helped one product are likely to be just as relevant in the future when that offering comes to be replaced. They also form excellent established links with existing target markets should complementary offerings be developed that can be marketed as additions to the existing product lines (Figure 12.4).

	Introduction	Growth	Maturity	Decline
Market growth rate	Low	High	High	Low
Value added by channel	High	High	Low	Low
Personal computers	Hobbyist stores	Speciality retailers	Mass merchandisers	Mail order
Designer apparel	Boutiques	Better department stores	Mass merchandisers	All-price stores
Comment	Early adaptors and education	Volume and service	Lower cost channels	Low-cost channels
Objectives	**Attention**	**Interest**	**Sales**	**Struggle**

Fig 12.4 Distributors' role at different stages of the product life cycle

Managing conflict in distribution channels

An important feature of an effective distribution network is the degree of cooperation and connectedness that exists between those involved. However, there are many opportunities for conflict to occur, especially at the interfaces between members, both vertically, at different levels, and horizontally, between intermediaries at the same level. Conflicts arise when one member perceives problems with the behaviour or performance of another. This could be related to the division of responsibilities, or perhaps an attempt to gain a disproportionate share of resources or profit. It could also apply where one company seems to be underperforming and thus adversely affecting the total chain. Perhaps the greatest problem is when the goals of the various partners diverge to the extent that incompatible actions are undertaken. This illustrates how important it can be to fully understand the attitudes, values and motivation as well as the activity cycle, competencies and capabilities of potential partners.

It is much easier to avoid or resolve conflicts caused by the lack of clear roles and boundaries than ones where there are fundamental differences in objectives. Interestingly, research by Katsikeas (1992) found a greater level of conflict within distributive links in domestic markets than between exporter–importer relationships in international markets. This could indicate that greater attention is given to the choice of international partners or, as suggested by the researcher himself, geographic distance between parties allows more freedom and thus defuses some problems.

It is likely that there will always be some issues about which channel members do not agree. As Ford (1998) suggests, 'there are seeds of conflict in all relationships'. If the differences are not resolved they can easily build frustration, and can increase the relationship 'distance' between partners. However, not all conflict is destructive; positive benefits can come from what is termed *functional* conflict. This is where issues such as new developments or suggested improvements to services are considered, and where other problems are brought to the surface and resolved to the benefit of all parties. In order for harmony and loyalty to exist there must be regular two-way communications and sufficient commitment on the part of all partners to dispel any climate of mistrust and suspicion. If such a situation is created it is likely that resolution of conflict will not only be facilitated but positive future benefits will often emerge.

Conclusions

This chapter is entitled 'channel management and value-added relationships'. The focus is thus on the strategic issues that contribute to the value of an offering as seen by the final consumer in a chain. For this end user the purchase decision is made on the basis of everything that is presented, positive or negative, tangible or intangible. Customer satisfaction is derived from everything that is then received. It is, therefore, obvious that choices regarding distribution channels are not just about reaching customers and achieving satisfactory levels of availability, but they are about augmenting an offering by adding valuable features and closing the distance between the offer and the potential purchaser.

Although there can be transfers of ownership as intermediaries purchase the offering in its differing forms as it passes along the channel, the most important purchase is that by the end user. All links in a network are, therefore, dependent upon this final purchase and the demand that derives from it. Hence it is in the interests of every member of a distribution network to consider their actions with regard to the effect these will have down through the channel. Nevertheless each member will always try to achieve their preferred individual position, and even to optimize it, perhaps at the expense of the overall performance of a total channel. It is important that channel leaders recognize the objectives of other members and try to agree compromise arrangements otherwise differences can cause serious conflict within the channel.

There are two major areas of new channel decisions: first, the appropriate structure and, second, the choice of participating members, independent or corporate. For established networks the decisions are about reengineering a channel and about changes in membership or in the responsibilities or roles of individual members (distribution process reengineering).

Structures are long-term decisions. They cover the way in which the primary activities of outbound logistics, marketing/sales and service are to be performed. Effective channel choices can enhance value by providing high, or extraordinary, levels of service. Both direct and indirect channels are possible as well as a hybrid mixed system. Whichever system is chosen, it is critical that the roles of each member and the boundaries of responsibilities are clearly defined. Channels work because of good structures; they thrive when there is mutual support from committed members. However, most channels are 'controlled' by one member utilizing its power to take a leadership role. Usually it is this channel leader that initiates reviews of the network structure, but all individual members should review their own contribution in the light of their specific objectives and capabilities. Such a review can reveal interesting marketing opportunities for any organization.

There are seeds of conflict in all distribution relationships. When these relate to differences between the objectives of individual members and those of the whole network, they can be very difficult to resolve. Because of this each member must decide their own level of commitment to a particular channel. From the position of the channel leader it is critical to choose the best long-term partners and then encourage cooperation within the channel. Conflict can be both functional and dysfunctional. If it is encouraged as part of an open and developing series of relationships then it can be a positive force for improvements within the channel. The lessons of relationship building are perhaps most critical when practised within a distribution network.

KEY POINTS

12.1   The role of channel links is a major strategic issue. It should be reappraised so that the notion of an integrated distribution network stretching from initial supplier to final consumer is constructed. All members of the network should be viewed as partners.

12.2   Effective channel choice requires both a decision on channel structure, with the roles in each part of the structure, and decision on the level of corporate activity, direct and indirect, by the leader within that channel.

12.3   Most channel designs will be constructed by a channel leader who will exhibit power over the other members. Leadership is said to rely on four factors: economic power over the network, non-economic power

---

over the network, dependency of other channel members and the willingness to lead.

12.4 In trying to decide on whether direct or indirect channels offer the best option a number of factors will need to be considered. These can be grouped as: market/customer factors, product characteristics and company variables.

12.5 Channels should be regularly reappraised (distribution process reengineering).

12.6 Conflict in channels can be both functional and dysfunctional. If it is encouraged as part of an open and developing series of relationships then it can be a positive force for improvements within the channel.

QUESTIONS

12.1 Why should organizations consider building distribution partnerships with other independent companies in order to reach their final consumers?

12.2 When deciding a channel structure what groups of factors are likely to be considered? Give examples of each and suggest how they might affect a channel decision.

12.3 What are the issues that determine which organization will become a channel leader?

12.4 What is the role of distribution process reengineering and when should it be undertaken?

Bibliography

Bucklin, L.P. (ed.), *Vertical Marketing Systems*, Scott Foresman, 1970.

Cespedes, F.V. and Corey, E.R., Managing Multiple Channels, *Business Horizons*, July/Aug., 1990.

Christopher, M., Customer Service and Logistic Strategy, in M.J. Baker (ed.) *The Marketing Book*, Butterworth Heinemann, 1994.

Czinkota, M.R., Kotabe, M. and Mercer, D., *Marketing Management*, Blackwell, 1997.

Day, R.L., Michaels, R.E. and Perdue, B.C., How Buyers Handle Conflict, *Industrial Marketing Management*, Vol. 17, Aug., 1988.

Ford, D., *Managing Business Relationships*, Wiley, 1998.

French, J.R.P. and Raven, B., *The Bases of Social Power*, University of Michigan Press, 1959.

Heide, J.B., Interorganisational Governance in Marketing Channels, *Journal of Marketing*, Jan., 1994.

Hooley, G. and Saunders, J., *Competitive Positioning*, Prentice Hall, 1993.

Johnson, R. and Lawrence, P.R., Beyond Vertical Integration – the Prize of Value Added Partnerships, *Harvard Business Review*, July/Aug., pp. 95–101, 1988.

Jones, T.O. and Sasser, W.E., Why Satisfied Customers Defect, *Harvard Business Review*, Nov./Dec., 1995.

Katsikeas, C.S., The Process of Conflict in Buyer–Seller Relationships: A Comparative Analysis, *Journal of Marketing Management*, Vol. 8, 1992.

Kotler, P., *Marketing Management: Analysis, Planning and Control*, Prentice Hall, 1997.

Lambin, J.-J., *Strategic Marketing Management*, McGraw-Hill, 1996.

Mathur, S.S., Talking Straight About Competitive Strategy, *Journal of Marketing Management*, Vol. 8, pp. 199–217, 1992.

Murray, J.A. and O'Driscoll, A., *Strategy and Process in Marketing*, Prentice Hall, 1996.

Narus, J.A. and Anderson, J.C., Rethinking Distribution, *Harvard Business Review*, July/Aug., No. 4, 1996.

Stern, L.W. and El Ansary, A., *Marketing Channels*, 5th Edn, Prentice Hall, 1996.

RELATIONSHIP MARKETING AND COMPETITIVE ADVANTAGE

13

CHAPTER

INTRODUCTION

At the start of this book it was said that 'Marketing is based on an incredibly simple but powerful idea, that of achieving a profitable exchange between a supplier and a customer. . . . marketers must make things happen. Relationships do not just happen in a world typified by overproduction, where all customers have an abundance of choices. The exchange has to be created by investment and effort'.

As shown in Chapter 8, once decisions have been taken on *where to compete*, it is necessary to try to achieve a competitive position in the mind of each of the chosen customers. This can take time. Whatever the position at any specific moment in time, weak or strong, the next step is to build upon it by making promises to those potential customers, and delivering satisfaction by keeping those promises.

There will need to be a trade-off between the position occupied and the promises made (and kept). Where a supplier has a weak position it will need to compensate for this by making stronger promises supported by adequate guarantees that those promises can be met. At the other extreme a strong position by itself is a form of promise, and so this situation is likely to require less in the way of additional, overt, promises. This is especially true if the customer already has reliable evidence from previous experience that expectations will be met. It is this state which is the goal of *relationship marketing*.

Grönroos (1996b) argues that 'every single customer forms a *relationship* with the seller'. Relationships themselves can be casual and loose, or committed and tight, as well as the many positions in between. They start forming with the first contact between a supplier and a potential customer. They develop with every subsequent interaction. Levitt (1983) considered the development of relationships over time when he wrote 'The relationship between a seller and a buyer seldom ends when the sale is made. In a great and increasing proportion of transactions, the relationship actually intensifies subsequent to the sale. This becomes the critical factor in the buyer's choice of seller the next time round'. In addition to the time factor in developing relationships, the multiplicity of different contacts that take place each contribute in their own way. As Ford (1998) says, 'each interaction, such as the exchange of products, services, money or social "chit-chat" is an episode in the total relationship. . . . Each episode is affected by what has happened before in that relationship and will affect what happens in the future. Even the most important purchase isn't an isolated event. . . . Future episodes might be affected by actions, attitudes or experiences from many years before'.

The key point is that future exchanges are heavily dependent on all previous experience. There is much evidence to suggest that where close relationships exist, then future satisfying marketing exchanges are very likely to continue to take place.

Over the past two decades relationship marketing, sometimes termed *strategic business partnershipping*, has exploded into prominence in both marketing literature and thinking. Recently one of the key promoters, Evert Gummesson (1997), has reviewed this progress and suggested that 'much of what is currently written about RM is theoryless, a stack of fragmented philosophies, observations and claims which do not converge in the direction of an emerging theory'. He decries the presentation of RM as a new promotional package, or a new type of (direct contact) marketing based on advances in information technology. Rather he suggests it is a 'paradigm shift, requiring a dramatic change in marketing thinking and behaviour; not an add-on to traditional marketing'.

In many ways he is correct to warn against fragmentation; there are many diverse actions masquerading under the guise of relationship marketing. It is important that the role of RM is defined and then the extent to which it should be included as part of strategic marketing can be assessed.

The simplest definition is one from Grönroos (1996b), who suggests that relationship marketing is:

> the management of a firm's market relationships.

Of course our sales colleagues will suggest that they have been doing this for years, and marketing has only just caught up. Salespeople certainly know the basic economic facts that:

1. It is more expensive to acquire a new customer than it is to retain an existing one.
2. The longer the history of links between a supplier and a customer, the more profitable the relationship.

Salespeople also adopt as good practice the building of databases covering the necessary information about customers and contacts which is often included in the advice on building relationships. One area where both marketing and sales will agree is with Drucker's (1968) view that 'there is only one purpose for an organisation, that is to create and retain a customer'.

Historically the emphasis in transactional marketing has been on the development and promotion of a competitive *total offer* in order to create customers, and the measurement of loyalty as a discriminator in segmentation studies aimed at finding other similar customers, the traditional tools used being the controllable variables of the marketing mix.

The result of a shift in marketing thinking to focus on relationships should lead to the ability to manage all the *episodes*, interactional exchanges, with customers in a more strategic manner. To achieve results it will be necessary to involve every department within an organization, and its distributive partners, in coordinated activity aimed at offering specific benefits to the right customers. This goes beyond even the enlarged marketing mix. It is this widening of scope which relationship marketing can add to the continuing sales focus on personal direct links with customers. By considering all the factors affecting a relationship, more options become available to use as part of an enlarged marketing mix, but the output still ought to be seen as part of the ongoing process of differentiated target marketing.

Study of the benefits of developing relationships with specific customers or groups will lead to the strategic choice of those who should receive greater resources with enhanced levels of augmentation, and, at the other extreme, those customers who should be offered no more than a basic deal, and finally those who should be dissuaded from buying because their needs cannot be met in full. This is a key part of managing the mix of customers. The choice of target segments is very much a strategic decision relating to *where to compete*, and the development of suitable offers is necessary to *compete effectively*.

Some relationship management techniques can be used to strengthen the links between exchange partners and this can prove to be a positive advantage in the competitive arena. But these are some of the fragmented activities Gummesson criticizes; they are not relationship marketing. Acceptance of Grönroos' definition involves a commitment which has to stretch across the whole supply network. As Kotler (1997) states, 'marketing can make promises but only the whole organization can deliver satisfaction'. In fact the role of marketing in fostering a customer-oriented service culture which can support all the network activities is a necessary condition for undertaking relationship marketing.

Organizations have to decide their strategic priorities. A relationship marketing consortium will emphasize the development and maintenance of mutually satisfactory, long-term relationships with chosen customers, while a more traditional exchange marketing company will concentrate on the satisfaction of some specific needs and wants of customers. These are not exclusive choices; in fact, they are complementary, and the distinction may seem unnecessarily trivial, but the focus is very different. It is the need to emphasize the relationship above all else which Gummesson (1997) stresses when he concludes that RM requires a dramatic change in marketing thinking and behaviour. He describes it as a paradigm shift and definitely not an add-on to traditional marketing.

However, not all markets, nor all organizations, nor all occasions, benefit from this new, relationship-based, thinking. There are obvious examples of one-off transactions where the seller is the initiator and the stimulus–response paradigm is the most appropriate – for instance, a gift shop in a tourist resort, a participant at a car-boot sale or the seller of other low-involvement products such as an umbrella or a kettle. It can also apply to high-involvement purchases. An estate agent selling a house, as well as the vendors themselves, and even perhaps the choice of university for a student, are examples of this type of situation. In these obvious examples there are no major benefits from long-term relationships and so the marketing emphasis will be on constructing a good offer for a single transaction. Of course there could be a need for effective pre-purchase contact to build awareness and confidence, and there is definitely a need for post-purchase satisfaction, especially if it can be beneficial to good 'word-of-mouth' recommendations, which will encourage other customers in the future.

There are other less obvious exchanges where the buyer is likely to undertake a series of purchases over time, but where each purchase event will be independent of the others. Provided the products offered on each separate occasion reach the basic expected level of quality and meet the customer's needs effectively, then there is little to be gained from a strong relationship. This could include a local authority asking for tenders for specific building contracts, or an airline flying on a major route alongside several other well-known carriers. It can also include low-value consumables such as a pad of paper or a litre of milk.

Of course there may be some positive feelings towards a particular seller in any of these examples, but these will not necessarily lead to high levels of repeat purchasing. There can be a high level of 'promiscuity' by the buyers, who offer no exclusive loyalty to any one supplier. The situation where there are multiple suppliers, all able to conform to the specification, and each able to be considered on every purchase occasion is termed an 'always-a-share' market by Barbara Jackson (1985). In these markets the investment and commitment required to build strong relationships needs to be assessed carefully to evaluate the benefit of going deeper than the ability to satisfy the basic needs every time. A relationship programme must be judged by the mutual benefits, both economic and non-economic, that accrue to both parties from a series of exchanges.

The marriage metaphor

Over the past 15 years the analogy between building business relationships and personal relationships (marriage) has been utilized extensively. Certainly there are some interesting parallels between them, and by considering the personal aspects of relationship development it is possible to arrive at a better understanding of the business issues. Levitt (1983) first used the analogy, with comments such as 'The sale merely consummates the courtship, then the marriage begins. How good a marriage depends upon . . .' and 'Buyers want vendors who keep promises, who'll keep supplying and standing behind what they promised. The era of the one night stand is gone. Marriage is both necessary and more convenient'.

Other authors have continued to describe the similarities (see Hunt and Morgan, 1995; Buttle, 1996) and in 1987 Dwyer *et al*. added the concept of divorce. The linking stages seem to be:

- meeting (awareness),
- dating (exploration),
- courting (expansion),
- marriage (commitment), and possibly
- divorce (dissolution of relationship).

While the language of personal relationships is obviously dated, it is only recently that the basis of the gradual development, moving towards ever closer partnerships over time, has been challenged.

Professor Tynan (1997) reviewed the analogy and declared that:

> the marriage analogy has outlived its usefulness. . . . While some parallels do exist in the domain of relationship development, the metaphor fails to deliver on issues concerning the number and nature of the parties involved in the relationship, on the attendant costs and benefits, on the willingness of the parties involved and on the 'ideal' timescale of the relationship. . . . The concentration on one form of a monogamous and successful marriage has excluded many parallels in the full range of relationships. . . . In the real world both human relationships and marketing relationships can be functional as well as dysfunctional. Metaphors including stalking, rape, prostitution, polygamy and seduction may be more appropriate than marriage to describe the full range of relationships which occur.

In fact there is a lot to learn from *all* types of personal relationships, not just marriage. After all, business relationships are not impersonal; they depend entirely on the people who represent the supplier and the customers. There are interesting parallels with the Chinese concept of *Guanxi*, which involves different levels of personal commitments and connections (Arias, 1998). While it is essentially a social network, the links are carried into business relationships. In this respect it is important to establish social and personal credibility with the people in a potential exchange partner organization prior to any business relationship. One of the key elements of *Guanxi* is that of reciprocal obligations which last over an indefinite period of time. These are 'banked', to be repaid when the time is right. It is misleading to identify *Guanxi* with relationship marketing, but the emphasis on credibility and trust within a culturally different relationship structure can be usefully extended. In particular, there is the spectrum which ranges from the very close relationships within a family group, where there are strong obligations to attend to all of a partner's needs, to the opposite situation of loose relationships with strangers where transactions are conducted on a purely economic basis. In the middle there are types of *Guanxi* relationships involving a mix of social obligation and benefit alongside the economic factors. If relationships are not defined by a tightly worded 'marriage' contract then there could be many of the elements of *Guanxi* present where regular exchanges by loyal customers take place.

But even when considering corporate entities as the partners in a slightly looser relationship, it is still possible to benefit from advice drawn from marriage. Hunt and Morgan's (1995) recommendations for business are:

- choose your partner carefully
- structure the partnership carefully
- devote time to developing the relationship
- maintain open two-way communications

- be entirely trustworthy.

These could equally apply to a marriage. Tynan suggests further lessons from marriage such as the support activities of 'pre-marriage counselling, marital agreements and marriage guidance need a parallel in the marketing world'.

It is important to point out that not all personal relationships progress to a marriage, monogamous or polygamous, and it is equally appropriate that not all marketing partnerships have to, or even are able to, develop beyond the friendship stage. Krapfel *et al.* (1992) identified important prerequisites that need to be present if a relationship is to be worth building into an ever closer partnership. These are the generation of mutual value from the increasingly close links, and the congruence between the interests/objectives of both parties. Both of these usually exist between close distribution partners, but they are not always both present in other 'buyer–seller' situations.

If only one of these prerequisites is met, say congruence of interest, but without any obvious additional benefits as a consequence of the two parties 'living together', then the relationship should resemble that of a friend, a trading partner who at best warrants some special attention. If, on the other hand, there are obvious reductions that can be achieved in the exchange transactional costs but no commonality of interest, then there are difficulties even in establishing a 'marriage of convenience' as short-term negotiations and win/lose issues dominate. This is the case between many food manufacturers and major grocery supermarket chains. A survey of Dutch food companies showed the five most important issues for the parties to be:

FOOD MANUFACTURERS	GROCERY RETAILERS
1. CONTINUITY OF TRADE	1. PRICE
2. LEVEL OF DISTRIBUTION	2. SHARE OF TOTAL RETAIL MARKET
3. INFORMATION EXCHANGE	3. STORE 'OWN LABEL' PRODUCTS
4. SHELF SPACE	4. SHOP IMAGE
5. QUALITY OF PRODUCTS.	5. IN STORE MERCHANDISING.

It will be noticeable that there is no overlap here, hence supporting the view that it will be extremely difficult to build long-term partnerships in this market-place, the only possible exception being the suppliers of the store's 'own label' products, who could both share many objectives with the retailer and profit from the mutual economic benefits available from working closely with their partner.

Krapfel *et al.* suggest that for partners and friends a more accommodating, collaborative style of management is appropriate. Is this also true of personal relationships? This contrasts with the more aggressive drive necessary in those other cases where no common interests exist. Are these situations similar to acts of 'prostitution' or 'rape'? Both of these acts are illegal in personal terms, but if their equivalent exists in a business relationship what is the likely outcome? And what will be the effects on future contacts?

It is interesting to compare such situations with the customer types described as 'mercenaries' and 'hostages' by Jones and Sasser (1995) (see Chapter 2). It will be remembered that mercenaries only deal if the 'price is right' or if they want a 'change of pace' from a more regular supplier. Such customers come and go but offer little commitment to developing relationships. Hostages are trapped into dealing because of the lack of suitable alternatives; they are *loyal* but are not *satisfied* by their current supplier, they do not build rewarding relationships, and are likely to defect quickly when a more acceptable option appears.

Relationship marketing and competitive advantage

Clinton Silver, once Purchasing Director of Marks & Spencer, told a conference that 'we are not looking for new suppliers in any of our existing product areas. We have the suppliers we want and, unless something goes wrong with the relationship, we will not search for new suppliers' (unpublished). The opportunity to develop a strong bonding which excludes others is a real competitive advantage for both parties. Within the relationship they can concentrate on developments to maintain the competitiveness of the network. Others, outside the partnership, have no leverage and therefore must look to other market areas.

Within a well-managed relationship nothing should be allowed to 'go wrong', although mistakes are more easily forgiven in strong partnerships. But both parties need to understand what is actually meant by 'things going wrong'. When working for an organization which supplied Marks & Spencer, I was called to the Baker Street HQ of Marks & Spencer to be told that my company had not come up with enough potential new product options. Although the basic product was entirely satisfactory, the retailer required new ideas which would add excitement within the range offered and thus enhance the shopping experience of their customers. The failure of the supplier to develop possible new products was seen as a failure in the relationship and it had to be addressed urgently. The problem in this case was that too much past attention had been given to ensuring that the quality and efficient delivery of the contracted product met the strict Marks & Spencer standards, and not enough effort had been focused on the customer and what that important customer wanted from the relationship.

If customers feel so satisfied that they are prepared to commit future purchases to a particular supplier then the relationship is offering real competitive advantages on top of any economic benefits that also accrue. But, as the above example shows, it is not the focus on products that creates satisfying relationships, but rather the strong understanding of each other's needs. However, as Buttle (1996) states 'RM is not philanthropic, it is a means to an end'; that end is profit for the participants.

The modern market-place is one where, in the words of Aijo (1996), there is 'unlimited consumer choice, a higher level of competition and an ever-increasing pace of change. Companies find themselves having simultaneously to lower their costs, improve efficiency, raise the levels of quality and service, as well as speeding up innovations'. If stable links with loyal customers can be established then a supplier can put greater efforts in coping with the market conditions. This gives obvious benefits to the supplier, who does not have to utilize scarce resources in continually searching for and creating new customers.

However, buyers too have to experience benefits to justify their continuing loyalty. If technology is advancing and competition is driving down costs, this must happen both within and outside a relationship. A relationship is not an excuse to halt progress, rather it is a context in which progress can be more focused to deliver benefits to customers as well as suppliers.

Fournier *et al*. (1998) suggests 'in their role as relationship partners, companies (suppliers) need people (customers) to think of them as allies and friends, but more often than not they come across as enemies. Companies claim to offer solutions to consumers' problems; but in fact, they are creating more problems than they solve'. If competitive advantages are to be achieved it will be because of a small number of loyal advocates who view their supply partner as an ally.

Loyalty can be a misunderstood concept. All the major UK supermarket groups have their so called loyalty cards, but do these produce loyal customers? In fact they do not use the word 'loyalty' on the cards, and this is appropriate as there are many shoppers who hold the full set of Sainsbury's Reward Card, Tesco's Club Card and Safeway's ABC Card. None of these retailer schemes actually rewards exclusive loyalty, although all offer a small discount to card holders who achieve specific (low) purchase levels. More effective are the type of turnover-based 'overriding' discounts used in some business markets. Here the discount level is continually increased as the spend rises above agreed levels. The growing level of benefit that comes from continued loyalty is therefore reflected in the scheme. This meets the requirement of a good promotional scheme in that the benefits of developing stronger relationship links are rewarded, and of course these increases help in binding customers to a particular seller, thus increasing the switching costs. But while this can be related to competitive advantage it is really a promotional device and not a move to committed relationship marketing.

In a later chapter other techniques for building strong relationships will be considered. However, in order to assess the effect of the shift to a relationship marketing orientation on the ability to achieve sustainable competitive advantage, three questions must be answered:

1. Does the use of relationship marketing lead to a higher retention rate with regard to existing customers in the light of competitive offers?
2. Does the use of relationship marketing lead to a greater share of a particular customer's total business?
3. Do firms undertaking relationship marketing achieve greater levels of profitability when compared to firms not engaged in long-term relationships with customers?

Unfortunately no single, prescriptive answer exists to all questions and so the consideration of these issues must be based on specific contexts and particular inter-company relationships.

However, the first issue, the increased ability to retain customers, can be almost a self-proven hypothesis. A successful relationship can be described as one where customer defection is low, relationships are longer and it is easier to defend a market position. But, as already discussed, not all relationships are successful in these terms, and there is no real evidence that the random use of relationship marketing techniques actually leads to successful partnerships. What is more relevant is that failure to focus on specific customers will leave more opportunities for competitors to attack. Kalwani and Narayandas (1995) report from their empirical research that 'there is a growing trend towards single sourcing by US manufacturers who are slashing their vendor lists dramatically. Consequently, suppliers that do not focus on their existing customers might lose the entire business to a focused competitor. Because these long-term relationships typically have a horizon of five to seven years or more, it means that the suppliers lose those customers for *good*'.

As to the second question, 'share of customer's total business' refers to that percentage of a customer's annual (or lifetime) purchases which are placed with the supplier. This is an effective measure of loyalty, and the relevance can be appreciated when the actual lifetime value of a customer is estimated. For instance the Pizza Express company talk about the £3000 pizza. This is their forecast of the actual spend by an average customer over a 5-year time horizon. Obviously the difference between a 60% share and a 20% share of business is considerable, but the key question is whether a pizza company can establish a strong relationship with its customers. It is unlikely to be the variety available or even the taste of the product which leads to loyalty, but possibly could be the service level which is the important critical success factor. Barbara Jackson (1985) gives an example of a shipping (transport) company where the adoption of a focused relationship marketing strategy led to a wider spread of actual business customers. However, the company failed to achieve the desired high proportion of the business available from many of their new and existing customers as a low-priced competitor proved effective in an 'always-a-share' market-place – the type of market where every contract is a separate event. The shipping company practising relationship marketing was considered for most contracts, but only obtained a small number of them. The example demonstrates that relationship marketing does not always offer the expected returns.

The third question was one of the hypotheses tested by Kalwani and Narayandas (1995) as part of their research using cross-sectional and longitudinal information from US data sources. They concluded that 'supply firms in long-term relationships with select customers are able to retain or even improve their profitability levels more than firms that employ a transactional approach to servicing customers'. While this is not necessarily true in every context, the US research does indicate some performance advantages from achieving long-term partnerships. There will always be problem areas, such as the shipping company, where the cost of the relationship marketing activities is undoubtedly higher than their low-priced competitor. This means that high profitability does not follow the investment in building relationships in every specific case.

The appropriate context for relationship marketing

There is a strong feeling, demonstrated in much recent writing on marketing, that relationship building is now a critical component in any marketing-oriented company. In general this is true, as the basis of strategic marketing is creating and keeping customers. However, there are some situations where intense effort and perhaps a great deal of investment is essential in order to retain a particular customer; others where it is not so necessary. It is always important to understand the chosen customers, and if relationship marketing is, as Grönroos declares, the management of a firm's market relationships, then it is always present as part of ongoing marketing operations. The more strategic decisions will revolve around the level of investment required and the ongoing costs of building up a strong close relationship with different groups of customers, when compared first to the potential long-term returns from trading with those specific segments and second to the expected outcome if less investment is made and a less intense relationship developed.

There will be some potential relationships where the time horizon is lengthy and there is a congruence of interests linking seller and buyer. For the industrial component suppliers to manufacturing companies, mentioned above, this is obviously the case. As long as the partners are carefully chosen and there is mutual commitment to form a close partnership, then the appropriate conditions exist for investing heavily in building up the relationship. This will involve focusing the whole supply organization on the chosen customers and their many needs, in particular those that go beyond the supply of one particular component.

Alternatively, there will be other customers who require a one-off, short-term product or service with no subsequent follow-up and no continuing relationship. It is possible to put this type of buyer at one end of a spectrum and the deeper relationship customer at the other. This illustrates the two extremes of marketing exchanges. Then, as Jackson (1985) says, 'others, in real situations, will generally occupy less extreme points along the spectrum'. The position of each will depend upon the product/service characteristics, how they fit into the customer's activity cycle, and the objectives of both seller and buyer (Figure 13.1).

Building and maintaining close relationships is likely to involve significant allocation of resources, in particular by the seller. This is likely to go beyond the sales and marketing functions and could even involve the allocation of production facilities and the modification of processes. In a strong relationship the buyer could also be encouraged to modify its activities so that mutual benefits can be met.

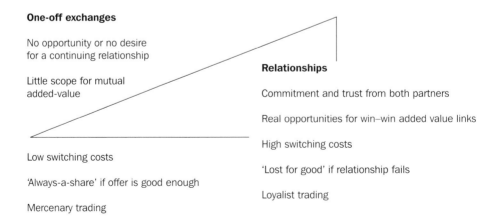

One-off exchanges

No opportunity or no desire for a continuing relationship

Little scope for mutual added-value

Low switching costs

'Always-a-share' if offer is good enough

Mercenary trading

Relationships

Commitment and trust from both partners

Real opportunities for win–win added value links

High switching costs

'Lost for good' if relationship fails

Loyalist trading

Fig 13.1 A spectrum of relationships

A supplier of fresh chickens to supermarket giant Sainsbury's agreed to receive orders for up to 40% of its output at 4.00 p.m. every day. The product is perishable and had to be on the supermarket shelves by 8.00 a.m. the next morning. This was made more difficult by the logistics of delivering to hundreds of locations throughout the UK. While a pattern of demand emerged over time, every day was different, depending on individual sales in each store the previous day. Chickens are sold by weight from small (1.2 kg) right up to extra-large (2 kg+), and the orders specified precise numbers of boxes for each weight. However, on any one day it is impossible for the supplier to know how many of each weight will be available for sale as the poultry received from the farms, while of a constant age, is of variable weight. So a complex operation was set up to pre-pack a given quantity of each size with Sainsbury's labels and prices prior to the detailed order being received, the balance being packed after the order came in. The chilled distribution vehicles were already scheduled with departure times, the closer destinations being dispatched last. Meeting the precise needs of the stores involved use of a highly sophisticated computer program. But inevitably the production had to plan on having many more chickens available than the customer required. As a perishable commodity these extras could not be kept even for one more day so they had to be sold unbranded through wholesale meat markets, or possibly frozen. As both alternative routes are unprofitable, they had to be kept to a minimum.

The relationship with Sainsbury's was strong – it had to be the major source of profitable sales for the supplier – but to accommodate both parties certain compromises were agreed with respect to flexibilities in the order and methods of joint working. There was a mutual dependency and the complexity of the integrated processes meant that it would be very difficult for either party to switch to another partner. Nevertheless, the arrangements for one large customer dominated all activities of the supplier, who still had to market the 60% of output not required by Sainsbury's. Therefore the supplier had to develop other customers where a great deal of variation was possible in the product offered on a daily basis.

For this poultry company, and for many others, the management of its relationships meant allocating its resources differently for its various customers. There were long-term investment decisions to enable Sainsbury's requirements to be met, but these affected both that trading and all other customers. Generally such situations are not unusual, especially in business-to-business marketing. As Ford (1998) suggested, 'Customer relationships vary widely in their nature and importance. Some may be individually insignificant, some may be distant, impersonal, even hostile and confrontational. It is, however, common for a company in business markets to have a relatively small number of important, close customer relationships on which its future depends'.

It is these 'important close' customers, critical to the supplier's future business, where increased investment in respect of their needs is warranted. They are the ones with whom the deepest relationships should be formed, and they should be placed at that end of the customer spectrum. For many companies it is possible to develop a relationship portfolio which highlights these 'cash cow' partners, separating them from other customers, similar to Figure 13.2. Developing and managing such a portfolio requires a great deal of thought, analysis, planning and investment, and is actually more important than the product portfolio. It is necessary to have separate relationship strategies for those who are today's *cash producing* profitable customers, those who are the *stars* and/or *problem children* of the future, and those *dog* customers where business should be discontinued.

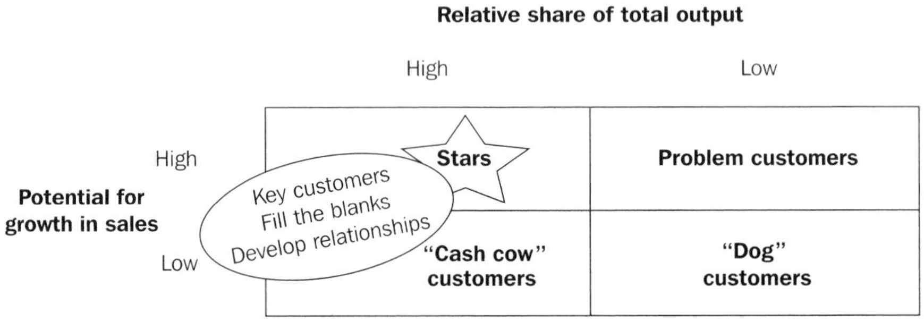

Fig 13.2 Adapting the Boston Consulting Group matrix to customer groupings

There are likely to be no more than 20% of all customers who warrant extra special interest and attention. It could be as basic as the top 100 customers and top 50 prospects who are considered as the critical relationship customers, although such a numeric cut-off is probably too simplistic.

Added-value relationships

Traditional marketing puts an emphasis on winning the competitive battle through an offer of superior value. Relationship marketing switches the emphasis from competition within the triad of customers, competitors and our own organization to a specific focus on the efficient management of the dyadic supplier–customer relationship. Of course it would be naive to ignore competition completely, as the focus on the dyad can occur only when a customer has committed itself to work with a particular supplier. Usually this will be as a result of a comparative evaluation which includes alternative offerings and competitor organizations, although it could be as a result of an existing social relationship (Gummesson (1987) mentions friendship and ethnic bonds as possible examples). It could even possibly be as a result of 'mega marketing' which has effectively reduced the extent of free competition.

Irrespective of the motivation, economic or social, the basis of relationship marketing must be the acceptance of an interactive approach together with the desire to create a win–win situation. In this both parties benefit so it is a true added-value relationship where mutual value is generated from ever closer links. A supplier will typically want to put extra effort into building up the relationship with that small group of critical customers. Such effort is warranted only if it is reciprocated by the customers in question. A key question must be the consideration from the customer's position of whether the seller is one of their really critical suppliers. Relationship marketing is cooperative and it is therefore necessary to understand how important a particular supplier (say, firm A) is for each of its customers. It could be that the product class is of low interest to all customers. It might be that a customer has a large number of supply links which are more important: maybe firm A and its products are considered only when a repurchase situation occurs. If this is the case then too great an effort to get close to the customer by the supplier could be seen as irrelevant or even annoying. In this situation it might be enough to set up a system which made a habitual straight re-buy both convenient and cost effective. This happens with the renewal of car insurance from Direct Line and others who utilize a well-worded reminder, linked to a well-constructed financing deal, just a few weeks prior to the renewal date. It also applies to the delivery of home heating oil, with the tank being topped up every month on a regular basis irrespective of usage. These activities are less demanding for the customer by putting the onus onto the systems employed by the supplier. The relationships are not particularly deep but trust is necessary, and provided the reliability is maintained they can be both relevant and yet beneficial for each party. The moral is that a close relationship does not have to involve excessive direct contact, it just has to be tailored to the situation so that it meets the requirements of both parties. In this way it adds value just as much as a more active link in another context.

Grönroos says:

> a key requirement underpinning a relationship marketing strategy is that any supplier knows the long-term needs and desires of customers better and offers added value on top of the technical solution embedded in consumer goods, industrial equipment or services. Customers do not only look for goods or services, they demand a much more holistic service offering including everything from information about how best and most safely to use a product, to delivering, installing, updating, repairing, maintaining and correcting items they have bought. And they demand all this, and much more, in a friendly, trustworthy and timely manner.

This is quite a shopping list, but most good relationships are not exclusively one-way demands by the customers; at best they should be open exchanges so that the benefits accrue on both sides. All relationships will involve a mix of positive and negative, as well as desirable and undesirable, aspects. What determines the continued involvement by the parties concerned (if they have that kind of choice) is the extent of the *net* added value they receive.

Added value for customers can come from additional services, or a holistic total offering. At the extreme this will lead to individually customized offerings. Utilizing modern technology can offer economies of scope, as opposed to economies of scale. For instance, it is now possible to have your personal selection of music put onto a CD in a record store, thus giving variety without crippling added costs. Further examples of personalized products have already been given in Chapter 5. These illustrations of *mass customization* in practice relate to offers that can be made available to all buyers, providing added value within loose relationships.

For the few really important customers, *focused customization* has to go further, but it is usually a worthwhile investment. Issues which lead to value were discussed in Chapter 7, and value was there described as multidimensional as well as being variable over time. It is a very personal measure and, almost certainly, different for each individual customer. This makes it a very difficult concept to evaluate. It must be remembered that perceived value can occur both from desirable added features and services, as well as from reductions in the customer's sacrifice, the cost of obtaining a satisfactory offering.

Added value for suppliers also involves a trade-off between extra benefits and greater costs. The main benefits come from the two economic drivers of relationships. The first involves the cost of creating a customer, the second the financial advantages from retention. Many researchers consider that it is some five or even ten times more expensive to acquire a new customer than it is to continue trading with an existing one. In general this has not been challenged, and there is additional evidence of the superior financial performance of companies with a low customer defection rate, such as credit card company MBNA, to reinforce the message. Of course part of the benefit of low defection also comes from the advantages of dealing with the same customers over a period of time. This is due to the experience effect, which increases as more interactions occur between a supplier and a customer. It derives from learning about each other and then finding ways of driving down the transaction costs, thus creating a more profitable series of exchanges.

The investment costs of developing a close relationship are usually thought to involve:

1. the cost of building up a database covering the necessary information about customers and contacts
2. the development of customer-oriented service systems
3. the cost of extra direct contacts with customers.

These are actions that can easily be justified in a marketing oriented company. If they are really to help in the development of a relationship then the result of this investment must be felt as a benefit by customers. The database information and extra direct contacts must not be seen as an invasion of the customer's personal space because if they are seen as producing increased pressure then they will be counterproductive. If they offer tangible advantages because the knowledge and contacts are of real value then this is one way of passing over additional benefits to customers. Investments that are not able to be utilized in giving value to customers are purely self-indulgent and do not foster long-term relationships.

There has been work in the field of psychology with regard to interpersonal relationships where attempts have been made to measure the 'returns' for each party in an exchange. The aim is to identify and measure individuals who feel that their relationship is *equitable*, that is, they get as much as they give; those who feel severely *underbenefited*, that is, they get much less than they give; and those who feel *overbenefited*. The experience of psychologists is that the principles of a fair exchange and equity play a significant role in intimate relationships and, especially in the short term, this makes compatibility very hard to achieve. Perhaps this is an area where lessons can be learnt with regard to business relationships. However on a pain–pleasure index the way a supplier measures the costs of its investments is likely to be very different from the basis used by a buyer to assess the benefits received. If a small sacrifice by a supplier can produce a large benefit for a customer, and then that customer repays the investment with increased loyalty, an ideal win–win situation is created.

Interdependence, trust, commitment, cooperation and intrusion

There is a good deal of research into the factors that contribute to good, and bad, relationships. Perhaps the most important issue to take into account is that companies that wish to build strong relationships must give up some of their independence in committing to work with a partner. Kumar's (1996) study into 400 manufacturer–retailer links found that a company's level of trust and its satisfaction with the relationship was highest, and the level of perceived conflict lowest, in situations in which there was a high degree of interdependence. Effective relationships require partners to make contributions, and the greatest contribution is to commit to the network. In the main, Kumar was studying relationships within the distribution network, where the need for integration is greatest. It is more difficult to extend this work to individual consumers. Within a network the decision to commit in this way has to be a strategic decision taken in the light of all the implications.

To succeed as partners, companies must be able to trust each other and to make a 'leap of faith' in believing that each is interested in the other's welfare, and that neither will act without considering the effect on the other. This is supported by Morgan and Hunt (1994), who demonstrate the negative effect that opportunistic behaviour can have on the development of trust. The opposite effect is present when trust demonstrated by one partner in another leads to similar trust in return. This positive cycle of trust influences a range of exchange variables such as communication and feedback, mutual problem solving and partners accepting each other's common goals. It is a prerequisite for collaboration and coordination, and for risk and revenue sharing.

As Selnes (1998) states, 'trust in the supplier plays an important role in terms of reducing the perceived risk in extending the scope of a relationship'. Dwyer *et al.* (1987) add 'where the partners have trust in one another then there will be ways by which the two parties can work out difficulties such as a power conflict, low profitability, and so forth'. If trust exists and a strategic decision has been taken to sacrifice some degree of independence, then the conditions exist to encourage commitment to a close relationship.

A series of regular purchases is not, by itself, a committed relationship; this is only achieved when the partners cooperate with each other because of their joint desire to make the relationship work and to achieve mutual goals, although, again, this is more obvious in business relationships than consumer markets. Commitment positively influences the degree to which a partner is willing to accept or adhere to another's specific requests or policies. It also reduces the likelihood that a partner will leave a relationship.

Good, customer-oriented, marketing should include the supplier working with potential customers to develop mutually 'profitable' solutions to the problems of satisfying needs. The relationship marketing task is to work to solve a wider group of problems related to all the interactions and the ways the two parties can work together. Obviously, conflict can occur in any relationship, although conflict within distribution channels was specifically discussed in Chapter 12. All problems are best approached in an open constructive way. A history of previous productive working and communications can increase the belief that problems can be solved in a functional or beneficial way. In many relationships there is a 'reservoir of goodwill' that encourages such beliefs. Amicably resolved disputes (or functional conflict) can actually increase the effectiveness of a relationship because problems are brought to the attention of all partners and mutually acceptable solutions created.

While this section has, so far, considered the more positive aspects of relationships, there can be damaging disputes and serious consequences if trust is destroyed. No partner should be taken for granted; they are not stupid, and if they believe the relationship exists simply to exploit them and make another sale, they will seek to end the links.

In addition to the negative feelings of exploitation, there is another critical area, which is the need to respect the privacy of a partner by accepting boundaries to the depth of any involvement. A company which shows no regard for the individual privacy of its customers could undermine the confidence and perception of trustworthiness, and thus adversely affect the development of a closer relationship.

In the attempt to understand customers and to build up long-term relationships, suppliers in both consumer and business markets try to build up databases of relevant facts. These are often established without the consent of the customer, and could contain information from a wide variety of sources. Similar techniques are employed in the closely related field of database/direct marketing. In this area it is stressed that there is no excuse for using inaccurate databases. In both database marketing and in relationship marketing initiatives, if the data are well used for the purpose for which they were intended then few problems occur. If the data are abused, sold, manipulated or otherwise distorted, and the results of this are experienced by the customer, then that customer has every right to feel used, and to react against the perpetrator. This usually comes to light because an unwanted, and often irrelevant, contact is made, and this can be traced back to some personal information held by a supposed partner.

It is necessary to know a lot about your partners and potential partners, especially if deep relationships are the objective. It is therefore stupid to risk that development by a casual approach to the gathering and use of the very personal facts that are necessary to support the growth of such a partnership. The short-term gains are rarely worth the effect on the chances of achieving a long-term strategic goal.

The problems with the implementation of relationship marketing go deep. Fournier *et al.* (1998) report that:

> when we talk to people about their lives as consumers, we do not hear praise for their so-called corporate partners. Instead, we hear about the confusing, stressful, insensitive, and manipulative marketplace in which they feel trapped and victimized.

Companies may delight in learning more about their customers than ever before and in providing features and services to please every possible palate. But customers delight in neither. Customers cope. They tolerate sales clerks who hound them with questions every time they buy a battery. They muddle through a plethora that line grocery store shelves. They deal with the glut of new features in their computers and cameras. They juggle the flood of invitations to participate in frequent-buyer rewards programs. Customer satisfaction rates in the US are at an all-time low, while complaints, boycotts, and other expressions of consumer discontent rise. This mounting wave of unhappiness has yet to reach the bottom line. Sooner or later, however, corporate performance will suffer unless relationship marketing becomes what it is supposed to be: the epitome of customer orientation.

Multiple buyer–seller contacts

One of the key issues identified by Gummesson (1987) as being a reason to challenge the traditional marketing concept is the presence of 'many headed' customers and 'many headed' suppliers. The terms customer and seller are widely used, but what do they mean? The dictionary definition given in Chapter 2 is 'a customer is a person with whom one has dealings' so for individuals it is easy. But there are different influencers for most individuals, and when considering organizations it can become extremely complex. Organizational buying centres are seen to include *deciders*, *influencers*, *users* and *the rest* but the actual contact can involve many others not in the traditional buying centre. The same is true for suppliers. Contacts are not exclusively restricted to certain chosen times and with specific chosen people, and so, as Ford (1998) indicates, many interactions occur. These are perhaps the 'moments of truth' described in Chapter 10 and each interaction is an episode contributing towards the total relationship.

The control of these multiple contacts is primarily an operational matter and will be discussed in Part V. However, no strategic decision on *how to gain competitive advantage* through the management of the relationships with chosen customers can be taken without understanding the level of commitment required from the whole organization. It has already been said that marketing can make relevant promises to the selected customers, attracting them with a mix of a competitive total offering and other valuable reasons to enter into a relationship. However, it takes the whole organization, and supply network, to work in a consistent manner in order to achieve a continuing satisfactory experience for the buyers.

Gummesson's new marketing (1987) and Grönroos' (1990) redefinition of its role were both designed to support the delivery of satisfaction within the context of multiheaded interactions. The emphasis was directed towards *management responsibility* and the role of the *part-time marketers* in delivering against the promises made. The total network must be structured in a way that enables all contact episodes to be coordinated and which fosters the appropriate approach to each one of the different chosen target segments or individual customers. The policies adopted have to show consistency so that any embarrassing episodes where one part of a network, say finance, is interacting in a way different from another, maybe sales, just cannot occur. Systems to improve coordination can be introduced, but only if the top management take responsibility for and facilitate such operations.

Part-time marketers are the actual contact personnel at all levels within the network, and many of them are not in a primary marketing role. The influence of such people when delivering the specific service for which each is individually responsible is obvious. Doing this in a consistent and planned way requires both a high level of coordination and the 'dramatic change in marketing behaviour' which Gummesson demands. This does not come about without a major commitment to operate in this way, and this requires that strategic decisions are taken affecting the whole network.

Conclusions

Relationship marketing has come to dominate marketing thinking as the new millennium starts. It is not altogether new, having strong roots in all those areas where customer contact has traditionally been important, such as business to business, services and personal selling. In fact, it is fundamentally a reappraisal of the application of the basic marketing concept but one that interprets customer needs extremely widely. It is the implementation of a proper marketing orientation.

Of course the economic drivers are based on higher profitability through fewer upfront customer creation costs, and from the benefit of experience when dealing with an exchange partner over an extended period of time. But the underlying philosophy is based on the achievement of a win–win situation where both parties benefit economically, and perhaps socially, through commitment to a relationship.

Relationships can be close and deep or very loose and casual, and many points in between. What is best in one situation is not necessarily right in another, even within the portfolio of customers of a single supplier. In fact most suppliers will have only a small number of links which require extra levels of attention and which will benefit from ever closer relationship links. Many of the closest relationships will be with network partners who have to work closely together to achieve real satisfaction for the final consumers.

Relationships are developed over a long period of time. Every episode or interaction contributes towards its evolution. But a series of transactions is not, by itself, a close relationship. Relationships require trust and commitment, and the closer the links the more a participant has to sacrifice its independence in order to demonstrate this commitment. However there are real risks of going too far and invading the 'space' of a partner in an inappropriate way. The definition of relationship marketing, suggested by Grönroos, that it is the management of a firm's market relationships, probably offers the best description. The actual strategic choices that have to be made within this role of managing market links involve a great deal of careful analysis and planning.

There are parallels with many types of personal relationships, although few commercial partnerships are as focused as a monogamous marriage. While there are a number of strong, close, contractual 'marriages' between some distribution partners, most relationships involve differing degrees of friendship, but whatever the depth of the links it is always necessary to know, understand and respect your partners.

There is some evidence that a total commitment to relationship marketing can produce benefits such as increased loyalty, longer term strategic thinking, a focus away from price and an atmosphere where problems can be resolved more easily. However, adopting a customer-focused approach requires investment in time and money with no short-term returns, as well as commitment and support from all staff and relevant network partners.

The level of investment required is not always appropriate, for instance where supplier switching costs are low or stand-alone purchase events are common. Of course, there will always be some customers who will never be profitable so suitable strategies have to be devised for these. It is also important to remember that markets are dynamic, changing over time, therefore the scope and depth of all relationships must be reviewed at regular intervals.

If an organization takes the strategic decision to adopt a *customer relationship* focus or orientation, as opposed to a *customer-need fulfilment* focus, then it will involve everyone in that organization, as well as a real change from traditional marketing thinking and behaviour. Building strong relationships with selected customers can lead to real competitive advantages, but only if:

- all the implications are considered and accommodated
- full commitment and trust exist on both sides
- market conditions exist for mutual benefits to be experienced.

KEY POINTS

13.1 Relationship marketing is the management of a firm's market relationships.

31.2 Not all markets, nor all organizations, nor all occasions are suitable for relationship-based thinking. There are obvious examples of one-off transactions where the seller is the initiator and the stimulus–response paradigm is the most appropriate.

13.3 Relationship marketing is sometimes likened to a marriage, with aspects of meeting (awareness), dating (exploration), courting (expansion), marriage (commitment) and possibly divorce (dissolution of relationship). However, 'the concentration on one form of a monogamous and successful marriage has excluded many parallels in the full range of relationships. . . . In the real world both human relationships and marketing relationships can be functional as well as dysfunctional. Metaphors including stalking, rape, prostitution, polygamy and seduction may be more appropriate than marriage to describe the full range of relationships which occur' (Tynan, 1997).

13.4 For a good relationship to develop it is necessary to choose your partner carefully, structure the partnership carefully, devote time to developing the relationship, maintain open two-way communications and be entirely trustworthy.

13.5 Three key questions regarding the decision about whether to invest in relationships are:

1. Does the use of relationship marketing lead to a higher retention rate with regard to existing customers in the light of competitive offers?
2. Does the use of relationship marketing lead to a greater share of a particular customer's total business?
3. Do firms undertaking relationship marketing achieve greater levels of profitability when compared to firms not engaged in long-term relationships with customers?

13.6 Relationships are only justified if they offer a win–win outcome. Both partners must benefit from the relationship or they will not make the sacrifices necessary to restrict their freedom and commit to the partnership.

> **13.7** It is vital that anyone considering a relationship-based marketing strategy understands the issues and implications of interdependence, trust, commitment, cooperation and intrusion. In particular, issues such as intrusion can affect trust. A customer who feels the relationship does not offer them some advantages will seek to end the links.

QUESTIONS

13.1 Is it possible to identify market factors which would suggest that a relationship marketing approach is not appropriate?

13.2 What is the role of two-way communications in developing a relationship?

13.3 If a relationship requires investment and customers require added value from relationships, how is it that relationships are worth building?

13.4 What is a 'many-headed' supplier–customer relationship? How might this be controlled to ensure such contacts assist in the building of long-term relationships?

Bibliography

Aijo, T.S., The Theoretical and Philosophical Underpinnings of Relationship Marketing: Environmental Factors behind the Changing Marketing Paradigm, *European Journal of Marketing*, Vol. 30 No. 2, 1996.

Arias, J.T.G., A Relationship Marketing Approach to *Guanxi*, *European Journal of Marketing*, Vol. 32 No. 1, 1998.

Barnes, J.G., The Quality and Depth of Consumer Relationships, in M. Bergadaà (Ed.) *Proceedings of the 24th EMAC Conference*, ESSEC, 1995.

Buttle, F. (Ed.), *Relationship Marketing: Theory and Practice*, Paul Chapman, 1996.

Dibb, S. and Simkin, L., *Marketing*, 2nd European Edn, Houghton Mifflin, 1994.

Doyle, P., *Marketing Management and Strategy*, Prentice Hall, 1994.

Drucker, P., *The Practice of Management*, Pan, 1968.

Dwyer, F.R. Schurr, P.H. and Oh, S., Developing Buyer–Seller Relationships, *Journal of Marketing*, Vol. 51, 1987.

Ford, D., Gadde, L.-E., Håkansson, H., Lundgren, A., Snehota, I., Turnbull, P. and Wilson, D., *Managing Business Relationships*, Wiley, 1998.

Fournier, S., Dobscha, S. and Glenmick, D., Preventing the Premature Death of Relationship Marketing, *Harvard Business Review*, Jan./Feb., 1998.

Grönroos, C., Marketing Redefined, *Management Decisions*, Vol. 28 No. 8, 1990.

Grönroos, C., The Rise and Fall of Modern Marketing, in S. Shaw and N. Hood (Eds) *Marketing in Evolution*, Macmillan, 1996a.

Grönroos, C., Relationship Marketing: Strategic and Tactical Implications, *Management Decisions*, Vol. 34 No. 5, 1996b.

Grundlach, G.T. and Murphy, P.E., Ethical and Legal Foundations of Relationship Marketing Exchanges, *Journal of Marketing*, Vol. 57, October, 1993.

Gummesson, E., The New Marketing: Development of Long Term Interactive Relationships, *Long Range Planning*, Vol. 20 No. 4, 1987.

Gummesson, E., Relationship Marketing and Imaginery Organizations, *European Journal of Marketing*, Vol. 30 No. 2, 1996.

Gummesson, E., Relationship Marketing as a Paradigm Shift: Some Conclusions from the 30R Approach, *Management Decisions*, Vol. 35 No. 4, 1997.

Hooley, G. and Saunders, J., *Competition Positioning*, Prentice Hall, 1993.

Hunt, S.D. and Morgan, R.M., Relationship Marketing in the Era of Network Competition, *Marketing Management*, Vol. 32 No. 2, 1995.

Jackson, B.B., *Winning and Keeping Industrial Customers*, Lexington Books, 1985.

Jones, T.O. and Sasser, W.E., Why Satisfied Customers Defect, *Harvard Business Review*, Nov./Dec., 1995.

Kalwani, M.U. and Narayandas, N., Long-Term Manufacturer–Supplier Relationships: Do they Pay Off for Supplier Firms?, *Journal of Marketing*, Vol. 59, 1995.

Kotler, P., *Marketing Management: Analysis, Planning, Implementation and Control*, 9th Edn, Prentice Hall, 1997.

Krapfel, R.E. Jr, Salmond, D. and Spekman, R., A Strategic Approach to Managing Buyer–Seller Relationships, *European Journal of Marketing*, Vol. 26 No. 2, 1992.

Kumar, N., The Power of Relationship Marketing, *Harvard Business Review*, Nov./Dec., 1996.

Levitt, T., After the Sale is Over, *Harvard Business Review*, Sept./Oct., 1983.

Morgan, R.M. and Hunt, S.D., The Commitment–Trust Theory of Relationship Marketing, *Journal of Marketing*, Vol. 58, 1994.

Murray, J.A. and O'Driscoll, A., *Strategy and Process in Marketing*, Prentice Hall, 1996.

O'Malley, L., Patterson, M. and Evans, M., Intimacy or Intrusion? The Privacy Dilemma for Relationship Marketing in Consumer Markets, *Journal of Marketing Management*, Vol. 13, 1997.

Selnes, F., Antecedents and Consequences of Trust and Satisfaction in Buyer–Seller Relationships, *European Journal of Marketing*, Vol. 32 No. 3, 1998.

Tynan, C., A Review of the Marriage Analogy in Relationship Marketing, *Journal of Marketing Management*, Vol. 13 No. 7, 1997.

14
CHAPTER

EXPEDITIONARY MARKETING AND NEW PRODUCT DEVELOPMENT

INTRODUCTION

Advertising guru David Ogilvy (1983) once said 'try to inject NEW into your headlines because the consumer is always on the lookout for NEW PRODUCTS, or NEW ways to use an old product'. While he may not be correct about the extent to which consumers seek out new products, there is no doubt that new offerings do create excitement and interest in a market-place. The opposite position is not so well encapsulated in the ditty: 'if you always do what you've always done; then you'll always get what you've always got'.

Marketing people should not be seduced by the attractiveness of new product development, but rather they should see it as just one of the strategic options that must be considered when evaluating future opportunities. In fact the well publicized failure rates for many types of new products should encourage caution, especially with respect to untried new-to-the-world products or new products targeted at new market areas. If a company considers the high potential of existing products against the high risk of new offerings then a balanced view can be taken.

However, the high potential of the older products will be realized only if they continue to remain relevant to their markets. Products don't decline because of the product life cycle. Decline takes place because the offering has been allowed to become less acceptable in the basic role of meeting the needs of customers. In some cases, say where radical new technologies have been developed, it is better to move on, allowing an obsolete product to be deleted while, possibly, replacing it with a new offering. In other situations the introduction of appropriate modifications to some part of the offering will ensure that the product continues to thrive.

New product development covers everything from minor adaptations right through to radical new-to-the-world ideas. There is a distinct difference between the modifying of an existing product (incrementalism) and the development and launch of a new offering (innovation). It is obvious that in the case of incremental changes there is a key role for marketing management to play within the new product process. In particular, it should be marketing people who draw up the specifications for the required changes and they have the responsibility to ensure that the revised offering is introduced to existing customers in an appropriate way. This is part of the regular product/market management role. It has a short- or medium-term focus, but the decisions are strategic in that they are vital to the future performance of an organization.

New product decisions are especially important if a relationship marketing focus predominates. Within such relationships the emphasis is on satisfying chosen customers as their needs and wants change over time. Therefore, all proposed changes to an offering should be negotiated, perhaps going further by involving some of the key partners within the development process. Apart from the general benefit of customers' opinions, there are two other specific advantages from such involvement: first, a direct response as to how any changes might affect future trading and, second, an opportunity to build stronger links through commitment to the modified offering. This happens increasingly in the grocery food market where manufacturers work together with major retail groups to develop both store own label and branded new products.

Strategic marketing also has an obvious part to play in the wider innovation process. Doyle (1998) defines innovation as 'developing and delivering products or services that offer benefits which customers perceive as new and superior'. He goes on to suggest that it is only by continually updating existing offerings and adding new ones that an organization can hope to maintain its profitability. He is certainly correct with respect to product updating, but it is not so easy to justify every new product addition. In fact, it might be counterproductive if a range is constantly enlarged by new products, and there are many advantages from the effective pruning of a product portfolio, especially if this increases the focus on the really important areas of business.

Aaker (1998) uses the term *pre-emptive strategy* when referring to innovations. These are new business opportunities which give an advantage because competitors are inhibited or prevented from copying or counteracting them. Straight copies of existing products with no additional advantages seldom succeed. Every new product needs to be supported by some rationale which could persuade a customer to buy. Doyle classifies innovations into those developed because *new needs* have arisen, and those which update by presenting *new solutions* to replace an established offering.

Innovations imply changes. Most visibly, this is seen as a change in the output (offerings), but it usually also involves changes in inputs, with different skills and capabilities required to produce the new product/service. There are increasing risks as an organization moves away from its existing competence base. A competence is the sum of learning across individual skill sets and, as such, can include any primary activity of an organization. The concept was developed by Hamel and Prahalad (1994) and discussed, with specific examples, in Chapter 4.

An important distinction has to be made between core and non-core competencies. An offering is the output from the integration of many internal activities, and for customers it is the totality of the net benefits received that is vital to the measurement of satisfaction. All organizations have a very large number of competencies but only a few are absolutely essential for success. These are the core competencies – those skills and technologies which really contribute to profitable exchanges. Innovation, in the form of a new product offering, can be achieved by creative changes in the way existing competencies are utilized, but it is more often necessary to acquire some new capability or competence in order to support a specific new output.

The first, critical, marketing strategy decision is said to be the consideration of *where* to compete, although this is closely linked to the offerings to be made. In Chapter 4 it was suggested that a review of both:

1. the existing product/market area, and
2. new product/market opportunities

is necessary when developing future product/market strategies.

Within the existing customer group there will be opportunities to introduce either new offerings that deliver better solutions to existing needs, and/or additional products that satisfy new needs. However both categories will have a greater chance of adoption if these existing customers have previously been fully satisfied with the supplier. If, however, there are some existing customers who are currently dissatisfied, such as those described earlier as 'hostages', then for this group it is most critical that emphasis should be on developments that deliver a new and better solution to their needs. This might, possibly, avoid the more extreme forms of 'terrorism' should these customers get the opportunity to defect to another supplier. Hostage customers are unlikely to be very receptive to additional products that increase their level of business with a supplier with which they are dissatisfied.

It is always appropriate to consider all the ways of increasing trading with the 'loyal advocate' group of customers. New developments should form part of a targeted strategy aimed at retaining this group of satisfied existing customers, and it is to be hoped that they have enough confidence in their supplier to consider any new offerings against a background of strong trading links. Even so, this may not be enough if the new product offering involves displacing another 'strong' supplier. It is often forgotten that there is already a surplus of supply in many markets. Therefore, entering a new product/market area will usually involve taking business from some other organization, so it is important that those customers in the chosen segment are offered real added-value benefits in order to persuade them to switch.

Why develop new products?

New products are developed either to support an established position occupied by an existing offering, or, alternatively, to facilitate growth into a new product/market area.

In the first the emphasis is on defending an existing position, perhaps using a replacement product, in order to keep a relevant and competitive offering in a changing market-place. In a number of specific cases a fighting brand might be developed and launched directly against a competitor but expressly designed to help defend the established position. Developments such as these are undertaken as part of a strategy aimed at retaining existing customers and possibly increasing the sales to those customers. They can, therefore, also include further exploitation of strong relationship links as there could be opportunities to build additional business with additional offerings made to the same customer base.

In any defence situation it is best to be proactive, making changes before new competitors do, and in this way leading the development of the market. If an organization is forced to be reactive due to competitor activity, it is not so likely to be able to defend its position successfully. Hence this is the first reason for undertaking new product development.

The second, attack, situation will usually be chosen if the objective is to build new business by widening the scope of operations into new product/market areas. To be successful against an established competitor it is necessary to offer real advantages for customers. These can include any of the sources of competitive advantage discussed in Chapter 8, in particular those that lead to higher perceived value or lower costs. Doyle (1998) suggests that 'in the last decade a new breed of competitors have shown that it is possible – indeed, increasingly essential – to be both low cost and highly differentiated . . . offering customers the benefits of a stream of innovative products and a wide variety to choose from . . . These third generation competitors had both cost structures that could match their low-cost rivals and speciality products which could compete in innovation, design and performance with the best of the niche players'. This quotation illustrates the extraordinary requirements for an organization which wishes to enter a new market successfully. It emphasizes the importance of developing new solutions as one way to extend the scope of a business. This is the second reason for developing new products.

Growth strategies can also include new opportunities, which build on new needs that might have arisen, or capitalize on significant market changes that may have taken place. Abell (1978) has suggested that these strategic windows occur because of:

- redefinition of markets
- development of new primary demand
- availability of new competing technology
- channel changes.

In order to take advantage of these changes, and maybe to help create the conditions for change, an organization has to develop appropriate new products that reflect the new needs in the market-place. This is the final reason for product and competence development.

It will be noted that all of the above three reasons for developing new products are market focused. They cover

- retention of existing customers/users
- creation of new customers/users
- exploitation of new usage.

While there is also a role for speculative development, it only rarely leads to commercial success. However, where success does occur it is often spectacular and high profile. Products such as Post-It Notes, Walkman, Bailey's Irish Cream, Dyson cleaners, Body Shop, Apple personal computers and many others have all been developed in spite of sceptical management and discouraging research. Obviously new-to-the-world products which totally redefine a new market are unlikely to be developed if rational market decisions are made about which projects are going to be supported. Some well-publicized cases, such as 3M allowing employees time to speculate on personal projects, can pay back handsomely but it is not a reason to develop new products, just a creative way of accomplishing the 'thinking of the unthinkable' which removes the traditional constraints from the development process.

Doyle sums up the situation well when he writes 'invention is different from innovation. Many inventions fail to build markets. An invention is a new product; an innovation is a new benefit . . . Inventors, fixated by technical novelty, are particularly prone to undervalue the customer benefits. . . . Customers do not want new products, they want solutions which offer new and superior benefits'. He goes on to suggest four benefit criteria that a successful new product innovation should meet:

- *importance*: the benefits must be perceived as important by customers
- *uniqueness*: unless customers perceive the advantages as different the idea will not be valued
- *sustainability*: the benefits must be able to be sustained, and not easily copied by competitors
- *marketability*: the company should have the capability to market the new offering effectively.

The use of speculative methods can be justified but only if it is understood to be a bit of a gamble where an affordable investment is made, which an organization accepts may never pay back, but just might hit the jackpot.

A typology of new products

Tweaks

If an organization is studying its growth opportunities then the traditional Ansoff matrix is a valid starting point. Adopting a modified version of this 'product-market vector' but choosing to go even further than the adaptation by Hamel, the first consideration should be the least risky area of the existing products and markets, the top-left corner in Figure 14.1. Every organization should fully understand that this is its existing reference market in which all the possible options can be effectively evaluated. If the decision is taken to continue to operate within the current trading area, then it is important to *defend* the existing position and to develop ever closer, strong relationship links with specific chosen customers. Hamel used the term 'filling the blanks' when developing strategies for existing business areas, the task being to identify and then to tackle any gaps or weaknesses that might otherwise allow a competitor a chance.

	Existing competencies	New competencies/ old benefits	New competencies/ new products
Defending and extending existing markets	Fill the blanks Cost reductions	Premier plus 10 Improvements to existing products/ additions to existing lines	Premier plus 10 New product lines or new to the world products
Expanding into new markets	White spaces Repositioning	White spaces Additions to existing lines	Mega opportunities New product lines or new to the world products

Fig 14.1 Expeditionary marketing and new product development.
Source: Adapted from Hamel (1994)

By identifying the competencies that underlie existing products it is possible to appreciate more fully what is really being offered to our customers. Attention must be given to building from strength, not only incorporating low-cost modifications but also trying to increase the value added to each partnership through actions aimed at driving down the costs of each offering and every transaction. This will include every customer-oriented action which could add to the tangible and intangible benefits of an offering, the objective being to make it more difficult for challengers to attack, and possibly to assist in stealing some business from close competitors. While this does not have the excitement of innovation/expeditionary marketing, it is a very important area of new product and new competence development.

There is a continuing need to keep existing products both competitive and relevant given the ever-changing demands in a dynamic market-place. This involves introducing appropriate improvements to the offering at different points in time. These low-risk *tweaks*, incremental adaptations, should take place unceasingly, and they will require constant product development activities and possibly the acquisition of some new competencies.

Developments of this sort could include adopting new technological improvements and/or introducing new service initiatives which could help to further enhance customer value. 'Tweaking' is a prudent, necessary and regular review of an offering carried out in order to avoid what Johnson and Scholes (1997) call strategic drift. The necessary incremental changes will typically include the migration of features from the augmented product category into the expected product, as well as from the potential product to the augmented category as competitive offerings, and customer expectations, develop over time. See the discussion in Chapter 4.

'Premier plus 10' is the term used by Hamel and Prahalad to describe the development of those new competencies required for the future. It is still concerned with ensuring that an existing customer can continue to be satisfied with a competitive offering, and is derived from consideration of their needs over a five- or ten-year time horizon. In fact, it sometimes can take up to five years to acquire the necessary competencies and to apply them to customer needs so the time scale is not unreasonable.

Minor product and/or service modifications account for almost half of all new products recorded in the classic Booz, Allen and Hamilton (1982) study, where they are classed as

- cost reductions or
- improvements in/revisions to existing products.

Both are aimed at the existing market-place. Cost reductions are self-explanatory but should always be judged against the required level of expected benefits which will continue to be demanded by all customers. In fact, it is better to think of cost reductions as those developments that enhance the economic value of an existing offering. The other category, improvements to existing products, is specifically aimed at increasing the perceived value through appropriate product adaptations, and ensuring the continuation of a competitive advantage for the offering. Mercer (1996) suggests four areas for incremental changes:

features: making minor modifications to change what a product actually does

quality: improvements in those features valued by customers to give even greater levels of performance

style: updating the aesthetic aspects of a product to ensure it continues to be seen as appropriate for today's consumers

image: the subtle repositioning of an offer by manipulating the intangible elements and communicating them carefully.

The designations of 'filling the blanks' and 'premier plus 10' are essentially defensive, although both focus on positive actions designed to improve competitiveness. The actual strategies adopted will depend on whether the organization is a leader in its market as opposed to being one of the smaller challengers or market followers.

Twists

In contrast to the regular, low-risk new product tweaks, there are a number of more substantive attack strategies open to organizations wishing to penetrate into a new area.

The first of these involves the 'twisting' of current offerings or of the competencies of an organization. This could enable a company either to reposition its offering, making it more suitable for entry into a new market, or to make suitable additions to existing product lines to help widen the customer base. Twists will involve some additional risk but are likely to offer high returns on the investment. They are usually substantially based on the existing core competencies within the organization. Hamel and Prahalad recommend that a core competence should deliver customer value and competitive difference (advantage) as well as the potential to be extended into new areas. It is often necessary to 'twist' these competencies if such an extension is to be achieved.

The targeting of new markets or market segments in order to *expand* or *extend* a business while still utilizing existing competencies is an example of *repositioning* of the offering, that is redefining its market position. While any excursion into new markets is a form of a 'white spaces' attack strategy, Hamel and Prahalad actually suggest that the goal is 'to imagine opportunities to extend into new markets by creatively redeploying or recombining existing core competencies'. This perhaps highlights one of the possible requirements for entering new markets as it allows for consideration of and modifications to the way a total product is put together. This kind of 'twisting' is often necessary in order to be acceptable in a new market and is another role of product development.

It might also be possible to exploit changes in the primary demand for an offering by widening choice and extending an existing product line: for instance, a building contractor who offers a combined 'design and build' package in addition to the traditional service, or a bank choosing to use new technology such as SMART cards and electronic cash for use by 'personal' customers. The benefits received are increased, but the basic need can still be satisfied, probably utilizing the same umbrella brand name, but with the use of some new and many of the existing competencies perhaps applied in a different way. Such twists can offer advantages to both existing and new customers but, as they involve improvements and additions, they are still a low- to medium-risk strategy.

Twirls

The next more radical development can be thought of as 'twirls', where a new product line is offered in an attempt to enter or redefine an established market. The risk is much greater with new product lines and it is therefore essential to offer either new solutions or to meet new needs. All the evidence on new product failures shows that 'me-too' products with no real advantages have a very high failure rate.

A study of competencies should enable an organization to consider the full scope for new offerings. There will be some potential new product offerings where new capabilities are necessary and the products are possible only if it is feasible to acquire such assets. Most new offerings will require a rebundling of existing competencies, but the more radical the development, the greater the need for new competencies and it is this that increases the potential risk. One of the ways of reducing the risk is to add the required new products by acquisition rather than development. Of course it may be that a new competence is acquired rather than a whole new product. For instance, in the attempt to penetrate a new geographical market an organization might purchase a small local company in that market in order to acquire its selling skills, distribution locations and local contacts. These can be utilized with the addition of products from the parent organization, which can then be sold through the newly acquired channels.

Twinkles

The final category of newness, the 'twinkles' or new to the world products, are extremely rare: less than 10% of all new products. Typically they are high-risk, high-cost, long-development products. They could utilize a fundamental change in the basic technology, but are likely to result in a unique offering which really moves into the area of expeditionary marketing and mega-opportunities.

There is a continuing argument about the contribution of marketing as opposed to the technical input to new product development. While it is accepted that a complementary fusion of the two provides the best route for most product development, this is not completely accepted with regard to new to the world products. If there is a predominance of market issues with questions such as 'Who are the customers?', 'What do these customers want?' or even 'What business are we in?' then it is thought, by some, that major opportunities could easily be missed. This is especially true for those outside of the current activities which might lead to an entirely new market in which to compete. Nagel (1995) points out 'Overemphasis on marketing and/or the financial future can lead to a technological policy that is short termist. Business plans often have a two- to three-year time horizon, while technological development typically has a longer time-span, particularly before the investment made in the development of new technologies begins to be repaid and generate income'. Quinn (1998) reinforces this from his research stating that 'Time-horizons for radical innovations make them essentially *"irrational"* from a present value viewpoint'. His survey found that the time elapsed between invention, the technical idea and commercial production was averaging almost 20 years. As Nagel says, 'It is unlikely that a customer plans that far ahead. The development of new technologies, components and products is often started long before customer demand exists, so that the firm is able to meet the potential, future demand of customers. A firm cannot look ahead or predict with certainty the customer demand 20 years hence, but what it can do is build on its strength – its (core) technologies – and be ready to respond to changing technological needs'.

There are very real advantages for an organization if it is a successful first-mover into a new market. During the introduction and growth stages proactive initiatives by the pioneer will enable it to influence the establishing of new market norms, as well as pre-empting or even preventing competitors from entering the market. The evidence on pioneering organizations in both consumer and industrial markets seems to indicate both a higher market share and higher return on investment for these companies. However, Aaker (1998) warns that a pioneer without the resources and ability to exploit ideas can be vulnerable. He cites research that shows that only 50% of true pioneers survive, and there are a 'host of firms that have been successful in part because they were followers'.

Followers have the advantage of being 'second but better'. There are real opportunities for later entrants to revise their offerings and learn from the mistakes of the pioneers. The opportunities are greatest in the growth stage before all of the potential customers have adopted the new product. To achieve this a follower will have to respond rapidly to the pioneer, utilizing its own imitative development skills, while ensuring that the offering actually does improve on the initial offering.

The process of product development

From a marketing perspective, product development is the process that transforms an identified market need or opportunity into a new or modified offering that can be made available to customers. Usually it is seen as a series of stages ranging from the idea generation to the product launch. Each of these is considered necessary in order to proceed and to ensure that those products actually launched have the greatest chance of success. While technological quantum leaps usually fall outside this process, most other developments follows the *stage-gate* approach described by Cooper (1990). In this process both technical and marketing progress takes place in defined stages with a review, or gate, at the conclusion of each stage. At these review points a decision is taken on whether to move onto the next stage or whether to abort the project. Each of the gates involves a financial analysis as well as a forecast of the likely risks and rewards. These assessments become ever more detailed at each subsequent stage of the process.

Following a positive review, progression to a new stage will require a commitment of effort and resources, it will also deepen the emotional feelings of those employees involved in the process. It is for this reason that the evaluation at each gate should be carried out objectively by people external to the project. Remember the three filters, Figure 3.1. However, the review should be structured to allow a limited number of affordable speculative research and development initiatives to continue in spite of the financial analysis.

All new product projects start with an idea based on the identification of some market need or some potential area of opportunity. In general there are thought to be five gates (Figure 14.2) to be overcome for an initial idea as it is developed through to full-scale production and launch into a market. In fact there is a sixth test, that of the market itself, and there is still evidence that on average only one in every three new products actually succeeds in this final test.

While I worked in the Cadbury Foods Group, two decades ago, there was a myth that it required one thousand innovative ideas to produce one successful new product. This was based on the crude 'one in three' rule that only a third of all developments pass through each review gate, so:

1000 ideas are screened to become 300 new concepts
  300 concepts are evaluated to become 100 development projects
  100 projects are developed to become 30 prototypes
    30 prototypes are refined to become 10 products for final testing
    10 products are tested to become 3 products launched into the market
      3 products are launched – 2 fail, and only 1 succeeds.

This may seem fanciful, and the figures are idealized, but it does indicate the demands on the process, especially in the early stages. Obviously, less detailed analysis is required in the initial development but Cooper claims that 'the seeds of success and failure appear to be sown in the first few steps of the process'. Actually care is required at every stage of the process as it can also be shown that the later activities have a critical influence on determining success. Compromises made with respect to the final product make-up can often prove to be costly mistakes. It is possible to see evidence of products that have been launched and then subsequently failed. It is never known how many potentially successful products get aborted during the process and never actually reach the ultimate test of the market-place.

The detail of the stages and the actual management of the process is outside the scope of this book, but the strategic role of product development is a vital element within the marketing planning process. Much of marketing decision making relates to existing products in existing markets. For this area a programme of tweaks, incremental changes, involving only the two stages of modification and re-launch, is required. This is a very abbreviated process.

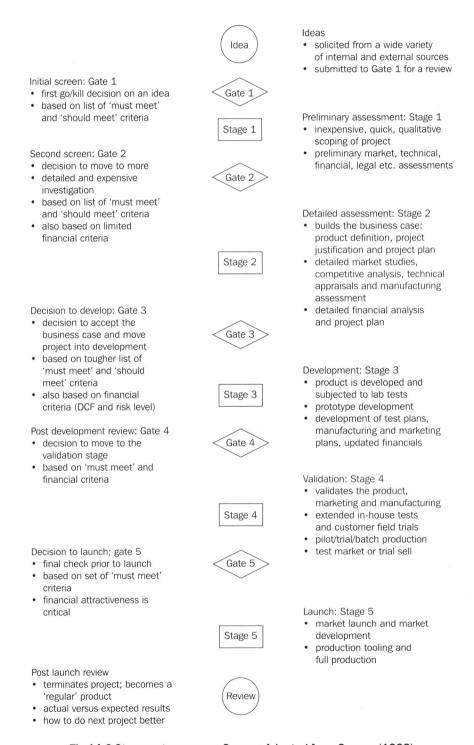

Ideas
- solicited from a wide variety of internal and external sources
- submitted to Gate 1 for a review

Initial screen: Gate 1
- first go/kill decision on an idea
- based on list of 'must meet' and 'should meet' criteria

Preliminary assessment: Stage 1
- inexpensive, quick, qualitative scoping of project
- preliminary market, technical, financial, legal etc. assessments

Second screen: Gate 2
- decision to move to more
- detailed and expensive investigation
- based on list of 'must meet' and 'should meet' criteria
- also based on limited financial criteria

Detailed assessment: Stage 2
- builds the business case: product definition, project justification and project plan
- detailed market studies, competitive analysis, technical appraisals and manufacturing assessment
- detailed financial analysis and project plan

Decision to develop: Gate 3
- decision to accept the business case and move project into development
- based on tougher list of 'must meet' and 'should meet' criteria
- also based on financial criteria (DCF and risk level)

Development: Stage 3
- product is developed and subjected to lab tests
- prototype development
- development of test plans, manufacturing and marketing plans, updated financials

Post development review: Gate 4
- decision to move to the validation stage
- based on 'must meet' and financial criteria

Validation: Stage 4
- validates the product, marketing and manufacturing
- extended in-house tests and customer field trials
- pilot/trial/batch production
- test market or trial sell

Decision to launch; gate 5
- final check prior to launch
- based on set of 'must meet' criteria
- financial attractiveness is critical

Launch: Stage 5
- market launch and market development
- production tooling and full production

Post launch review
- terminates project; becomes a 'regular' product
- actual versus expected results
- how to do next project better

Fig 14.2 Stage-gate process. *Source*: Adapted from Cooper (1993)

It is when the study involves new product lines or true innovative products that the full process must be followed through. This presupposes that all development is taking place within the organization. If an external agency is utilized to develop new ideas then it is best to consider this as an extension of the core organization and implement all stages of the process with emphasis on the evaluative gates being given by internal personnel. As has already been mentioned, there is another alternative arrangement, which is the acquisition of a new product by buying in one that has already been developed elsewhere. This is often simpler, certainly quicker, has a lower risk and is in most cases more expensive, but is not always available. If acquisition is being considered then the final review gates must be carried out with great care as part of the decision on the value of the purchase.

It has been said that:

> Having ideas is not difficult.
> Having unique ideas is more difficult.
> Bringing unique ideas to the market-place is still more difficult.
> Bringing unique ideas to the market-place, and succeeding in today's environment, and prospering in the future, is the real test.

There are immense time pressures to complete developments in the minimum possible time. These come about for three reasons.

1. When a project is being discussed *internally* it already seems established well before it is actually launched to customers. Therefore, there is an internal perception that the project is further forward than is the reality in the market-place.
2. The incredible speed with which *competitors* can copy a new offering in a dynamic market-place means that any advantage can be short lived, and continuous new developments are required to keep ahead.
3. In too many cases the need for a new product to offer is identified a little too late, when existing products have already started to decline. Therefore the replacement product is required almost instantly.

Because of such time pressures, an innovative leader may well wish to collapse the stage-gate process to allow some stages to be shortened with the aim of gaining lead-time advantages over competitors. In order to achieve this, strong links with customers and their involvement in the development process are real advantages.

Speed to market is also important as part of an effective follower strategy, followers being organizations that benefit from the pioneering work of others but that must themselves be structured and resourced to allow rapid evaluation of competitive moves, and singular effort to improve upon them. Emphasis here should be on the comparative aspects of the offering as the number-one success factor, according to Cooper, is a unique and superior product that delivers excellent benefits and value to customers. This complements Doyle's definition of innovation given earlier. However, producing a *superior* product is not a demand for a 'technical' focus although many benefits are derived from the tangible features, but it is the whole offering that must be assessed and improved. It might be that it is possible to meet customers' needs better due to some additional service such as 'we'll install and maintain your PC, removing all worries' (local computer store ad). History shows how IBM was able to capture the early computer market by offering a customer friendly, software included, financially affordable package, which solved many problems for early customers. IBM was thus able to overtake Sperry Rand, which was the pioneer, but offered only complex hardware. Likewise VHS video systems offered the desired benefit of access to a wide, ready to view, movie library and so overtook the technically superior, and earlier launched, Betamax from Sony, which lacked this extra 'ingredient'. These advantages are outside of the technological development activities and illustrate the importance of a strong marketing involvement focused on those issues valued by customers. In consumer markets understanding what is valued is especially vital in order to draw up improved specifications and to test results.

In industrial, business to business, markets the links between technical design engineers and customers is much closer than in consumer markets. Therefore there is less of a role for marketing to interpret requirements in such situations. Perhaps the major marketing role in these markets is to facilitate direct communications between the technical experts within the two partner organizations.

The factors that drive success

In Cooper and Kleinschmidt's (1993) longitudinal study of new industrial products he claimed to be able to identify the eight most critical factors that contribute towards new product success. Only one of these, the first, relates to the output and, as Cooper says, 'product superiority separates winners from losers more often than any other single factor'. Of course this could be a self-fulfilling statement as the 'superiority' of a product is evaluated by customers and therefore by definition a superior product ought to be successful. However, it is useful to look at the facts from this research:

- Products rated in the top third in terms of superiority exhibited a success rate in excess of 90%.

- Products rated in the lowest third in terms of superiority exhibited a success rate of below 30%.

In fact for the top 20% in the survey Cooper reported a success rate of an almost perfect 98% and there was no other part of his survey that indicated such a certain correlation with success. The success rate of the superior products is also backed up with high market share and achievement of high profit targets.

It will not come as any surprise to find that the seven 'ingredients' of a superior product, as suggested by Cooper, are:

- *unique attributes* and characteristics for the customer, not available from competitive products
- good *value for money*: positive economic impact on the customer
- *meeting customer needs* in a way superior to competing products
- excellent *relative product quality* compared to competitive products, and measured in terms utilized by customers
- superior *price/performance characteristics* relative to competitive offerings
- product *benefits* or attributes perceived as being *useful* by customers
- highly *visible benefits*: very obvious to customers.

These include both of the categories of *features* and *quality* mentioned earlier with respect to incremental changes, but exclude *style* and *image* which are equally part of every offering. An obvious question therefore is to establish the impact of these other elements upon product success. Cooper reports some findings in the industrial chemical market, where *superior customer service* and *technical support* stood out as the next important categories. *Image/reputation* was much further down, in fifth place behind sales force and technical competence. Nevertheless, he found there was still a positive correlation between image and success in industrial markets. It is to be expected that style/image and reputation will figure more strongly in the evaluation of new consumer product success.

As to the rest of the study, there were a number of issues related to the new product process itself that were identified as important when determining success. These included the use of cross-functional project teams, said to speed up the development time scale, and the necessity that good definitions of the project requirement are agreed by all parties prior to the start of development activities. As Doyle says, 'Larger organisations are split into functions and often operate at different sites. Knowledge about customers' needs and how they might be resolved is no longer unified. Sales, manufacturing and R&D staff report to separate departmental heads. Functions develop their own goals, often jealously guard their own territories and expand their own culture. Communicating information, priorities and direction then become a major problem. Not surprisingly, in many large organisations innovation languishes'.

A key issue in the process is the way the evaluation gates, the 'various go/kill decision points in the innovation process' are handled. In fact, these decision points are thought to be the weakest steps in the development process but, ironically, they can be decisive when determining the outcome. At each of these evaluation gates explicit results should be presented by the project team so that a decision can be made regarding progression to the next phase/stage. It is critical that the evaluations are objective and carefully considered as it is very easy to continue with a project because of the internal momentum it has generated, rather than because of the potential of that product to generate additional business. Because of this, a team of independent, objective, experienced managers should have the responsibility to review the situation critically and, if the decision is to continue, to set clear targets for the next stage. See also issues discussed in Chapter 3.

A surprising statistic from Cooper's (1990) study of over 1000 development projects was that, prior to launch, marketing activities accounted for just over 8% of the input as measured in days spent on the project, and even less in terms of money spent. Amazingly, detailed market studies, marketing research, were all too often omitted. In fact, there is a correlation showing that when more effort goes into marketing activities, the success rate of products that get to be launched into the market rises. Successful projects had, on average, just over twice as much spent proportionally on seeking customer input and feedback. This is not to belittle the importance of technical activities, but rather to emphasize the necessity of achieving a balance between marketing and the other development inputs.

An important advantage recorded in projects where there was a greater level of marketing input is a sharper focus. This results in more effective selection in project reviews and better adherence to time schedules throughout the process.

Just as good practice can be developed from the factors that lead to success, so errors to avoid can be highlighted from a study of new product failures. Of course some of these serve to re-emphasize the positive actions required. In general, six major causes of new product failure have been identified as:

1. *The better mousetrap no one wanted*: products with unique features not able to attract sufficient customers.
2. *Me-too products*: imitative products which offer *no* advantages to customers.
3. *Technologically deficient dogs*: products fundamentally flawed in their design.
4. *Price crunch products*: products priced at levels above the customer's evaluation.

5. *Competitive losers*: products that lost out to more aggressive competitors, either due to poor competitive analysis or perhaps an inappropriate launch strategy.
6. *Laggards*: products that appeared in the market too late, after the opportunity had passed.

Conclusions

New product development has two roles within any study of competitive advantage. First is the effort required to defend an existing position and to ensure that current offerings are always relevant and competitive in spite of ever-changing market conditions. The other is based on the desire of many organizations to grow (from strength!) and this can be achieved by identifying, then filling, gaps in both existing and new market areas.

The commonest and most successful areas for new products involve the modification, or even replacement, of existing offerings, often within the confines of existing market relationships. It is best to think in terms of a revised *total* offering as all elements, positive or negative, tangible or intangible, are actually evaluated holistically by a customer. This is why it is so important to understand customers and to attempt to fill the blanks with regard to the total competitiveness of the whole offering. The defensive role of filling the blanks and premier plus 10 are the more mundane tasks of marketing management, but they are also the most likely to generate a fast pay-back in terms of return on investment.

Innovation is more exciting, dramatic, expensive and high risk. There are ways of controlling the risks. One of the most successful is to listen to customers and to try to integrate them into the new product process. In fact customers are an excellent source of new product ideas, and bringing them into the development helps to gain commitment to the output.

There is nothing fundamentally wrong with 'creatively' stealing competitors' products. However, the emphasis must be on the additional creativity that enables an imitator to capitalize on someone else's earlier work. There are advantages for 'fast followers' that improve the offering (second but better), and that build on the market development undertaken by the pioneers. There are also gains to be had in any market where an existing benefit is delivered in a more acceptable (or affordable) manner. In fact, most of the really new products are still aimed at satisfying an old established need. What is unlikely to succeed is an imitation that fails to offer any reason for a customer to switch to the new product.

By studying market trends, and, in particular, closely watching competitors' actions, it is possible for any organization to ensure that it is ready to react to moves in the market but this must be supported by some commitment of the product development capability to protect an existing position against surprise competitive moves. It is possible that the necessary reaction will involve buying short-term time by marketing and promotional activities, in order to allow the more technical developments to take place. Reactive product development is necessary, just as proactive development. An innovative organization could easily structure its process to be working on the next development even before the current initiative has been launched.

The risks with new products are threefold:

1. It is very difficult to assess new market opportunities as customers have no reference points (norms) against which to judge the new product and its benefits.
2. Developing a new market involves a high requirement for customer/ market education. This takes time and money, with no guarantee of success.
3. Even if the education is successful in changing attitudes and behaviour, and an initial trial is followed by repeat demands, there is always a risk that another organization will enter the market with an improved offering – one it has been able to concentrate on while the pioneer focused primarily on market development.

Nevertheless, expeditionary marketing can offer rewards to companies prepared to take the risks. The key is the development of a 'superior' product, but the way the stage-gate development process is handled can affect the successful outcome. All developments need to progress from the initial idea through to the final product/service ready for commercial test in the market. At the end of each part of the development process an evaluation should be made before further materials, money and human resources are committed to further work. The integration of technical and marketing functions will ensure that these evaluation gates provide opportunities for an objective review of the probabilities of success. Success depends upon both effective technical development and appropriate marketing action, both focused on satisfying customers. Many ideas fail to negotiate the gates and there is evidence that the quality of the reviews have a real bearing on the best choice of continuing projects at any one time.

Twinkles, or new-to-the-world-products, are likely to be rejected in the review process. These projects have a lengthy time horizon, and the chances of payback are very small. However if it happens, the actual returns from a radical new development can be huge. Hamel and Prahalad appropriately call them mega-opportunities. Therefore, where possible, within any process room should be allowed for a few speculative projects alongside more certain developments.

KEY POINTS

14.1 Marketing people should not be seduced by the attractiveness of new product development, but rather they should see it as just one of the strategic options which must be considered when evaluating future opportunities.

14.2 New products are developed either to support an established position occupied by an existing offering or, alternatively, to facilitate growth into a new product/market area.

14.3 True expeditionary marketing is about developing new markets for the future. While having ideas is not difficult, bringing unique ideas to the market-place, succeeding in today's environment, and prospering in the future is the real test.

14.4 New products should meet the criteria of importance, uniqueness, sustainability and marketability.

14.5 As shown in Chapter 3, there are four categories of new products: tweaks, twists, twirls and twinkles.

14.6 The new product development process should include different stages of development activity, each reviewed at an appropriate time (the stage-gate process).

14.7 Remember that two out of every three new products are likely to fail. Some of the reasons are rather obvious!

QUESTIONS

14.1 What are the implications for a marketing strategist in the activity to *tweak* an existing offering as compared to the development of a new-to-the-world product (*twinkle*)?

14.2 How is it that in too many cases the need for a new product to offer is identified a little too late, when existing products have already started to decline?

14.3 How can an appreciation of an organization's competencies lead to the development of new products?

14.4 Suggest a framework of key questions for the final gate of a process, so that the offering can be assessed just prior to the decision to launch onto the market. How might the validity and reliability of the answers be ensured?

Bibliography

Aaker, D., *Strategic Market Management*, 5th Edn, Wiley, 1998.

Abell, D., Strategic Windows, *Journal of Marketing*, July, 1978.

Ansoff, H.I., *Corporate Strategy*, McGraw-Hill, 1965.

Ansoff, H.I. and McDonnell, E., *Implanting Strategic Management*, 2nd Edn, Prentice Hall, 1990.

Booz, Allen & Hamilton, *New Products for the 1980s*, Booz, Allen & Hamilton, 1982.

Cooper, R.G., The Stage-Gate System: A New Tool for Managing New Products, *Business Horizons*, May/June, 1990.

Cooper, R.G. and Kleinschmidt, E.J., Screening New Products for Potential Winners, *Long Range Planning*, Vol. 26, 1993.

Dibb, S., Simkin, L., Pride, W.M. and Ferrell, O.C., *Marketing Concepts and Strategy*, 3rd European Edn, Houghton Mifflin, 1997.

Doyle, P., *Marketing Management and Strategy*, 2nd Edn, Prentice Hall, 1998.

Hamel, G. and Prahalad, C.K., *Competing for the Future*, HBS Press, 1994.

Johnson, G. and Scholes, K., *Exploring Corporate Strategy*, 4th Edn, Prentice Hall, 1997.

Kotler, P., Armstrong, G., Saunders, J. and Wong, V., *Principles of Marketing*, European Edn, Prentice Hall, 1996.

Mercer, D., *Marketing*, 2nd Edn, Blackwell, 1996.

Moran, W.R., Why New Products Fail, *Journal of Advertising Research*, April, 1973.

Nagel, A.P., A Framework for Technological Strategy, in Bruce and Biemans, *Product Development*, Wiley, 1995.

Ogilvy, D., *Ogilvy on Advertising*, Multimedia Publications, 1983.

Quinn, J.B., Managing Innovation: Controlled Chaos, in H. Mintzberg, J.B. Quinn and B. Ghoshal, *The Strategy Process*, Revised European Edn, Prentice Hall, 1998.

Vandermerwe, S., The Market Power is in the Services; Because the Value is in the Result, *European Journal of Management*, Vol. 8 No. 40, 1990.

WHEN TO COMPETE: STRATEGIC WINDOWS

15

CHAPTER

INTRODUCTION

Today's marketing takes place in fast-moving dynamic market-places. Development times have been dramatically reduced in many industries, and life cycles have been cut short as new competitive offerings appear. Of course this is most apparent with the rapid growth in high-tech markets, fuelled by intense fast and flexible new product development. In these industries the choice of pioneer or follower does not exist; there is only one way and that is to be first, beating everyone else to the new technological breakthrough.

The focus on fast and furious activity is not apparent in all markets, but whereas speed is not always critical, achieving the optimum timing for new initiatives can be a vital component of success in every market. It has been suggested that there are only limited periods of time during which the 'fit' between the key requirements of a market and the particular competencies of a firm in that market is at its greatest.

In other words, in a dynamic market *windows of opportunity* open when the market conditions are most receptive to an initiative, but there are also periods when these windows are firmly closed. In fact it is just as bad to be too early with a new product as it is to be too late.

The suggestion that there are 'strategic windows' of opportunity which both open and close was first made by Derek Abell (1978). He considered the more revolutionary market changes when the climate might possibly be ripe for dramatic changes that capitalize on major new opportunities. He suggested four relevant situations:

1. Development of new primary demand as markets grow and develop.

2. Redefinition of markets, significantly widening the product benefits expected by customers.
3. Availability of new competing technology that can deliver benefits in a new, more effective, way.
4. Channel changes and other market structure modifications which dramatically affect the way benefits reach customers.

These windows should not be seen as mutually exclusive as, for instance, the availability of suitable new technology made channel changes possible in the case of direct home banking.

The impetus for most of Abell's changes can be seen as somehow external to the market. Nevertheless, organizations should not be reactive in their strategies, just awaiting the opening of the windows; they have to be proactive, working hard to create the right atmosphere in which new initiatives are acceptable. In this it is necessary to explore strategies that will assist the opening of the strategic windows.

Much of the recent writings on time has focused on reducing lead times and speeding up the period necessary to launch new or modified products, and this is critical in those markets where there is a culture of rapid developments. In other areas the customers can be extremely wary of changes. However, it is not the fact of change itself which tends to worry customers, but rather it is the uncertainty as to the effect of a change. Therefore the handling of any changing situation requires attention to be given to the management of uncertainty and the creation of a positive feeling of enhanced benefits as a result of the changes. This applies both to proposed product modifications and to initiatives aimed at deepening the relationship links with selected customers.

The classic work of Everett Rogers (1962) on the diffusion of innovation suggested that there are five groupings of consumer types in any market, each with a different behavioural pattern when it comes to adopting a change. He defines an innovator as 'someone who is relatively earlier in adopting new ideas when compared to others'.

Rogers' groups are:

- innovators
- early adopters
- early majority
- later majority
- laggards.

While innovators/early adopters are more ready to accept new offerings than the majority, they still require a stimulus to initiate trial, and equally they do have to be receptive to the new ideas. It is often necessary to communicate information to particular customers in order to create the right climate prior to a new product launch or some other changes. Also, actions designed to deal with uncertainty are necessary whenever attempts are made to open a strategic window. These activities, planned to 'manipulate' attitudes and to ensure a window is open when required, are vital marketing tasks

It is not only the development of new initiatives that requires appropriate timing; it is also important when making any changes to an offering. Much attention naturally focuses on the introduction of new products. This is one of the most exciting areas of marketing. The problems associated with the elimination of products from a range are rather neglected by comparison. They are, nevertheless, critical as they affect the relationships with customers, some of whom could well be fully satisfied with a product that is to be cancelled. Decisions cover both the right time to pull the plug on a newly launched initiative and accept that it has not met organizational expectations, as well as the action necessary when a previously successful existing product seems to have reached the end of its viable life in the market. In the latter case the established product will almost certainly have achieved a position with its customer group, and so decisions as to the value of this 'franchise', and how to preserve, exploit or otherwise extend it, are critical. The timing of any proposed changes is perhaps the most important part, having a crucial role in the successful achievement of changes.

Strategic windows

When a new product is launched the key marketing roles are to:

- *ensure* the product is available for all potential new users
- *educate* the target customers, especially the innovator/early adopter groups, as to the enhanced benefits of the new offering, while trying to dispel fears about the changes
- *persuade* customers to try the product, or to discuss a contract, in a way that actually minimizes the risks to the customers.

Until enough customers are seduced or cajoled into trying a new product, the combination of heavy distribution and promotional expenses together with small sales revenues usually leads to a loss, or a very low level of profit.

It becomes very important to minimize the financially difficult launch period, and to hasten the move through to a period when promotional spending can be reduced while sales actually grow fast both in respect of repeat orders from innovators and first orders from new adopters.

A number of reasons are suggested for the slow growth of many new products. These can involve the supplier's internal operations, for instance the delay in completing the production line for Cadbury's Wispa after its successful test marketing. Other reasons can centre on financial issues, maybe the cost of finding suitable locations and setting up regional outlets, and in some other cases slow growth is a result of prudent management, the need to eliminate problems before going 'global'. The major cause of delay, however, is external: it is the reluctance of many customers within the target market to change their patterns of behaviour and switch to the new offering.

Some potential customers require little encouragement to switch from their current supplier, perhaps because they are unhappy (dissatisfied, 'hostages' previously with little choice but to trade with a competitor). Others are the 'mercenary' type who reassess what is on offer every time and, where appropriate, switch to the one offering the 'best' value on each occasion. Yet others, 'innovators', are predisposed to consider new offerings and to try them because of some internal drive. All of these are categories where the switching costs are comparatively low so it is important to identify these segments. It can be extremely beneficial to target initial effort towards these groups and thereby to maximize the potential from early adopter customers.

Additionally, external changes can reduce the stability of existing markets, and this inevitably increases the number of customers prepared to reappraise their buying habits, and possibly prepared to switch suppliers. Abell's strategic windows relate to four major categories of market evolution where market stability is threatened, although there are other occasions that could be considered equally advantageous.

When there are changes in the macro-environment, such as the availability of new technology, the customer can be focused onto the new situation and thus encouraged to reappraise competitive offerings. However, Abell could equally have included changes in any of the macro factors such as political decisions, new legislation or macro-economic shifts. Unlike technological advances, some of these others can be influenced by what Kotler terms 'mega marketing' – 'the strategic co-ordination of economic, psychological, political and public relations skills to gain the co-operation of a number of parties in order to enter and/or operate in a given market' – as mentioned in Chapter 8. This adds a new dimension to the concept of 'windows' by indicating that there are actions, not part of traditional marketing, that can help to open up an opportunity and, by changing the market conditions, improve the chances of success.

Within the task environment, competitors can inadvertently allow a window to open for rivals; for instance, the problems Perrier encountered with contaminated product in 1994, leading to their product being withdrawn from the market. Although they handled the subsequent events quite well, competitors were able to gain additional positions in the market and, in many cases, these gains have been consolidated.

Putting a rival under sustained pressure can also force mistakes by even the best of companies. A decade of intense marketing activity, including the high-profile promotion surrounding the 'Pepsi challenge', is thought to be the main reason for the launch and subsequent withdrawal of New Coke in 1985. Although now confined to history, as Coca Cola has recovered from the setback, the events of the mid-1980s did give PepsiCo a real opportunity. At the time *Business Week* (1986) published an article on 'what makes Pepsi different?', suggesting it is 'the fast-moving, risk-orientated style of management with an exquisite sense of timing'. While acknowledging that 'Pepsi uses the same type of research, advertising agencies, and test-marketing tools as its rivals', the article asserts that 'its managers also recognise that marketing is more than a science based on exhaustive numerical analysis. It's a bare knuckle sport where instincts are important'. Hamel likes to call this 'strategic intent' – the ability to achieve greater results because of the extra motivation and commitment to winning by the employees in an organization.

But no company can actually rely on competitors making mistakes and thereby opening up a market. Therefore, it is usually necessary to try to create such opportunities, perhaps by changing the basis of customer evaluations. Two of Abell's strategic windows relate to possible ways of affecting the task environment with the aim of finding a point of leverage that could lead to a new market opportunity. These are

- redefinition of markets
- channel changes.

The first of these is the result of reconfiguring an offering, making it more acceptable by substantive changes to both the core and the augmented product levels. Redefining the benefits so that customers value the new mix is more than a few additional features or some extra promotion. It involves careful consideration of the customer's activity cycles, and from the understanding of how a class of products is used it is possible to develop a new package. Example of design and build construction contracts and fully integrated software/hardware systems are both examples of such thinking.

The channel changes can come from a review of marketing channels (see Chapter 12), although the impetus could come from a third party 'channel leader' such as Toys R Us with children's toys, or ISDN technology affecting the way business is conducted.

The final strategic windows situation highlighted occurs specifically in the growth stage of a new market. A pioneer will have invested time, money and effort in order to make customers aware of the benefits of a new class of products. It might, possibly, have taken advantage of one of the above types of windows to facilitate entry. But in spite of beginning to build successfully, it may still be operating in a situation where the market norms have yet to become firmly established, and where many potential customers have yet to fully adopt the new product. There is much evidence that for really innovative products there is an enhanced risk of a less than satisfactory performance. In this situation there are real opportunities for early entry by new competitors (fast followers) to build on the work done by the pioneers in creating initial awareness. It requires developing an offering (product/service) that has a comparative advantage over the pioneer. It is usually necessary to ensure the modifications actually eliminate some of problems experienced by the pioneers, but the advantage for the follower company is that it can concentrate its initial efforts on this product development while pioneers have to try to develop the market. It is only after producing a satisfactory revised product that attempts should be made to create new primary demand; that is, to 'capture' new customers who have yet to come into the new market, perhaps the early adopters and early majority types.

The product adoption process

It will be obvious already that it is dangerous to group all customers together and treat them as a homogeneous segment. In business to business trading this is less prevalent than in consumer markets. But any organization that does not understand the differing needs of its individual customers will obviously be condemned. This is appreciated with the offering but it is often forgotten when it comes to the readiness of those customers actually to make a purchase.

For industrial buyers it is likely that the complex buying behaviour, the involvement of many people as deciders or influencers as well as the operation of 'buying committees' means it is easier to understand the differences in the speed at which decisions are made. It is also possible that the culture of some companies as risk adverse can be identified, as well as knowing which firms are always ready to adopt the latest technology. Therefore marketing strategies will be tailored to suit each type of company, and to work within the time scale for that specific firm.

There are also pressures on consumer buyers, especially when an individual purchaser is considered as part of a unique social system both within their own family groups and outside with peer groups. Some people are innovators, prepared to take a risk in order to be the pioneer or leader in a particular area, maybe a new clothing trend or a novel type of food.

As mentioned earlier, Everett Rogers (1962) identified five groups with very different attitudes towards new products. He plotted them on a normal distribution, and this indicates that they are part of a continuum rather than distinct homogeneous groups. The names he gave were:

- innovators (3%): willing to take risks and/or keen for a change
- early adopters (13%): accept new ideas carefully, usually based on their own assessment
- early majority (34%): deliberate in actions but often rely on some recommendations as to adoption
- late majority (34%): sceptics, adopt only after a majority have already tried, susceptible to personal influences
- laggards (16%): suspicious of any change, take a long time to come round.

Innovators are willing to try new offerings as soon as they are launched, while laggards are very conservative in their habits and extremely reluctant to change. But even laggards do change eventually as old products are removed from the market, or when an offering is well into its maturity phase.

It is vital to understand the attitudes of the different customers in each chosen target market as it can be seen from their attitudes to new products that timing is a critical issue. The windows of opportunity will therefore open and close at different times for each of Roger's groups of customers.

Some organizations will want to focus on the innovator group. These companies will require constant product development and they will try to change their product offering before any competitor has copied them. This is particularly apparent in fashion retailing where the risks of getting things wrong are very high.

Most companies will want to offer their products to a wider market than the innovators. But even here it is critical that each group is explored and the maxim of the *right product, for the right price, in the right place, and at the right time* can be applied. In the attempt to satisfy the needs of as wide a market as possible it will be necessary to develop appropriate support packages that reflect the different needs and differing time scales of each group. The early majority group are deliberate in their product decisions and they will want to have information about a product and possibly a guarantee in case it fails to perform. The sceptical late majority require more experiential evidence, possibly a personal endorsement or some other proof that many others have already tried the offering and found it suitable. Only then will they commit to a purchase.

When launching new products and attempting to take buyers through the necessary stages of *awareness – interest – evaluation – trial – adoption* the critical issue of the *right timing* must always be considered.

Managing the product portfolio

The study of product policy, consideration of the product range, and the balancing of a portfolio are all well discussed in traditional marketing planning texts. These give a great deal of attention to the issues of developing new products and the roles of meeting new customer needs, filling gaps in the range and replacing the weaker products that are about to be withdrawn. Less attention has been given to the actual process of withdrawal and the critical importance of timing in implementing such decisions. This could be because elimination of products is a highly emotive area of marketing management. Most products have internal supporters, such as a senior manager who first introduced the product x years ago, or the operations group who have been responsible for its production over many years, or even accountants who worry about the reallocation of overheads.

Issues about the importance of a specific product as a past creator of positive feelings inside an organization tend to lead to the postponing of replacement decisions until well past the optimum time for such action. The effect of an outdated product within a range can act as a negative influence on a company's image and reputation.

In today's economic climate most companies are multi-product, i.e. they handle a multitude of offerings, whether they are in manufacturing, wholesaling or retailing. If the product range is left to grow unchecked then there are problems of resource allocation and coordination, with effort being spread too thinly over a wide range. Sir Adrian Cadbury, then Chairman of Cadbury Schweppes once said of a specific deletion 'I'm personally sorry to see it go because I enjoy the product . . . however we have too many lines and if we put the same marketing effort behind a smaller range we can afford to give better value to the consumer. We will attempt to make up the lost revenue by more activity over a reduced number of lines'. This might be good news for the consumer but it was a blow for the particular product manager at that time.

Increased competition can have an adverse affect on firms even in normal circumstances, but the situation is worsened if the company is carrying a weak product. In addition, if the profitable life of a product is considered in terms of the product life cycle then there are three important trends to consider:

1. Life cycles in many markets are getting shorter as competition increases.
2. Competition reacts more quickly to new initiatives so the period of comparative lead is rapidly decreasing. Thus pressure on price, and hence profitability, is tending to build up at an earlier point in time.
3. The minimum weight of promotion (advertising and promotion) needed to keep a product in a consumer market during the saturation stage is increasing.

Every product that lingers in the portfolio is a costly burden. It can be argued that some managers are complacent so long as the product sales cover the variable costs (marginal costing). However, this tends to overlook some important 'hidden' costs:

• Weak products tend to consume a disproportionate amount of management time.
• Weak products often require frequent price and stock adjustments.
• Low-volume products involve short production runs with costly set-up times.
• Because a company offers a less popular product this can lead to customers doubting the other offerings from the company.
• While weak products remain there can be delays in the R&D for replacements and this could be the biggest threat to the future.

The reasons for considering elimination of a product can range from external environmental changes or revisions to the structure and definition of a market (major strategic windows, as above), through to poor performance (competitive issues and customer satisfaction). In all situations the prospects for future long-term profitability can be questioned, and the possible detrimental effect on valuable and scarce company resources can be evaluated.

When considering withdrawal four main areas have to be examined:

1. internal resource availability issues
2. internal management issues
3. external customer-linked issues
4. external competitive issues.

Internally the question must be asked about how resources could be reallocated if a specific product were eliminated. Could they be put into a direct replacement or are they required to support some other initiative? If the latter then what are the implications of a withdrawal with no replacement?

Although there is no overt correlation between product elimination and management attitudes, there will be an effect. Experience has shown that some managers become very attached to products, particularly if they have nurtured them and seen them develop. In these cases any decision becomes emotional and more a matter of pride. Management attitude may also be influenced adversely if the product elimination has negative career repercussions such as job loss.

Externally the key is the effect on the ongoing relationship with customers. The opinion of key partners must be sought and the most likely customer reaction should a product be discontinued must be judged objectively. However, many of the changes considered will be the result of modifications to an old product so that, although it is being withdrawn, a new, improved, version is immediately introduced in its place. This type of action helps to strengthen relationships. However, when total withdrawal is considered the value of continuing relationships with the affected customers has to be considered from the supplier's viewpoint. It is also possible to be manipulative by considering the degree of a customer's dependence upon a product or a supplier, and reacting accordingly. If customer goodwill is to be retained for some other reason, maybe another product bought by the same customer, then some level of compensating benefits offered to cover an elimination could well be required. This could be the continuation of spare parts over a prolonged withdrawal cycle, or perhaps helping to set up alternative arrangements for a few key customers.

Elimination decisions, as well as replacement decisions, are dependent on the competitive activity within a market. In some markets it can be a real problem if sales are lost by hanging onto an old product for too long. If a competitor gains a position and sales as a result of competing against an old product, then those sales and those customers could be lost for good.

Consideration of these four aspects might lead to conflict, with each indicating a different best time frame for the change. In all cases the external views, perhaps seen as opportunities and threats, should be paramount, especially with regard to the timing of any alterations. In practice this does not always happen and too often internal issues are considered, with the result that inappropriate timing is employed, leading to a detrimental effect on a relationship, and the loss of a valued customer.

Conclusions

If organizations are to remain relevant within their markets they must know both *how to compete* and *when to compete*. As the competitive dynamics of the marketing environment change and positions are challenged, it is necessary to modify or in some cases dramatically alter an offering. It does not matter whether the appropriate changes are evolutionary or revolutionary; they must be relevant and they must be carried out at the optimum time with reference to the effect on customers.

However, customers vary in their attitudes and willingness to adopt changes. Those that are receptive must be identified fast and targeted as their experience as early adopters can reassure and encourage the more reluctant majority. It is, however, possible to take advantage of external conditions which make acceptance of changes more likely. These are the strategic windows of opportunity. It is even possible to influence some of these factors and so actually manipulate a window and thus improve the chances of a change being acceptable. The overall message of strategic windows is that the market conditions are critical to successful market entry and therefore launching new developments is appropriate only when a window is seen to be open.

Strategic windows can also occur in the markets your organization is trying to defend, giving opportunities for competitors to enter. It is possible that marketing mistakes could be one reason a market is opened up. If product quality is allowed to deteriorate and there are failures in previously accepted standards, then customers are likely to reappraise issues. This can also happen when any change is made, especially the withdrawal of an existing offering.

The management of the product range involves launching new products as well as eliminating ones that no longer fulfil internal objectives and external needs. It is just as important that the timing is right for a withdrawal as it is for a new product launch. Products must not be withdrawn too early, and they certainly ought not to be retained well past their 'sell by' date. Therefore, the concept of strategic windows that both open and close, are determined by external environmental and competitive forces, but can be influenced by marketing/mega marketing actions, is just as relevant in a product withdrawal situation as in new developments. As with everything in marketing, the final test is the effect upon the final consumer.

KEY POINTS

15.1 Much attention in marketing texts has been given to issues of where and how to compete. The critical question of timing is often ignored. Three specific areas need to be considered: (i) the strategic windows of opportunity which dictate when it is more auspicious to launch a new product; (ii) the differing behaviours of customers, which sees them accepting new initiatives in very different time frames, and (iii) the need to get the timing right when deleting a product. This is necessary to maintain the maximum effectiveness for the supply company, and create the minimum dissatisfaction from loyal customers.

15.2 Derek Abell suggested four 'windows of opportunity': development of new primary demand as markets grow and develop; redefinition of markets significantly widening the product benefits expected by customers; availability of new competing technology which can deliver benefits in a new, more effective, way; and channel changes and other market structure modifications.

15.3 There can be other windows such as one caused by a competitor's blunder, or certain external environmental pressures, perhaps new legislation, can also create new oportunities.

15.4 Everett Rogers suggested five groups of consumers based on their attitudes towards new product adoption: innovators, early adopters, early majority, late majority and laggards.

15.5 Industrial companies also show differences in their adoption behaviour.

15.6 Deleting products is more an emotional than a financial process. Some managers as well as some loyal customers will resist product withdrawal so the timing is always a matter of opinion. However, there are a plethora of hidden costs associated with weak products and these could bring an organization down.

QUESTIONS

15.1 How can a supply company redefine its market in an attempt to open a strategic window of opportunity?

15.2 In what ways could new legislation be considered to open a strategic window in a market?

15.3 What is the importance of categorizing customers as innovators, early adopters, majority (early or late) or laggards?

15.4 Suggest some of the hidden costs involved in retaining a weak product in a range.

Bibliography

Abell, D., Strategic Windows, *Journal of Marketing*, July, 1978.

Ansoff, H.I., *Corporate Strategy*, McGraw-Hill, 1965.

Avlonitis, G., Project Dropstrat: What Factors do Managers Consider in Deciding whether to Drop a project?, *European Journal of Marketing*, Vol. 2, 1993.

Dibb, S., Simkin, L., Pride, W.M. and Ferrell, O.C., *Marketing Concepts and Strategy*, 3rd European Edn, Houghton Mifflin, 1997.

Greenley, G.E. and Bayus, B.L., A Comparative Study of Product Launch and Elimination Decisions, *European Journal of Marketing*, Vol. 28, 1994.

Hamel, G. and Prahalad, C.K., Strategic Intent, *Harvard Business Review*, Vol. 6 No. 3, May/June, 1989.

Hamel, G. and Prahalad, C.K., *Competing for the Future*, HBS Press, 1994.

Hamel, G. and Prahalad, C.K., Strategy as Revolution, *Harvard Business Review*, July/Aug., 1996.

Kotler, P., Armstrong, G., Saunders, J. and Wong, V., *Principles of Marketing*, European Edn, Prentice Hall, 1996.

Rogers, E. *The Diffusion of Innovation*, Free Press, 1962.

Stalk, G., Time – the New Source of Competitive Advantage, *Harvard Business Review*, Vol. 66, July/Aug., 1988.

Vandermerwe, S., The Market Power is in the Services; Because the Value is in the Result, *European Journal of Management*, Vol. 8 No. 40, Dec., 1990.

EVALUATION AND SELECTION OF STRATEGY

IV PART

This section contains just one chapter, Chapter 16. However, the issue of strategy selection is a critical stage in the marketing strategy process. In order to decide which direction an organization should follow it is probable that several alternative actions will have to be considered. In fact there are so many different considerations arising because of the elements discussed in Parts II and III that it would be surprising if the strategy process did not generate a large number of options. The *suitable* ones must be identified and then evaluated to assess their *feasibility* in the light of known competencies and resources. Further assessment is also important as to the possible/probable *acceptability* given predictions about the future environmental pressure. On some occasions an iterative procedure will be followed, first screening out those that are totally unsuitable and then reviewing again to make a more careful judgement, especially with regard to the scope of organizational capabilities required to give the strategy selected the best chance of success.

Since the evaluation process is dependent on the opinions of managers and consultants, it can sometimes be both subjective and a little blinkered. There is no procedure which can totally eliminate such problems, but discussion of the issues can help make people aware of the risks.

Chapter 16 covers the evaluation of the various options against a background of complexity and uncertainty as to the future. The key questions revolve around the tests of suitability, feasibility and acceptability; of course, these also have to be located in the future. It is also necessary to discuss the concept of *rationality*, and yet allow that decision making can include some degree of considered judgement. It should be remembered that George Bernard Shaw suggested 'all progress depends on unrational men'. By allowing this view the possibility of selecting actions which require extraordinary effort, such as that described by Hamel in the concept of *strategic intent*, is not ruled out. In any case *evaluation* should never be seen as a process for eliminating the more radical options.

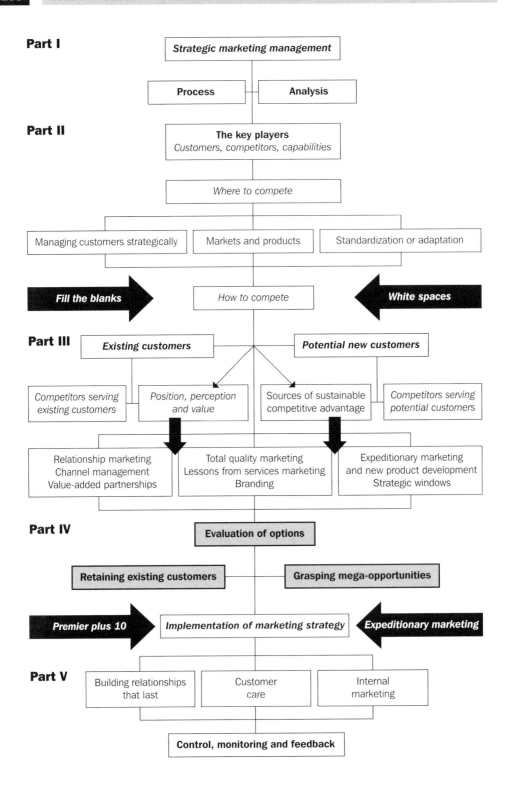

EVALUATING STRATEGIC MARKET OPTIONS

16

CHAPTER

INTRODUCTION

Maybe no reminder is necessary but marketing is based on an incredibly simple but powerful idea, that of achieving a profitable exchange between a supplier and a customer. The chapters so far have concentrated on the key aspects included in the highest level strategic marketing decisions:

- Where to compete:
  - Who can we serve?
  - What do they need?
- How and when to compete:
  - How can we satisfy customers ?
  - How can we ensure we are (and remain) the supplier of choice?

It is very easy to forget these simple questions when faced with the wide range of decisions that are part of the day to day tasks of marketing management. Remember that Aaker (1995) rightly says that the scope of a business is defined 'by the products it offers and chooses not to offer, by the markets it seeks to serve and not serve, by the competitors it chooses to compete with and to avoid'. Such choices about where and how to compete help to define strategy and shape strategic options.

But it is also easy to forget that strategy forms the link between an organization's objectives and the implementation necessary to achieve those objectives. Therefore a key precursor for strategic choice is the answer to the question 'What do we want to achieve as an organization?'. The answer will determine the corporate objectives, and act as a basis for decisions regarding corporate and marketing strategy.

There can be many options open to an organization so, ostensibly, the decision maker's task is to evaluate each of these to determine the most appropriate strategy for the future. In practice a number of options are discarded early, or not even considered, perhaps suffering from a similar filtering out process to that discussed in Chapter 3 with regard to analysis. The restrictions that can occur include limits on the width of search for ideas worthy of consideration, the interpretations (mentality filters) utilized, and the use (abuse) of power to include or exclude certain options from those to be evaluated. Of course some limit on the number of options is desirable, but there is a risk that inept filtering might ignore some of the more interesting but unconventional ideas, or reject out of hand a proposal that seeks to break the comfortable, established rules of competitive action that exist in many industries.

Porter (1996) has warned about the failure to distinguish between operational effectiveness and strategy. He suggests that in many cases management tools have taken the place of strategy. While there is a superabundance of theories and models, all supposed to assist in the making of 'marketing' decisions, these are only appropriate if the main aim of deciding a direction and scope for an organization is paramount.

Recent writings by eminent professors have sought to show strategy as a major initiative. For instance Hamel and Prahalad (1996) suggest it is *revolution*, giant leaps as opposed to incremental improvements. Certainly there is a need to explore the 'revolutionary' mega-opportunities as these can offer the best options for new, high potential profit, areas in the future, but even here the focus on chosen customers soon becomes critical. Porter describes competitive strategy is about being different, choosing a set of activities to deliver a unique mix of value to customers. In many cases organizations already have a basis for their future based on their current activities, although actions must be planned that retain or extend competitive advantages.

Strategy does not always require change. A perfectly acceptable strategy in some circumstances could be no change, but every strategist should guard against complacency as past success can be a real barrier to much needed future change. A good strategic thinker should be able to review what an organization is able to do by taking a dispassionate and objective view of the competencies and capabilities that it possesses. As a result it might be possible to define existing operations in a completely new way.

In practice actions and results speak louder than words. Strategies are not about some underlying logic based on well-crafted arguments and elegant analytical models; they are, in essence, a series of coherent decisions that can be implemented in the future. They will be remembered, finally, by the results that follow on from the decisions made and how the operational activities undertaken help to meet the organizational objectives. Strategies should be proactive, whether the decision is to grasp some major new activity or to consolidate a current position. Relationships do not just happen in a market where all customers have an abundance of choices, and to achieve ongoing profitable business requires creativity, investment and effort.

In a dynamic world with a future that is difficult to predict, strategic decisions that are well founded on the basic principles of achieving customer satisfaction stand more chance of success. This is because any resulting strategy must be evaluated from the viewpoint of the customer, who is the ultimate judge. Decisions such as offering low price in the hope of high volume, or using heavyweight promotional activities, or maybe adopting a strategy of slipstreaming (following) a brand leader could have as much to do with the availability of organizational resources as with the wants of customers.

A useful framework for evaluating decisions is the one suggested by Johnson and Scholes (1997). It considers them in relation to the objectives of an organization and its stakeholders on the basis of:

* suitability to meet objectives
* feasibility of achievement
* acceptability to stakeholders in the organization.

This has been modified for this text to suggest:

* suitability to meet customer needs in a competitive environment
* feasibility of achievement given organizational resources
* acceptability to customers.

This is not dissimilar from the strategic decision triangle in Figure 16.1. This triangle draws on the work of Noorderhaven (1995), who has reviewed the three broad categories of strategic decision making theory, and has suggested that they have meanings within the four concepts of complexity, uncertainty, rationality and control.

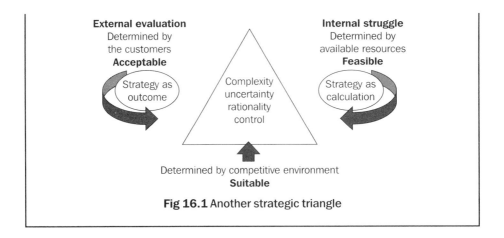

Fig 16.1 Another strategic triangle

The role of analysis

It is important to differentiate between analysis and evaluation. *Analysis* represents a structure and method for gaining information relating to external markets and internal assets. *Evaluation* is the study of options in the light of company capabilities and attitude to risk.

When the question of where to compete has been resolved, then the organization will have already made a fundamental strategic commitment. This will determine its chosen environment and, as Murray and O'Driscoll (1996) write, 'its context for action is given. It must then strive to compete, survive and prosper within the forces at work in the chosen marketplace and within the general profit potential of that industry. At the same time, it must accept that most of its learning, and therefore the character and value of its resource base, will be shaped by the chosen environment. Both environment and organisation will evolve and adapt interdependently'.

It has already been argued that effective decision making must be underpinned by a good marketing audit. In particular the analysis of a specific product/market area should highlight the few really important critical success factors in the market. These will fall into two categories, the necessary or expected features that must be present, and the energizing attributes that augment an offering and help to achieve some form of sustainable competitive advantage.

As already mentioned in earlier chapters, it is important to consider strategy as a response to external opportunities and threats as well as to internal strengths and weaknesses within the confines of acceptable risks. It is sometimes difficult to identify opportunities that move away from conformity with industry norms, and many strategic choices will inevitably be continuations of the past. But for either it is necessary to have a thorough understanding of customers, competitors, and the internal organization and to evaluate options while appreciating these issues in a competitive context. Without this any recommended strategic move will be purely instinctive. The aim is to achieve a competitive position and good strategists understand their markets and can anticipate most competitive reactions.

Formal audits must be carried out critically and the commonly used SWOT analysis is one way of focusing on the key problems and opportunities. But, as McDonald (1989) states, 'The SWOT device (Strengths, Weaknesses, Opportunities and Threats) whilst potentially a very powerful, analytical device is rarely used effectively'. This is an appropriate warning, although it is usually necessary to use a SWOT or an issue–impact analysis to identify those factors that must be tackled. It is only with this knowledge that it is possible to assess whether a proposed strategy does actually address the relevant issues.

The basis of strategic choice

The highest level decisions which relate to what we want to achieve and where we want to or should compete both seem misleadingly simple. But they are critical because they define the scope of an organization's operations and they shape many of its actions. It is only after consideration of these questions that it is possible to decide a suitable strategy on *how and when we should compete*.

Of course these decisions are not simple, nor are they totally sequential, independent or unrelated. The complexity comes from the array of choices available, the vast number of issues that can impact upon the focal organization so that it is not possible to scientifically assess the outcomes of any action, and the multiple stakeholders who each have a vested interest in any future decision. Noorderhaven (1995) likens strategic choices to a game of chess, except that in the latter there is a finite number of possible legal moves whereas business decisions are boundless. Nevertheless the comparison is justified because 'the number of contingencies is sufficiently large and there is not one clearly overriding factor'.

For an organization with existing operations – most companies – the first decision is whether to remain in their current markets and whether these are producing a return sufficient to meet corporate objectives. If the answers are yes and yes, then consideration can be given to defending an established position and ensuring a long-term future. New developments could be seen as a luxury rather than a necessity, although as Hamel and Prahalad (1994) rather dramatically ask 'is management fully alert to the dangers posed by new, unconventional rivals? Are potential threats to the current business widely understood? Do senior executives possess a keen sense of urgency about the need to reinvent the current business model? Is the task of regenerating core strategies receiving as much top management attention as the task of reengineering core processes?'. The warnings are given, and even maintaining an existing position can be fraught with uncertainties.

In the situation where current performance falls short of the objectives or targets, then it is obvious that some additional developments will be required. Any decision on a new direction would do well to take some account of those assets already available such as internal company capabilities or, equally important, external assets based on existing trading links and the attitudes of current customers. These were considered earlier under the two categories of partnership-based assets and customer-based assets.

However, any decisions will be extremely subjective, dependent on the vision of the company and what Hamel and Prahalad (1994) terms the 'genetic diversity' within the firm. 'Corporate genetics' are the 'set of biases, assumptions, and presuppositions about the structure of the relevant "industry"; about how to make money in that industry; about who is, and who isn't, the competition; about who are, and who aren't the customers; what they want or don't want; which technologies are viable and which aren't; and so on' that every manager carries around in his or her head. They include the 'beliefs, values, and norms about motivation of people; the right balance between cooperation and competition; relative importance of shareholders, customers, and employee interests' – in fact, everything that adds up to the knowledge base of the average executive within an implicit but dominant company paradigm. Of course the message is that the tighter the paradigm, the less easy it becomes to move away from it. With a degree of genetic diversity a wider focus and a more diverse set of options become apparent. However it is more than the options, it is the evaluation of those options that is driven by the organizational paradigm; this can mean that few decisions are ever taken which involve any move outside existing competencies. Compare this with the mentality filter in Chapter 3.

In many ways this bounded attitude stems from an unknown level of uncertainty about the outcome. If a situation is complex but stable, then it is possible to compute a 'best' strategic option. Where there are uncertainties due to the lack of understanding outside of a known management frame, or due to a perceived inability to predict the reactions of customers and/or competition, then finding a 'best' choice is much more difficult.

However, even under conditions of uncertainty, it is still possible to arrive at a rational decision. Rationality does not equate to an exhaustive analytical process, it can always include some degree of considered judgement. As Harrison (1987) suggests, 'all that is necessary to make a choice a rational one is that an objective exists and that the decision maker perceive and select some alternative that promises to meet that objective'. This can be modified by Simon's (1957) famous concept of *bounded rationality* that suggests that 'people act *intentionally* rationally, but only limitedly so'.

So far this section has addressed some aspects of complexity, uncertainty and rationality, which all affect strategic decision making. These together ensure that making choices is not a simple act. A final concept, control, is also necessary if choices, once made, are to be implemented. Some measure of control must be present if decisions are to go beyond the planning stage. Without the influence or power to put decisions into practice at the operational level there would be a local emergent strategy, but no chosen considered strategy would exist and there would be little point in evaluating such options. Of course this is not an attempt to stifle creativity, flexibility and speed in responding to market and customer changes; bureaucratic control can be very counterproductive in dynamic markets, but it is necessary that any empowerment should be bounded by some shared decision on how to act: a type of *umbrella strategy* where broad decisions are made, say, to the general direction of 'where do we want to compete?'; maybe, for example, in high quality/high profit markets where high tech can be exploited or, alternatively, with large customers with whom a strong relationship can be developed or some other decision. Under an umbrella strategy the operating managers then have the power to act within the guidelines but have flexibility to decide specific issues of detail at a local level.

Evaluating strategic options

The choice of product/market(s) – where do we want to compete? – sets the context within which all other decisions can be taken. The choice is highly judgmental, but certain aspects of a market are likely to be considered in helping to make the decision. As already mentioned, Aaker (1995) summed up the scope of a business as 'the products it offers and chooses not to offer, the markets it seeks to serve and not serve, the competitors it chooses to compete with and to avoid', although perhaps this definition based on products, customers and competition could be seen as too specific if a flexible, tight/loose strategy is to evolve.

Initially all 'products' and all 'customers' are available, but based on some measure of *attractiveness* it is possible to make rational judgements which reduce the choice to either a small group of potential markets or a list of preferred characteristics to be present in any market considered. The decisions on how to evaluate the attractiveness of a specific market involve areas of detailed analysis.

The classic analysis of attractiveness is contained in the nine-cell GE matrix, which also includes a study of the competitive strength of a supplier. Other similar matrices are the Shell Directional Policy Matrix, and the Arthur D Little product-market evolution portfolio. Each is a logical refinement of the heavily criticized Boston Consulting Group (BCG) box with its colourful categories of *cows*, *stars*, *problem children* and *dogs*. The replacement of the single BCG dimension of market growth with the more complex multidimensional *market attractiveness* on the vertical axis, and, on the horizontal, using measures of *competitive strength* instead of the single dimension of relative market share makes the nine-cell alternatives far stronger as analytical tools. A composite of these matrices is given by George Day (1984) and shown in Figure 16.2.

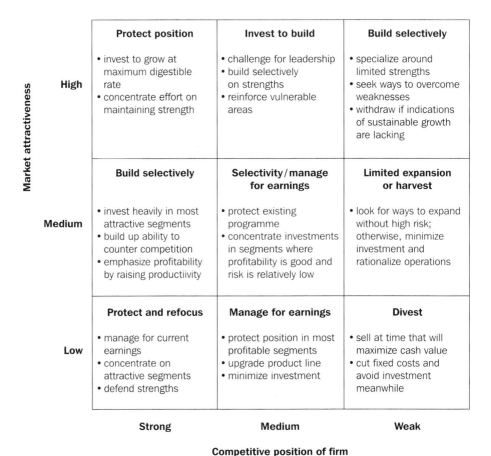

Fig 16.2 A market attractiveness/company capability portfolio matrix.
Source: Day (1984)

This matrix can be used to recommend relevant strategic choices for different combinations of situations, but the effectiveness depends entirely on the realistic identification and evaluation of market attractiveness and relative competitive strength. The position identified by analysis and discussion has to be based on an objective and unblinkered view of these two dimensions if the strategies indicated are to be appropriate. This is considered later in this section.

Murray and O'Driscoll (1996) suggest that a worth while market choice matrix will 'usually display more potential segments than the company is capable of serving. A creative business definition analysis should ensure this'. He suggests drawing a diagonal line on the matrix as shown in Figure 16.3(a), and crudely eliminating all those markets that fall below the line, even though Day suggested *managing for earnings*, and possibly *limited expansion* in some of these cases. The use of the matrix is to focus on the good opportunities and to filter out unlikely directions where weaknesses or unattractive market situations exist. Piercy (1997) is much more direct (see Figure 16.3(b)), suggesting that where strength and attractiveness are strong this should be the *core* business, and where they are weak is a 'dead end' option.

Even more dramatic is Piercy's description of an *illusory business*: a highly attractive opportunity which offers everything required from a market, but where company capabilities and strengths mean the best that could be achieved is a weak position. Piercy bluntly says 'these segments are an illusion because the market looks great – but no pay-off is possible'. It is of course possible to envisage opportunities to build capabilities to reap future rewards. This involves forecasting several years into the future, still expecting the segment to remain attractive, and investing accordingly. This is where Day suggests building selectively and seeking ways of overcoming existing weaknesses. However, as Murray and O'Driscoll say, a 'disaster scenario would be one in which capability is acquired or built through heavy investment only to find that by the time it is available and operational the segment has become unattractive'. This is an example of strategic windows closing, and there are many such examples given the time involved in building up capabilities.

There can be a situation where current capabilities are strong, but the market unattractive – often yesterday's markets. If there are genuine reasons to expect that the market can be revived then there are opportunities but all too often such predictions are just wishful thinking. Piercy again summarizes well, saying these matrices offer 'a crude and often uncomfortable view of markets'; they are very useful because they 'force an organisation to face up to realities'.

So how are attractiveness and strength measured? The answer could be seen as an entirely subjective process, as evaluation criteria have to be identified and the

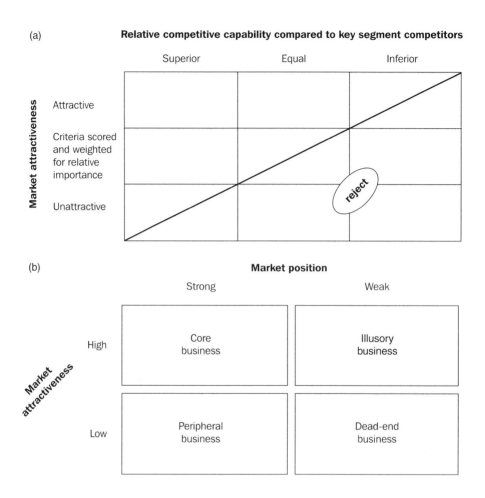

Fig 16.3 (a) Compare this with the industry attractiveness/business strength matrix, derived from the General Electric and Shell Directional Policy matrices (Figure 4.9). (b) Market attractiveness/market position matrix.
Sources: (a) Adapted from Murray and O'Driscoll (1996); (b) Piercy (1997, p. 171)

appropriate weightings of their relative importance decided. Actually, there is a need to pull away from the subjective nature and to try to take a dispassionate view of the issues so that the criteria that are finally used are the most relevant in the eyes of an objective observer. Avoiding the mentality filter. Initially a list of those things that are important should be developed, perhaps using an external consultant or more simply by brainstorming such a list. Issues linking to attractiveness could include:

- market dimensions
  - market size and opportunity
  - growth prospects
  - low level of external threats
- competition issues
  - weakness of established competition
  - barriers to new competitive entry
- customer issues
  - desires and expectations that can be satisfied
  - 'compatibility' between activity cycle of customers and competencies of supplier
  - opportunities to build a relationship
- internal 'fit'
  - acceptable level of risk
  - ability to concentrate resources
  - complements other activities
- 'social' issues
  - conserves scarce resources
  - emphasizes good citizenship.

A detailed study of the operations of market members, in particular their customer activity cycles (CACs), should point to a key basic dimension which could be very important in deciding attractiveness. This is the potential for developing strong collaborative relationships with customers. At this initial stage it is the criteria themselves that have to be developed; an evaluation based on the relative importance of the chosen criteria is the next stage.

Each of the criteria that is to be used must be considered both individually and in comparison to other criteria. The aim is to establish first which criteria are really important and to follow this up by showing the relative level of that importance. Although the discussions at this stage again risk a degree of subjectivity, it is critical that appropriate measures are developed in order that all possible options can be assessed and no false, illusory, opportunities are followed just because a market seems large or participation in a segment offers excitement.

The individual measures could involve asking how each criteria could help to establish the suitability and acceptability of a particular option in its particular competitive market-place. It should also be possible to evaluate the feasibility of actually making it happen with known capabilities. In so doing the list of initial criteria will be reduced to ones that really are considered necessary tests of future opportunities. The actual criteria chosen will be different for each organization depending on the ambitions it has and the risks it is prepared to accept.

Having chosen the criteria to be used in evaluation, it will be obvious that some are more important than others. This is then recognized by allocating different weightings to each. The weightings are yet another area where judgement is involved, so it is again an area for careful discussion and consideration. How does an organization decide that an option compatible with existing resources is more important than one which avoids head on competition, for instance? It is difficult to do this, but it must be achieved, and the relative weightings will reflect the values and internal attitudes inside an organization. A wide involvement of key opinion formers in the discussions on the relative weightings will help to establish a sound basis for the evaluation process. This wide involvement is necessary to ensure internal support for the evaluation process since by its very nature some future projects will be adopted and some rejected. To have such decisions accepted requires belief in the evaluation process and agreement that the methods used are appropriate.

It is quite easy to design a table showing the various criteria and their relative weightings, and this can be used to evaluate the options available (Table 16.1). The use of such tables might seem mechanistic and prescriptive, but it is an excellent way of forcing objective consideration of the factors involved.

The criteria will be put into the table – there may be more or fewer factors than in Table 16.1 – then an evaluation of each option can be made. Weighted scores are a combination of the previously agreed weightings and the individual criteria score. Those scoring the highest will be the ones to consider as the most attractive routes to follow. It is the belief of the author that measures related to the acceptability to

Table 16.1 Criteria and weightings for evaluation

Criteria	Weighting	Score	Weighted score
Criterion 1			
Criterion 2			
Criterion 3 (suitability)			
Criterion 4			
Criterion 5			
Criterion 6 (feasibility)			
Criterion 7			
Criterion 8			
Criterion 9 (acceptability)			
Criterion 10 (risk)			

customers are the most important. Of course no option can be adopted if it is not suitable both within an organization and in the competitive environment. It should be possible to exhibit more objectivity with regard to the internal factors; it is much less easy to affect the external competitive/environmental issues, even by adopting a form of mega marketing (see Chapter 8) in a strategy.

While it is possible to criticize theories that imply strategic actions are shaped mainly by external forces, in particular because of the complexity and the multitude of combinations of environmental variables, it is essential to try to evaluate the *feasibility* of achieving targets within a chosen market context. This requires an honest assessment of the strengths and weaknesses so that no-hope situations (dead-end options) are avoided. This emphasizes the role of strategy as a *calculation* rather than a happening, although this can sometimes be a dangerous miscalculation.

It is possible to see examples of organizations that achieved success in spite of all the apparent odds stacked against them. Hamel and Prahalad (1994) use the term 'strategic intent' and give examples of successes over the past two decades such as Honda compared to Volkswagen, Canon compared to Xerox, Compaq compared to IBM and, in the US, Wal Mart compared to Sears. A UK example might be Body Shop compared to Boots. As Hamel and Prahalad ask, 'where would you have put your money?'. They answer, 'Without the benefit of hindsight, most investors would probably have been tempted to back the firms which had the strongest reputations, greatest technological riches, and deepest pockets; these firms could hire the most talented people, had sizeable market shares, and established worldwide distribution'. Of course, we now know that all lost out, in varying degrees, to firms with fewer visible resources. In these examples the outcome belies any calculation as to the obvious feasibility of success. In retrospect it is possible to see that the strategy adopted by the smaller challenger was more suitable, but success often had more to do with internal stubbornness and the refusal to give up in spite of the odds. Success relies on strong individuals, such as Anita Roddick of the Body Shop, who did not evaluate the options but just adopted a position in which she believed. The successful cases are well documented; the failures, which are the majority, are most often forgotten.

For any strategy to succeed it must be more than suitable, feasible and acceptable in a competitive market-place – it must also be acceptable to the influential 'stakeholders'. These 'stakeholders', such as financial investors, organized unions and even suppliers, are able to exert a form of environmental pressure on many firms. In the case of the Body Shop only the initial investors had anything to lose if the strategy, and the embryonic company, failed. With established corporations there is more to lose, so fewer risks are taken as more stakeholders worry about their investments and seek to protect the past rather than gamble on the future. Noorderhaven (1995) talks of strategy as a 'ritual dance' with a level of symbolic action. This can be possible in an 'open system' where activities are undertaken to influence stakeholders to support particular strategic decisions.

Risk, market dynamics and competitive strategy

All options will involve a degree of risk as it is impossible to predict future activities of customers and even more difficult to predict competitors with any degree of certainty. The same applies to the wider marketing environment and the effect that external changes could have on the potential outcome of an option. While assumptions will have to be made in order to evaluate an option, it is necessary to consider the risks to the organization should some of the underlying assumptions prove inaccurate.

Continuing in the existing markets with the existing customer base should be the least risky of all options. It is the one where existing knowledge and contacts should make future predictions more reliable. All other initiatives include something new – new customers or new products/competencies – so there will always be an increased risk because of the move into the unknown dimensions involved. Supporting any decision will be dependent upon the prevailing market conditions. For an existing market this will include considerations such as whether the firm is a market leader or a follower. For entry to a new area for the organization it is perhaps a question of whether the market is relatively young and growing or whether it shows mature, stable characteristics. Different strategies are appropriate for pioneering activities, market following, challenging a leader or defending an existing position.

The study of market situations and market evolution will highlight different characteristics which will be good indicators of the risks involved. In every case where there is a new initiative, it is necessary to persuade customers to change their established habits and norms. The chances of achieving a change of behaviour is a measure of the risks, and this does affect the market attractiveness discussed earlier. Obviously the position and strength of competitors is another input when assessing the chances of success and the risks associated.

Some companies, especially those in particularly unstable or fast moving environments, have attempted to evaluate the wider external risks separately from the market dynamics of customers and competitors. Shell Chemicals, which uses scenario planning to test strategies, has developed a two-dimensional environmental risk versus business sector profitability matrix. This allows closer attention to be given to apparently attractive customer markets and to consider a wider number of variables. Shell also constructs scenarios of the most likely and worst case conditions which it sees as possibly occurring in the future. These are used to determine the risks of strategies in these different situations, and to minimize the overall risks to the company. The impetus for much of Shell's planning stems from the major oil crises in 1974 and 1978 when exceptional changes in the wider environment had dramatic effects on plans that were then in place. Shell also selects key employees to work for a short time, maybe a year, in a section that does 'think the unthinkable', taking a critical and dispassionate look at all the proposals in future strategies. This has two benefits for Shell: first, proposed plans are subject to rigorous testing to ensure they are robust and well based, whatever the future, and, second, the employees are trained to think objectively and critically, which is an excellent training for future senior managers of the company.

The logic behind Shell's evaluation of the wider environmental factors is that it is not easily integrated into an evaluation of market attractiveness as it requires a very different type of analysis. In many marketing plans a basic PEST analysis (see Chapter 3) looking at the macro-environment is often conducted separately from the market-focused issues. Unfortunately it is rarely used as a forward-thinking basis for testing strategy against the range of potential opportunities and threats that can occur. But if contingencies are to be established and the full risk of possible different 'futures' is to be considered then more attention needs to be given to the type of thinking undertaken by Shell.

In assessing risk it is also possible to carry out a *sensitivity analysis*. This is a useful technique that tests the effect that changing key assumptions has upon the expected outcome of a strategy. It has become more widely used as computer models of markets have enabled many changes of the different assumptions to be studied. All options are re-evaluated for each possible change and the recalculated outcomes illustrate the sensitivity of a strategy to each of the key assumptions. In some cases little will actually change, but this type of analysis will highlight those critical factors which could have a major effect on the outcome of a specific strategy. Sensitivity analysis is sometimes called a 'What if?' analysis as this is the type of question that has to be asked. Its use helps to develop a better understanding of the risks involved with an option should the future not turn out as originally foreseen.

Strategic choices

The discussions so far have looked at the evaluation of market options in order that those that are not suitable, feasible or acceptable are rejected. Those that do meet the tests are then able to be compared with each other and their different outputs and required inputs studied. The evaluation stage should yield a reduced list of options which are all within the capabilities and resources that can be acquired by an organization. The next stage is to make choices as to which options should actually be adopted. There should also be no more options than the organization can effectively handle properly. Nothing is more certain of disaster than trying to capitalize on a market opportunity while restrictions exist as to the resources necessary to undertake the tasks involved.

At this stage the chosen options can be brought together and the results compared with the overall corporate objectives set by the organization. This is an application of a planning technique known as 'gap analysis'. If the predicted outcomes fall short of targets there is a problem; if they exceed the set objectives then, at least, the plans are suitable for immediate adoption. In cases of shortfall it is usual to revisit the options but this can be dangerous and organizations should avoid arbitrarily increasing forecasts too far. It is possible that the present organization is incapable of reaching its objectives given its resource base without stretching outcomes beyond acceptable limits. In this case alternative strategies such as acquisition or alliances could be considered at a corporate level.

Even if it looks as though objectives can be met on one measure, say short-term profitability, there could be other targets to be achieved such as establishing a high-quality position in a market area, or becoming the market leader, where the consolidated plans still fall short. The achievement of strategic targets should not be considered as just a short-term aim but should look to the longer term and lay foundations for that rather than milking today's assets at the cost of the future. Where there are no realistic solutions to meeting targets within the planning time horizon it will be necessary to review the objectives themselves and adjust them to reflect reality.

The first and most important option will usually be the continuation of current strong trading positions. With some investments already made, and the presence of what have been termed customer-based assets, the requirement is to build to enhance relationships, fill the blanks and ensure a profitable future. This is the least risky option as many of the customer and market variables are known. In markets where repeat business is required it is hoped that investment in relationships will lead to an ongoing series of future exchanges. There is a difference between defending a market position by continuing investment in brands, quality delivery and other components of high perceived value, and, on the other hand, focusing specifically on individually chosen customer groups in order to build deeper relationships in existing markets. This difference must be recognized because work required to enhance the value of an offering involves different actions and marketing emphasis from that aimed at strengthening trading links with customers. Of course such activities are not mutually exclusive, although they do have different risks and rewards, and the results will be measured in different ways.

There will be occasions when the investment required to develop stronger relationships is greater than the expected return. So, in spite of the feasibility and acceptability of the option, building deeper links is not always the most suitable means of achieving corporate objectives. Such a situation exists when there is always a chance of a share in a particular customer's business, but due to the behaviour of that particular customer, or other market factors, it would not be cost effective to go beyond each separate transaction. What is necessary is to carefully choose those customers where it is worth investing in a deeper relationship, and those where it is not so important. This is not always shown up in a more general evaluation of options.

Continuing with existing trading positions is attractive only if there are realistic prospects of increased business in the future. In such circumstances extra investments are justified either to enhance the value of an offering or to increase the value of a deeper buyer–seller relationship. If there are signs of decline, maybe falling profitability or loss of market share, then the root causes must be identified and hard decisions taken. This usually involves a choice as to whether it is better to try to counteract the competitive or environmental changes and attempt to rebuild a position, or to manage an orderly withdrawal to get the greatest return from the existing assets and invest these into new developments. As discussed in Chapter 15, it is important to be aware of the strategic windows of opportunity in order to identify the most favourable conditions for different actions.

For all decisions it is the long-term effect on customers that has to be the prime consideration. It must never be forgotten that existing customers, whether satisfied or not, can influence other potential customers. So the consequential effect of any action should be considered at the same time as any decision on the most attractive options available.

Doyle (1994) says 'companies run into a crisis when organizational inertia prevents a sufficiently rapid and decisive change in strategy to meet new industry conditions'. The golden rules for any organization are that it should not be:

• blinkered when considering options
• unrealistic when evaluating options
• protective when faced with change.

Hamel reckons there are three kinds of business organizations: *rule makers* – the pioneers who first established the market, *rule takers* – the followers and later entrants who play by the given rules, and *rule breakers* – revolutionaries who reinvent the future.

The first two groups are sometimes worried about changes, even when faced with evidence that their traditional markets are threatened. In today's market-places there are no inaccessible markets, although Microsoft is close to such a position. But even Microsoft can be challenged, maybe through mega marketing and the US competition laws rather than by conventional marketing strategy. Rule makers and rule takers must decide when to forgo the past and attempt to redraw the market norms in order to deter the innovative rule breakers from outside the industry gaining a foothold. The inertia resisting change is usually well placed within an organization. As Hamel warns, 'senior management is often the repository of orthodoxy, not the source of radical innovation'. However, the message should now be clear that although existing products in existing markets might be the least risky choice, even in this 'safer' domain there are risks and hard decisions with regard to both the short-term and long-term futures. Decisions must be proactive if an organization is to maximize its return from the established position over an agreed time scale.

When it comes to decisions on options that do not fall into the 'safe' existing areas then it is necessary to give extra consideration to competitive advantage. Since a new offering usually has to replace an existing (competitive) offering, the new one must be capable of first attracting customers to try it, and then to buy it over again (repeat business). The evaluation of market attractiveness will need to be modified by measures of the feasibility of success. This includes the probability that product development can come up with an offering that is competitive and can be offered at a price customers can afford. It will be remembered from Chapter 14 that there are six major causes of new product failure. Three of these – me-too products, price crunch products and technological dogs – are options where the new product offered has no advantages for customers. If a new offering lacks competitive advantage it should be held back until this aspect can be improved. But it must not be overdeveloped as another failure category is the 'better mousetrap no one wanted' where the product has many features but not the ones to energize customers. Nor must the continued development take so long that the new product is a laggard in that it misses the strategic window of opportunity. This is also a real risk in the common situation where an attractive option is identified, but time is required to develop a suitable new product. In fact, where an opportunity has been identified the strategic choice is most often whether to commence or continue product development rather than actually launching immediately into the new product/market area.

The final category of new product failures is the competitive loser. Even when a new product has been developed, and seems to compare favourably with competitors already in a market, it is still possible for it to fail due to an inappropriate or ineffective launch strategy, which fails in the light of competitive reaction.

Example

The UK's leading brand of milk shake is Nestlé's Nesquik. During the 1970s Cadbury's developed a product which marketing research indicated was superior. This new product was launched in test market conditions in the southern TV area. Nestlé responded by exceptionally heavy promotion and media activity in that area, and this prevented the Cadbury product from achieving its sales targets even though the additional marketing activity meant the sales of all milk shakes (product class) reached levels more than double anything previously achieved. The strong established brand (Nesquik) was therefore able to utilize aggressive marketing and promotion to prevent the new entrant from achieving customer trial, and after a few months Cadbury's withdrew from the market altogether.

Strategic intent

To actually implement strategy requires a high level of commitment and effort from all those involved. This is especially necessary if it is going beyond a simple indicator of direction into the energizing of a whole organization in order to overcome severe resource limitations and still successfully achieve a result. Hamel and Prahalad suggest the measure used should not be one of organizational resources but one of employee resourcefulness, and they encapsulate this in the term *strategic intent*. This is the 'dream that energises the whole company which is often more sophisticated and more positive than a simple war cry'. The problem is that strategic choices are usually made by senior level managers, and yet the implementation of strategy relies on all employees. It is no use relying on deliberate directions if those employees do not share a sense of commitment and purpose beyond their short-term routine tasks. Strategic choices must be made, taking account of activities where all employees can be motivated. As Hamel says, 'if a compelling sense of direction is lacking, then few employees will feel a compelling sense of responsibility for competitiveness'. These issues will be covered in the next few chapters but, because of the need to consider issues of implementation, no decision on future direction for an organization and the choice of options to be adopted is complete without an appreciation of how to make them happen internally as well as externally.

Conclusions

Marketing strategy is about where, how and when to compete. In dynamic markets these questions have to be considered and reconsidered on a regular basis, and decisions have to be taken as to the future directions to be followed. The need is to develop a coherent set of decisions that can be implemented for the future. These must help an organization to create and retain customers, and must therefore offer those existing and new customers something of value when compared to alternative offerings aimed at satisfying the same needs, wants, desires and expectations.

Strategies can be seen as the link between objectives and the implementation necessary to achieve those objectives in a competitive arena. There will be many possible alternative ways of operating, and each of these must be considered so that decisions can be made on which are the most appropriate. The decisions will be made in the light of all the variables, including the environment, competition, customers and company resources. In fact, unless strategies meet the tests of suitability, feasibility and acceptability they are likely to lead to failure in the market-place.

Strategy can be seen as an *outcome*, suitable to meet objectives, a *calculation*, involving feasibility in practice, and a *set of actions* that have to be acceptable to all the stakeholders of the organization. Decisions as to the choice of strategies have to be taken under conditions of complexity and uncertainty, and they may not be entirely rational. In particular, the choice will have to include an assessment of acceptable risk for the organization as a whole. It will also require a study of how to motivate employees both to adopt a strategy and to implement it with maximum commitment and resourcefulness.

The process of generating options, evaluation and choice is critical to the future of every organization. It should be allowed the time and effort, and the top management support, necessary to ensure that the decisions taken are those that have the greatest probability of success, success being the profitable and long-term future of the organization.

KEY POINTS

16.1 Strategy is about generating options and selecting from these options.

16.2 It is important to differentiate between analysis and evaluation. Analysis represents a structure and method for gaining information relating to external markets and internal assets. Evaluation is the study of options in the light of company capabilities and attitude to risk.

16.3 Evaluation is based on value judgements filtered through those managers who participate in the decision process. The need is for objectivity and the reality often involves bias.

16.4 One way of assisting objectivity is to draw up the evaluation criteria and weightings at a relatively early stage in the process. A wide involvement of key opinion formers in the discussions on the relative weightings will help to establish a sound basis for the evaluation process.

16.5 Piercy warns of the illusory business: a highly attractive opportunity which offers everything required from a market, but where company capabilities and strengths mean the best that could be achieved is a weak position.

16.6 There are many techniques available to study strategic choices into the future. One of the most interesting is the use of scenarios in order to test against a range of possible and less probable conditions.

QUESTIONS

16.1 Strategic decisions are about what to do in the future. How can proposed actions be judged in respect of the future conditions in a market, and what problems are inherent in such an analysis?

16.2 The evaluation process involves managers who have to decide what to study and how to assess issues. There is a possibility of bias in these issues rather than an objective, impartial view. This is usually due to the preconceptions of those managers. What steps could be taken to avoid too much subjectivity?

16.3 Discuss the attitude to risk likely to be present in each of Hamel's kinds of companies: rule makers, rule takers and rule breakers.

16.4 Evaluation is often seen as a rather negative process in which reasons for not taking some actions are explored. How can an evaluation process incorporate the more positive aspects of strategic intent while still ensuring that a company does not either overextend its resources, or enter any illusory markets?

Bibliography

Aaker, D., *Strategic Market Management*, Wiley, 1995.

Ansoff, H.I., *Corporate Strategy*, McGraw-Hill, 1965.

Davies, A., *The Strategic Role of Marketing*, McGraw-Hill, 1995.

Day, G.S., *Strategic Market Planning, The Pursuit of Competitive Advantage*, West, 1984.

Doyle, P., *Marketing Management and Strategy*, Prentice Hall, 1994.

Hamel, G. and Prahalad, C.K., *Competing for the Future*, HBS Press, 1994.

Hamel, G. and Prahalad, C.K., Strategy as Revolution, *Harvard Business Review*, July/Aug., 1996.

Harrison, E.F., *The Management Decision-Making Process*, 3rd Edn, Houghton Mifflin, 1987.

Hooley, G. and Saunders, J., *Competition Positioning*, Prentice Hall, 1993.

Johnson, G. and Scholes, K., *Exploring Corporate Strategy*, 4th Edn, Prentice Hall, 1997.

Lane, D., *Systems Dynamics in Shell*, Wiley, 1996.

McDonald, M.H.B., Ten Barriers to Marketing Planning, *Journal of Marketing Management*, Vol. 5 No. 1, 1989.

Murray, J.A. and O'Driscoll, A., *Strategy and Process in Marketing*, Prentice Hall, 1996.

Noorderhaven, N., *Strategic Decision Making*, Addison Wesley, 1995.

Piercy, N., *Market Led Strategy Change*, 2nd Edn, Butterworth Heinemann, 1997.

Porter, M., What is Strategy?, *Harvard Business Review*, Nov./Dec., 1996.

Simon, H.A., *Models of Man*, Wiley, 1957.

IMPLEMENTATION AND CONTROL OF STRATEGY

V

PART

The five chapters in this last section are concerned with some of the specific topics that ultimately affect the realization of a desired strategy. Strategy can be seen as the link that runs from corporate objectives through to the action necessary to achieve those objectives. It does not conclude with the implementation, as the monitoring of results is necessary both to review progress and so that the strategy development cycle can restart in new conditions and with revised targets.

While *evaluation* is a key decision event within the strategy process, the actual choices depend for their success on many internal factors which can directly influence performance. It is important to consider *implementation* in terms of what is really necessary to enable the chosen strategy to be undertaken under the specific market conditions likely to prevail. For a customer the important issues are the *positioning* of the supplier, *promises* made and the influence or *persuasion* exerted. The internal actions must reflect these and reinforce them in a consistent and complementary way. Chapter 17 looks at implementation issues in a general way, and Chapters 18 and 19 follow up the specific internal and external perspectives. First, Chapter 18 focuses on the customer and looks at the promises made, especially with regard to the management of levels of *expectation* and *satisfaction*. The relevant issues of *quality* and the role of *customer care* are followed by a discussion on *recovery*; that is, how to retrieve a situation if things go wrong and a customer complains. Chapter 19 turns further into an organization by concentrating on the key human resource, people employed in every role in any organization. The concept of *internal marketing* is covered, especially its roles in the two areas of achieving a *customer orientation* with a drive for *strategic consistency*.

Chapter 20 then looks in a deeper way at the relationships that can be built between a supplier and a customer. Where *relationship marketing* is appropriate, building

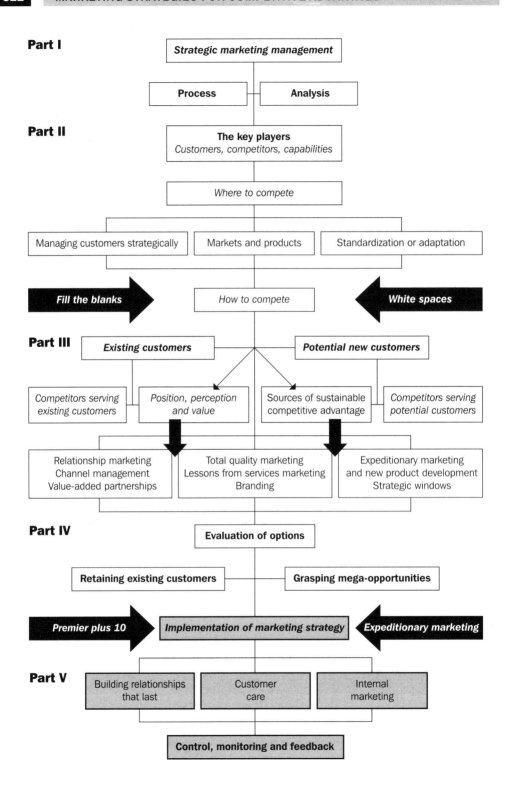

such links requires a shift in organizational culture and the achievement of this is covered, along with other issues, in developing a relationship marketing orientation. As has already been discussed in Chapter 13, not all situations are suitable for relationship marketing but where the benefits exist and the strategic decision has been taken to utilize it, there must be a complete change affecting the whole organization. It is important to stress that relationship marketing is not an addition to the marketing mix but a totally different way of thinking and operating with respect to customers.

Chapter 21, the final chapter, reflects the need for *monitoring* and *controlling* activities. This is a vital check on performance and hence the final topic, but it feeds into the new requirements and new analysis for future decisions. The idea of *feedforward* activities, positive impetus for future correction action, is stressed as opposed to feedback and blame. Control is considered from three different aspects: individual self control, small group social control and corporate cultural control. The chapter studies different control measures, both strategic and tactical, and the data required for effective measuring of what is happening. If the feedforward principle is actually applied then the whole cycle of strategy development can begin all over again.

IMPLEMENTING MARKETING STRATEGY

CHAPTER 17

INTRODUCTION

'Enough about strategy – let's see some clever executions!' This was a headline of an article by Thomas Bonoma in 1988. As he says, strategic brilliance cannot compensate for dim tactical follow-through. It does not matter how much thought and cleverness has gone into the strategic options and strategic choices, it is the implementation of the resulting decisions that is seen and judged by the customers.

Henry Mintzberg (1987) reinforced the message by his studies of deliberate, intended strategies and how these are often 'remodelled' by a kind of emergent strategy which appears in practice and affects the resultant activities. As he says, 'for a strategy to be truly deliberate – that is to have been realised exactly as intended – would seem to be a tall order . . . [especially due to] interference by market, technological or political forces'. But, as he also suggests, the emergence of a consistent strategy without any planned intentions is also unlikely and lack of consistency will not satisfy customers. If the investment of time and effort that goes into developing new competitive options is to be realized then it is important that the intended strategy should form the basis for future action. There might be a few 'emerging' variations within agreed boundaries due to the requirements at the points of delivery, but the substantive direction and prepared game plan should drive all the activities affecting the chosen customers.

One particular problem is that those whose job it is to implement the plans have rarely had the privilege of seeing the full range of inputs that were available to those who finally decided the strategic direction. Therefore, those charged with implementing do not always understand the rationale behind decisions, nor why one strategic option is being adopted above the alternatives. It is critical to success that the chosen options are more than acceptable. In fact, the aim must be to generate real commitment to implement strategy as intended wherever possible.

Marketing is not about capturing customers and holding them as 'hostages' because these customers will move on as soon as a better proposition is available; they are the loyal but dissatisfied customers discussed in earlier chapters. The marketing task is to create satisfied customers who wish to return on their own terms. They will do business in the future because they like what is offered and, more importantly, trust an organization to keep the *promises* it makes to customers. This aspect of customer retention was considered as a source of competitive advantage in Chapter 8. The programmes of action that are developed from agreed strategies must be designed to achieve desired results through satisfying the chosen customers.

An alternative 7 Ps framework, relating to strategic issues and including such concepts as *positioning, promises, persuasion* and *power*, was proposed in Chapter 8 as part of the discussion on how marketing can achieve its objectives. If we now consider the original, operational 7 Ps framework from Booms and Bitner (1981), which reflects the actual controllable variables of marketing activities, it will be more appropriate to the task of implementation. This framework encapsulates all the elements of the marketing offering that are seen by customers. While the customer judges the ingredients of the mix in different terms to a supplier, the categories of *product, price, place, promotion, people, process* and *physical evidence* are a good focus for the implementation of strategy. Of course, these elements must also be seen as inputs that affect the sources of competitive advantage such as quality, branding, value-added partnerships and positions. However, they also represent the most widely remembered model of operational marketing, and it is a model that is often known by people working in all the other functional (non-marketing) areas of a business. Each component individually and all components taken together are the total offering delivered to a customer in the hope of satisfying a need or meeting an expectation.

Bonoma (1985) decried what he called 'democratic even-handedness' in marketing operations, whereby in the organizations he researched there seemed to be an adequate level of attention generally across all the components of the mix, but insufficient emphasis on the specific factors that actually create the competitive advantage. He suggested that successful organizations had a 'real facility for handling one or two (critical) marketing functions with greatness or at least flair, and competence at the remainder. No marketers are good at everything, but the most able concentrate on doing an outstanding job at a few marketing subfunctions and an adequate job with the remainder'. Of course the concentration is required on the specific subfunction that actually energizes customers and creates a stimulus for them to trade.

Bonoma differentiates between *marketing programmes*, which integrate all the separate elements of the marketing mix into a coherent, consistent whole, and *marketing actions*, which lead to effective handling of individual parts of the mix. In order to achieve strategic objectives systems must be devised to allocate the tasks to suitable employees, who might not be marketing staff, as well as organizing these efforts and monitoring the resulting implementation.

In just the same way as strategies have to be designed to offer sustainable competitive advantage, so the implementation has to reflect this in reality. Customers have to actually see what it is that makes a product/service offering unique and attractive. As Piercy (1997) says, 'customers could not care less about impeccably planned structured marketing programmes. They are only concerned with the value of what we offer them'. Strategic decisions cannot be considered as 'good' or 'bad' without seeing the results, in practice, following implementation of those decisions.

The borderless organization

This is a term used by David Aaker (1995) after quoting from an American symposium of CEOs where it was suggested that an organization should 'break down the horizontal barriers between functions and the vertical barriers between organizational layers [thus] encouraging employees to collaborate with one another . . . and turn their creativity into productivity'. This is necessary for the implementation of plans as, looking at the operational marketing mix, the tasks involved to deliver the 7 Ps are organization-wide. It is, of course, possible to establish who contributes directly to each element and actually meets the customers, as well as identifying those who support this interface. Reiterating the words of Kotler (1997), 'marketing can make promises, but it takes the whole organization to deliver satisfaction'.

Piercy rejects terms involving the word marketing because '*markets* are more important than marketing, and markets and customers are the responsibility of every manager in a company, not the "property" of marketing specialists'. In fact, this emphasizes the need to focus attention and responsibility for markets onto those areas where it belongs in an organization. That is *everywhere*, the purpose of all *business* being to 'create and retain a customer' (Drucker, 1968). If there is a marketing department then most activities relating to the market/customer will be seen as belonging there; if no such autonomous function exists then it will be necessary for every employee to become customer/marketing oriented.

The definition of marketing in an 1880 Webster's dictionary is:

1. The act of purchasing in a market;
2. Articles in market; supplies.

This shows the *market* focus before marketing became seen as a business discipline. Even now the way some marketing departments are conceived and constructed leaves a lot of room for problems while diverting others away from the required level of customer orientation. Van Mestag (1988) reported 'sometimes the people engaged in marketing research, advertising and sales promotion are lumped together and called the marketing department, which may or may not have a marketing manager. Product development, pricing, distribution, customer service and public relations could well be housed elsewhere undoubtedly under several other functional headings.' Whatever the reason for this type of arrangement, usually to do with inter-functional struggles and departmental autonomy, the result is that the 'crucial attribute of marketing does not get a chance', that crucial attribute being the achievement of a position in the minds of customers that is more than the sum of the individual parts of an organization's activities.

Antony Brown (1995) of IBM has suggested that 'There are now two types of organization: those with a marketing department and those with a marketing soul . . . the latter are the top performing companies, while the former, steeped in business traditions of the past, are fast disappearing'. It is not necessary for a marketing department to exist in order to successfully implement a marketing programme; what is necessary is the marketing orientation (soul) and a way of ensuring that everything offered to customers integrates into a coherent, consistent and competitive package which delivers real advantages for a purchaser.

Marketing orientation

The need for a marketing orientation throughout an organization has been present in marketing literature for a long time. It has not always been as dominant a requirement in management and operational studies, thus suggesting that it is not as widely accepted outside of marketing. However, there is enough appreciation of the underlying issues for believing that there could be a shared understanding of the key components of the concept. These are

1. the customer is central to all activities
2. a business thrives by satisfying customers
3. considerations must extend beyond customers to consider the activities of competitors
4. internal activities must be prepared in the light of uncontrollable external events.

Attempts have been made to suggest how to implement a marketing orientation, especially in a medium to large organization where personal contact is difficult because of the numbers of employees. Techniques such as internal marketing (see Chapter 20) and many organizational schemes are a possible answer. Free dissemination of information, as suggested by Jaworski and Kohli (1993), is another. In fact these authors, who fully understand that information can be a critical source of power within an organization, define a marketing orientation specifically in terms of the level of information flow.

However, exchange of information is not enough – unless actions are taken as a result then nothing is achieved. Slater and Narver (1995) suggest that

> A market orientated culture can achieve maximum effectiveness only if it is complemented by a spirit of entrepreneurship and an appropriate organizational climate, namely, structures, processes and incentives for operationalizing cultural values. Thus, the critical challenge for any business is to create the combination of culture and climate that maximizes organizational learning to create superior customer value in dynamic and turbulent markets, because the ability to learn faster than competitors may be the only source of sustainable competitive advantage.

The concept of a learning organization has a resonance in organizational dynamics, and where a business can learn it should be possible to reduce internal conflict and move towards a more integrated and better focused operational output. However, learning is not the same as reacting to everything that is said, especially in the area of customer complaints. Learning must involve the sensible use of all relevant information, and the checking of some intelligence to ensure a balanced reaction. Information sourced from customers is obviously vital but as Piercy warns there is nothing fundamentally wrong with most customer feedback: 'most of the ways things can go wrong reflect how the results are *used* and *abused* – the goal is to learn and improve, not to "police" the company'. The following five rules are drawn from Piercy's work.

1. Don't over-react to isolated criticism: check out the impact and respond accordingly.

2. Don't react only to those things you think are important: unless responses are made to things customers think are important then the point could be missed.
3. Don't under-react to criticism: never underestimate feedback and fail to take necessary action.
4. Don't be defensive: good learning accepts all criticism as a positive opportunity to learn and improve. If it is used to find excuses or to punish then it is negative and counterproductive.
5. Don't allow customer feedback to be used to fight internal battles: internal conflict can sometimes be positive and constructive, but not if an internal culture exists which focuses on interdepartmental issues instead of external market-based activities.

On a more positive note, Piercy suggests that some companies that 'do focus on what is value to their customers, and who do listen and learn, go much further – they are obsessional and almost overpowering'. He uses the widely known examples of Ray Kroc of McDonald's with an obsession based on *quality*, *service*, *cleanliness* and *value*, and Terry Leahy of Tesco, who, according to a press report, has an obsession 'not with the graphs that show good performance, but rather with the customers who shop in the stores. Leahy's mantra is "customer". The word creeps into every sentence to the point of irritation. But to Leahy it is the crux of the business and the focus'.

These examples of customer focused obsession refer specifically to chief executives. For a wider marketing orientation it must be reflected, although perhaps not quite so compulsively, throughout all parts of the entire organization.

The marketing mix

The marketing mix has been used to describe the different elements of a marketing programme for almost 50 years. In the 1960s Neil Borden (1965) reduced it to twelve internal and four external components and this was further truncated to the 4P framework a few years later. The effect of this reduction has led to an oversimplification of the mix and a worrying misunderstanding as to its role and scope. Used casually, the 4 Ps are a strategic snare which particularly allows descriptions of product and place that are inadequate and sometimes misleading. The 4 Ps are also rather production oriented as they focus on what is to be offered and not on the receipt by customers of an *acceptable*, *affordable* and *available* offering.

Many writers have attempted to correct the limitations of the 4 Ps by the addition of yet more Ps, elements that are also important and happen to start with the letter P.

Perhaps the best of these comes from the 1981 review of the mix by Booms and Bitner, which expanded it to 7 Ps specifically to deal with the marketing of service products. In fact the additional elements of people, processes and physical evidence are applicable to all offerings and should always be included if a framework of easy to remember words beginning with the letter P is to be used. Paul Fifield (1998) suggests the use of the P-words is an invaluable *aide-mémoire* for harassed marketers. However, harassed marketers should worry about taking too many shortcuts and not giving enough attention to the full scope of each of the components.

- Product is more than product; it is the augmented offer, including services and all intangible contacts.
- Price is more than money paid; there are other non-financial sacrifices to consider, and anyway customers do not just compare prices, they measure values.
- Place is a poor way of describing how products are made available to customers. Too often it becomes geographic and yet place has nothing to do with location.
- Promotion sounds short term. It would be better if all communication links between buyer and seller (two-way) were studied.
- People count, especially in interactive situations. They matter prior to a purchase, they help deliver satisfaction at the time of a purchase, and are involved in building relationships following a purchase. People are not just employees; they could work for partners or intermediaries, or they could just be independent influencers.
- Processes are about the impersonal operations on the one side, and the processes and systems that affect motivation and quality control on another. The processes employed have a direct effect on final satisfaction.
- Physical evidence perhaps has more to do with place than the usual interpretation of the earlier P. All tangible evidence surrounding the delivery of a product/service is included here.

In some ways it might be better to reduce the marketing mix to 3 Ps – position, promises and persuasion. These were all discussed in Chapter 8. The point is that each of these three elements can be expanded to cover some part of whatever is being offered to customers:

- Positioning involves all the preconceptions about a product/service held by the customer as well as the perception as to the specific offer.
- Promises are the totality of everything the supplier says and does which communicates the offer.
- Persuasion can cover the methods utilized to influence customers to deal with one supplier rather than another.

Whatever is included or excluded in a marketing mix, it will always be possible to criticize its use if it is presented as a collection of discrete individual elements. A market offering is *everything* presented to a potential customer, tangible or intangible, positive or negative, necessary or unnecessary, valued or not valued – in fact, all that is in the marketing mix, and more. Customers judge offers as a whole, total entity, therefore the coherence and consistency of all the component parts are evaluated. A comparison will be made as to how each of the available offers is perceived to match up to the basic needs and wants of each individual customer. They are not assessed on the menu of factors to be found in each separate category of a nominal marketing mix, however many P-words are used.

Unique offerings: achieving a competitive edge

There are many marketing people who would agree with Bonoma that the 'democratic even-handedness' of an offering does not really give a competitive edge that can be promoted. Bonoma suggests playing to marketing strengths and handling one or two (critical) subfunctions with flair, although the rest obviously require competence. The critical elements that have to be identified are sometimes termed the *unique selling propositions* (USPs). The idea of selecting a USP to exploit is strongly supported in advertising theory and selling tactics. The logic behind the concept suggests that by promoting only one (at most two) benefits to the chosen customers, a stronger, more powerful message can be developed. The proposition can reflect a dominant requirement of the customer group and its promotion can be used to establish a strong position in the market-place.

The word 'unique' is important as the use of a USP is aimed at differentiating one offer from all others, as well as energizing customers who value the chosen attribute. A USP may be based on any part of the marketing offer, tangible or intangible, but it needs to come from the features that augment a product rather than those that are expected from all competitive products. It could involve anything from a valuable integral benefit through to the quality of service and delivery support. There may be several unique features in any offering, but care should be taken in promoting too many differences as this could lead to a confused position in the minds of customers. The USP is often communicated in the media headlines that are sometimes used to promote a product.

Apart from the specific single USP it is also important that the total offering should be competitive in its market-place. This means that the marketing mix, with all its individual elements, should reflect a combination of attributes and features not matched by existing competition, and difficult for new competitors to copy. Provided the unique aspects of the mix are valued by customers, the total mix will be competitive. However, selecting a specific USP is still usually the best way to promote the offering.

Consistency, coherence and cohesiveness

Earlier in this chapter it was said that it is not necessary for a marketing department to exist in order to successfully implement a marketing programme. But it is necessary to ensure that everything offered links to form a consistent, coherent, cohesive and competitive package which delivers real advantages for a customer. The operational plans will be developed from the more general strategic options, but it is sometimes difficult to draw a clear line between strategy and tactics. Often the strategists will also be involved in the implementation, both because this encourages greater commitment and, as Fifield notes, 'they find it irresistible'. All planners know the importance of implementation if the strategy process is finally to prove its value, and many fear that their plans will be corrupted if they are not involved at the final stage. Therefore the development of specific programmes is a key part of the process.

The first requirement is for the individual components, and the whole integration of these, to be consistent with the overall strategy. The programmes must reflect the strategy and be designed to contribute to its achievement without any contradictions.

Coherence means the logical or orderly relationship of the individual parts – a form of horizontal consistency or congruity. The decisions as to the promotional effort should be sympathetic to and supportive of the product features. The price message ought to reflect the value position; the people and processes must not detract from the tangible elements of the offering and so on. Since the different components of an offer are likely to be constructed and delivered by different parts of an organization, there needs to be an overall 'product champion' who draws up a total game plan, briefs the various people involved, monitors everything offered and evaluates this from a customer's perspective. This is the traditional role of brand/product management. Many organizations today do not have large corporate marketing departments that cover all the specialist roles of marketing, and the product manager (champion) role can be undertaken outside of a functional area, but there must be an individual charged with the task of making everything happen in an coherent way if the programmes are to be effective.

Cohesion is the final consideration and it is also a key brand/product management role. Not only must the components of the marketing mix be consistent with the overall strategy and coherent between each other, but the totality of the offering, how the components come together as a unified whole, is the ultimate test as seen by customers. The unity and mutual attraction of the components can achieve a form of synergy which ensures the total offering is greater than the sum of its individual parts. This will be reflected in a strong position, and possibly a powerful brand image which can be exploited for the future.

Conclusions

Implementation of strategy is the final, critical examination. All the thinking and research will then be exposed to the ultimate test of a hostile and changing external environment. It is at this stage that the strengths of a strategy are revealed.

The first task is to ensure that the programmes developed actually reflect the strategic options chosen. Changes should only be allowed if they are small ones of detail and if the overall planned direction remains unaltered. Where major deviations which change direction emerge it is usually due to the problems of generating appropriate actions from the stakeholders involved. This is a failure of implementation.

The programmes themselves will involve many staff from across an organization. Most of the elements of the so-called marketing mix will rely on staff who are not part of the marketing department, if such a department actually does exist. There is a real task to be undertaken to deal with this, it is the need to control the coherence of the individual components delivered to customers, and to ensure they integrate into a cohesive whole.

For the total offering to be competitive it will need to pass a test of uniqueness with regard to other offerings. The unique features should be ones valued by customers, and are usually additional to the expected features in the mix. One or two individual features of unique status and exceptional value to customers can be selected for specific promotion. These unique selling propositions are what should energize customers to buy, and contribute towards the achievement of a strong position in a chosen market.

In order to achieve coherent and cohesive implementation of strategy it is beneficial to identify a 'product champion' who can take overall responsibility for effective delivery. If this is done well the resulting offering will actually seem to be greater than its constituent parts, which is where real competitive performance is achieved.

There is a distinct difference between adequate execution of a marketing pro-gramme and a really strong marketing performance which manipulates the balance of an offering to achieve something special.

KEY POINTS

17.1 It does not matter how much thought and cleverness has gone into the strategic options and strategic choices, it is the implementation of the resulting decisions that is seen and judged by the customers.

17.2 All marketing implementation revolves around making promises to customers, and then keeping those promises. Marketing can make promises, but it takes the whole organization to deliver satisfaction.

17.3 A marketing offering is *everything* presented to a potential customer, tangible or intangible, positive or negative, necessary or unnecessary, valued or not valued – in fact, all that is in the marketing mix and more.

17.4 Implementation really requires a positive marketing orientation. Brown (1995) suggested that 'There are now two types of organisation: those with a marketing department and those with a marketing soul . . . the latter are the top performing companies, while the former, steeped in business traditions of the past, are fast disappearing'.

17.5 While it is not necessary for a marketing department to exist in order to successfully implement a marketing programme, it is necessary to ensure that everything offered links to form a consistent, coherent, cohesive and competitive package that delivers real advantages for a customer. Customers judge offers as a whole, total entity, and therefore the consistency, coherence and cohesiveness of all the component parts are evaluated.

QUESTIONS

17.1 If marketing implementation is about making and keeping promises, how can issues of persuasion of, and power over customers be viewed from the market-ing operation's standpoint?

17.2 Why is it important for effective implementation to achieve a 'borderless organ-ization' where employees collaborate with each other?

17.3 The 4Ps and 7Ps frameworks for remembering the scope of the marketing mix are invaluable *aides-mémoires* for harassed marketers. Explain the problems that could arise with each component if marketing programmes accept short-cuts and marketers do not give enough attention to the full scope of each of the components of the traditional mix.

17.4 What is a USP? How can the emphasis on one proposition be justified while attempting to achieve a consistent, coherent and cohesive presentation of everything that is seen by a customer?

Bibliography

Aaker, D., *Strategic Market Management*, 4th Edn, Wiley, 1995.

Adcock, D., Bradfield, R., Halborg, A. and Ross, C., *Marketing Principles and Practice*, 3rd Edn, Pitman, 1998.

Bonoma, T., *The Marketing Edge*, Free Press, 1985.

Bonoma, T., Enough about Strategy – Let's See Some Clever Executions!, *Marketing News*, 13 February 1988.

Booms, B. and Bitner, M.J., Marketing Strategies and Organisation Structures for Service Firms, in J. Donelly & W. George (Eds) *The Marketing of Services*, American Marketing Association, 1981.

Borden, N., The Concept of the Marketing Mix, in G. Schwartz (Ed.) *Science in Marketing*, pp. 386–397, Wiley, 1965.

Brown, A., The Rise and Fall of Marketing, *Marketing Business*, February, 1995.

Dibb, S. and Simkin, L., *Marketing*, 2nd European Edn, Houghton Mifflin, 1994.

Doyle, P., *Marketing Management and Strategy*, Prentice Hall, 1994.

Drucker, P., *The Practice of Management*, Pan, 1968.

Fifield, P., *Marketing Strategy*, 2nd Edn, Butterworth Heinemann, 1998.

Hamel, G. and Prahalad, C.K., *Competing for the Future*, HBS Press, 1994.

Hooley, G. and Saunders, J., *Competition Positioning*, Prentice Hall, 1993.

Jaworski, B.J. and Kohli, A.K., Market Orientation; Antecedence and Consequences, *Journal of Marketing*, Vol. 57 No. 3, 1993.

Kotler, P., *Marketing Management: Analysis, Planning, Implementation and Control*, 9th Edn, Prentice Hall, 1997.

Mintzberg, H., Five Ps for Strategy, *Californian Management Review*, Fall, 1987.

Morgan, R.E., Katsikeas, C.S. and Appiah-Adu, K., Market Orientation and Organisational Learning Capabilities, *Journal of Marketing Management*, Vol. 4, 1998.

Murray, J.A. and O'Driscoll, A., *Strategy and Process in Marketing*, Prentice Hall, 1996.

Piercy, N., *Market Led Strategic Change*, 2nd Edn, Butterworth Heinemann, 1997.

Slater, S.F. and Narver, J.C., Market-orientation and the Learning Organization, *Journal of Marketing*, Vol. 59, 1995.

van Mestag, M., *Think Marketing*, Mercury Books, 1988.

18 CHAPTER

SATISFACTION AND CUSTOMER CARE

INTRODUCTION

Mahatma Gandhi is reputed to have written 'A customer is the most important visitor on our premises. He is not dependent on us, we are dependent on him. He is not an interruption of our work, he is the purpose of it. We are not doing him a favour by serving him, he is doing us a favour by giving us the opportunity to do so'. This certainly sums up the role of a customer, and it should indicate the supreme need for caring for that customer.

The basis of marketing and business success is the creation and retention of customers and this involves meeting the requirements of chosen customers better than the competitors – thus not only satisfying those customers but doing so in a hostile competitive environment. For the customers the offer will be assessed in terms of utility and comparative value. For the supplier the measure is one of quality – *product quality*, *service quality*, *relationship quality,* but all defined in terms of how well these different elements of the offering deliver value to customers. In fact it is sometimes said that the most important single factor affecting a business's performance is the quality of its products and services relative to those of competitors. Quality has already been discussed in Chapter 9. It is a widely used term in management and, as a result, has been defined in many different ways. It is often considered as a measure of excellence; it certainly means 'pleasing' consumers, so perhaps the best definition of quality is that it is everything that leads to long-term customer satisfaction. Achieving this aspect of quality is obviously the best way to care for customers.

In simple terms, *satisfaction* occurs when a customer's expectations are either met or exceeded. The reality is a little more complex in that the crucial question is whether a customer's *perception* of the 'total product' as received, including the intangible features, actually compares to their expectations. Customers evaluate products, services and relationships against some personal set of criteria, which includes the perceived benefits and costs, *value* being the computation of the perceived benefits of ownership when reduced by both the cost of acquiring a product and the cost of ownership. It may be that the evaluation is based on criteria that are not properly understood by the supplier.

Customers receive more than a simple commodity product when they enter into any transaction. The total offering is *everything,* both tangible and intangible, favourable and unfavourable, that is received in an exchange. Prior to a purchase customers will form their own *expectations* as to what they are likely to receive and the probable costs. One of the inputs will be the *promises* made by the supplier about a particular offering; another is the experience properties if a previous purchase has taken place, or if some positive or negative 'word of mouth' recommendations have been received. Further input will include all the tangible cues designed to add credence properties to an offering and give customers confidence in the supply company, as well as the customer perception of such intangible issues as company image, brand reputation or relationship value.

There is a vital relationship between promises and the total product actually offered. Customer satisfaction, and the development of long-term relationships, is heavily dependent upon the promises both made and kept. Effective marketing therefore involves more than the development of acceptable, competitive offerings; it includes the crucial management of customer expectations through the promises made to prospective buyers. This is another dimension of customer care.

It is obviously important that any promises made are not exaggerated as this will lead to a serious risk of customer dissatisfaction after a purchase if the expectations are built up too much when compared to what is actually possible. However, marketing has to develop a balance to ensure that the prior expectations of customers about a particular offering do not fall below what is actually being offered. If they do then the supplier will be at a competitive disadvantage in any comparative evaluations made as part of a customer's decision making. This could mean that a trading exchange might never be achieved. Therefore managing expectations is critical to both competitive success and to customer satisfaction.

Even with limited marketing input an offering will 'acquire' a level of expectation which becomes the customer's benchmark of satisfaction when a purchase exchange finally takes place. After a purchase every customer has the additional input, either positive or negative, from their experience, which, when set against the expectations that existed prior to buying, enable them to judge satisfaction. Where there is a perception that experience exceeds expectations there will be satisfaction with the offering received. The opposite indicates dissatisfaction and this might lead to a complaint, unwelcome word-of-mouth publicity or even the loss of a customer.

Kotler (1997) once stated that 'customers are attracted by promises and retained through satisfaction'. He went on to say, 'Marketing can deliver the promises, but only the whole company can deliver satisfaction'. The level of satisfaction and the experience properties of an offering can only be assessed after a purchase. However, the total offering usually includes some intangible features, and these can have a disproportionate effect on an evaluation of the whole. All intangibles are subject to variability and this inevitably means that the satisfaction experienced by customers is also variable, with the service delivery sometimes falling short of what is required. The *defining moments* in any customer exchange are often the actual 'service encounters' between the parties.

It is the interactions with customers – the *moments of truth* – where levels of customer care are most obvious. The perception created at these times can be critical to the achievement of customer satisfaction. Gummesson (1991) described the contact staff as 'part-time marketers', people whose prime job is not marketing, but because of their interaction with customers have an influence on the delivery of an offering. Moments of truth are usually thought of as direct personal contacts, but they could be remote such as a telephone call, or even more impersonal, maybe a letter or an invoice. However, each contact has a bearing on the customer's perception of the levels of care shown by the supplier. The skills and training of all contact staff should be of a sufficiently competent level because the supplier has to put a great deal of trust into these employees. Sometimes there are only a limited number of suitably skilled personnel.

A large number of complaints, as well as some customer defections, are caused by the unhelpful attitude of some contact employees. In Chapter 10 it was reported that in some industries over 90% of service staff are in so-called dead-end jobs, those with low basic wages and little prospect of promotion. In spite of this it is necessary to find ways of ensuring that all contact staff really do care for the customers of their organization.

Customer care obviously embraces everything that is done for a customer. The prime test of good care is satisfaction but the reasons why it is so important are much deeper. The key point is that future exchanges are heavily dependent on all previous experience. There is much evidence to suggest that where high levels of satisfaction exist then customers are very likely to continue to trade with a supplier. The basic economic facts are:

1. It is more expensive to acquire a new customer than it is to retain an existing one.
2. The longer the history of satisfactory links between a supplier and a customer, the more profitable the relationship.
3. High satisfaction is especially important to encourage good word-of-mouth recommendations, which will encourage other customers in the future.

It has often been said that the 'Quality of a product is remembered long after the price is forgotten'. The opposite is also true, and a poor quality experience will decrease the value received as well as the level of satisfaction. Of course, there are times when things do go wrong, and when they do the result can be overwhelming.

Kevin Gavaghan, former Marketing Director of the Midland Bank, once said 'As a percentage, the error or failure rate is minimal. . . . But for the individual consumer, the real rate is made more real by the fact that the topic is money and the failures always occur in front of a supermarket checkout or late at night, or abroad or in an emergency. . . . And like the product, the memory has a long life and is spread by word of mouth' (Gavaghan, 1993). His message might refer to the customers of his bank, but the point is that problems occur in awkward places and at awkward times and this makes them more acute. The negative impact of a problem is dramatically increased by the multiplier effect whereby every dissatisfied customer may tell at least 10 others about the problems.

In spite of all the quality assurance and controls it is very difficult to achieve zero defects. Even if this seems to be possible, every organization should think about possible contingent actions should the worst happen. There are a number of simple rules that can help to reduce the impact if a problem occurs. Basically these are *act fast*, *recover the situation*, which is more than replacing a faulty part, and *consider the value* of a satisfactory recovery and not the cost.

There are four main themes to customer care which must be seen both individually and as an interdependent set. These are:

- ensuring satisfaction
- managing expectations
- quality interactions (good moments of truth)
- recovering after complaints.

Customer care as ensuring satisfaction

Achieving high levels of satisfaction is the best way of caring for all those customers with whom an organization wishes to trade. For anyone else, outside of the group of chosen customers, a different strategy is necessary to avoid discontented but unwanted customers. However, satisfaction is not an absolute measure, and in a dynamic marketing environment the factors that lead to satisfaction are continually being reappraised, with customers becoming increasingly sophisticated as well as more critical in the way offerings are assessed. It is apparent that there is now 'unlimited' consumer choice, a higher level of competition and an ever-increasing pace of change in most markets. To respond to this most organizations find that they have to operate on many fronts such as simultaneously reducing costs and improving efficiency, reducing prices while raising levels of quality and service, and speeding up innovations in order to keep customers in the face of intense competition.

At the level of the individual customer there is another problem in that each customer is different. Each perceives things differently, and requires a different mix of benefits for their individual satisfaction. While it might be possible to segment a market on the basis of these criteria, it is likely to result in a very different grouping from a segmentation carried out using alternate discriminators such as customer descriptions, product use and usage, or profit potential. It is arguable whether a useful actionable segment will be found from the criteria of individual satisfaction, so the real, different requirements of each customer will have to be accommodated in individual marketing mixes if each is to be properly satisfied.

As Pine *et al.* (1995) say, 'Customers, whether consumers or businesses, do not want more choices. They want exactly what they want – when, where, and how they want it – and technology now makes it possible for companies to give it to them'. The concept of *mass customization* has already been discussed in Chapter 5, and real satisfaction is the result of such policies. Of course it is not always possible, even with modern technology, to give every customer an individual offering, but it is easily possible to go close to this with personalized mixes of the elements that make up the total offering. An offering can be divided into the tangible features, service features and image features. In a differentiated market it is possible to modify some of these features to provide a close match for specific customer requirements.

In particular, some of the differences demanded can be accommodated at the level of personalized delivery and support, the intangibles of the sales and customer contact occasions. In this it is possible to utilize the heterogeneity and inseparability of service features to positive advantage in delivering satisfaction. While not so easy with tangible product features, even here it is becoming possible, by creative use of new technologies, to achieve a measure of customization. Examples of this were given in Chapter 5, but in many cases the fully customized offering was only part of a total range, and sales of standardized products, at the right price, still continue because customers make their own, individual choices based on their personal trade-off between features and value.

Studying the five most important dimensions of service quality, as developed in the SERVQUAL model (see Chapter 10), can be useful in a wider application than just services (Table 18.1). The categories include all the dimensions of quality as suggested by David Garvin (1987) and it is possible to relate them to customer requirements to act as an indicator of the aspects that are really critical when attempting to satisfy a customer (see Chapter 9). Research needs to be undertaken so that the important aspects of each are established, and these can then be reflected in the personalized marketing mix for each individual customer.

There is a commonly accepted wisdom that satisfied customers are also loyal, repeat customers. In fact, this is not always the case as has been explored by Reicheld (1996), who reminds readers that 'it is not how satisfied you keep your customers, it's how many satisfied customers you keep!'. Of course there will be *loyalists* who are both loyal and satisfied and who consider a supplier and its offering so superior to the competition that they continue to buy regularly. On the other hand, there are *mercenaries*, as discussed in Chapters 2 and 8, who exhibit no loyalty, considering each exchange as a separate event, and re-evaluating potential suppliers on every purchase occasion. All customers have a free choice to decide between competitive offerings, and it should not matter if dealings are with loyalists or mercenaries because the aim should be maximum satisfaction for both groups. This should be the objective of any effective customer care programme.

Table 18.1 Dimensions of quality

SERVQUAL	Examples	Garvin's dimensions
Tangible aspects	Facilities, appearance and equipment	Performance, durability, features
Assurance	Knowledge, security, professional credibility	Conformance
Reliability	Ability to perform dependably and accurately	Reliability
Responsiveness	Willingness to help and promptness	Serviceability
Empathy	Care, courtesy and attention as perceived	Perceived quality

Other strategies will have to be devised in order to try to convert mercenaries into repeat buyers. It might be possible to do this by adding some extra, unexpected service which enhances an offering in an unforeseen, but wholly acceptable, way. By increasing the value and satisfaction for the customer over and above the desired level of expectation it is possible to produce some measure of *unanticipated value* and maybe some customers could be converted. However, there are many mercenaries whose behaviour has more to do with a cautious overall attitude to purchase decisions, and they will not be changed by a 'one off' special offer. Of course, this type of conversion strategy is not part of ongoing customer care.

Customer care should include everything that could maximize the level of satisfaction for a purchaser both during and after a sale. It includes the elements of the basic offer as well as the after-sales support expected, such as service, installation, training and maintenance. All too often, such activities are seen as bolt-on extras and not as an integral part of the marketing mix. If they are important to achieve satisfaction, and if they are expected by customers, they must be given the status and attention due to them alongside all the other elements that are critical to achieving customer satisfaction.

Customer care as managing expectations

Satisfaction is measured by the differences between what is perceived to have been received by a customer and the prior expectations of that customer. In the traditional marketing concept the suggested starting point is the establishment of the needs and wants of customers before working out how to satisfy them. Two problems arise directly from this. First, it is sometimes difficult actually to satisfy a customer in every way demanded and so some compromises have to be made, which reduce the absolute level of satisfaction possible. This could involve price being not as low as desired due to the need to include a special feature. The second problem is that expectations are not always the same as needs and wants. Customers make their own compromises, and if they do not believe a particular combination of features can be found within available and affordable boundaries they will modify their expectations accordingly. Hooley (1993) explores these gaps in his study of quality marketing.

However, it should not be left to a customer to unilaterally amend expectations. Marketing involves promises made to customers and these are a vital input into the development of expectations. As was said in the introduction to this chapter it is dangerous to promise too much as this increases expectations above the level that is realistically possible. It is also stupid to promise too little, or to fail to include a key component in the promises made, even if this could lead to a level of unanticipated value. This is a situation where an organization could place itself at a competitive disadvantage. The real task is to ensure that both expectations and perception are as close as possible to the reality of the offering that can be delivered.

This could involve efforts to change a customer's expectations by communication and realistic promises. It is easier to raise expectations by offering more, while hoping competitors cannot match it, although, as has been shown, the expected level of a product class is continually being changed as features that once were 'plus' energizers, which augmented only one offering, are copied so that all competitors include them, and customers get used to them and expect them as standard. This is the migration of product features between the different levels of a total product discussed in Chapter 4 (see Figure 4.7).

It is less easy to offer less. However, this can be achieved if a compensating benefit of equal or greater value is also included: look at the success of the 'no-frills' airlines – minimal on-board comforts, no food, no films, no harassed flight hostesses rushing to serve drinks and duty free. The new airlines offer a basic service from one airport to another, but they succeed by giving a different benefit – cheap fares – which suits a substantial number of passengers. On a short-haul (say one-hour) flight in Europe, how many passengers really want a tray of food? If they can fly from the UK to France for half the regular fare then there are those who will go for it. They have adjusted their expectations and are satisfied by a basic product. Of course there are other passengers who expect more and would really complain if by mistake they ended up without the extras they desire. These passengers are not the target of the price-busters. Organizations that make realistic promises and deliver against them should have satisfied customers, but only if those promises are up-front and strong, thus deterring customers who have different requirements and different expectations.

It should be the role of the marketing manager to stop consumers from making unsuitable choices, at the same time as encouraging others to trade. This requires promises to be highly visible and to help prospective customers to base their expectations on reality. Perhaps too much honesty could be seen as dangerous, as I found when working for a short time as a commission-based life insurance salesman. However, the problem of misleading customers always has a negative pay-back – witness the pension mis-selling scandal in the UK. In fact, when insurance companies put exclusion clauses in the small print of their policies they are failing to be honest with their customers. They have only themselves to blame if customers who expect more than is offered turn on them when headline promises are found to be false. The insurance industry is now cleaning up its act but it still has some way to go. It may be legal to add disclaimers in small print, but it is hardly ethical and it is extremely poor marketing if ongoing business is the objective. Products like insurance are very difficult for a customer to evaluate and so the clues as to expectation come from a variety of sources. Perhaps the success of Marks & Spencer in financial services has more to do with higher expectations of fair trading, based on the strong company image, than it has to do with the products actually offered.

While it cannot be proved that satisfied customers eventually develop into loyal buyers, what can be shown is that dissatisfied buyers, whose expectations have not been met, will be vociferous in condemning a supplier. And they will not keep it to themselves but will spread the message, becoming *terrorists* who are rightly destructive if they have been misled by a supplier over what to expect.

Customer care as quality interactions

While customer care can be measured as satisfaction and determined by expectations, it is often delivered during the interactions between a customer and a supplier. Moments of truth are the critical incidents when customers come into contact with an organization and experience the (different) levels of service and quality. This is customer care at its most direct. People are critical to the moments of truth because during a contact an individual employee 'becomes' their company. They are the direct representative of the company and they are operating on behalf of the whole company, so in the eyes of the customer they are that company.

Often the people involved are not senior managers but fairly junior operatives who may be in so-called dead-end jobs. Front-line staff who have the highest level of contact with customers should be aware of the needs and expectations of those customers. They should fully understand their role and the scope they have in satisfying customers. A wonderful article about banking in Florida entitled 'Mickey Mouse marketing' contrasts the training of front-line bank staff with the policies of the Disney Corporation (Pope, 1979). At Disney, if your job 'interfaces' with the public (customers) in any way whatsoever, you are considered 'on stage'. If you do not meet the public you are 'back stage'. As they say, one job is not more important than another; it takes both to put on a 'show', but this does focus the attention of front-line staff on their role.

At the Midland Hotel in Manchester there was for many years a notice above the door to the staff entrance reading 'you are now going on stage'. This is the same philosophy as Disney, but it does emphasize that any staff member could meet a customer. The 'on-stage' staff have to be trained to display a high degree of interpersonal skill, show good knowledge of their organization, adopt a professional approach and sustain this image even under pressure. The 'back-stage' staff need to realize they are supporting the direct contact employees, perhaps thinking of their colleagues as customers within an internal supplier–customer chain.

Of course, a lot has been written both in marketing and in human relations management about how to ensure quality delivery of the moments of truth. There is, however, a downside to the situation. The quality of service offered by front-line staff is only as good as people themselves, their training, the processes and systems that support them, and the commitment they feel towards the organization which employs them. If they feel the organization does not care about them, then it will obviously be that much harder for them to be positive as representatives of the company. Therefore, for all front-line staff, and especially for those in the dead-end jobs, it is necessary to adopt policies that show the organization as a fair employer that looks after its staff. Perhaps this can be achieved by utilizing high-profile, high-visibility activities so the front-line contact staff feel part of an overall team. More of this will be covered in Chapter 19.

There are two distinct approaches to achieving a quality performance in respect of the contact employees of an organization. The first is the use of standards-based quality control techniques to monitor performance. However, control measures can sometimes be extremely threatening to staff. The other approach is culture based, developing a strong attitude within the company that recognizes the importance of customers and the interactions with them. There is a real distinction to be made between a standards-based approach as compared to one founded upon an organizational culture in which employees commit themselves to company values and strive to deliver high levels of quality to customers. The latter is a true marketing orientation and is necessary if moments of truth are to deliver the levels of quality contact expected by customers.

There are many opportunities to encourage contact with customers rather than just waiting for the customer to approach the supplier. These are especially valuable after a sale, where they can help to build strong relationships and develop repeat business. The type of contact and the balance between good business and intrusive behaviour has to be planned carefully. It might involve a regular ongoing dialogue and maybe a formal maintenance or service contract, but it could be restricted to a single communication which asks if everything is working as expected. The level and effectiveness of the after-sales contacts can dramatically affect the satisfaction levels as evaluated by customers.

Kotler has reported that 'most companies operate customer service departments. The quality of these varies greatly. At one extreme are customer service departments that simply turn over customer calls to the appropriate person or department for action, with little follow-up as to whether the customer's request was satisfied. At the other extreme are departments eager to receive customer requests, suggestions, and even complaints and handle them expeditiously'.

Customer care as recovering after complaints

The economist Adam Smith wrote that the 'real price of anything is the trial and trouble of acquiring it'. That is worth remembering in the normal course of events, but it is even more important when things go wrong so that trials and trouble increase. Complaints are one of the most important areas of customer care but often they are sadly neglected. They are an invaluable source of information direct from customers, and should enjoy a key role as a critical form of marketing research.

There are two reasons for taking complaints seriously. First, they usually indicate that something has gone wrong with an offering and a customer is not satisfied. A good marketing person will want to investigate further to get to the cause of the complaint and put it right for the future. However, that is not the first action that should be taken. The second aspect of complaints, and the one that requires prompt action, is the need to put things right for the customer and certainly to avoid any negative effects due to the complainant telling other potential customers. In fact complainers are often customers who actually care about the supplier – they bothered to complain, when many might have just walked away, transferring their business to a competitor.

It is possible to cover the two aspects in parallel, with some staff investigating the cause and seeking to correct things for the future, and others working directly with the customer to recover their confidence. There are companies who try to investigate first and keep customers waiting before compensating them for the problems. This is usually justified on the basis of the cost of 'frivolous' and unsubstantiated complaints. However, thankfully, such incidents are quite rare, and it is more important to make good for the 95% of those with genuine problems without undue delays than it is to test the validity of every claim before action. With the availability of effective computer databases it is easily possible to keep records of those with a complaint and thus monitor multiple incidence. In fact, a number of firms that compete in the same industry also cooperate on this by using a combined database that is effective in identifying persistent complainers.

The sequence of events that should be employed with regard to complaints is:

Encourage → Recover → Investigate

Levitt (1983) suggested that 'one of the surest signs of a bad or declining relationship is the absence of complaints from the customer. Nobody is ever that satisfied, especially over an extended period of time'. If no complaints are being heard then it is not because everything is perfect, it is because even your best customers don't want to tell you things aren't right. By encouraging complaints, making it easy for customers to register their problems, a great deal of valuable market feedback is obtained. The value should be recognized by rewarding those who complain by putting even small things right. Encourage complaints, publish contact numbers, operate freephone lines, but above all develop a reputation for always wanting to ensure complete customer satisfaction.

The complaints department should not be tucked away as a part of operations, and must not be seen as a place where problems can be hidden, but neither should it be an area where there is a 'blame' mentality. If an open attitude that focuses on achieving satisfaction, based on constructive criticism and effective problem solving, can be established then the organization will be close to achieving a powerful marketing orientation.

Encouraging complaints is just one way of establishing the size of any problem. The dialogue with customers is a real bonus, and there is evidence to show that where customers actually complain they are much more likely to continue to purchase from that same supplier. This is especially true if the complaint is resolved quickly. When they don't complain and the loss is significant then over nine out of every ten will *never* buy from the supplier again.

This leads on to the second activity – the recovery of a customer. Goodman and Malech (1986) quoted from a report carried out by the US Office of Consumer Affairs. This shows that for complaints in excess of $100 the percentage of customers who will buy again from the supplier is:

- non-complainers: 9%
- complaints not resolved: 19%
- complaints resolved: 54%
- complaints resolved quickly: 82%.

For smaller losses the figures are even higher, with 95% of those who have their complaints resolved quickly continuing to trade.

The rules of recovery are:

- act fast
- recover not replace
- think value not costs.

The evidence for acting fast is shown above. The longer a problem drags on, the more positions become entrenched. It is easier, and cheaper, to solve things early. Fast action can be further enhanced by trying to anticipate problems and establishing contingency plans. This is not the same as accepting that regular mistakes will occur – efforts are still required to eliminate problems – but it is spotting areas where, if the worst happens, someone already knows what to do or how to reach someone who could handle things.

I arrived late one night at Miami Airport after a long flight. Somehow my suitcase was mangled in the baggage transfer and most of the contents ruined. The harassed ground staff just wanted to get home, it being the last flight that night. They had no authority to do anything to help and after an increasingly heated exchange left me with a form to fill in and a large polythene bag in which to put the torn clothes. You can imaging my fury on returning the next morning when all I was offered was $100 and no apology as 'these things happen all the time!'. In fact, the customer service staff suggested this was standard compensation, whatever was damaged. After half a day of effort a senior manager was eventually persuaded to increase the compensation ten fold, but this was little compared to the ruined contents, half a day of hassle, and a further few hours of shopping. The final words of the vice president were 'maybe I ought to leave a contact number with the night crew, but they can't be trusted with money!'. This whole episode could so easily have been handled better. Many readers will have similar stories to tell.

Recovery is more than replacement. For my suitcase the $1000 barely covered the contents and certainly did nothing for the time wasted for the trial and trouble involved. Recovery could be the same as *replace plus* – that is, replace and add something for the trouble.

There is, however, one issue relevant to service offerings: due to its perishability a poor service, once experienced, is more difficult to replace. The examples given in Chapter 10 are repeated here. If a haircut goes wrong, the customer has to wait for the hair to regrow. Restitution is completely impossible if a train arrives late; the only option is to compensate passengers in some other way. Of course, many services can be repeated, but the repeat service is not a clone of the original, nor is it a ready-made 'service product' taken out of stock to replace a defective experience.

Investigation is quite separate from customer care. Obviously it is necessary to identify the causes and rectify problems, but this is not the prime concern of a dissatisfied customer. Later they might consider the matter, especially if they are contemplating buying again. If investigation has shown up the problem and this has been corrected why not communicate that to the customer? They should have already been compensated but knowing that the problem has been dealt with will always help rebuild confidence and dispel any lingering worries about the next purchase.

Conclusions

Customer care means doing everything possible to look after the existing customers of an organization. The focus is on ensuring satisfaction for these customers and that involves creating a 'customer first' culture throughout an organization. However, this is entirely appropriate since the creation and retention of customers is the prime role of a business. And, as Gandhi said, we are dependent on customers. The customer is doing us a favour by giving us the opportunity to serve them (in a competitive environment).

There are four aspects of customer care that have to be understood:

1. what the customer understands by satisfaction
2. the key role of expectations within satisfaction
3. the crucial involvement of people and service experiences
4. that recovery is required should customers complain.

As far as satisfaction goes, it is created by meeting the expectations of customers. Even this can be difficult to assess as different customers perceive and evaluate the components in many different ways. Quality is best defined as the achievement of customer satisfaction. This applies to product quality, service quality and the quality of the relationship between supplier and customer. In fact, the total offering is a complex mixture of all these components, and each regularly requires revision and representation as the balance changes in a dynamic market-place.

While each component of a marketing offering requires attention, it is possible to identify one or two that set the offering of one supplier apart from others and become the key propositions in a trading situation. These should be the ones that stimulate and energize customers, and special attention and effort should be put into the achievement of satisfaction in these areas.

It must be remembered that satisfaction is not the same as loyalty, although the failure to satisfy can easily lose customers. Reicheld wrote 'There's nothing wrong with measuring satisfaction. The problems begin when satisfaction scores become a goal unto themselves, independent of customer loyalties, rewarding careers for employees and superior profits to investors'.

Expectations are a major input to satisfaction. This is what a customer has decided, in advance, they will receive by trading with a specific supplier. It is greater than the *expected product*, which is the minimum that is expected from all possible suppliers who are considered. The augmentation of an offering by one supplier, reflected in the promises made by them, creates a level of expectation that the company has to achieve if customers are to be satisfied. It is critical that this level is neither too high, and unattainable, nor too low, and uncompetitive. Managing the expectations of customers is an important part of marketing operations, and no supplier should be afraid of scaring off customers if their expectations are unlikely to be met.

The moments of truth are the short periods of contact between a supplier and a customer. This is where service is experienced and it involves employees from any part of an organization. The description of them as moments of truth is apt as they are defining moments in any relationship. Problems can sometimes occur because many such contacts are with front-line staff in low-paid jobs. While low paid, they should not be allowed to become low status. The 'interfacing' with customers is critical to long-term satisfaction and requires special attention within every organization.

If things do go wrong it is not enough to replace or repair a defective element. Because of the trouble caused and the hassle in trying to get things put right, a customer has been involved in more 'costs' and these should be recognized. If they are not, satisfaction will suffer. There is good evidence that fast action resolving complaints will keep customers, but if dissatisfied customers just walk away they are lost for good. So the initial requirement is to encourage complaints as a vital dialogue with customers and important feedback as to the performance in the market. Complaints must be given a high priority with regard to customer satisfaction. First, respond to the customer and do what is necessary to put things right – the risks of not doing this are really too large! Then find and correct the cause of the problem, and thank the customer for bringing it to the notice of the organization. Complaints should be seen as positive feedback to assist the future, and not treated as an opportunity for a blame culture which is destructive to future customer care.

KEY POINTS

18.1 Customer care is an important aspect of both marketing strategy and marketing implementation.

18.2 Satisfaction occurs when a customer's expectations are either met or exceeded. The reality is a little more complex in that the crucial question is whether a customer's perception of the total product as received, including the intangible features, actually compares to their expectations.

18.3 Customer care is ensuring satisfaction. It should include everything that could maximize the level of satisfaction for a purchaser both during and after a sale. That involves all the interactive elements of the basic offer as well as the after-sales support, such as service, installation, training and maintenance expected by customers. If they are important to achieve satisfaction then they must be given the status and attention due to them.

18.4 Customer care is managing expectations. It should not be left to a customer to unilaterally amend their expectations. Marketing involves promises made and these can be a vital input into the development of expectations.

18.5 Customer care is quality interactions. Customers come into contact with a supply organization in the critical incidents known as moments of truth, when they experience the (different) levels of service and quality. This is customer care at its most direct. During these moments of truth contacts an individual employee 'becomes' the company in the eye of the customer. It is therefore crucial that these interactions are anticipated, planned and controlled, and those employees involved trained to ensure quality delivery.

18.6 Customer care is recovering after complaints. In spite of all the quality assurance and controls, it is very difficult to achieve zero defects. Even if this seems to be possible, every organization should think about possible contingent actions should the worst happen. There are a number of simple rules that can help to reduce the impact if a problem occurs. These are: act fast, recover the situation, which is more than replacing a faulty part, and consider the value of a satisfactory recovery and not the cost.

QUESTIONS

18.1 Suggest the key activities associated with customer care that relate to ensuring satisfaction. Give an example to illustrate the points made.

18.2 Suggest the key activities associated with customer care that relate to managing expectations. Give an example to illustrate the points made.

18.3 Suggest the key activities associated with customer care that relate to quality interactions. Give an example to illustrate the points made.

18.4 Suggest the key activities associated with customer care that relate to recovering after complaints. Give an example to illustrate the points made.

Bibliography

Calonius, H., The Promise Concept, research report, Swedish School of Economics, Helsinski, 1987.

Carlzon, J., *The Moments of Truth*, Ballinger, 1987.

Dibb, S. and Simkin, L., *Marketing*, 2nd European Edn, Houghton Mifflin, 1994.

Doyle, P., *Marketing Management and Strategy*, Prentice Hall, 1994.

Drucker, P., *The Practice of Management*, Pan, 1968.

Garvin, D.A., Competing on the Eight Dimensions of Quality, *Harvard Business Review*, Nov./Dec., pp. 101–109, 1987.

Gavaghan, K., *Marketing Week*, Vol. 15 No. 45, 29 January, pp. 42–3, 1993.

Goodman, J.A. and Malech, A.R., The Role of Service in Effective Marketing, in V.P. Buell (Ed.) *Handbook of Modern Marketing*, McGraw-Hill, 1986.

Grönroos, C., Marketing Redefined, *Management Decisions*, Vol. 28 No. 8, pp. 5–9, 1990.

Hart, C.W., Hesketh, J.L. and Sasser, W.E. Jr, The Profitable Art of Service Recovery, *Harvard Business Review*, July/Aug., 1990.

Hooley, G., Market-Led Quality Management, *Journal of Marketing Management*, Vol. 9, 1993.

Hunt, S. and Morgan, R.M., The Commitment–Trust Theory of Relationship Marketing, *Journal of Marketing*, Vol. 58, July, pp. 20–38, 1994.

Jones, T.O. and Sasser, W.E., Why Satisfied Customers Defect, *Harvard Business Review*, Nov./Dec., 1995.

Kotler, P., *Marketing Management: Analysis, Planning, Implementation and Control*, 9th Edn, Prentice Hall, 1997.

Levitt, T., After the Sale is Over, *Harvard Business Review*, Sept./Oct., 1983.

Murray, J.A. and O'Driscoll, A., *Strategy and Process in Marketing*, Prentice Hall, 1996.

Parasuraman, A., Zeithmal, V.A. and Berry, L.L., SERVQUAL Scale for Measuring Consumer Perceptions of Service Quality, *Journal of Retailing*, Vol. 64 No. 1, 1988.

Pine, B.J., Pepper, D. and Rogers, M., Do You Want to Keep your Customers Forever?, *Harvard Business Review*, March/April, 1995.

Pope, N.W., Mickey Mouse Marketing, *American Banker*, 25 July, 1979.

Ravald, A. and Grönroos, C., The Value Concept and Relationship Marketing, *European Journal of Marketing*, Vol. 30 No. 2, pp. 19–30, 1996.

Reicheld, F.F., The Satisfaction Trap, *Customer Services Management*, Dec., pp. 51–53, 1996.

COMPANY CAPABILITIES AND INTERNAL MARKETING

19

CHAPTER

INTRODUCTION

There are two slightly contrasting views of internal marketing. The first is based on the application of external marketing techniques to the internal market-place in order to propagate messages to all employees. This is sometimes viewed as an attempt to sell (or market) the corporate mission, or to get commitment to a particular strategy. This view has applications to change management as well as to the human resource management (HRM) tasks of motivating and controlling. Perhaps the notion of trying to 'sell' a predetermined 'product' should worry good marketers, who might prefer to adopt a more customer-oriented position and apply their marketing skills in a less directly promotional way. This opens up a debate as to what internal marketing is. In particular, is it a concept that should be discussed, a philosophy that ought to be imposed or a set of management tools that can help implementation programmes?

The second view sees all organizations as networks with every person or department receiving an input and producing an output, the output becoming the raw material further down the line and, eventually, reaching the external customers. It is, therefore, possible to reduce an organization down to micro units each establishing a relationship with both supply departments and customer departments. Every dyadic link can then be considered as part of the total operation of the company.

If a small operating department or business unit is seen as an entity in its own right, it is fair to ask it to consider its output as 'product' and the departments it supplies as 'customers'. Then it is possible to apply the principles of the marketing concept to evaluate the quality of that output and reconsider the exchange to see how things should be developed for the future. Of course, it is not a true exchange because although the output flows forward, there is no reciprocal compensation coming the other way. The only rewards come in a job well done and the absence of complaints made to the CEO. This is a situation not unlike public sector marketing.

It might be instructive to consider make or buy decisions on the output of every (independent) department. If they were each free-standing profit centres could they survive? And what would they charge? Of course a similar system has recently been tried with a major UK organization – the National Health Service. The results of the internal market are now being unravelled, but one lesson is clear: without employee motivation and the achievement of a consistent culture, no internal market can ever work. This returns us full cycle to the first form of internal marketing. The key question here is whether 'a marketing orientation' or 'a need for internal cooperation' can ever be considered as a 'product' and if so how useful external marketing techniques are in achieving a specific dissemination of such organizational cultures.

It is certainly true that no marketing strategy, or other strategy, can be implemented without effective customer contact, and this involves all internal staff, as well as staff at partner distributors. These employees, and in particular the part-time marketers – staff who meet customers but whose primary functions are not marketing – are the people who can ensure a product and, especially, a service meets customer expectations. They are the people who are close to the customers all the time. They can usually tell more about the performance of existing products than any carefully structured research programme and they can sometimes actually spot opportunities that might lead to great new product ideas. They are obviously a critical resource within any organization.

While employees are obviously vital to quality delivery as well as an excellent source of feedback, it is debatable whether they should really be considered as 'customers' of their organization. Perhaps the organization is really their customer! However, because of the vital role of specific, non-marketing, employees in the implementation of marketing programmes, it is essential that the question of how to achieve the required motivation and coordination is properly addressed. Of course a great deal of what is sometimes called internal marketing can also be seen as HRM. There are already many tried and tested motivational techniques available to managers, so the question must be: can marketing offer any skills which could improve on what already exists? It is also necessary to ask who should take ultimate responsibility for the implementation of marketing programmes that require wide participation of employees. Is it the marketing manager or the direct line manager?

Bringing together the two aspects of internal marketing, it is perhaps possible to see it in terms of the relationships and interactions that exist between two specific, and distinct, groups of internal employees. This could include the marketing management group interacting with the part-time marketers, which is related to the first view above. It also encompasses the individual supply–customer dyads throughout an organization, which is the second view. In both cases communications have a vital part to play, although in the first the objective is both educational and/or achieving influence over the behaviour of others (motivation/control), whereas the second sees a less formal, although equally vital, role based on casual contacts and effective feedback.

Reynoso and Moores (1996) have suggested six common steps for internal marketing. These can be summarized as:

1. Creation of internal awareness
2. Identification of internal groups (suppliers and customers)
3. Identification of expectations of internal customers
4. Consideration of requirements by internal suppliers and identification of capabilities necessary
5. Delivery of expected 'product/service' to internal customers
6. Measurement of quality and levels of satisfaction.

Internal awareness

One of the better definitions of internal marketing is actually quite an old one from Grönroos (1985), who suggests its role should be 'to create an internal environment which supports customer-consciousness and sales-mindedness amongst all personnel within an organisation'.

The satisfaction of customers is a comparative measure. But achieving it will require the delivery of those success features critical to the expectations of the specific customers. The internal competence of a supplier to deliver this depends in part on the physical resources available, but perhaps even more importantly it depends on how the contact employees deliver the intangible elements of the offering. At one extreme these might require extraordinary levels of service but in any situation they will at least have to demonstrate an obvious feeling that the supplier's staff care about satisfying customers.

To be able to care in this way it is necessary to understand the expectations of customers and how the organization as a whole intends to meet them. It is therefore very important to discuss with the front-line employees, who are often far removed from the regular customer research and the decisions on strategic positioning, the things for which they are to be responsible. In fact, a recent US study by Gilly and Wolfinbarger (1996) suggests employees take a great deal of interest in and are greatly influenced by the advertising messages that their company aims at its customers. The problem comes when this is the only message and the emergent strategy is therefore constructed in a lopsided way.

While it is often said that every organization should appreciate its assets, especially its workforce, less is said about how to give them the specific tools that will enable them to do the job required. There are many training programmes that focus on some mythical 'king' customer, but few actually seek to identify the specific issues that are really important to customers. The general point about customers being vitally important is already well understood, but if marketing is seeking to find ways of complementing the HRM training it must be in the area of the specifics, not the generalities. This means helping to create awareness of the critical issues such as actual service levels, the dimensions against which customers measure quality, or even which customers are particularly important and which should be offered alternative arrangements. What actually matters to our customers is how we can help the part-time marketers to deliver what we know they expect.

In considering the components of a competitive 'total' offering, the tangible resources required are reasonably obvious, and even the core competencies as reflected in necessary skills can be identified. What is less easy to establish is how far these can be leveraged to create a greater level of capabilities than is apparent, so that a 'better' offering can be made to customers.

There is also a question of the relationship between strategy and structure. Knowing what the customers expect is only half the battle; operating in the most appropriate infrastructure is also vital. If the contact employees are aware of the specific details of customer expectations then they can recommend the best balance between capabilities and competencies and how such activities should be structured. The term 'architecture' (see Chapter 2) has been used for those links involving employees, suppliers and external customers. A strong architecture built upon an established network of relationships, contracts or understandings between partners can provide an important source of competitive advantage for a company, and it can influence the behaviour the partners involved. Similarly, a strong architecture is required internally as a basis for effective operations. It is possible to achieve this by evolution but it can require revolutionary techniques such as those proposed in business process reengineering, which assesses whether there is an overall, better way of organizing things.

While awareness of the supreme position of customers may be achieved easily, and messages about specific requirements also communicated, there is still a major problem in actually implementing programmes. Most organizations are comprised of a number of 'political' subgroups. To deliver the message is not enough; as most marketers realize, it is the results that actually count. As Flipo (1986) says:

> every member or group inside a firm develops a strategy which tends to prioritise its own interest over co-operative behaviour as concerns other groups and members. The best case for such a group occurs when it increases the importance of its own interest without giving up co-operative behaviour. According to behavioural theorists, the more powerful an inside group is, the more it can achieve this best case. Power here means being able to impose one's own view on an internal issue against possible opposition. It has the same meaning as that used when studying power in a channel of distribution.

Unfortunately the marketing team rarely has this level of power when set against production, with greater numbers, and finance, who seem to bring everything down to figures and payback periods. Srikanthan *et al.* (1986) bemoan this: 'it is often suggested that marketing management tends to ignore the financial control systems and information produced by accountants and to rely on "intuitive feel" for the business as a basis for decisions. . . . Why do accountants allow this situation to continue when, in most companies today, the production environment is subject to good day-to-day financial control systems and all major investment decisions are subjected to rigorous financial analysis?'. This is an *accounting orientation*, and while there are some difficult to control marketing budgets, it does indicate how it may not be enough to raise the awareness of a customer orientation if every customer focused investment has to be measured against some rigorous financial measure.

Identifying internal groups

On one hand this is easy – it is any group that interacts with or requires to get a message across to another internal group. However, the practice can be more complex because most organizations are comprised of the political subgroups described above. Marketers already know something of the difficulty of changing behaviour from their external activities.

If launching a new product externally then there are real advantages if groups of innovators and early adopters can be identified. The diffusion of innovation externally, with adoptions taking place at different times, leads a marketer to segment a market and first target the opinion leaders, or other influencers among the innovators. Internally, the same approach is possible. Segmentation can be applied within an organization, although it might come down to a segment of one. Internal access to the different groups is relatively easy; knowing which ones to approach first is a direct application of marketing thinking.

But in some situations the internal group is determined by the organizational structure in place. A useful model here is the value chain from Michael Porter (see Figure 2.7). He identified two categories of organizational activities:

1. primary activities, through which a company adds value to its inputs for those customers prepared to pay for the output.
2. support activities, required to support the primary value-adding activities both now and in the future.

Between each of the activities in the primary category there must be strong operational linkages. These are the dyadic exchanges with direct internal customers and internal suppliers. These primary suppliers and customer groups can easily be identified by constructing a value chain. Although primary activities stretch from original input right through to final output and the external customers, there is usually a restrictive flow between each department along the chain. So each 'supplier' will have only a small number of 'customer' groups to consider, and, unlike external marketing, there is no choice as to which of these internal groups can be a 'customer' and which cannot. These are predetermined by the organizational structure and the flow of primary tasks. However, it is still necessary to understand the needs of the 'customer' groups properly.

For the support functions it is different. They are not part of the primary activity chain. They have to interact with many different internal groups across the organization, and they do not always have close proximity to some of their internal 'customers'. The output of support activities, staff functions, is often less tangible than the primary groups and often will be advisory. These groups, which include the marketing planners, will have more reasons to try to find effective ways of disseminating (marketing) their output to potential user groups.

In addition, there are many stakeholder groups that have an exchange relationship with the focal organization. It is important to understand their role, and the benefits they offer to an organization. Marketing externally to financial stakeholders is already accepted as necessary; they are treated as 'customers' for the corporate message. The same thinking has to be applied to internal stakeholder groups such as works committees, local trade union branches and others who have a genuine interest and influence over the performance of the organization.

Each of these internal groups, whether primary, support or stakeholder, would benefit by thinking about their role as a 'supplier' within the organization structure. They can then understand why they should identify their 'customers' and also explore the flexibility that exists with regard to the 'products' offered. Rather than take the inputs and outputs as fixed by long internal tradition, by adopting an *internal marketing orientation* they could begin to ask the relevant marketing questions: What do our customers want? How do our customers judge quality? How strong is the relationship with our customers? What developments are required to strengthen the links? Who could be the competitors (maybe an outside supplier)? The last question should focus on the rather revealing debate which forces an internal department to really think about what it is contributing to the well-being of the whole organization.

Identifying the expectations of internal customers

The basis of the marketing concept is *find needs* and *fill them*, although, as shown earlier in this book, there are more subtle aspects to marketing, especially the building of relationships. There is every reason to apply basic marketing thinking regarding the needs of customers to internal markets. Just because things have always been done in a particular way does not mean it is what is required, nor does it mean that it is right.

Example

> When I joined one company as marketing manager, I looked at the internal sales statistics and found they were not analysed by customer or product type. Both these categories were already part of the input so the data did in fact exist. At first the request for a different breakdown of the sales figures was met with refusal because 'the previous marketing manager had never required such details'. Only after some internal negotiations were the statistics produced, and they made very interesting reading, enabling a better focus to be developed for the company trading.

Ling and Brooks (1998) undertook a quality audit of internal customers using a SERVQUAL type questionnaire. The objective was to identify the intangible expectations of such customers. The results were interestingly similar to the external measures but did include two additional categories as relevant. These are *proactive decision making* and *attention to detail*. One external intangible category, *security*, was not rated as important internally. The complete list of expectations from a quality internal service is:

- Reliability
- Responsiveness
- Communication
- Credibility

- Competence
- Courtesy
- Understanding the customer
- Access
- Proactive decision making
- Attention to detail.

Marketing theory would suggest exploring these expectations (doing customer research) and then taking steps to ensure that they are met in a way that satisfies the customer. It is arguable whether many internal supplier departments ever do this properly, and ever do it proactively, probably because there is no organizational culture aimed at satisfying internal customers. Perhaps the contribution of internal marketing is to demonstrate to internal colleagues that there can be real benefits, not just extra work, from such an approach.

Identifying required capabilities of internal suppliers

This is the obverse of internal customer expectations and there will be a 'satisfaction gap' if the supplier is unable to deliver the required product. Although the internal marketing programme is aimed at the individual internal links, the combined total of all internal operations integrates into the capabilities, competencies and resources that a company 'owns' and can deploy to satisfy the external customers.

For primary activities the closeness between supplier and customer means that, given good internal communications, most problems can be worked out. In the wider context of change management and the need to achieve a company-wide acceptance of a particular strategy, it is much more difficult.

Piercy and Morgan (1991) once suggested that internal marketing was the missing half of the marketing programme. In particular, they wrote about the internal marketing gap that can exist between the part-time marketers who have to implement programmes and the planners and strategists who devise them. As this often involves changes to routines for the implementors, there is a lot of discussion in their paper on the power of the groups involved and the political nature of accomplishing the changes. Examples from Piercy's consulting work sometimes involved utilization of mega marketing techniques (involving support from senior directors) in order to achieve the aims. They always have a significant communications input, although internal communications used different media from those external to the organization. The most important part of the internal marketing mix was often the 'price' to be paid by the internal customers. Where the price of adopting changes is high then compensatory benefits are required (Figure 19.1). These must be part of the capabilities of the internal supplier (those who want to achieve the changes). It is obvious to everyone that propaganda is never going to be effective.

Rational	Opportunities given up
Power	Loss of control, staus, initiative
Political	Psychological adjustment to change

Fig 19.1 Dimensions of price in internal change programmes

Delivery and measurement of quality internal products

In some ways this has already been covered with the SERVQUAL list of expectations. Quality is the meeting of those expectations. There are many beliefs that internal customers have about their internal suppliers, some positive, some negative. Of course, both are relevant. They do not have to be true; it is enough that a customer perceives them to be true. The problem within an organization is that it is difficult to change 'suppliers' and to find a better offering. What has to happen is to learn the lessons of relationship marketing, ensure a two-way dialogue between the parties, and then make a commitment for the future.

Pfau *et al.* (1991) reported on a study undertaken by the Hay Group which questioned employees in several industries about the quality of services delivered by internal suppliers. They found that 'the primary factor distinguishing service units that provide superior service was management style. Managers in outstanding departments actually did things differently – and this appeared to influence employees' commitment to quality and their views of the entire organization'. Leaders of highly ranked units tended to:

- Involve their people in a formal planning process, with clear and realistic goals.
- Create a unit structure that encourages people to get involved in decision-making processes and gives them the information they need to make effective and timely decisions.
- Emphasize working with other people and units in the organization and breaking down barriers.
- Communicate clearly, encourage constructive criticism and open discussion of conflicts, and solve problems quickly.
- Insist on high-performance standards, hold people accountable for achieving performance objectives, and reward superior performance.

• Create challenging opportunities and a sense of personal satisfaction.

As can be seen, this is not the task of internal marketing but has a much wider corporate relevance. It is a list of those things that lead to good management generally. The debate is not about what has to be achieved inside an organization to ensure success externally; it is how it can be achieved and whether marketers with particular skills can assist the process.

Internally yours

The contribution that can be made by internal marketing is well summarized by Keith Thomson (1991), a consultant working in the field:

> Internal marketing isn't about hype, and 'selling' things, like for example, a 'mission statement'. It is fundamentally about marketing anything in an organisation that needs to be bought by the internal target markets within that organisation. This includes training, and all forms of motivation, education, information, strategy, plans and many other internal 'products' and 'services'.
>
> To the internal marketer the problems of skilled labour and motivation can be looked at as simply ones of 'reaching and teaching' internal markets. If this can be done with messages that make them, as customers, want to change their attitudes and approach, then this marketing-based methodology must be explored.
>
> Internal marketing is the fusion of four 'key disciplines', practised as one within an organisation. These are: marketing, human resources, training and behavioural sciences. The concept of internal marketing is that it simply treats the employee as an internal customer not as someone to be patronised and ordered around. It is unique in that it 'matches' the needs and values of the work force with the aims and objectives of the organisation. These aims, objectives and virtually everything else the organisation wants to put over to the people within it, are therefore treated in marketing terms as internal products and services.
>
> Why internal marketing succeeds is because it *does* see these as internal products. It treats the internal customers in as sophisticated a way as an external customer (if not more so). And it provides the creativity to counteract the traditionally boring forms of internal communication, like memos and company magazines – backed up by tried and tested techniques like research, design, development, testing and launch promotion.
>
> Whichever way you look at it, marketing, including internal marketing, has a vital role to play in the future of any organisation, it does this through matching its needs to those of its internal customers.

Conclusions

The quotation from Thomson has already covered much of the discussion on internal marketing. There is often a desire by marketing people, who are judged by results delivered by the operations of others, to try to impose themselves upon others in the organization. This is likely to be counterproductive. Also, some marketers believe that since the phrase 'internal marketing' includes the word marketing, they should somehow be instrumental in directing the whole programme. However, this is wrong. There is no reason for a marketing department to try to increase its influence over the internal management roles, even if they directly affect marketing programmes. Such attempts will cause conflict with others equally involved in the internal activities. In fact Rafiq and Ahmed (1993) suggest that such programmes should not be the sole responsibility of any single department. This is not only because of a desire to avoid inter-departmental conflict but because of the real contributions that can be made by many different managers. Marketing skills and thinking form just one of these.

There is sometimes an assumption that marketing techniques can be applied everywhere and they will solve a problem and lead to 'customer' satisfaction. However, good marketers will realize that there are always limits to what can be achieved. The techniques to be used must be chosen carefully, and there are often opportunities to combine marketing skills with others. What marketing can offer is a different way of thinking and a range of skills not always available elsewhere. They are not supreme, but neither should others reject them because they offer different methods. In the use of communications there is no doubt that marketing experience is a tremendous asset, and with regard to research techniques they have a lot to offer. The important thing in the debate on internal marketing is that everyone has to agree the desired objectives of the organization, and then the best available methods can be selected to achieve them.

KEY POINTS

19.1 There are two contrasting views of internal marketing. The first considers the application of external marketing techniques to the internal market-place in order to propagate messages (such as a new strategic direction) to all employees. The second sees all organizations as networks with every person or department receiving an input and producing an output. Thus, each can be viewed as both a customer and a supplier in a large supply chain.

19.2 Marketing techniques and skills can assist internal motivation and the dissemination of information to facilitate a consistent performance from employees. However, they should not dominate as many other functional areas have a great deal to offer. The best situation has a fusion of marketing, human resources, training and behavioural sciences.

19.3 There are internal segments of employees in organizations in just the same way as there are external customer segments. Each segment could require a different (internal) marketing offering.

19.4 Applying the marketing mix categories to internal issues can require a measure of creative thinking. For instance:
new strategy = product, opportunity given up = price.

19.5 Attention internally to every employee will assist an external programme because of the direct interactions between employees and customers.

QUESTIONS

19.1 Which marketing skills can be particularly useful in assisting the attainment of a marketing orientation within an organization?

19.2 Do you think that the study of the *adoption* process (new product acceptance by innovators, early adopters, laggards etc.) has a relevance to internal marketing? If so, give an example to illustrate the issues.

19.3 If an internal department has identified both its *internal* customers and its *internal* suppliers, what type of research might be appropriate to evaluate the needs, wants and expectations of these exchange partners?

19.4 Would you agree that internal marketers should be more aware than their external colleagues of the *political* nature of exchange trading and also more cognizant of the role of *power* in the internal application of mega marketing strategies?

Bibliography

Drucker, P., *The Practice of Management*, Pan, 1968.

Flipo, J.-P., Service Firms: The Interdependence of External and Internal Marketing Strategies, *European Journal of Marketing*, Vol. 20 No. 8, pp. 5–14, 1986.

Gilly, M.C. and Wolfinbarger, M., *Advertising's Second Audience: Employee Reaction to Organizational Communications*, Marketing Science Institute, 1996.

Grönroos, C., Internal Marketing Theory and Practice, in T.M. Bloch (Ed.) *Services Marketing in a Changing Environment*, American Marketing Association, 1985.

Gummesson, E., Marketing Orientation Re-visited, the Crucial Role of the Part Time Marketer, *European Journal of Marketing*, Vol. 25 No. 2, pp. 60–75, 1991.

Kotler, P., *Marketing Management: Analysis, Planning, Implementation and Control*, 9th Edn, Prentice Hall, 1997.

Ling, I.N. and Brooks, R.F., Implementing and Measuring the Effectiveness of Internal Marketing, *Journal of Marketing Management*, Vol. 14, 1998.

Murray, J.A. and O'Driscoll, A., *Strategy and Process in Marketing*, Prentice Hall, 1996.

Pfau, B., Detzel, D. and Geller, A., Satisfy your Internal Customers, *Journal of Business Strategy*, Nov./Dec., 1991.

Piercy, N. and Morgan, N., Internal Marketing – The Missing Half of the Marketing Programme, *Long Range Planning*, Vol. 24 No. 2, 1991.

Rafiq, M. and Ahmed, P.K., The Scope of Internal Marketing – Defining the Boundaries between Marketing and Human Resource Management, *Journal of Marketing Management*, Vol. 9, 1993.

Reynoso, J.F. and Moores, B., Internal Relationships, in F. Buttle (Ed.) *Relationship Marketing*, Paul Chapman, 1996.

Srikanthan, S., Ward, K. and Meldrum, M., Reducing the Cost of the Marketing Game, *Management Accounting*, Nov., 1986.

Thomson, K., Internally Yours, *Marketing Business*, Sep., 1991.

BUILDING RELATIONSHIPS THAT LAST

CHAPTER 20

INTRODUCTION

In Chapter 13 the concept of relationship marketing was discussed in connection with competitive advantage. However, the concept is worthless unless it can be implemented in an organization. Such relationships do not just happen in a market where all customers have an abundance of choices – marketers must make things happen. Remember that it is only the management of a firm's market relationships in a way that focuses on the customer links.

Grönroos (1996) has argued that 'every single customer forms a *relationship* with the seller', and this develops with every subsequent interaction between customer and supplier. Levitt (1983) also considered the development of relationships over time when he wrote 'In a great and increasing proportion of transactions, relationships actually intensify subsequent to a sale. This becomes the critical factor in the buyer's choice of seller the next time round'. However, it only 'intensifies' if actions are taken to build a deeper relationship by continuing contacts over time. Future purchases are heavily dependent on the quality and perception of previous contact experiences.

Relationships can be close and deep or very loose and casual, and many points in between. What is best in one situation is not necessarily right in another, even within the portfolio of customers of a single supplier. They start forming with the first contact between a supplier and a potential customer, and they move through stages of development as described in Chapter 13. These could be:

- Meeting (awareness)
- Dating (exploration)
- Courting (expansion)
- Marriage (commitment) and possibly

• Divorce (dissolution of relationship).

Moving a relationship from the initial meeting through to total commitment (marriage) involves significant investment of time and resources, maintaining open two-way communication with customers, and being entirely trustworthy in keeping promises. There are increased costs, which usually include:

1. the cost of building up a database covering the necessary information about customers and contacts
2. the development of customer-oriented service systems
3. the cost of extra direct contacts with customers.

The second of these often extends beyond the sales and marketing functions and could even involve the allocation of production facilities and the modification of processes.

Regarding the third point, there will already be some contacts taking place between a buyer and a seller. In building relationships more contacts are sought. David Ford (1998) uses the term *episode* to describe all these interactions, including the exchange of products, services and money, as well as social 'chit-chat', which is equally important. He suggests that 'Each episode is affected by what has happened before in that relationship and will affect what happens in the future. Even the most important purchase isn't an isolated event. . . . Future episodes might be affected by actions, attitudes or experiences from many years before'.

Relationships are developed over a long period of time. Every episode or interaction contributes towards its evolution. But a series of transactions is not, by itself, a close relationship. Relationships require trust and commitment, and the closer the links the more a participant has to sacrifice their independence in order to demonstrate this commitment. However, there are real risks of going too far and invading the 'space' of a partner in an inappropriate way.

These episodes or contacts take place at many levels within *many-headed* customer and *many-headed* supplier organizations. Part-time marketers are often the actual contact personnel at different levels within a marketing network, and they are employees whose primary role is not marketing or sales. Their influence when delivering the specific service for which each is individually responsible is obvious. Doing this in a consistent and planned way requires a high level of coordination, and the control of these multiple contacts is a vital operational matter necessary if relationships are really to benefit and develop.

> Once an organization has taken the strategic decision to concentrate on developing customer relationships then it will be important to involve everyone in that organization and ensure that all the implications are considered and accommodated. It could also require a real change in organizational culture, what Gummesson (1997) suggests as a 'paradigm shift, requiring a dramatic change in marketing thinking and behaviour'. Building strong relationships with selected customers can lead to real competitive advantages, but only if full commitment and trust exist on both sides, and market conditions exist for mutual benefits to be experienced.
>
> Strong relationships are founded on the 'old-fashioned' values of respect, trust and keeping promises. They are also ones where a basic requirement is the acceptance of a mutual dependency together with the desire to create a win–win situation for both parties, with the added value for both generated from ever closer links.

Building a database

Understanding customers is a key element in all discussions on marketing, not just relationship marketing. It can be extremely important to profile a customer and to examine links between characteristics and purchase behaviour. The usual purpose of such analysis is to enable a product/service package to be developed which best matches a specific customer, and to identify the most appropriate ways of communicating with those customers. This is the basis of the marketing concept.

To process the information and manipulate it in previously unknown ways, more and more companies are building up databases on their customers and prospective customers using the power of computer technology. The information used should be current, accessible and useful for marketing purposes, but it should also be information that the customer would agree to. There are too many examples of sensitive facts being put into a database and causing problems or embarrassment. So when it comes to gathering information, it is necessary to do this carefully and not to be intrusive so that there is no invasion of a customer's privacy.

When trying to build deeper relationships these data become even more important. The better understanding there is of a customer's activity cycle (CAC, see Chapter 2) the more chance there is of satisfying the wider needs of that customer. The way the data are used is critical, but it is first important to decide what data are required, especially the facts about the customer's attitude to forming closer links with their suppliers. Of particular relevance to relationship marketing are their views as to the restrictions that such arrangements might involve, and the items of value that would be expected in return. As already mentioned in Chapter 13, relationship marketing requires commitments by both suppliers and customers. There is little point in a supplier committing to a relationship policy if all their customers are unlikely to value the closer links, and are not prepared to make a commitment in return.

In considering how to build relationships, a lot can be learnt from colleagues who have been building relationships for years. Anyone in personal selling will know that you do not get many sales by being pushy or ill-prepared. You get sales either because the purchasers knows precisely what they want and then hands over an order without any interaction, or because they have confidence in the salesperson and trust their ability to produce a solution to a problem for the purchaser. This contrasts *order taking* and *order making*. To be an order maker, who continues to trade with a chosen number of customers over time, requires a customer focused approach based on the qualities of *thoroughness*, *dependability*, *honesty* and the ability to *deliver promises*. These qualities are also required from a supply company as a whole in relation to all its customers. Of course, for both salesperson and company, it is the perception of customers regarding these attributes that actually counts.

Good salespeople know that the way they are seen (perceived) by their customers extends beyond a trading relationship and a business problem into personal feelings. All relationships benefit immeasurably when the buyer believes that the salesperson has a real interest in them as people. The same is true of personal relationships. By inbred ability and instinct, a good salesperson will remember what matters to their individual customers, and when they meet them they will utilize this information. They will also ask appropriate questions to establish more relevant details. Through this the salesperson establishes trust, and then 'exploits' this as a basis for relationships with the individual customer which, hopefully, leads onto further order making.

Sometimes it is necessary to 'cheat' a little. For example, a sales training manual recommended that after every call the salesperson make a positive record of the issues discussed and all facts gleaned, including personal details about the people met. Between appointments this should be developed further so that anything learnt is added to the information file. Before the next call this should be scrutinized and all relevant facts remembered again so that when meeting the buyer these can be used to show real knowledge and interest in the buyer. The manual even suggested the importance of knowing if the buyer supported a particular football team and then ensuring the score in the last match is known. Many salespeople now utilize portable computers in order to record and remember such facts, maybe not exactly 'cheating' but certainly a way of assisting the memory.

A database has a similar primary role for a supply company trying to develop a relationship. It can give personal details which might make personalized communications and individualized offers possible. Even the basic ability to compose 'personal' letters, addressed to an individual, could be beneficial in some circumstances, although customers are not stupid and could see this as an *expected* part of a trading exchange. They certainly then expect their name to be spelt correctly. The presence of errors in a database is guaranteed to offend customers and prevent the development of trust in a supplier. There are, of course, many situations where the front-line staff, such as receptionists or service engineers, are not personally acquainted with particular customers. If a well-organized, up-to-date, easy-to-access customer information record exists then it is much easier for these part-time marketers to show customer-oriented behaviour.

In addition, the database can reveal opportunities for cross-selling and other new opportunities, perhaps assisting the targeting of new products. However, care is required as the aggressive, pushy approach to contacts with customers will have as little chance of success if founded on database marketing as it has when used by direct salespeople. In addition, such behaviour, if handled badly, can damage fragile relationships.

This is enough about the role of a database, but how is one built to support these activities? First, it is important to understand that there is an enormous amount of data available from accessible sources and, even with modern computing, there is a real risk that the absolute quantity will overwhelm any system. Selecting the right data requires decisions about which items are required to be known. It also dictates the software required. Trying to include too many fields could be counterproductive as there is only one purpose for collecting data: to enhance the exchanges with customers.

There are many commercially available packages which are really massive libraries to hold the data, effective manipulators to link different items together, and efficient retrievers of processed information. But the software will not make all the decisions on what is, and what is not important. There may be some use of regression analysis and other statistical methods to assess if sales are actually dependent on any of the independent variables available, but in general it is the role of managers to define the important attributes which they wish to record. There are a lot of consumer data available in computerized form such as the electoral role, census figures, credit agency records, and membership lists. Different sources are available for business data. These can usually be made compatible with most systems and so input into the database quite easily. But it should be remembered that it is costly to fill up the computer memory with unnecessary data, so, before leaving it all in the system, every category must be tested for significance. Those that are important should be retained, the others dumped. This is more a qualitative task to be undertaken by marketing managers than a systems analysis exercise.

A great deal of the information from secondary sources can be merged with internal data from guarantee cards, sales records or, for retailers, EPOS (electronic point of sale) data. The latter is captured every time a customer uses their 'loyalty' card in an appropriate retail outlet. Another source could be customer complaint details. A number of valuable marketing lessons can be learnt from lapsed or unhappy customers. Organizations that can identify them and investigate reasons for customer defections can take steps to reduce future occurrences, and thus retain customers for longer periods of time. This has an enormous positive effect on profit.

The rationale for merging data from different sources and then studying the significant links is very simple. There is a need to match an offering to an individual customer. The degree of customization will depend on many factors, but without a comprehensive database, it could be more difficult to achieve. This is also paralleled when looking at sales techniques. In face-to-face situations, a salesperson can modify the intangible aspects of an offering and even present the tangible features in a different way, thus customizing it to meet the requirements of a buyer. Of course salespeople use their own abilities to decide what is appropriate and allowed. Computers require complex criteria to be programmed in order to achieve similar results. There are expert systems available to help in this respect, which learn from experience by utilizing artificial intelligence. By the time this book is published these developments will have moved on so that today's limitations become tomorrow's opportunity.

These systems, even with new developments, will still utilize the same basic data, and so existing databases can be transferred as more sophisticated manipulation is found. But a database is only as good as its input and maintenance. Databases take time to build up, especially if some items which are now considered important are from some previously unexplored area. Therefore collection of data can never start too soon, and the effort is rarely wasted. The major problem, then, is the accuracy of the data, and the routine updating to ensure changes are accommodated correctly. This is outside the scope of this book, but the implications should it not be achieved can be drastic. The bottom line is that incorrect information about customers will lead to fewer satisfied customers and weaker relationship links, precisely the opposite of what is required.

Customer oriented service systems

A lot has already been written in the previous chapters on the subjects of customer care and the need for employee commitment to customers. Relationship marketing depends on *marketing as practised* not *marketing as planned*. It is the way a customer is treated that determines the strength of feeling they have towards their supplier.

Christopher *et al.* (1991) suggest there can be significant benefits in defining a *customer service mission* in order to give a clear statement of intent and to define a future position based on stronger customer relationships. As they say, 'such statements are never easy to construct. There is always the danger that they will descend into vague "motherhood" statements that give everyone a warm feeling but provide no guidelines for action'. They therefore offer a model based on the work of David Norton (1988) (see Figure 20.1).

The shared concepts are obviously the 'product' when undertaking an internal marketing exercise. The competencies, or in Norton's words 'do-wells', are critical, and these have to be identified, not by senior management but by those who have to carry out the contacts, the part-time marketers who will have a better understanding of what they require to deliver in a customer focused way. The components of the mission/vision are shown in Figure 20.1 and the need for leadership to stretch the organization is obvious.

But the levels of service will be enhanced or impeded by the systems in force, in particular the empowerment given to the front-line staff, part-time marketers, to take actions that benefit customers. In fast-food restaurants, such as McDonald's, the systems are carefully prepared and predetermined, and here they do seem to work. In other organizations rigid prepared ways of operating can be too inflexible and actually fail to be customer oriented. Looser systems enable more adaptation, but of course this is the very difficult area of service marketing (see Chapter 10), where variability and inseparability can prove problematic. The trade-off between control and devolved capability is one that all service organizations have to face.

Shared concepts	Competencies	Vision
How will we compete?		Combine the essence into a statement that:
How will we make money?		
How will we hold it together?	Identify what we have to do well in order to achieve the shared concepts	• Describes the future state
		• Stretches the organization
How will we produce value for our stakeholders?		• Excites the participants
How will we make this a good place to work?		• Creates a home for everyone

Fig 20.1 Developing a customer service mission. *Source*: Adapted from Norton (1988)

Successful relationships are developed when everything received by a customer is complementary and together increases the value of the partnership. This requires all episodes, or interactional exchanges with customers, to support the total offering, and this is dependent on the attitudes, commitment and activities of employees. They must perform in a consistent customer-focused way or the relationship will not thrive.

In order to have a customer-oriented system it is necessary to create the right culture, choose and train the right people, structure them appropriately, utilize the right technology and processes, and allow time for all these to gel together. The final question in Figure 20.1 is 'How will we make this a good place to work?' – this is actually crucial: as has already been said a happy, well-motivated workforce will reflect their positive attitudes in their work and this is primarily caring for the company's customers. But also reiterating what was said in Chapter 18, customers react negatively to inconsistencies and poor coordination when they suffer from it. Mary Larson (1996) gives an example that now seems rather too common when telephoning a company and being answered by the notorious recording 'your call is very important to us; please stay on the line'. As she says, the 'programme is doomed to fail the moment that same customer, when finally connected to a (*real*) person is told to call another number for the information or service he or she wants'.

The result of a shift in marketing thinking to focus on relationships should lead to the ability to manage all the contact episodes in a more appropriate manner. To achieve results it will be necessary to involve every department within an organization, and its distributive partners, in coordinated activity aimed at maximizing customer satisfaction. Relationship marketing focuses attention on personal direct links with customers. But unless those moments of truth are worth while episodes, the customer will not respond and will reject the formation of closer links.

Multiple buyer–seller contacts

The aim of relationship marketing is to make every chosen customer feel unique and special. However, in business-to-business markets both the customer and the supplier are organizations with many employees. In these markets there are inevitably multiple contacts between different people in different roles from each organization. Even in consumer markets there is a possibility that an individual customer can have contact with more than one employee of the supply company, say a grocery supermarket. For all such situations episodes occur on several different levels, some contacts being deep and involved, some casual and general. However, they all add together to form a total picture, and the perception of the customer will be more positive if all these moments of truth are consistent with one another. Since some of these encounters will be planned and others only chance meetings it is quite difficult to control the overall pattern unless all employees opt into a strong customer-centred culture, which can then pervade all contact events.

Two-way communications

The last few sections will have shown how fragile company operations can be, and how easily things can go wrong with the result that relationships are damaged. However, it is sometimes possible to retrieve the situation, and even one or two mistakes can be overlooked if the overall supplier performance is good. A key part of recovering a situation is to encourage a two-way communication flow between supplier and customer. As with all customer complaints, there must be encouragement to make contact whenever anything goes wrong. This then enables a start to be made on recovering the situation. But it should not just be when things go wrong that contacts should take place. Regular communications are critical to every exchange, and are a major ingredient in the general development of closer relationships.

In trying to build such links a supplier should get to know, and try to open communications with the key people within a customer business, or, in person, with an individual key consumer. For business-to-business marketing it is these key people who provide information, or who can influence colleagues; they are the decision makers and influencers found in any industrial buying centre. Regis McKenna (1991) suggests, 'what you want to do is have your customers educate you about how their companies work and what they need. In turn, you want to use that information to develop a product and then educate customers back through the infrastructure so they know why your product is unique, why it works so well and what it really brings to the market in terms of benefits'.

The ideas expressed by McKenna are leading to mass customization, the ultimate extension of which is a segment of one, a single customer. It should be obvious that extra added value for customers can come from the provision of a personalized total offering as opposed to a standard item. In many markets this is still an ideal to be aimed for, but over time many markets, both industrial and consumer, are moving, imperceptibly towards its realization. But even if this remains just a dream, there is a great deal to gain from direct person-to-person contacts with customers. They can be used, as many salespeople already know, to present product features in a new and different way, thereby giving a customer a chance to perceive an offering as individual, personalized and unique. If customers can be made to feel special then they will be more willing to commit themselves to a closer relationship in the future.

Most good relationships are not exclusively one-way demands by the customers. At their best they should be open exchanges so that the benefits accrue on both sides. Most relationships involve a mix of positive and negative, as well as desirable and undesirable, aspects. Utilizing communications is very important as a means of ensuring that exchanges are open, and that the mutual benefits are discussed and understood.

Two-way communications are also useful in helping to facilitate the sharing and exchanging of information between the parties. While databases might be used to store information, the actual event of sharing is a real indication of the existence of commitment and trust in a relationships. Once received, all information must be treated with respect, and of course mutual respect is a prerequisite for a successful partnership. Encouraging the giving and receiving of relevant information is a positive step in building a relationship. Of course the information itself helps both parties to understand more about the other, and the aspirations and fears each has about the relationship.

The exchange of sensitive information is less likely than the exchange of sales and marketing data. For instance a poultry company (see the example in Chapter 13) was once asked by Sainsbury if it would reveal some internal costings on the production of free-range chickens. This was considered going too far beyond the accepted boundaries of privacy, and in spite of a close relationship in other ways this request caused some problems between the parties. This situation was actually sorted out, but if a company does not show any regard for the individual privacy of its relationship partner it could undermine the confidence and trust that should exist, and thus adversely affect the relationship itself.

To succeed as partners both companies have to be able to trust each other and to believe that each, while interested generally in the other, will never demand too much from the other. Talking together and exchanging views is the best way to achieve this.

Commitment, trust and loyalty in relationships

Committing to a relationship involves perhaps a smaller sacrifice for a supply company, which wants to try to secure future business with existing customers, than it is for one of their customers, who could be asked to give up the freedom to choose between and negotiate with alternate sellers. Rarely are suppliers asked to commit to an exclusive, single customer arrangement, although some customized offerings are often produced, whereas single-source supply deals are quite common. Commitment means accepting an obligation that restricts freedom. Of course this is accepted only if there is some attractive compensating benefit. With a supply company the obligation is that it will keep its promises, which also has a lot to do with building trust as well as demonstrating commitment.

Whatever the current position in any specific relationship, the next step for the supplier is always to build upon it by making further promises to their customers, and then delivering satisfaction by keeping those promises. Every time this happens there will be an increase in the level of confidence and satisfaction felt by the customer. This creates trust and this develops into the conditions where a relationship can develop further.

When trust is shown by the actions of one partner this can stimulate a reciprocal reaction from the other leading to similar trust in return. This becomes a positive cycle of trust which can then influence a number of other areas such as communication and shared information, mutual problem solving and acceptance by each of compatible goals. It is a prerequisite for collaboration and coordination, and for risk and revenue sharing.

Building relationships is rarely a steady progression with clear objectives along the way. More often it starts casually, then as interactions/episodes take place, one party decides that there are greater benefits possible if a closer relationship is formed. If conditions are right, and communications exist, then the relationship moves on, and the parties decide upon the depth of their future involvements. In order for the right conditions to exist there must be sufficient knowledge of each other's goals and values, which is rather deeper information than is usually included in a database. But the basic data about each other's operations do, of course, require use of a database. There also needs to be customer-oriented systems in place with the supplier, and complementary systems with the customer, as well as the regular two-way communications which facilitate the operations of both.

Creating these conditions, and investing in the necessary infrastructure and modifications to ways of working, is a real statement of commitment and trust. But, as has been said in Chapter 13, it is very easy to destroy trust, the obvious way being by opportunistic behaviour whereby one party steps outside the agreed partnership operations. Trust relies upon both parties and demands that neither will act without considering the effect on the other. No partner should be taken for granted; they are not stupid, and if they believe the relationship exists simply to exploit them and make another sale, they will seek to end the links.

Loyalty is not the same as satisfaction, although in many cases it depends upon satisfaction. It is best defined as the continuing emotional commitment given by a customer who expects, in return, that their needs will be met satisfactorily. Loyalty results in repeat business occurring because a customer wants to (or has to) continue trading with a supplier. If they 'have to' – the hostage situation – then there is no strong commitment, so relationship marketing is focused on those free-choice customers who continue to trade with a particular supplier because they 'want to'. Loyalty is not easily bought, and exclusive loyalty is the exception rather than the norm. The reasons why a particular customer becomes loyal are often difficult to understand, although there are approaches and conditions that help to develop a positive perception, and to reinforce associated behaviour.

There are many customers who are loyal to more than one supplier in the same industry. They may consider it prudent to have two acceptable alternatives, or they may have a preferred second choice if the original is not available, or if they want a short-term change to their regular habits (change of pace brand). This must be accommodated, and if a supplier properly understands the customer will be seen as acceptable loyal behaviour. While loyalty can embrace such polygamy (see the marriage metaphor in Chapter 13), it will find it very difficult to accept promiscuity and other opportunistic behaviour.

Conclusions

The past few years have seen an intense focus on relationships as a way to build a sustainable competitive advantage. The roots of relationship marketing go back to small traders and the nineteenth century, well before marketing and mass markets were developed. The idea of building a long-term link with a customer which thrives because both parties benefit from the close ties has parallels in many areas. However, there are still some markets where it is just not suitable to invest in the relationship, usually because the investment is unlikely to be rewarded by increased business. This is not to say that satisfaction does not count; it obviously does, but building relationships is more than satisfaction, and it requires deeper and more restrictive links than in traditional transactional trading.

Where the conditions are right, building strong relationships offers opportunities to 'fill the blanks' so that there are no gaps that a competitor could exploit, the aim being to hold onto specific existing customers and develop the links so that both parties benefit from real added value as a result of the closer arrangements. Once the decision has been taken to concentrate on relationships with chosen key customers, or even all customers, then a number of activities are necessary in order to build the links. These activities start with a move away from traditional marketing methods, product emphasis, and stimulus–response programmes, a paradigm shift which changes the focus of an organization. Relationship marketing requires the emphasis to be put on satisfying customers by developing joint programmes which offer quality interactions, rather than supplying products which are thought to offer a number of defined and required benefits.

If this is to be achieved then three main actions are required from the supplier:

1. Understand the chosen customer as never before, including motivations and the full customer activity cycle, to see how all offerings fit into this pattern.
2. Focus all the people in the organization and all the systems onto customer satisfaction.
3. Encourage as much direct contact as possible, at all levels, between the supplier and customer, and take steps to ensure these contacts are consistent with one another.

Then don't rush things, and certainly don't abuse the trust that a customer places in the supplier by allowing closer links.

Over time partnerships will develop, although closer ties will involve both sides giving up some of their freedom of choice. To compensate for this there must be benefits identified which show that the relationship is offering more by way of compensating for the freedom that has been forgone. The relationship has to be based on a win–win philosophy where added benefits are derived from replacing conflict with cooperation. Accepting the loss of freedom is a real positive undertaking, and a relationship will not develop unless both parties make a commitment of this sort. Commitments will not be made unless there is a degree of trust existing. This must be honoured as any action which lessens the trust will be destructive in a relationship. The ultimate sign of a good trading relationship is regular business from loyal customers.

Over time, markets will change. They are dynamic and a close relationship that seems valuable now has to be reassessed at regular intervals to decide its true worth when set against the costs involved in the future. Marketing that is aimed at managing the customer relationships also has to be hard-headed and consider long-term profit. Relationship marketing will require a great deal of up-front investment, and there will be little in the way of short-term payback. But the longer trading continues with a specific customer the more opportunities can be found to benefit from lower transaction costs. Individual customers could be at different stages in the development of their relationships, and this means there will be differences in the various customer profitabilities so it might be necessary to manage a portfolio of customers to identify the cash cows and the dogs. However, some relationships are exclusive; others allow a degree of multiple trading. Unless this is recognized there will be a great deal of disappointment if a relationship building programme is initiated and the results seem to involve some mixed trading.

Building relationships is not easy; it requires commitment from everyone within the organization as well as from prospective partners. Relationships can be rewarding, but they can also be fragile as all inconsistencies and failures are open to scrutiny. While in good relationships some mistakes are forgiven more readily, especially if effective two-way communications exist, this happens only if the future benefits remain attractive. Anyone involved in a relationship programme should understand that logic is not a good guide. Most relationships are based on the perception of those involved as to the benefits accruing, but human nature is unpredictable, and even where there seem to be completely satisfied customers they could still move away, ending a relationship with little warning.

KEY POINTS

20.1 Building a relationship can be achieved more easily if an organization develops a suitable database to profile specific customers and to examine links between customer characteristics, their activity cycles and purchase behaviour. The way the data are used is critical, but it is first important to decide what data are required, especially the facts about the customer's attitude to forming closer links with their suppliers.

20.2 Relationship building can benefit from a customer-oriented service system which focuses the supplier's employees onto the customer. These part-time marketers, who have to meet customers, will perform better if they have a good understanding of what those customers require. The levels of service will be enhanced or impeded by the systems in force, in particular the empowerment given to the front-line staff, part-time marketers, to take actions that are of value to customers.

20.3 When building relationships it must be appreciated that there could be multiple contacts between different people in different roles from the selling organization with the buyer(s). Since some of these encounters will be planned and others only chance meetings it is quite difficult to control the overall pattern unless all employees opt into a strong customer centred culture which can then pervade all contact events.

20.4 Good relationships are not exclusively one-way; at their best they should be open exchanges so that the benefits accrue on both sides. Most relationships involve a mix of positive and negative, as well as desirable and undesirable, aspects. Utilizing two-way communications is very important as a means of ensuring that the exchanges are open, and the mutual benefits are discussed and understood.

20.5 Committing to a relationship can involve a smaller sacrifice for a supply company, wanting to secure future business with existing customers, than for a customer because they are being asked to give up the freedom to choose between and negotiate with alternate sellers. Commitment means accepting an obligation that restricts freedom, but there has to be some attractive compensating benefit.

20.6 Trust is necessary if relationships are to develop. When trust is shown by the actions of one partner this can stimulate a reciprocal reaction from the other party. This can become a positive cycle of trust, which can then influence a number of other areas such as communication and shared information, mutual problem solving and acceptance of compatible goals.

QUESTIONS

20.1 What can marketers learn about building relationships from the experience of effective sales people?

20.2 Why might commitment to a relationship involve a lesser sacrifice for a supplier than for a customer?

20.3 Building relationships will naturally increase the flow of information between the two parties. Some could be confidential, and all should be treated with respect. How should this be handled when specifying the type of database to be constructed?

20.4 How frequently should relationships be reviewed?

Bibliography

Buttle, F. (ed.), *Relationship Marketing: Theory and Practice*, Paul Chapman, 1996.

Christopher, M., Payne, A. and Ballantine, D., *Relationship Marketing*, Butterworth Heinemann, 1991.

Dwyer, F.R., Schurr, P.H. and Oh, S., Developing Buyer–Seller Relationships, *Journal of Marketing*, Vol. 51, 1987.

Ford, D., Gadde, L.-E., Håkansson, H., Lundgren, A., Snehota, I., Turnbull, P. and Wilson, D., *Managing Business Relationships*, Wiley, 1998.

Fournier, S., Dobscha, S. and Glenmick, D., Preventing the Premature Death of Relationship Marketing, *Harvard Business Review*, Jan./Feb., 1998.

Grönroos, C., Marketing Redefined, *Management Decisions*, Vol. 28 No. 8, 1990.

Grönroos, C., Relationship Marketing: Strategic and Tactical Implications, *Management Decisions*, Vol. 34 No. 5, 1996.

Gummesson, E., Relationship Marketing and Imaginery Organizations, *European Journal of Marketing*, Vol. 30 No. 2, 1996.

Gummesson, E., Relationship Marketing as a Paradigm Shift: Some Conclusions from the 30R Approach, *Management Decisions*, Vol. 35 No. 4, 1997.

Hunt, S.D. and Morgan, R.M., Relationship Marketing in the Era of Network Competition, *Marketing Management*, Vol. 32 No. 2, 1995.

Jones, T.O. and Sasser, W.E., Why Satisfied Customers Defect, *Harvard Business Review*, Nov./Dec., 1995.

Kalwani, M.U. and Narayandas, N., Long-Term Manufacturer–Supplier Relationships: Do they Pay Off for Supplier Firms?, *Journal of Marketing*, Vol. 59, 1995.

Kumar, N., The Power of Relationship Marketing, *Harvard Business Review*, Nov./Dec., 1996.

Larson, M., In Pursuit of a Lasting Relationship, *Journal of Business Strategy*, Vol. 17 No. 6, 1996.

Levitt, T., After the Sale is Over, *Harvard Business Review*, Sept./Oct., 1983.

McKenna, R., *Relationship Marketing, Successful Strategies for the Age of the Customer*, Addison-Wesley, 1991.

Morgan, R.M. and Hunt, S.D., The Commitment–Trust Theory of Relationship Marketing, *Journal of Marketing*, Vol. 58, 1994.

Murray, J.A. and O'Driscoll, A., *Strategy and Process in Marketing*, Prentice Hall, 1996.

Norton, D.P., Breaking Functional Gridlock; The Case for a Mission-Oriented Organisation, *Stage by Stage*, Vol. 8 No. 2, 1988.

O'Malley, L., Patterson, M. and Evans, M., Intimacy or Intrusion? The Privacy Dilemma for Relationship Marketing in Consumer Markets, *Journal of Marketing Management*, Vol. 13, 1997.

MONITORING
AND
FEEDBACK

INTRODUCTION

The real test of strategy is not the plans made, nor the thoroughness with which key issues were considered during the planning stage, neither is it the quality of implementation of the decisions taken: the real test of strategy is the results achieved, which can be only seen in retrospect. Marketing is an activity where performance suffers from a high degree of risk due to the uncontrollable nature of customers and competitors. This is particularly apparent with the launch of new products. Previous chapters have covered the important issues of implementation and effectiveness, but as strategies are being implemented it is essential to monitor performance regularly and use the feedback to ensure everything is 'on track' or, if not, to stimulate appropriate action.

Control systems are utilized to assist responsible managers in knowing whether their organization is meeting its desired objectives, and if not to identify areas for remedial action. In Chapter 1 the SFA acronym (suitability–feasibility–acceptability) was shown to also stand for survey → feedback → action, which is the core of all management processes, sometimes termed a *closed-loop* system. The difference between planning and control lies in the way this is applied. In the planning process the internal and external factors are surveyed and then this information is used to plan the optimum future course of action. This can be thought of as survey → feedforward → action, feedforward being used to describe the way information is used. Feedback is different in that it considers the results actually being obtained, which can then stimulate corrective action (if necessary). This is the control process. Therefore, there are two roles of surveys. The first, a formal review, is the initial step of any planning process applied as feedforward; the second is the regular, ongoing monitoring of trends and tracking of actual performance, which is feedback. There are, of course, many overlaps in the audits (surveys) because the resulting information/analyses that are used to plan the future action can also be a control check on current activities (feedback). Kotler (1997) actually refers to the marketing audit as a *control* instrument used for periodic reviews of marketing effectiveness. Consequently, analysis is required both as the starting point of the marketing planning process, and as the final measure at the end of the cycle determining whether the strategies adopted and the implementation activities are really delivering against the objectives of the organization.

The control and reappraisal role should be both interpretative and diagnostic. The aim should be to consider current outcomes and assess if they are consistent with agreed objectives. It is not an activity aimed at identifying past mistakes. Actual results are compared against the targets set and, if unsatisfactory, tactical changes can be made to the current activities. There is, of course, plenty of evidence to show that changes in a dynamic marketing environment can upset even the best of plans. However, problems are not always due to environmental changes; the reasons behind failure to achieve objectives might equally be the result of poorly thought out plans, or difficulties with the implementation of those plans, or a combination effect. Hence the feedback has to be diagnostic, able to identify where things are possibly going wrong.

It is, of course, essential to have a good total understanding of how the different environmental, competitive and implementational issues can affect the outcome of a strategy. In particular, it is important to be able to differentiate between those real changes which require immediate reactions and those which can be carefully studied and evaluated, and then used as part of the input in a future planning cycle. It is not always necessary to make changes just because targets are not being achieved. Inappropriate reactions can make a situation worse, and it might be that the targets were just too ambitious given the conditions in a specific market-place. Luck and Ferrell (1979) differentiate between *tactical* control and *strategic* control. Tactical control concentrates on the implementation of plans, including modifications that might possibly have to be made to the marketing mix. Strategic controls are wider in scope and review the assumptions made in the plans which, if shown to be incorrect, could lead to them being reformulated and, perhaps, a change of strategic direction.

Every organization has to decide for itself which elements of performance and which environmental factors should be monitored. But the raw data are not sufficient alone they must be developed into useful marketing information which can be used to monitor performances. In Chapter 3 a warning was given about excessive analysis (*paralysis by analysis*: an unhealthy obsession with numbers, analyses and reports), therefore the controls should be based on a few well-thought-out specific measures, and not on masses of data. Although modern technology does help reduce and analyse data, the tracking of performance is best done without an over-abundance of information. All information must have a purpose; its value is derived from the use to which it is to be applied. As has already been said in Chapter 3, information is like a jigsaw puzzle, each piece helping to make the overall picture clearer. But for control purposes the key is to first identify if there is a problem by tracking general results, then, if things are not on target, to institute more detailed investigations in order to see if corrective actions are possible.

There are vast numbers of different control measures. The ones chosen have to reflect the objectives being pursued and the importance of particular issues to an organization. Control should not be based on what just happens to be available, it should be based on measures with which the organization can feel comfortable, and this could involve adapting standard controls and setting them in the context of a particular organization. While there are many universal measures such as market share, sales growth and profitability which will be present in most control packages, the actual checks used have to be specific to a particular situation and to each individual organization. They will be based on the expected performance and will compare actual results with the targets set. In Chapter 3 it was suggested that a marketing audit should comprehensively cover all those areas which could affect a company's commercial performance over a defined period, and for planning purposes an audit will embrace a wide evaluation of many issues. For control, however, it will be much narrower, and it is acceptable for the analysis to be a little mechanistic and routine at the general review level. If a reasonable set of performance standards exists then comparisons with these will ensure that managers know whether their results are satisfactory or unsatisfactory. But this means it is necessary to have a framework for control analysis that can assist in drawing out the really vital issues.

What is also critical is the objectivity of the people who review performance. It is very easy to try to make excuses for below-standard performance, suggesting that it might be due to circumstances outside the control of an organization, or arguing that a failure is a short-term problem that will correct itself in a future period. This may be the case, but it is dangerous to rely on such convenient explanations. If a manager sees their credibility, or even a salary bonus, dependent on performance, then it is tempting to take a subjective view to see things in terms of the effect on the manager and excuses for past results rather than taking corrective action for the future. This is a risk which it is difficult to overcome as line managers must be involved in the control process, and there can be problems if harsh penalties are imposed for failure. There can often be a very real problem of managers tackling those things which improve only the measured performances in the short term rather than the issues that actually matter to an organization. For instance, where customer satisfaction surveys are linked to salary it is tempting to concentrate on the factors being measured instead of overall satisfaction and how to convert this into repeat business. As such, the measures should be chosen carefully to avoid an inappropriate focus.

In addition to the formal controls there are also informal controls in organizations. These are part of the control framework both because they can be very effective and because they sometimes conflict with the more formal controls. Wilson and Gilligan (1992) look at these at three levels – individual, small group and corporate – suggesting that:

- Individual self control is where 'individuals set their own personal objectives and attempt to achieve them . . . monitoring their own performance and adapting their behaviour whenever necessary. . . . This can lead to high levels of job satisfaction but it may fail to achieve the outcomes sought (by the organisation)'.
- Small group social control exists when 'groups set their own standards of behaviour and performance with which group members are expected to conform. . . . Whenever a member behaves in a deviant way by violating a group norm the other members will attempt to use subtle pressure to correct the deviance'.
- Corporate cultural controls are the 'accumulation of rituals, legends and norms of social interaction within the organisation'. Johnson and Scholes (1997) called these collectively the paradigm or cultural web which dictates much of what happens, and is an extension of social controls within the total organisation.

This chapter will look at the issues surrounding formal controls, both strategic and tactical, while accepting that it can only be a very general indication as so much of the specifics has to be developed in the context of a particular organisation and its detailed objectives. Much has been written recently regarding the so-called learning organization. While many of the activities of all organizations could be construed as learning, the intensity of activity, when coupled with a drive to improve, and a positive climate which rejects blame for past mistakes, sets some organizations apart from others. The process of organizational learning and the facilitating factors are distinguished by the way they are undertaken in such companies.

Performance measures

If performance targets and objectives are to be useful as a control standard they must be measurable and exist within predetermined time parameters. In addition they must also be measured at regular intervals, chosen to be long enough to ensure a true reflection of events but early enough to allow remedial action to be possible. It is no use working against annual budgets if the monthly figures show a trend that might respond to some more immediate activity. In fact controls at the product/market level usually operate on a weekly, monthly or quarterly basis with data compared to the previous year. There is a great deal to be learnt from trend data where existing (continuing) products are being studied although different controls are required for new products. For some organizations such as retail stores or JIT manufacturers daily sales or stock data can be a vital part of a control information system. The message is that the controls have to reflect the objectives and ways of working of the organization concerned.

For some specific marketing objectives the targets could be set some years in advance. Perhaps this could involve the desirable level of unprompted awareness or the number of distribution points achieved. Such growth targets are common with new products although should not be exclusively confined to recent launches. There could easily be targets for repeat purchase levels, brand loyalty or market share which are regularly monitored in marketing organizations. Obviously the achievement of such targets is dependent on the effectiveness of the marketing programmes, maybe advertising or sales activities, and these can be increased or decreased relatively easily. To have future targets is fine but in these cases it is useful to agree a series of intermediate targets to be achieved every few months en route to the ultimate goal.

However, although marketing spending can be calculated, its effect is not a function of levels of expenditure. The link is much more illusory. Organizations should not be afraid to cancel campaigns that do not seem to be working, and to invest further in those that are. Marketing expenditure is often considered as discretionary because of the absence of direct links between spend and results so it is inevitable that it is sometimes cut as a way to boost short-term profits. Such actions can, of course, be dismissed as short-term thinking but it should be seen as an understandable reaction, especially where very large marketing budgets are involved. The best that a marketer can do is to specifically agree measures and intermediate targets that are responsive to changes in marketing activity,

Performance measures can be applied to every aspect of business, but it is not possible to generalize about the actual factors to be controlled in any specific situation as these will vary from organization to organization. Generally the emphasis should be on measures that reflect an organization's objectives as well as its future position within its chosen market areas. At the highest level there will be a number of primary objectives which will require achievement of specific marketing goals. These usually cover annual sales turnover and profit levels for existing products and specific growth targets for new products. The need to achieve these targets will usually determine the short-term marketing tactics. On occasions an organization has the 'luxury' of concentrating on longer term marketing goals such as market share but this is not always compatible with direct contributions to profit.

Although decisions regarding the actual performance measures are specific to every organization, it is possible to suggest a framework for this. Perhaps the simplest framework is the one proposed by Wilson and Gilligan (1992), who suggest 'The level of a responsibility centre from a control viewpoint can be evaluated by obtaining answers to three pairs of questions':

Quantity
    How much was accomplished?
    How much should have been accomplished?
Quality
    How good was that which was accomplished?
    How good should it have been?
Cost
    How much did the accomplishment cost?
    How much should it have cost?

In most organizations financial measures such as profit or return on investment are seen as paramount. The achievement of these (corporate) objectives is equally important to marketing as to other functions but sometimes marketers try to avoid direct financial responsibility. As Bureau (1994) says 'it will help the marketing function's efficiency if it has a recognized profit contribution responsibility, and that it is considered as an organisational profit centre. The marketing function can then be called upon to explain shortfalls against budgeted targets, product by product, and is expected to recommend short-term remedies to these problem areas, should this be necessary'. However, care must be taken so as not to consider such measures in isolation. Marketers should be acutely aware of the trade-offs possible between long-term profitability and short-term results: after all, today's advertising could be cut to help achieve this year's profit levels. There are also trade-offs between quality, long-term relationships and current sales. In agreeing which control targets to use the possible compromises have to be embraced, and a lot can be gained by considering several measures together. For example, market share can usefully be considered in conjunction with future purchase intentions, sales should be evaluated in the light of levels of unfilled orders and numbers of customer complaints, and profitability (whether company profitability or profitability analysed by product or by customer) requires many other issues to be studied in order to establish whether it is a level that can be repeated in the future.

In considering quality it should be obvious from Chapter 9 that total quality is synonymous with customer satisfaction, and requires a company-wide marketing orientation. However, marketing managers do not, and should not, have hierarchical line control over all those involved in producing and delivering a product offering to customers. Therefore, some performance measures will be required across functional boundaries, and, as such will require coordination at senior management level.

It is usually accepted that control reports should be pitched at the appropriate level for a particular individual's level of responsibility. The operating managers thus receive control reports on the operational issues that they influence. However, because of the interactive effect of actions decisions on corrective action should be taken at a higher level. Because senior managers often receive summary reports they will require detailed breakdowns of a situation before action can be initiated. There is often a time problem here so it is important that any problem is spotted early enough for both the investigation into its cause and the implementation of corrective action to take place.

Data for control purposes

When performance standards have been agreed the next step is to decide what data are relevant, and then to develop a system that can provide it in a speedy and accessible form. There are two areas of data that must be studied as part of the monitoring of activities. The first relates to the assumptions made about the external environment, including the activities of competitors. This includes changes in both the macro-environment such as political or technological developments or, maybe, the unforeseen alteration in a well-established trend. It also covers changes in the 'task' (close market) environment. The second area is the outcome of strategy as reflected in the results achieved by an organization. Results are more than current profit or sales figures; for marketers they include the results of marketing programmes in achieving specific levels of product performance in the marketplace.

For the measurement of outcomes there is a great deal of operating data covering profitability (company, product and/or customer), product sales and growth, segment performance and other customer issues which can be obtained from internal company data, which record every transaction made by an organization. The problem is that this is often accounting or production information and it is necessary to transform this by building in marketing requirements at an early stage, thus ensuring data are collated in a way that allows general marketing control information to be reported and detailed interrogations analysis of specific aggregations (e.g. customer type or product range) to be carried out.

Internal data cannot give market/customer feedback although it is possible to utilize customer complaints data as a crude indication of satisfaction (or dissatisfaction). Most customer information is obtained directly using external studies, either by conducting customer questionnaires, or specific tracking surveys commissioned for the purpose. Market information also requires external surveys such as the evaluation of measures such as 'advertising awareness' or 'customer attitudes'. Market research studies can be expensive if commissioned on behalf of a single organization. For many key variables there is no alternative, and the organization has to evaluate the trade-off between the known cost of obtaining regular customer/market information and the risk of not acquiring the data, which could lead to a failure to control the marketing effort.

However, since much of strategy depends on assumptions about the dynamic marketing environment, there should be systems set up to highlight trends in the market at an early stage which assist the regular reappraisal of strategy to be undertaken. For this appropriate external marketing research data can often provide the necessary warnings. Many organizations set up customer panels or other continuous research facilities in order to track the most important aspects of usage and attitude that have a bearing on current products and future purchase intentions. Such panels must be recruited and administered in an objective manner as the aim is to pick up the early warning signals regarding the overall product/market strategy of the company. Alongside such an objective panel it is prudent to establish an effective feedback structure so that possible informal information, such as that picked up by the field salesforce in their regular contacts with intermediaries and customers is passed back for validation and evaluation.

Sometimes it is possible to acquire data in a less expensive, coordinated way by utilizing research studies undertaken on behalf of several, competing, organizations. This is known as syndicated research and is offered by organizations such as AC Neilsen, AGB and Taylor Nelson, who undertake industry studies then offer the results to individual companies. In some cases, such as the UK poultry industry, the trade association commissions the Neilsen surveys, retail sales and stock checks every eight weeks, and the six-figure cost of the research is split between association members. Surprisingly a lot of syndicated research is arranged through trade links or utilizing independent arbiters. An example of the latter occurred in a major UK industry where all the major companies agreed to supply specific sales/stock data to an independent, and trustworthy, organization, actually a major accountancy firm. In return, they received total industry figures for comparison with their own inputs. This, and other cooperative research, gives the same data to each company, but each will use it in their own specific way to control their own performance.

Most control data are *quantitative*, which allows easy comparison of results with the specific targets, and the variances can then be enumerated. However, 'customer behaviour' and 'two-way relationships' are examples of issues that are difficult to quantify. If they are considered important enough to monitor, this will involve the use of more *qualitative* controls. Numerical/financial measures should not be utilized nor seen as more important just because of the ease of assessing variances. In the area of 'service quality' there is now the well-established SERVQUAL measure, which has enabled this vital qualitative aspect of an offering to be monitored in an objective way.

The best approach to the identification of suitable control data and data sources is to start by agreeing the issues that must be monitored, as well as the time intervals appropriate to that issue, then decide the best way of measuring performance. Only then can the most relevant data source and methodology for acquisition be identified. Finally, implement the control against targets and ensure the information is passed to the manager(s) with responsibility for that operational outcome. This should be done in a timely manner. The specifics for any one organization are impossible to cover in a general section, but the decisions over this area can be far-reaching in ensuring the effectiveness of any marketing organization.

Strategic control

The results being achieved by an organization should be formally reviewed at regular intervals, maybe every month and certainly every year. While some deviations from targets can be identified as short-term events that will soon be corrected by tactical actions, continued shortfalls against targets indicate a more serious problem and require more fundamental action with a review of the whole strategic direction. It is usually better if such problems can be spotted at an early stage in order that the strategy can be reconsidered and relevant changes can be considered. Problems may be the result of environmental changes or the failure of some strategic action to produce the required outcome. It is necessary to find out the underlying cause of the problem rather than implementing an inappropriate 'knee-jerk' reaction. The key strategic variables can usually be identified and studied, but strategic control systems are sometimes not very effective in achieving rapid corrective action because of the length of time involved between development of strategy and the implementation. They often have a greater effect on future planning than on remedial action for current strategy.

Strategic control is about getting relevant facts to the appropriate company manager in the most effective way. As Dickson (1994) says, 'it is about getting the information into the hands of the teams and individuals that execute the decision-making and implementation processes. It is not about getting information into the hands of management four layers above the process and four months later'. He goes on to suggest:

> To avoid being buried in output data from routine marketing activities, many marketers use an exception management reporting system. It reports only exceptional results, those that deviate significantly from what was planned or budgeted. When this occurs, the system reports the situation in detail. For example, it may present the results of the previous five reporting periods so a visual trend analysis can be taken to help diagnose the cause. The benefits to the manager are obvious. He or she can focus attention and management on the exceptions, good or bad. Many production, accounting, and marketing systems already have this capability, and, if not, their report writing can be modified to accommodate such triggers. Immediate exception reporting is a crucial part of total quality management because TQM requires that deviations from accepted performance be corrected immediately.

While exception reporting highlights problem areas, there is still a need for some regular tracking and publishing of certain key measures, both inputs (assumptions) and outputs. These can act as strong motivators of staff and play a role in both social and cultural control, because while these controls are based on deviations from the norm, they benefit hugely from positive messages being broadcast rather than always emphasizing the problem areas.

For all measures trigger points have to be agreed and built into the control system. For instance a 20% shortfall in sales will usually provoke an immediate investigation into the cause, but should a smaller variance (say 5%) have the same effect? In fact 5% might be acceptable in a single reporting period, but if such a negative result is repeated, persisting for two or three months, then this could be another trigger that would initiate action. The actual systems and the specific triggers are of course specific to each organization.

Control for new product launches

One particular area requiring more continuous control based on effective control and objective targets is product development activity. The basic 'stage-gate' process of new product development was described in Chapter 14. Each of the review gates is a crucial part of the control process. Objective assessment of the issues at each of the gates is important as the risks of new product failure are very high. It is tempting for managers closely involved to accept slightly lower performances than are really necessary, but this could lead to real problems at a later stage when the product is launched.

After the launch it is absolutely essential to have unambiguous targets for distribution, brand awareness, levels of customer trial, and repeat purchase, planned at short time intervals and agreed prior to the launch. These market measures are more relevant than financial returns at this stage. During a new product launch period extra marketing expenditure is usually allocated in order to achieve market entry with sufficient critical mass to sustain future sales. Few organizations expect to achieve immediate profits. If the performance is failing by not reaching the targeted market measures it might be possible to increase the short-term launch spending and so ensure the product can establish its niche in the market. This might adversely affect short-term profit but once the product is established this can be looked at. If the product fails to achieve a competitive position during the launch then it is likely to be one of the many failures where there is no point trying to build sales at a later time and it should be withdrawn without wasting further effort.

There is, however, another consideration regarding new product monitoring. If a real market opportunity exists, and competitors have not yet reacted, then it might be possible to modify an offering and have another go. This is especially true in emerging markets (new-to-the-world). In these markets a strategy of continuous market testing and fast product iteration (revising and relaunching) can be very effective. This type of strategic activity should not be based on launching products before they are ready, but it should be accepted that in these emerging markets the needs, wants and expectations of customers are often not fully understood. They may even still be developing. One of the main reasons why this type of iterative activity is not very common has been identified by Hamel and Prahalad (1994). They suggest that the feedback from a new product launch rarely distinguishes between product offerings that are not quite right and those that are aimed at an illusory opportunity which does not actually exist. This is intensified within an organization as failure is often personalized.

Hamel and Prahalad suggest:

if a new product does not live up to expectations then it must be somebody's fault . . . there is more often a 'search' for culprits than for lessons when initial goals are not reached. . . . With risk so personalised, it is not surprising that when failure does occur, there is often a race to get the *body to the morgue before anyone can do an autopsy.* The result is a missed opportunity to learn.

This rather colourful quotation well describes the reality in many companies. It would be so much better if the blame culture did not exist and companies saw every event as a chance to learn.

Organizational learning

Organizational learning has always been around and it has been studied by management writers for over 40 years. In some ways all organizations undertake some collective learning, but there are some companies that really excel in this, and it has been suggested that the capability to learn faster than your competitors is a powerful form of competitive advantage. A learning organization will make a long-term commitment to improving performance through knowledge acquisition, and they will support this by developing an open, blame-free culture.

There are two schools of thought concerning the benefits of learning. The first contends that behavioural change is required for evidence of learning; the other view is that learning can be deemed successful purely though a change in perceptions. What is agreed is that the objective of all learning activity is to achieve and maintain a sustainable competitive advantage and to strive for superior customer value. Argyris (1977) suggested that learning could either be *adaptive* or *generative*. The first is the so-called single-loop system where errors are identified and lessons learnt but the underlying policies and assumptions are not challenged. In a generative situation everything is studied in an unprejudiced but often very creative way.

Learning involves a four-stage process, as in Figure 21.1. In the first stage, acquisition, data are sought from internal and external sources in order to get a comprehensive view of opportunities. This is then processed into *useful* information before that information is shared by dissemination throughout the organization. The key to learning is the positive attitude to the information and the resulting attempts to improve because of it. A study of the many writings on learning suggests

| Knowledge and data acquisition | Processing to create information | Dissemination of information | Utilization to improve performance |

Fig 21.1 Four-stage learning process

there needs to be a suitable climate and culture for improvements to occur. Four facilitating factors have been identified as being complementary to a learning culture. These are:

1. *Experimentation*: this involves questioning the current status quo within an organization and searching externally for new ideas. This creative thinking is particularly important for generative learning.
2. *Teamwork/cooperation*: teams are important as they enable positive interactions and sharing ideas. Day (1994) believes that in order for an organization to learn, there must be a consensus on the meaning of information. This is fine as long as it takes place in a questioning climate and does not degenerate into negative *groupthink*.
3. *Awareness of the environment*, with sufficient knowledge of the elements that could affect performance. This must allow for a dual focus on both the external influences and the internal capabilities in order to maximize opportunities.
4. Use of appropriate *technical and human systems*. Such systems greatly facilitate the implementation of learning ideologies. Technological/ computer-based systems have already massively increased the ease of access of knowledge. Human systems need to be in place to control the knowledge. Slater and Narver (1995) propose an 'organic structure which is decentralised, with overlapping personal responsibilities
    and few constructional constraints on information flows in all business functions'. The climate of openness will then encourage creativity, communication and learning.

Conclusions

Control activities are the way organizations monitor their performance and ensure they are moving in the desired direction. They are the ultimate process in the strategic activities undertaken. Successful controls are part of a learning loop whereby decisions are made, implemented and then evaluated. Good control ensures that action can be taken to correct performance if necessary, but it also forms part of the learnt input, which should lead to better decisions in the future.

The control processes, performance measures and relevant data have to be determined by each individual organization, and must be specific to its particular needs and objectives. There are many diverse systems in use; some are standard packages designed to be used in parallel with the other internal systems, others are custom built for a specific organization. What is necessary in any system is that it delivers relevant and timely information to the right managers, and that those managers are both directly involved in the making of strategic decisions and have the responsibility to ensure that performance meets expectations. There is no point in flooding these managers with unnecessary information, therefore an exception reporting system will provide sufficient control provided it concentrates on the really important measures of company performance.

Control should cover the outputs, both financial and market based, which together provide measures of performance. These are sometimes conflicting and the trade-off between market success and financial returns needs to be recognized. Control should also cover the uncontrollable variables of marketing as represented by the external environment and the assumptions made as inputs to the strategy process. Control is part of the closed-loop feedback system, but all organizations must look forward and continue to prepare for the future so control should also be seen as playing a role in the feedforward activities of a company. In fact, just as strategic decision making is an ongoing activity in every successful organization, so control is necessary as a parallel process which cannot be seen as anything other than a continuous dialogue from the market-place to ensure the results are actually being achieved.

KEY POINTS

21.1   Instead of a survey → feedback → action process, sometimes termed a closed-loop process, monitoring for strategic decisions should seek to apply a survey → feedforward → action process, feedforward being used to describe the way information is used.

21.2   Every organization has to decide for itself which elements of performance and which environmental factors should be monitored. But the raw data are not sufficient by itself; they must be developed into useful marketing information, which can be used to monitor performances.

21.3   Performance targets and objectives are useful as a control standard but they must be measurable and exist within predetermined time parameters. In addition, measurement should be undertaken at regular intervals, chosen to be long enough to ensure a true reflection of events but soon enough to allow remedial action to be possible.

21.4   Most control data are quantitative, which allows easy comparison of results with the specific targets, and the variances can then be enumerated. However, marketing often requires the use of good qualitative measures for control.

21.5 Marketing managers must establish their own balance between paralysis from too much data, and the reliance on instinct by using too little of the available data.

21.6 New products require their own specific controls.

21.7 Feedback and blame are not appropriate in a process that is looking to improve tomorrow's performance. A new climate and different culture will lead to more positive actions for the future.

21.8 A learning organization is not a short-term fix. Implementing a learning and control system needs careful planning and continuing support.

QUESTIONS

21.1 Explain the difference between a feedforward control system and a feedback system. What are the advantages of each?

21.2 What performance measures might be appropriate for an industrial capital goods supplier? Compare these with those that might be used by a fast-moving consumer goods manufacturer.

21.3 What are the four stages of the learning process? Suggest how the future effectiveness of learning might be increased for an organization of your choice.

21.4 What categories of data could be relevant as an input into a marketing monitoring and control system?

Bibliography

Aaker, D., *Strategic Market Management*, Wiley, 1995.

Argyris, C., Double Loop Learning in Organizations, *Harvard Business Review*, Sept./Oct., pp. 115–125, 1977.

Bitner, M.J. and Booms, B.M., The Service Encounter: Diagnosing Favourable and Unfavourable Incidents, *Journal of Marketing*, Vol. 54 No. 1, pp. 71–84, 1990.

Bureau, J., Controlling Marketing, in M. Baker (Ed.), *The Marketing Book*, 3rd Edn, Butterworth Heinemann, 1994.

Davies, A., *The Strategic Role of Marketing*, McGraw-Hill, 1995.

Day, G.S., Continuous Learning about Markets, *Californian Management Review*, Summer, pp. 9–31, 1994.

Dickson, P.R., *Marketing Management*, 2nd Edn, Dryden, 1994.

Fifield, P., *Marketing Strategy*, 2nd Edn, Butterworth Heinemann, 1998.

Prentice Hall, 1997.
Luck, D.J. and Ferrell, O.C., *Marketing Strategy and Plans*, Prentice Hall, 1979.
McDonald, M.H.B., Developing the Marketing Plan, in M. Baker (Ed.) *The Marketing Book*, 3rd Edn, Butterworth Heinemann, 1994.
Slater, S.F. and Narver, J.C., Market Orientation and the Learning Organisation, *Journal of Marketing*, July, pp. 63–74, 1995.
Wilson, R.M.S. and Gilligan, C., *Strategic Marketing Management*, Butterworth Heinemann, 1992.

INDEX